THE REBIRTH OF SUSPENSE

FILM AND CULTURE SERIES

FILM AND CULTURE

A series of Columbia University Press

Edited by John Belton

For a complete list of books in the series, see the Columbia University Press website, https://cup.columbia.edu/books/series.

Hollis Frampton: Navigating the Infinite Cinema, by Michael Zryd
Perplexing Plots: Popular Storytelling and the Poetics of Murder, by David Bordwell
Horror Film and Otherness, by Adam Lowenstein
Hollywood's Embassies: How Movie Theaters Projected American Power Around the World,
    by Ross Melnick
Music in Cinema, by Michel Chion
Bombay Hustle: Making Movies in a Colonial City, by Debashree Mukherjee
Absence in Cinema: The Art of Showing Nothing, by Justin Remes
Hollywood's Artists: The Directors Guild of America and the Construction of Authorship,
    by Virginia Wright Wexman
Film Studies, second edition, by Ed Sikov
Anxious Cinephilia: Pleasure and Peril at the Movies, by Sarah Keller
Spaces Mapped and Monstrous: Digital 3D Cinema and Visual Culture, by Nick Jones
Play Time: Jacques Tati and Comedic Modernism, by Malcolm Turvey

THE REBIRTH OF SUSPENSE

Slowness and Atmosphere in Cinema

RICK WARNER

Columbia University Press
New York

Columbia University Press
Publishers Since 1893
New York   Chichester, West Sussex
cup.columbia.edu

Copyright © 2024 Columbia University Press

All rights reserved

Library of Congress Cataloging-in-Publication Data
Names: Warner, Rick, 1977– author.
Title: The rebirth of suspense in cinema / Rick Warner.
Description: New York : Columbia University Press, 2024. | Series: Film and
    culture series | Includes bibliographical references and index.
Identifiers: LCCN 2024012061 (print) | LCCN 2024012062 (ebook) |
    ISBN 9780231212700 (hardback) | ISBN 9780231212717 (trade paperback) |
    ISBN 9780231559522 (ebook)
Subjects: LCSH: Thrillers (Motion pictures) | Slow cinema. |
    Experimental films.
Classification: LCC PN1995.9.S87 W37 2024 (print) | LCC PN1995.9.S87 (ebook) |
    DDC 791.43/6556—dc23/eng/20240401
LC record available at https://lccn.loc.gov/2024012061
LC ebook record available at https://lccn.loc.gov/2024012062

Printed and bound by CPI Group (UK) Ltd, Croydon, CR0 4YY

Cover design: Noah Arlow
Cover image: From *Under the Skin* (2013); directed by Jonathan Glazer. Shown:
Scarlett Johansson. A24/Photofest © A24.

For Gigi and Bridget

CONTENTS

Acknowledgments   ix

Introduction   1
1. Suspense in Slow Time   21
2. Minimal Thrills   52
3. The Ambient Landscape   86
4. Ailing Bodies on the Threshold of Action   120
5. Gothic Uncertainty, Bordering on Horror   154
6. Streaming the Undead Energies of "Film"   186

Notes   223
Index   277

ACKNOWLEDGMENTS

When my research for this book was in its earliest stages, I received crucial feedback and assistance from Kyle Stevens, who invited me to give a talk at Appalachian State University in 2018. Further encouragement came that same year from the Whitney Humanities Center at Yale University, where I took part in a symposium on contemporary art cinema, receiving formative advice from Dudley Andrew, Francesco Casetti, Oksana Chefranova, Michael Cramer, Angela Dalle Vacche, Aaron Gerow, and Joe McElhaney. In 2021, I presented a draft of a chapter to the Global Horror Studies Research and Archival Network at the University of Pittsburgh, where I benefited from comments by Charles Exley, Chika Kinoshita, Akira Lippit, Angela Ndalianis, and especially Adam Lowenstein. My debt to his friendship and generosity goes beyond what I have the space to recognize here. Also in 2021, my research drew support from the Film Studies Research Seminar at King's College London. I am grateful to Mark Betz, Jin-hee Choi, Victor Fan, Elena Gorfinkel, Laurence Kent, Iain Robert Smith, Bélen Vidal, and Catherine Wheatley for their feedback, which nudged me to refine my morphology of suspense. On another occasion, I benefited immensely from a roving discussion with Elena, who offered guidance and helped me convince myself that I was onto something with this project.

At the University of North Carolina at Chapel Hill, I have been the fortunate recipient of support from the Carolina Asia Center (my thanks to Ji-Yeon Jo and Kevin Fogg in particular) as well as from the Institute for the Arts and Humanities. My heartfelt thanks to the undergraduate students, class of 2021, who nominated me for the Chapman Family Teaching Award I received in combination with my IAH Summer Fellowship.

My gratitude goes to the following individuals who offered valuable feedback and encouragement at some point: Sam Amago, Dudley Andrew (again), Clint Bergson, Matthew Bernstein, William Brown, Ana Maria Burkett, Steve Carter, Marsha Collins, Taylor Cowdery, H. M. Cushman, Tiago de Luca, Eric Downing, Mary Floyd-Wilson, Nick Forster, Alex Greenhough, Amelie Hastie, Josh Heaps, Matt Holtmeier, Lanie Hopson, Dean Hurley, Steffen Hven, Sam Ishii-Gonzales, Karla Jimenez, Geoff King, Tom Lamarre, Marcia Landy, Dominic Lash, Shayne Legassie, Dom Lennard, Josh Martin, Meta Mazaj, Kristi McKim, Dan Morgan, Wakae Nakane, Angela Ndalianis, Miguel Penabella, Wyatt D. Phillips, Murray Pomerance, Michael Renov, David Roche, Richard Rushton, Steve Rybin, Jordan Schonig, Robert Self, Girish Shambu, Halynna Snyder, Rob Spadoni, Doug Stark, Kim Stern, Kyle Stevens (again, a surrogate brother), Jeremi Szaniawski, Zack Vernon, Patricia White, Gavin Whitehead, Jessica Wolfe, Justin Wyatt, and Dan Yacavone.

I thank my two editors at Columbia University Press, John Belton and Philip Leventhal, who were enthusiastic about this book from day one. It has been a pleasure to work with the whole team at Columbia. I also wish to thank the anonymous reviewers of the proposal and final manuscript and Alexander O. Trotter, who compiled the index.

Alternate versions of some material included in this book have appeared previously in *After Kubrick: A Filmmaker's Legacy*, edited by Jeremi Szaniawski (New York: Bloomsbury, 2020), and *Screening American Independent Film*, edited by Justin Wyatt and W. D. Phillips (New Brunswick, NJ: Rutgers University Press, 2023). My thanks to the publishers for their permission to rework that material here.

Special thanks to my brilliant colleagues and friends in Film Studies at UNC Chapel Hill. I am blessed to be in the company of Gregg Flaxman, Martin Johnson, Inga Pollmann, and, most recently, Daelena Tinnin-Gadson. Discussions with Inga, astute thinker of cinematic mood, were helpful at multiple stages of this project.

My mother, Arlene Warner, and sister, Jennifer Burgess, have been a constant source of support since the day I decided to go to graduate school. Talking about Hitchcock's films with my mother in my youth during a month-long Turner Classic retrospective on the director was one of the initial sparks for my fascination with suspense. My father, Richard Warner, passed away after a bout with illness in 2019. He was often in my thoughts as I completed this book—his frequent words of encouragement, his inspiring work ethic and attention to detail. I know he would have been proud of this study and eager to discuss it.

Most profoundly, I thank my wife and best friend, Gigi Warner, who has contributed to this book in indispensable ways, whether serving as editor or dialogue partner. Her good cheer, laughter, intellect, love, and powers of observation have steered me through the low points and the high points of this project. I am grateful for the many sacrifices she has made so that I could finish this manuscript, and I promise to reciprocate.

In April 2022, our daughter, Bridget, entered the world and rearranged our lives for the better. I cannot wait to watch with her some of the films investigated in these pages. This book is dedicated to both Gigi and Bridge—and to our future of seeing and talking about all sorts of movies together.

THE
REBIRTH
OF SUSPENSE

INTRODUCTION

I am trying not to do the cliché. I'm getting away from dark shadows and wet streets, you know. And the black cat that goes along the wall, and somebody looks out of the curtain. These are old-fashioned things. So, I say to myself, "I don't want to do that anymore; I want to do something different: I will do it with nothing, *and make the audience wonder. I will add suspense and mystery by having . . . the air, the sun." There would be nothing more attractive than to have a beautiful scene in the country—gorgeous, lovely—and a brook, you know, that babbles along. And you look down, and under the brook there's a dead body.*

—Alfred Hitchcock

As Alfred Hitchcock keenly understood, "suspense" is a domain of cinematic style and spectator experience that needs constant reinvention lest it languish in overfamiliarity, losing its power to unnerve and enthrall us. The very term comes with plenty of baggage. Its mention calls to mind reductive genre labels and poster art with piercing eyes, heavy shadows, sniper crosshairs, and ominous or alluring figures in silhouette. It cues a mental montage of dramatic clichés beyond Hitchcock's litany. One thinks of slowly rotating doorknobs, ticking clocks, coiling staircases, subjective tracking shots that align us with the gaze of a not-yet-identified stalker, last-second rescues staged by means of crosscutting, and so forth.[1] Many of these trademarks of suspense stem from Hitchcock's formative impact on later filmmakers working in the thriller and horror genres, and several can be ascribed to the influence of D. W. Griffith and Fritz Lang as well. A customary international genealogy of cinematic suspense might start with Griffith, Lois Weber's film *Suspense* (1913), Louis Feuillade's crime serials *Fantômas* (1913) and *Les vampires* (1915–1916), and the Weimar cinema that profoundly informed Hitchcock's ways of crafting suspense, such as the work of G. W. Pabst.[2] From there, one could trace all manner of stylistic reiterations around the globe. After decades of reuse in films rolled out for mainstream and exploitation markets, the vocabulary of suspense in popular cinema has become even more shopworn than the director of *Psycho* (1960) could have foreseen.

Even as Hitchcock's influence has contributed to such oversaturation, this introduction's epigraph reminds us that Hitchcock increasingly sought to deliver suspense in *minimalistic* ways, with the goal of conjuring mystery and anxious expectation out of nothing more than a pastoral landscape in the middle of the day. He returns to this ambition in his famous conversation with François Truffaut, arguing that directors ought "to stop time, to stretch it out" more frequently. He singles out the crop-duster scene in *North by Northwest* (1959), in which Roger Thornhill (Cary Grant), having been set up, waits alone and vulnerable in a quiet, desertlike space. "No darkness, no pool of light, no mysterious figures in windows," Hitchcock explains pridefully. "Just nothing."[3] This endeavor to generate suspense through reduced and muted conditions is consistent with a handful of moments in Hitchcock's films, such as the eerily calm stretches of *The Birds* (1963) that last an undue length of time by conventional standards. But Hitchcock's desire to "do it with *nothing*, and make the audience wonder" carries a deep tension in that his approach to suspense still necessitates the spectacular appearance of a crime or perilous threat: uneventful "nothing" leads to the discovery of a corpse or to a set piece involving an airplane and a fiery explosion.[4] In *Rear Window* (1954), *Vertigo* (1958), *Psycho*, *The Birds*, and *Marnie* (1964), Hitchcock distends time and relaxes narrative momentum in ways that defy the action-driven rhythms of Hollywood cinema. He flirts with radically pared-down modes of suspense, but the demands of plot and genre constrain that impulse: any ebb in the action, any pause for atmosphere, must flow back into melodramatic intrigue. Speaking to Truffaut, he wishes that "the genre of the suspense story," with its "rising curve" framework, didn't prohibit him from testing out looser, more open narratives in the manner of post-1945 European filmmakers whose innovations he envied.[5]

This is not another book about Hitchcock's mastery of suspense. My concern, rather, is to bring attention to how art-house films build suspense in alternative ways through slower rhythms, sparser audiovisual worlds, and gentler means of involving the audience. Hitchcock's films and public remarks remain a key reference for critical discussions of suspense, but the tendency to dwell on his methods has left us with a partial and distorted view of what suspenseful cinema necessarily looks, sounds, and feels like. One of my basic aims in this study is to redefine the concept and phenomenon of suspense by including more quietly virtuosic filmmakers such as Chantal Akerman, Pedro Costa, Jonathan Glazer, Kelly Reichardt, Lisandro Alonso, Lucrecia Martel, and Apichatpong Weerasethakul. Because *suspense* is a tag commonly reserved for genre-based, openly commercial filmmaking—not the art cinema with which these figures are associated—these names rarely if ever factor into discussions of suspense. But they are, to my mind, among contemporary cinema's most adroit practitioners of suspense, able to "do it with nothing" while exercising greater liberty and resourcefulness than Hitchcockian tradition permits. Indeed, they give us occasion to rethink the formal, affective, and atmospheric factors that bear on the spectator's encounter with enticingly uncertain and undecided events—particularly as slowness and duration structure this experience.

My purpose in this study is to salvage an account of suspense as it operates within and on the cusp of so-called *slow cinema*, an art-house tendency known for its prolonged shot lengths, sparing mise-en-scène, relaxed or stalled plots, and contemplative focus on quotidian events and landscapes. In other words, I pursue an uncommon understanding of the spectator's suspenseful encounter by turning to what may seem a disadvantageous source, given the refusals of the films in question to offer the kinetic stimuli and overpowering emotional manipulation with which we tend to align suspense generically. I am hardly the first, however, to detect forms of suspense in slow art-house cinema.

In an essay for a retrospective on the films of Pedro Costa in 2005, the eminent Japanese film critic and scholar Shigehiko Hasumi makes a curious claim about a lateral tracking shot that lasts for more than two minutes in Costa's *Ossos* (1997): "As the moving camera stays aligned with the walking man, a breathtaking suspense builds. This suspense is not anticipation that an unknown situation may arise; rather, it forms around the question of how long the certainty that nothing is likely to happen can be maintained. The viewer worries how long this scene will continue and has no choice but to keep staring at the screen so as not to be abandoned by the flow of the film."[6] This attribution of "suspense" to Costa's work might seem misplaced, but, for Hasumi, suspense in this austere, unhurried film has little to do with what happens next in the plot and still less to do with the psychological character alignment we find ourselves drawn into with Hitchcockian cinema. The term *suspense* in this case instead describes the spectator's anxious, dilated time of waiting on the threshold between nothing and eventfulness. It names our growing apprehension that "nothing" can continue for only so long but that it might continue indefinitely, a conflict that nevertheless rivets attention to the screen.

Hasumi's definition of suspense has an echo in Adrian Martin's consideration of Gus Van Sant's *Elephant* (2004), a slow-moving, temporally distended film that re-creates the Columbine High School massacre of 1999. Noting its "growing atmosphere of low-level (and eventually high-level) anxiety," Martin observes how suspense results from the subtlest formal operations, including but not limited to the mobile long take:

> Van Sant is exploiting, in a masterful way, one of the most basic and powerful properties of cinema as a medium: cinema not only gives us things to see, it plays on our mounting desire for this spectacle to at last *deliver* itself to us. One consequence of this is that when we talk about things like *suspense* or *tension* in movies we do not have to be talking about a specific, personalised hero in danger or a central, fictional conflict. Suspense and tension can come purely from the movement of a camera, the rising arc of a sound, a gradual change in the colour palette of the screen, the choreography of a body.[7]

These observations by Hasumi and Martin invite us to venture beyond the overly schematic ways in which suspense tends to be explained and canonized in film studies. Where Hasumi underlines the spectator's waiting game in the face of extreme yet hypnotic protraction, Martin stresses the uneasiness felt in and through our attunement to modulations of style and rhythm that may have little to do with our attachment to characters. In a similar vein, Yvette Biró, Annette Michelson, and David Bordwell have also called for unorthodox accounts of suspense in their engagements with minimalism, which, respectively, regard Hou Hsiao-hsien, Michael Snow, and Yasujirō Ozu as peculiar adepts of suspense.[8] What might it mean, from a critical standpoint, to displace and challenge the Hitchcockian model by examining *The Assassin* (Hou, 2015), *Wavelength* (Snow, 1967), and *That Night's Wife* (Ozu, 1930) as case studies in suspense? Such a change in vantage stands to alter our entrenched attitudes not only about suspense but also about the workings of slow-paced art films. After all, the category "slow cinema" comes with plenty of its own baggage. It suffers from taxonomies that impose a single aesthetic paradigm, usually predicated on the long take and specific modes of spectator response. Depending on the commentator, slow cinema either inspires contemplative wonder or revels in boredom by deliberately wasting time. In arguments that assign slowness a therapeutic value, it heals the spectator's overtaxed sensorium, restoring time for patient thought. For some critics, it uniquely caters to relaxation and even sleep, whereas for others it demands constant vigilance.[9]

Slow cinema, in fact, demonstrates each of these modalities yet none of them exclusively. If Tsai Ming-liang's *Days* (2020) elicits drowsiness as we sit through extended takes of nothing much happening in the way of narrative, the film rewards the wakeful attention it fosters through its fine-grained formal system.

Take the moment at the thirty-minute mark in which a silent long take of a mountain sunset, reflected in the glass facade of a rundown office building, is suddenly interrupted by an almost imperceptible vector of motion: a small cat catches the eye as it creeps into and across the frame. The animal moves inside the building but looks as though it scales a distant mountaintop mirrored in the facade—a playful superimposition that has been prepared for by earlier landscapes and a reflected-light motif (fig. 0.1). The delayed effect is thrilling if we are awake for it.[10] Tsai's slowness, even as it lulls us, primes us to expect and embrace delicacies of detail. Doesn't suspense texture our waiting, somewhat *im*patiently, for such mysteriously timed and contoured subtleties to emerge?[11]

But suspense has had no quarter in recent academic debates about cinematic slowness: if mentioned at all, it usually counts in the negative as something the films must nullify as part of their presumed opposition to the mainstream and the whirlwind speeds of global capital.[12] Yet some of slow cinema's most inventive variations flirt with genres where suspense is typically afforded pride of place—namely thriller, horror, and melodrama. A cinema of slowness doesn't have to affix itself to these popular genres to bring about the visceral suspense that both Hasumi and Martin describe, but in some cases slow cinema's structures of curiosity and anxiety tease us with generic borrowings. Think of *The Passenger* (Michelangelo Antonioni, 1975) or more contemporary productions associated with the slow mantle, such as *Humanité* (Bruno Dumont, 1999), *Day Night Day Night* (Julia Loktev, 2006), *The Man from London* (Béla Tarr, 2007), *The Headless Woman* (Lucrecia Martel, 2008), *Road to Nowhere* (Monte Hellman, 2010), *Once Upon a Time in Anatolia* (Nuri Bilge Ceylan, 2011), *Neighboring Sounds* (Kleber Mendonça Filho, 2012), *A Touch of Sin* (Jia Zhangke, 2013), *Stranger by the Lake* (Alain Guiraudie, 2013), and *Pacifiction* (Albert Serra, 2022). As these films attest through their invocations of the thriller in one or more of its guises, the term *slow cinema* names a variable field of global art cinema that freely combines with popular idioms, an aesthetic arena wherein some of the filmmakers who are said (or expected) to jettison suspense in fact do the opposite.

My interest in slow cinema's hybrid qualities is consonant with other recent efforts to decompartmentalize art cinema by questioning the rhetoric used by programmers, marketers, critics, academics, and cinephiles alike to separate "art" from entertainment fare as a sign of cultural distinction. Rosalind Galt and Karl Schoonover define "global art cinema" as a "mongrel" entity whose basic differences from both the mainstream and the avant-garde have always been compromised by "impure," ambivalent mixtures across institutional, commercial, critical, geocultural, formal, generic, exhibitory, and experiential levels.[13] In a similar spirit of embracing art cinema's global sprawl and aesthetic diversity, David Andrews and Geoff King have thoroughly examined the loose and porous boundaries surrounding the designation *art cinema* from the 1920s

6 Introduction

Figure 0.1 In *Days*, a tiny cat (*one row down, fourth glass panel from the right*) creeps across the frame and seemingly along the reflected mountaintop.

to the post–World War II years and through to its proliferation far beyond Europe from the 1960s to the postmillennial present.[14] Yet even as the "slow" impulse comprises one of the most vital art-cinematic strands at least since the 1990s (with clear roots in earlier art cinemas), its critical reception has insisted on rigid criteria of inclusion that overlook both its historical and newly emergent ties to popular cinema, as though to recognize such "impure" relations, including an investment in suspense, would be to forsake the subversive potential of slowness.[15]

Received scholarly wisdom about both slowness and suspense is frequently at odds with the sensibilities of artists who, *as part of their experimental tendencies*, set popular-film and art-film traditions on a continuum. When Apichatpong was preparing the slow, alcohol-enhanced scene of social bonding that transforms the protagonist's (Tilda Swinton) sense perception in *Memoria* (2021), he had in mind the boozy scene in Steven Spielberg's *Jaws* (1975) where the veteran Quint (Robert Shaw) recollects his horrific experience aboard the USS *Indianapolis* (fig. 0.2).[16] *Memoria* makes no overt allusion to *Jaws* but channels the mood and impact of Spielberg's famous scene, filtering it through an even quieter aesthetics of eeriness and a more muted confrontation with traumatic history. And we are as deeply "in suspense" with the one film as with the other. What we need, then, is a revised account of suspense that is fluid and ample enough to match Apichatpong's cinephilic imagination.[17]

This book thus makes a double intervention. It reconceives the aesthetic phenomenon of suspense by attending to its slow, art-house incarnations beyond

Introduction 7

Figure 0.2 *Memoria* (*top*) quietly borrows from *Jaws* (*bottom*).

the Hitchcockian paradigm. By the same token, this book's approach to suspense reopens and extends the critical conversation around slowness and its experiential affordances. Both *slowness* and *suspense* radiate fresh meanings when we defy protocol and consider the one by way of the other, as the films I study demand. Cinematic slowness, after all, entails more than a metrical fixation on the long take. It can be epistemological: "slow" as in hesitant to divulge information. What is suspense if not an encounter with a regime of withholding? Further, slowness can be affective and atmospheric, a modifier of mood, delicately profiled in time. The palpable slowness of Serra's thermonuclear "thriller" *Pacifiction* takes hold not through shot durations so much as through a languid, eerie feel that, along with the ambient sound, spans each cut and saturates the tropical environments and nightclub spaces onscreen, investing them with a viscous, radioactive atmosphere that is in dialogue less with the usual "slow" canon than with films such as John Cassavetes's *The Killing of a Chinese Bookie* (1976), R. W. Fassbinder's *Querelle* (1982), and Atom Egoyan's *Exotica* (1994), not to mention the moments of downtime in Alan J. Pakula's *The Parallax View* (1974) and Michael Mann's *Miami Vice* (2006) to which Serra's film alludes. Pace, we should keep in mind, is not just a matter of the cutting rate.

Redefining the Art of Screen Suspense

Suspense, let us straightaway acknowledge, is not simply a genre unto itself, even though Hitchcock sometimes speaks of it that way and even though commercial and critical discourses use the term as a pigeonhole. Rather, suspense is a flexible aesthetic process and viewing experience that may draw support from a wide array of genres.[18] It activates unknowingness by playing on our anxieties in the face of indeterminate and opaque events, pushing our sense of control into check. We are acclimated to the sensation of suspense well before we assume the role of cinematic spectator. According to the developmental psychologist Daniel N. Stern, the "suspense games" we play with a caregiver during infancy—peek-a-boo, walking fingers, tickle-tickle, "I'm going to get you!"— serve to usher us into interpersonal affective life. These games involve repetition as the child craves variation upon an established pattern—changes in speed, duration, rhythm, force, mechanism, direction, and so on. This anxious yet pleasurable state is a "mutual creation, a 'we' or a self/other phenomenon" that goes through cycles and "crescendos several times over" until the onset of fatigue or disinterest. But this interaction, crucially, is regulated by an imposed system over which the infant has little sway.[19]

Stern's conception of suspense—which turns on "vitality affects," or the elusive "rushes" of feeling by which humans dynamically experience the outside world[20]—differs from how film culture has pervasively come to classify the phenomenon. Stern's emphasis on variation has its complement in Hitchcock's insistence on avoiding clichés. Suspense figures for both as a game of uncertainty at the level of technique and sensory experience, but this isn't how we have been taught to understand suspense in film studies. I suspect that most cinema scholars, if pressed to offer a definition, would recite Hitchcock's famous distinction between suspense (the viewer is forewarned and epistemically ahead of the characters) and surprise (the viewer is jolted by a turn of events without having been readied for it).[21] This distinction typically comes with Hitchcock's hypothetical example of a scene in which a bomb detonates under the table of characters we are given to identify with: if the blast occurs suddenly, then we are surprised or shocked; however, if moments earlier the film shows us someone slipping a briefcase that we know contains a bomb underneath the table, then we find ourselves in suspense. We want to warn the characters of the danger but must sit through an agonizing stretch of powerlessness to do so, immersed in the drama but also made to feel our separation from the virtual world on the screen. Hitchcock maintains that suspense is the far "more pleasurable" experience because of its gradual "crescendo" structure, whereas surprise happens "like a bolt of lightning" and is "more difficult to savor."[22] In this account, what defines suspense is not radical uncertainty but, on the contrary, our superior levels of knowledge in relation to the dramatis personae.

Hitchcock's theories of suspense were deeply informed by what David Bordwell calls "a diverse ecosystem of murder narratives" across film, literature, theater, and radio plays of the 1940s. The "suspense story," which puts the audience in a state of psychological identification with an ordinary protagonist in extreme peril, became widely codified as a genre distinct from detective fiction and the whodunit.[23] Debates at the time in Anglophone literary circles shaped Hitchcock's habit of opposing suspense to the murder mystery: as he contends in writings and lectures, suspense above all caters to an emotional experience, but figuring out the murderer in an Agatha Christie plot is chiefly an intellectual exercise.[24] The trouble with this codification of suspense as a genre, which is very much still with us, is that, for all its convenience, it attends to just one, albeit highly familiar kind of suspense situation. Although it seems to stress affective considerations, it implies that the only feelings that count and call for scrutiny are those that are routed through the spectator's vicarious experience in a framework of identification.

This overly neat demarcation of suspense has had its equivalent in film theory, where the phenomenon has seldom met with sustained attention and has been addressed, for the most part, through the lens of cognitivist approaches to film experience. For decades, the most frequently invoked theory has been that of Noël Carroll, for whom suspense comes down to the viewer's mental and moral weighing of probability factors as the plot hangs in the balance. For Carroll, viewers weigh a desired, "morally correct" outcome against an undesired, "morally incorrect or evil" outcome that is more probable.[25] As Julian Hanich rightly observes, Carroll neglects "the *formal* as well as *experiential* aspect[s]" of suspense, and this rings true of many cognitivist understandings of suspense that reuse Carroll's arguments.[26] Lost in these studies are the visceral impressions, the *sensorial* and sometimes preconscious dimensions of embodied experience that bear on our suspenseful encounter with a phenomenal *world* onscreen.

Even Hitchcockian suspense calls out for a more sensitive and encompassing treatment of aesthetic experience. Let us take a scene from Hitchcock's spy thriller *Foreign Correspondent* (1940). Our protagonist is an American journalist, alias Huntley Haverstock (Joel McCrae), on assignment in Europe to discover if another world war is looming. He witnesses, or so he thinks, the assassination of a diplomat in Amsterdam and pursues the culprits in a high-speed chase until their car disappears in the countryside. Noticing that the sails of a nearby windmill are rotating against the breeze, he heads inside the mill to investigate. The scene moves to a tense but unhasty rhythm as we feel the slowing of pace in the aftermath of the car chase. What Susan Smith terms "shared suspense" is principally in effect: our level of knowledge is just as reduced as the character's.[27] The framing follows Haverstock's stealthy movements while immersing us in his limited point of view. The conversations he overhears (in muffled German) align us with his confusion in that they happen in a "foreign" language not translated as subtitles (let us imagine an English-speaking audience without German proficiency in the 1940s). Even if we gather the content of their hushed words, they allow no orientation. Like Haverstock, we don't know and can't know the complete narrative significance of the events before us.

But the *atmospheric* qualities of the scene—from the lightly expressionistic architecture of the windmill's interior to the sounds of its gears turning and creaking—give it a visceral charge that is closer to Smith's notion of "direct suspense," whereby we feel suspense in our own right, without this feeling having to pass through the prism of character subjectivity. We are brought into a "more direct, unmediated relationship to the film world" that plays out as sheer sensory encounter.[28] In our analysis of the windmill scene, we may miss this visceral dimension if we regard the atmosphere in figurative representational terms. It is tempting to view the setting as symbolic of the grinding forward of a plot that has yet to disclose itself, but that interpretation would omit how the sound design—which also includes wind, dripping water, and birdsong—sets our sensitivity on edge, holding us in suspense with an unnerving hypnotic force. There is also the fact that our experience includes a quasi-physical alignment with Haverstock, who is, after all, an embedded spectator in the scene. He almost loses a limb when his coat is caught in the wooden gears. Even when seeing the film for the first time, we know at some level that the protagonist, and for that matter the star actor playing him, will be spared, but we still squirm as he just barely frees his hand in retrieving the coat—a near-disaster magnified in close-up. In addition, when Haverstock finds that the "assassinated" diplomat is alive, the camera detaches from his point of view to track in toward the diplomat for emphasis. The camera declares its independent consciousness: in terms of suspense, this vector of motion doesn't just accent the drama but also alerts us to a directorial hand—an implied agent or entity that knows more than we do and seems to relish having us at its mercy. This scene alone indicates that the parameters of suspense need to be theorized more fully. Not *all* suspense hangs on plot uncertainties and psychological alignments with legible characters.[29]

My mission to challenge and rethink received understandings of suspense is preceded by Alanna Thain's *Bodies in Suspense: Time and Affect in Cinema*

(2017), a book that cannily reinterprets the formal and experiential resources of suspense. With strong investments in Brian Massumi's influential, Deleuze-inspired affect theory, Thain treats suspense not as a mere narrative device that elicits cognitive uncertainty but as a "force." Focusing on Hitchcock's *Vertigo* and films by other artists that in effect "remake" its experiments, Thain argues that the visceral force of suspense "deranges" time, *undoes* psychological identification, and pulls an embodied spectator, along with characters, into complex, nonlinear circuits of "anotherness." That is, suspense opens, multiplies, and disfigures identity instead of cementing it.[30]

Thain makes a valuable contribution to debates about "anomalous suspense," also known as "recidivist suspense," which refers to when spectators have a suspense-filled experience even when they already know the narrative outcome.[31] I suspect that most of us have had this feeling while reencountering a film. We *know* that FBI trainee Clarice Starling (Jodie Foster) will make it through the menacing gothic spaces she must navigate in *The Silence of the Lambs* (Jonathan Demme, 1991), leading up to the serial killer's labyrinthine cellar. Even so, we once again feel the pressing anxiety of her "uncertain" fate. Any assurance of knowing the outcome in advance is undercut by our surface anxiety that continues nonetheless. For purely narrative- and cognitive-based models, which turn on knowledge, anomalous suspense presents a quandary. Do we trick ourselves into thinking that we don't know where the narrative is headed, all the better to savor it anew? Have details of the narrative become so murky in our memory that we don't know *exactly* how events will be resolved? Thain shrewdly dismantles various scholars' efforts to explain this experience within the bounds of their knowledge-based and identification-based theories. In her dissenting account, anomalous suspense lays bare the fact that "the *passage to* knowledge is *as* significant, if not more so, than the outcome itself." She contends that if suspense endures in repeat viewings and is even nourished by them, it is because the corporeal and affective experience of film suspense goes beyond questions of knowledge. Suspense delivers a visceral charge that makes our interactions with it "direct," regardless of how narrative knowledge is distributed in relation to characters in the fiction.[32] Thain seldom uses the term *atmosphere*, but her ideas, especially those that engage David Lynch's audiovisual practices, lend themselves to what I delineate as *atmospheric suspense*, which aims to recover the sensory qualities that have been subtracted from the record where suspense is concerned.[33]

The Atmospheric Turn of Film Theory

One often runs across the word *atmosphere* in critical discussions of both suspense and slow cinema, but attempts to sketch a rigorous description of cinema's atmospheric dimensions have been few and far between. In recent years, however, film theory has seen a vibrant turn to atmosphere—or, rather, call it a *return* insofar as contemporary theorists have gone back to and expanded on pioneering accounts of film atmosphere put forward by classical theorists such as Jean Epstein, Béla Balázs, Walter Benjamin, and Siegfried Kracauer. Reimagining the concepts of aura, *photogénie*, *Umwelt*, ambience, milieu, and *Stimmung* as they pertain to the spatial and sensory characteristics of cinema, scholars such as Inga Pollmann, Robert Sinnerbrink, Giuliana Bruno, and Steffen Hven have reignited "old" debates regarding the aesthetic interface between spectator and screen.[34] Influenced by philosophies of atmosphere put forth outside of film and media studies, such as the work of Gernot Böhme and Hermann Schmitz,[35] this research branches off from decades of theoretical preoccupations with affect and embodiment across the humanities and joins a renewal of film phenomenology. Pollmann and Hven daringly recast the film diegesis as *environment*: that is, not merely a "text" with codes and meanings to be interpreted but also an atmospheric world with which the spectator has immersive, pre-reflective contact.[36] Also connected to this "turn" is Daniel Yacavone's study of film worlds, in particular what he theorizes as "cineaesthetic world-feeling."[37] This revival of interest in atmosphere is commemorated and advanced by Hven and Yacavone's coedited volume *The Oxford Handbook of Moving Image Atmospheres and Felt Environments*.[38]

My book contributes to this direction of thought by carefully examining the atmospheric workings of suspense in slow-paced art-house films whose tonal and sensuous aspects, while not ignored, have been relegated to overgeneralized registers of wonder and boredom in arguments looking to assign slow cinema a single group style and vocation. To speak of atmosphere is to underline the feel of the film's audiovisual world, and slow cinema, much more profusely and variably than has been noted, trades on *negative feelings* such as dread, eeriness, paranoia, and exhaustion, while bordering on suspense-laden popular genres instead of shunning them out of some inborn antagonism.[39] But what exactly constitutes "atmosphere" in the virtual medium of cinema? Not unlike suspense, atmosphere has been categorically dodged and diluted by certain critical tendencies. Consigned to mere "backdrop" and "setting," it is often taken as a decorative accessory for dramatic actions, its primacy revoked.

In fairness, atmospheres are equivocal in nature. Even when we sense them strongly, their sources and expressive devices can be hard to determine, let alone investigate. Across a series of related articles, Robert Spadoni has made crucial strides in this pursuit. Concentrating on horror films of the 1930s and 1940s (specifically their aesthetics and critical reception), he explains how atmosphere is a spatialized phenomenon that arises in and through the holistic combination of cinema's stylistic resources. Spadoni's thorough attention to style is what most enables him to ground atmosphere in concrete particulars as he defines it as the film's aesthetic "weather" system, referring not only to literal renderings of weather, which are privileged in gothic horror, but also to the variable stylistic process through which a film instills its spaces with "emotionality" and conveys to us something of their texture. Lighting, mise-en-scène (including architecture and landscape), editing, color, sound (from music to noise), cinematography, and actors' performances: all these expedients of style may charge the onscreen world with affective resonance and thereby weave a "seam of contact" between film and viewer.[40] *All* films, Spadoni insists, have atmospheres, not simply select genres and traditions such as German expressionism, film noir, horror, and melodrama, all of which are celebrated for their brazen atmospherics. A given film's atmospheric elements might come to the fore more tangibly in certain moments more than in others, claiming priority over the narrative, but never does the film, any film, altogether cease being atmospheric.[41] Indeed, as we will see again and again in this book, atmosphere can be as potent in diminution as in abundance. It can, in Spadoni's words, powerfully "gather and thicken" in the slowed and quietened "spaces opened up by sparse storytelling."[42]

Atmosphere, in short, is a sensorial quality that diffusely pervades a film's environments without necessarily being secondary to narrative and without being relegated to the background. The atmospheric elements of suspense are long overdue for theoretical and analytical inquiry. Is there not something inherently suspenseful—not just elusive—about atmosphere in itself? Though it is spatialized through concretely identifiable techniques, it retains a certain airiness for which the term *ambience* is appropriate, operating as it often does around the limits and borders of the visible. Atmosphere poses challenging questions that linger at the convergence point of sensation and cognition. If a given film's atmospheric world is charged with feelings, then *whose* feelings are they? If atmosphere closely relates to "mood" (as in the concept of *Stimmung*), does this mood belong to the space, or is it, rather, the projection of a human, inner-psychic state onto the surroundings? We could easily seek out subjectifying and objectifying approaches to atmosphere in the critical literature, opting for one or the other based on our preestablished preference, but that would neglect how films work through these matters in suspenseful ways. After all, a gothic film such as Jack Clayton's *The Innocents* (1961), adapted as it is from the ambiguous portrayal of ghostliness in Henry James's novella *The Turn of the Screw* (1898), quite deliberately leaves the distinction between "objective" and "subjective" undecided as we try to work out the difference between supernatural moments of haunting and the governess's fearful psychological projections.

Even beyond the realm of the gothic, the expressive operations of film atmosphere belong neither wholly to the object world nor wholly to a subjective experience, be it a character's or the viewer's. Distributions of affect may circulate freely between descriptive registers of "objective" and "subjective" as well as between "exterior" and "interior." In other words, far from being a fixed element of scenery, atmosphere is *liminal, mediating, and noncontainable* in ways that elude the customary parameters of analysis we bring to films.[43] To varying degrees depending on the formal system at hand, film atmosphere also *emanates outward* to envelop the spectator. What delimits an atmosphere, if anything, is precisely its grip on bodies.[44] Film history is shot through with stylistic and rhetorical devices that suspensefully play on our sense of exposure to atmospheric presences and mediations that leach from the film's world into our viewing space. The motif of hypnotic contagion in Kiyoshi Kurosawa's films, which I study in chapter 5, offers a case in point. These games of sensory address are not just rhetorical but also acknowledgments of the fact that "*atmos* (vapor) *sphaira* (globe)" extends the film's world to us by way of vibratory contact.[45] Indeed, atmosphere in cinema—in the very space of the theater—is at once "in the air" and "under the skin" of its perceivers.[46]

The dramatic systems of mainstream films typically find ways to stabilize these slippery questions through hierarchical emphases on plot and character over environment (and through prioritizations of foreground over background, center over periphery, onscreen over offscreen, pictorial over auditory, human over nonhuman, and so on). But, as we shall see throughout this book, slow art-house examples of suspense venture a different route by leaving their atmospheric ambiguities open and anxiously unresolved.

Because describing cinematic atmosphere makes essential the cognates *tone* and *mood*, let me spell out how these terms, as I regard them, mesh. *Tone* has a long-established place as a criterion of analysis in literary studies, where the term is generally taken to mean an "attitude" that a text assumes toward its own subject matter—a sentiment implied by an author, narrator, or inscribed agency, such as the speaker of a poem. This attitude, through which the literary work communicates something about itself, imbues the text and its stylistic features, informing the reader as to the intended response and interpretation.[47] Douglas Pye has adapted this conception of tone to the medium of film with insightful results,[48] but for our purposes "attitude" requires the addition of *sensorial resonance* if we are to understand the relationship of tone to atmosphere. Thinking of tone only as a stance or attitude can shortchange the word *tone*'s musical valences, which are in company with the qualities of pitch, accent, key, and timbre. Cinematic tone stems from the particular *feel* of the sound-image, not just from an inferred message.[49] Pauline Kael captures this affective quality in her review of Robert Altman's *McCabe & Mrs. Miller* (1971) when, in praise of the film's murky cinematography and deliberate obscuration of dramatic incidents and dialogue, she writes that "it's the *feeling tone* that matters"—not comprehension so much as our sensation of the oneiric somberness that runs through and characterizes the film's world.[50] Kael is concerned less with attitude than with a governing mood, as understood along the lines of *Stimmung*, with its conceptual fusion of "atmosphere" and "attunement."[51] Some film theorists prefer not to use the term *mood* because of its inherent anthropomorphism if we simply attribute human emotions to spaces and forms,[52] but, again, my sense allows for uncertainty and blurring between objective and subjective registers that a given film may negotiate in idiosyncratic ways. In my lexicon, *atmosphere* is the most encompassing of these three terms: it is the overall stylistic and affective system in and through which film space acquires tonal qualities that express and acclimate us to a mediating mood, be it faint or conspicuous, gradual or instant.[53]

Anxieties Amid Excessive "Nothing"

The stakes of considering suspense anew in relation to slowness and atmosphere stretch past matters of generic variation and hybridity to address nuanced experiences of spectatorship that have not been sufficiently taken into view. There is no suspense without anxiety, whether this prolonged uneasiness deepens into dread, escalates into heart-pounding thrills, or remains inchoate. That said, these anxieties need not be the product of a film's dramatic content alone, with the spectator reacting to what befalls the characters. What I have just explained about the impact of atmosphere reveals how a film's sensory reach and grip can tinge our encounter with apprehension, but I want to push further to account for anxieties that attend the *dispositif* of the cinematic viewing situation.

In his book *Film Is Scary* (2001), Kiyoshi Kurosawa asserts that watching a film in a darkened public auditorium constitutes a fearful experience of waiting at the mercy of the spectacle—no matter the genre in question.[54] Comparable notions have been explored by Thomas Elsaesser, Mary Ann Doane, Francesco Casetti, and many other theorists, including Christian Metz, for whom the viewer's primary level of identification with the film's technical apparatus involves not quite conscious anxieties that owe to the nature of the projected image, its double status as both absent and present.[55] The anxiety I want to gauge is not to be confused with the paranoia about emotional and ideological manipulation that one finds in theories of the apparatus from the 1970s, although my recourse to the French term *dispositif* bears a distant relation to that earlier line of thinking. A recovered byword in contemporary film and media theory, *dispositif* encompasses the technological "apparatus" of the medium as well as aesthetic systems of "arrangement" that "dispose" us to certain rules and habits of engagement. As regards cinema in its traditional setup, *dispositif* may at once comprise the theater space (architectural layout and immersive conditions orienting us toward the luminous, quadrilateral screen straight ahead) and the formal strategies that organize the film world. A comprehensive use of the term should factor in how these dimensions atmospherically interrelate.

My notion of dispositive anxiety takes cues from Elsaesser's little-discussed article "Narrative Cinema and Audience Aesthetics" (1973), where he writes of a fundamental, possibly very slight anxiety or "pressure" that is built into the viewer's captive engagement with the temporal processes of narrative cinema. This pressure—which mingles "the pleasure of anticipation, the discomfort of expectation, [and] even the anxiety of possible disappointment"—underpins our willful sense of surrender as we experience the film according to its imposed time sequences, fully expecting to be led somewhere by the story, to be galvanized and "released" in return for our voluntary "imprisonment." As such, this anxiety "demand[s] some form of 'management'" on the film's part through a dynamic of "energy transformation and emotional release." The film, while providing a "time-focus," must find a way to absorb, redirect, and supply an outlet for anxious energies that the viewing situation stirs up. Elsaesser theorizes the spectator's bodily, affective interface with the screen as a "channel, where energy flows in both directions." For the "channel" to function smoothly, the film, through its stylistic, rhythmic, and dramatic operations, must integrate and consistently control and redistribute this fundamental dispositive uneasiness. Any given narrative film, Elsaesser argues, "has no option but to be a time- and-energy manager," and he points to traditional narrative suspense in popular cinema as one such managerial instrument. Though he concentrates on Hollywood's ways of regulating latent anxiety, he insists that even avant-garde, nonnarrative, and European art films need time- and energy-management systems, the difference being they require of us "extra effort" to escape aggravation.[56]

Adrian Martin has applied Elsaesser's undervalued theory to slow, contemplative cinema and its buildup of "agitations" that, after much delay, occasions a "big bang" in the narrative—a structural dynamic to which Martin assigns an erotic system of energy management vis-à-vis the spectator.[57] For my part, I am interested in how slow films "improperly" administer anxieties intrinsic to the spectator's encounter. With many of the works I inspect in this book, it is as if we enduringly wait for the film to begin—for action to start—well into the running time as we find ourselves confronted with too much nothing, with "minimalist excess," to borrow an apt phrase from John David Rhodes's account of anxieties provoked by the reduced and slowed yet intricate style of Michelangelo Antonioni's *L'avventura* (1960), a relaxed "thriller" of sorts in which the thrilling plot vaguely dissolves no sooner than it begins.[58] Rather than redirecting dispositive tensions we feel before the screen, some, though not all, slow cinema preserves and redoubles them, inclining us toward the suspense Hasumi identifies when he mulls over the elongated tracking shot of the man walking in *Ossos*.

This kind of suspense has us swing between pulls of immersion and detachment, asking ourselves questions about the viewing experience and the film's manner of presentation—its delicate atmospherics, its strangely dilated, uneconomical timings. What, since Hitchcock's remarks in this introduction's epigraph, I have called "nothing" in reference to plot action is indeed something in the hands of slow cinema's virtuosi, something pitched between the banal and the mysterious that elicits in the spectator a layered waiting experience that does not congeal into a single, unvarying kind of response.[59] This "nothing" that is something in slow cinema often draws anxious attention, at least in part, toward the theatrical exhibition context and the physical environment of the spectator's encounter, a space that therefore is not just a vanishing mediator once it falls dark and the screen lights up.

In a particular manifestation of what Sarah Keller has called "anxious cinephilia,"[60] both the practitioners and critical supporters of slow cinema have expended much energy in paying tribute to the theatrical *dispositif* of cinema. This tendency has notably developed in step with and reacted to the film theater's inexorable displacement by a digital film culture with smaller, portable screens, streaming capabilities, and incontestably changed dynamics of spectatorship that skew toward distraction.[61] As we will see, a number of the films I discuss in this book clearly have the theatrical experience on their mind, as if paying their respects to an imperiled, lapsing arena of encounter, sometimes invoking it in their mise-en-scène. Tiago de Luca speaks for many proponents of slow cinema when he writes that slow films partake of a certain "mode of address that requires the film theater for their spectatorial contract to be fully met." Discussing Tsai's *Goodbye, Dragon Inn* (2003), which unfolds within a leaky, falling-apart film theater in central Taipei on its last night of commercial operation, de Luca describes how its stretches of actionless duration lead the spectator to reflect less on the film than on the process of viewing it. Tsai's "hyperbolic application of the long take," together with scenes of radical stasis that render void the image, "diverts attention away from the screen and onto the space of the film theater itself," including the nearby presence of other patrons.[62] In making this argument that slow art cinema caters to "a mode of spectatorship that reflects on its own phenomenology as a collective act of physical coexistence and lived experience in time," de Luca's essay allies itself with comparable claims by Karl Schoonover and Song Hwee Lim, who assert that slowness—as an affront to the speedy, labor-oriented routines of global capitalism—delights in the shared experience of wasteful, unproductive time.[63]

I agree that *some* slow films fit this diversional schema, but my chosen examples call for a more protean delineation of *slow*. While still acknowledging the significance of the viewing environment, my conception of suspense unearths different uses of slowness—and a more nuanced perceptual habitus that never quite licenses the audience (or, for that matter, the critic) to swivel entirely away from workings of style that more enticingly and mysteriously set forth something we are given to observe, something that may potentially make itself felt through its absence ("nothing" on the screen isn't always an invitation to disengage from the atmospheric world of the film). The critical demarcation of slow cinema as a sphere of boredom that impels us to focus not on the screen but on the theater space has often been based on a partial and thus less than accurate reading of Roland Barthes's article "Leaving the Movie Theater" (1975).[64] Barthes's essay is not about boredom. Instead, as a light riposte to the paranoia of apparatus theorists for whom the theatrical film *dispositif* was a subjugation chamber,[65] it reappropriates the maligned idea of cinema as "hypnosis" through Barthes's self-referential concept of the *double-bodied* viewer. He portrays himself as a viewer both attached to the image and distanced from it "at the same time": a spectator whose fixation on the screen is complicated by an equally hypnotic yet "perverse" pull toward "the texture of the sound, the hall, the darkness, the obscure mass of the other bodies, the rays of light." In espousing this eccentric way of "letting oneself be fascinated *twice over*, by the image and by its surroundings," Barthes doesn't sunder the one spectatorial body from the other. That is, he doesn't imply an absolute, once-and-for-all turning of attention away from the screen but rather an oscillatory, more or less concurrent dynamic of spectatorship—a compound state of pleasurable fascination derived from two contending and differently inflected sources.[66]

My conception of suspense seeks to uncover a suppler and more multifarious portrait of the slow-cinematic spectator. Chapter 1 provides a redefinition of suspense as it interlaces with effects of "suspension" in slow art cinema to produce a complex mode of spectatorship where attention shifts between multiple intensities of engagement. I trace this aesthetic back to Jean Epstein's underexamined version of suspense in his theory and practice, which predates and poses an alternative to the codification of suspense as a genre during the 1940s. Chapter 1 also supplies an expanded morphology of suspense (plot based, character based, structural, generic, perceptual, and, not least, atmospheric) that serves as the foundation for my refined arguments and analyses in the chapters that follow.

Exploring slow cinema's relationship to minimalism, chapter 2 recuperates an alternative lineage of suspense that stems from the spartan and minutely detailed work of Robert Bresson. I comparatively trace this style of suspense through readings of Bresson's *A Man Escaped* (1956), Chantal Akerman's *La captive* (2000), and Kelly Reichardt's *Night Moves* (2014). These films unfurl as minimalist thrillers that dwell on process and attune the spectator to rather subtle inflections of ambient sound, performing an anxious recalibration of attention that, in Reichardt's case, assumes ecological priorities. Chapter 3 further investigates suspenseful matters of sound by undertaking a more focused elaboration of ambience as it specifically involves the enclosure of a sensory point of view. My case studies here—Lisandro Alonso's *Jauja* (2015), Lucrecia Martel's *Zama* (2017), and Jonathan Glazer's *Under the Skin* (2013)—feature a questing protagonist whose plans are disrupted in part by an inhospitable landscape in which they are alien, a space whose aural ambiences encircle the spectator, too, but lack clear geometries of attribution as the sounds embody a force unmoored by the image. Chapter 4 then shifts attention to how fatigued, infirm, and reticent bodies resist readability in Costa's *Horse Money* (2014) and Apichatpong's *Cemetery of Splendor* (2015) and *Memoria* (2021). I comparatively show how these slow films, each of which is gently politicized as it revolves around motifs of therapy and traumatic history, instigate variations on character-based suspense that cross with both atmospheric and perceptual suspense forms. Another aim of this chapter is to exemplify how contemplation and suspense can intersect with decidedly surreal results.

In chapter 5, the porous boundary between popular and art-house cinema returns as I offer careful analyses of three horror-adjacent films directed by Kiyoshi Kurosawa: *Charisma* (1999), *Journey to the Shore* (2015), and *Creepy* (2016). Although Kurosawa rarely turns up in lists of directors affiliated with slow cinema, I relate his eerie, spectral, and dread-suffused work to gothic tendencies that scholarly studies have often overlooked in the international canon of slow cinema. Delving into matters of atmosphere as they activate the offscreen, I consider the ways in which Kurosawa's hybridized style conjures up suspenseful mediations that blend the negative affects of gothic horror with the wondrous and meditative impulses of slow cinema—a feat that occurs largely through sound.

Given that my case studies in suspense increasingly display uncanny and surreal traits, it is fitting that my final chapter turns to atmospheric slowness in David Lynch's *Twin Peaks: The Return* (2017), an eighteen-part serial "film" that hovers between cinema and television (as well as among popular, art-house, and avant-garde sensibilities) in our digital media environment. Taking leave of the movie theater as the implied arena of reception, I newly confront suspense in its multiple forms within the *dispositif* of digital streaming. I pursue the claim that *The Return* ruminates in self-conscious ways on changes to the viewing experience as suspense—what I call "medium suspense"—builds up around the unstable and uncertain status (technological, ontological, and phenomenological) of "film" in the twenty-first century. In response to Lynch's advice to watch the series with headphones, I show how headphonic sound, relative to a smaller screen, requires us to modify our working sense of ambience. The series' digital configuration of "film," I argue, becomes strangely bound up with Lynch's fiery play of atmospheric mediation that extends from domestic electricity to thermonuclear warfare.

As for methodology, I avoid frontloading a theoretical framework to be imposed onto all films that enter as my examples. What could be less heedful of suspense than forcing it, all too predictably, to illustrate Gilles Deleuze's time-image or a scaffolding borrowed from in-vogue approaches to affect and mediation? My claims find support in classical and contemporary film theories; ecological senses of atmosphere; various phenomenological arguments; affect theory; and, ultimately in chapter 6, theories of postcinema. But I go where the films carry me in the course of meticulous readings, with sensitivity not just to aesthetic form and texture but also to political and ethical considerations. Above all, I try to preserve how it feels to be in suspense—a feeling that can be stifled rather than described by the scholar's rhetorical pose of knowledge and mastery.

CHAPTER 1

SUSPENSE IN SLOW TIME

The tendency to concentrate solely on Hitchcock when discussing suspense arises in part from the need to narrow down the terrain. If we generally define suspense as a state of anxious uncertainty, then doesn't it encompass almost *any* film that has viewers grapple at length with the unknown and undecided? Responding to the narrative and emotional ubiquity of suspense, Martin Rubin argues for a quantitative definition: the question is not *whether* a film generates suspense but to what extent, how much or how little. The thriller, for Rubin, is where suspense finds its peak intensity, enthralling spectators through "sensational, sadomasochistic" games of withholding information and extending the intervals of uncertainty.[1] This process of delay and deferment, this torturous *stretching out* of experienced time, underscores the aesthetic relevance of suspense. To *suspend* (a term derived from the Old French *sospense* and the Latin *suspendere*) is to keep an outcome *in abeyance*, to leave an audience *hanging*, to hold someone in a state of *rapt attention*. Hitchcock is indeed emblematic for such a stimulus-response definition. As François Truffaut put it, Hitchcock's style manipulates us through a "constant play with the flux of time, either by compressing it or, more often, by *distending* it."[2] Hitchcock's public comments about suspense are formalist fantasies of absolute control over the spectator's sensory and emotional itinerary. To be in suspense is to be in thrall to a rhythmic and possessive operation. The sights and sounds aggressively *inflict* suspense. "You see, I am a great believer in making the audience suffer," he explained.[3]

Although Rubin's book gravitates toward mainstream thrillers, his account of suspense as falling on a range of intensities leaves open the possibility of its subtler existence at the other end of the spectrum, where slower rhythms prove vital. Despite much evidence to the contrary, film critics and theorists habitually associate suspense in its entirety with acceleration. For instance, Julian Hanich categorizes suspense, in contradistinction to dread, on the grounds of speed: "Dread is almost unmoving, quiet and slow—suspense is hectic, loud and fast." Accordingly, Hanich focuses on chases and countdown sequences when demonstrating the experiential dynamics of suspense.[4] Such rapid scenes, which have evolved from the crosscutting schemes of early cinema, enjoy a prominent position in the history of screen suspense, but they represent only one gear among others. More in line with Robert Spadoni's atmosphere-based definitions, I approach dread as a subset of suspense that reduces or removes any cause for optimism.[5] I return to this question later in this chapter as well as in chapters 2 and 5. The point to be stressed here is that no essential difference in velocity defines suspense. Nothing about the word *suspense* denotes rapidity, loudness, or frenetic energy. In fact, the legal contexts in its etymology refer to the slow, static prolongation of an unresolved issue, a frustratingly not-fast circumstance.

Instructive on this score is Raymond Durgnat's gripe, in the midst of his revisitation of Hitchcock's *Psycho* (1960) in 2002, that suspense—"a deceptively simple term"—is much in need of scholarly reconsiderations alive to the fact that it "comes in many kinds: 'low-key ominous' or 'climactic nail-biting,' 'pursuit-adrenaline' or 'haunted house creep with any-moment jump-out foreboding,' and so on." Calling for a groundswell of "PhD theses" on the subject, he proposes a broadened scale of suspense intensities: "10 as shrieking, 9 as heart-stopping, 8 as nail-biting, 6 as ominous, 5 as diffuse, and 4 or below as nil suspense." His own rethinking of *Psycho* paves the way for a refined atmospheric and temporal conception of suspense through his comparison of *Psycho* to Michelangelo Antonioni's *L'avventura* (1960). Invoking the latter film's notorious *temps mort* (dead time) and narrative lassitude, Durgnat seizes on the slower and more "minimalist" passages of *Psycho*, observing their atmospheric primacy by claiming they issue "less from plot than from *Stimmung*"—or, more specifically, from "lyrical *Stimmung*."[6] Imperfectly translated as "mood," "atmosphere," and "attunement" all at once, the German term *Stimmung*, as Robert Sinnerbrink explains, has to do with the disclosure of an aesthetic world infused with affective qualities that attune the spectator's engagement.[7] Durgnat's addition of "lyrical" implies slowness for the sake of mood, a quiet lingering in *Psycho*'s presentation of events that isn't first and foremost about narrative. For Durgnat, suspense subtly builds in the detours and the downtime surrounding the two murders at the Bates Motel: the shower scene and later stabbing of the private detective. *Psycho*'s lulling stretches augment attention to "micro-events and uncertainties," increasing sensitivity so that when the murder scenes do happen, we are all the more vulnerable to their visceral assault. But the intervening scenes, ostensibly more "boring," have a power of their own that is neither lost nor forgotten.[8] Durgnat's analysis of the film begs us to consider with care how suspense can awaken and shape attention to matters tangential to the plot—how it may deliver aesthetic payoffs for which the plot is mere pretext.

My goal in this chapter is to carve out a multipart conception of suspense in slow-paced art films where suspense falls mostly in the ominous-to-diffuse range on Durgnat's scale, even dipping into the nil. I want to highlight how suspense and what I define as "suspension" work hand in hand in these films instead of being opposed, and my argument, while offering many examples, will ultimately alight on Nuri Bilge Ceylan's *Once Upon a Time in Anatolia* (2011) and Alain Guiraudie's *Stranger by the Lake* (2013), two case studies that elegantly retime their thriller components to practice suspense by other means. But first, a more expansive definition and morphology of suspense is in order—one that compares but also finely differentiates popular and art-house varieties.

For an Expanded Morphology of Suspense

Suspense comes in many forms that may within a single film overlap, correlate, or work at odds with each other. The forms I sketch here are not neatly demarcated types so much as interacting levels, and their combinations may vary depending on the film's aesthetic priorities. Indeed, one of the main drawbacks of prevailing theories of suspense, such as Noël Carroll's and Edward Branigan's, is that they don't confront how suspense has changed since its classical Hollywood constitution, how it has evolved internationally along intersecting pathways within and outside the mainstream.[9]

Plot-based suspense is the most familiar. We anxiously wonder about the trajectory and consequence of narrative actions. This form of suspense, which puts the emphasis on the nextness of things (narrative eventuation and its pending outcomes), is typically conceived from the standpoint of the plot having already established itself and announced a crisis or problem. Will the meaning of "rosebud" be discovered? Who will win the face-off between gunfighters? Will our babysitting heroine survive Michael Myers's spree? Will Mrs. Chan and Mr. Chow's secret romance endure their claustrophobic milieu and prying community in Hong Kong of the 1960s? Will Charlie Chaplin's window-shopping Tramp—who is very taken with a nude statue—manage to avoid the trapdoor we see opening and shutting at random behind him? But there are other sorts of questions in plot-based suspense. The viewer's waiting for basic plot pieces to fall into place (which, in art cinema, might never come to pass without deep-seated and persistent ambiguities) can be suspenseful, too. The *incipience of plot* can pique anticipation as much as a looming result within the plot. Nearly all the films I investigate in later chapters delight in supplying their audiences with meager exposition: they dispense and clarify the narrative "inadequately" relative to orthodox practices. "Plot" consists not strictly in the tale (fabula) but also in its telling, its articulation (*syuzhet*).[10] Why and to what end does the film present narrative information in the manner that it does or in the temporal order that it does? To what extent is the narration reliable? Are we being primed for an M. Night Shyamalan–style twist, whereby a delayed disclosure asks us to read prior events anew? Thomas Elsaesser's influential concept of the "mind-game film," as Alanna Thain has illustrated, casts into relief how suspense forms around the complex ways in which a film imparts the rules of its world and narrative conceits. As part of the "game," this conveyance is filtered through a character's point of view, but that point of view tends to be pathological, while basic senses of identity and agency plunge into doubt and dispersion. Tracing enigmatic relations among plot, character, and the conceptual framework of the movie, Elsaesser's and Thain's respective precincts for the mind-game film stretch from popular to art-house and experimental examples, from Christopher Nolan's amnesiac thriller *Memento* (2000) to David Lynch's abstruse *Inland Empire* (2006).[11] I would add that plot-based suspense can also find expression in exercises of aesthetic modernism. Few would call Jean-Luc Godard's *Nouvelle vague* (1990) a "suspense" film, but its deferred, fragmentary, and mercurial plot is radically suspenseful, not just its noir-inflected dramatic situation (What will become of our central couple's power struggle?) but also its narrational devices (Whose voice-over is it that opens the film by stating against a black screen, "But I wanted this to be a narrative," as if the film in front of us is something else instead, perhaps an essay, having not yet made up its mind?). If one compares the contemporary mind-game film to antecedents such as Maya Deren and Alexander Hammid's *Meshes of the Afternoon* (1943) and Alain Resnais's *Last Year at Marienbad* (1961), it becomes clear that anxieties lining suspense may stem from interpretive pressure amid at least temporary vagueness and inscrutability, beyond or even in the absence of our concern for characters.

Character-based suspense is also a commonly recognized form that is more complicated and varied than received views allow. Its most normative forms play out when our suspenseful encounter is filtered through a character with whom we find ourselves "aligned" spatially and temporally, whether via structures of sympathetic identification or not.[12] These attachments, to borrow Susan Smith's useful terms, may be either "vicarious" (we fear *for* characters who are less privy to story information than we are) or "shared" (we fear *with* characters who know as much or as little as we do).[13] Most theories of suspense hinge on psychological identification with protagonists, but many suspense strategies openly frustrate that mechanism. Thain shows how David Lynch's *Lost Highway* (1997) suspensefully ruptures identification and unleashes "deranged" temporalities that attune viewers to "anotherness."[14] The sustained *suppression* of character identity and information can also occasion suspense of an unresolved order, and this can be understood as a subversion of the more familiar varieties of character suspense. Screen figures in slow cinema tend not to convey characterological depth. Their toned-down physical dispositions often evoke traditions of the Bressonian model, neorealist nonprofessional or still more curious registers of embodiment, such as the fatigued and dispossessed nonagents Elena Gorfinkel has examined.[15] Suspense in Lucrecia Martel's *The Headless Woman* (2008) evolves from the obstruction of identification where the largely unknowable Vero (María Onetto), who may or may not have hit and killed a child with her vehicle on a remote road, is concerned. Do we "identify" with the icy, impassive surface that is Jef (Alain Delon) in Jean-Pierre Melville's *Le Samouraï* (1967) (fig. 1.1) or with the aimless being that is David Locke (Jack Nicholson) in Antonioni's *The Passenger* (1975)? A related subvariant of character suspense that typically has little to do with identification takes effect when an uncertainty surrounds not only the intentions but also the basic capabilities of a character who has been *sparingly* established. In Charles Burnett's *To Sleep with Anger* (1990), the visitor Harry (Danny Glover) radiates an aura of semiconcealed menace and supernatural mischief across early scenes that portray his reunion with Los Angeles–based friends he has been long separated from, having kicked around the Deep South. The film's tone melds dark humor with family melodrama, surrealism, and intimations of gothic horror as Harry somehow upsets a baby in the womb and in a later scene at the kitchen table brandishes a large pocketknife to clean his fingernails, a rabbit's foot dangling from its handle as an amulet of sorts. What, we wonder, are the basic rules of the film's diegetic world? Do they permit the supernatural capacities Harry seems to embody? Enhanced by the film's atmospheric quaintness (drawn in part from African American folklore), character suspense here troubles any perceived bedrock of reality.[16]

I am not simply suggesting that there are two utterly different versions of character-based suspense, one of psychological identification (popular cinema) and the other based on the denial of identification (art cinema). If that distinction holds in a generalized sense where this book is concerned, it is also true that a given film may change back and forth between both varieties while it progresses. Even character-driven films may suspensefully refuse the audience entry to the central character's most crucially revealing thoughts and personal histories. Lynne Ramsay's psychological thrillers *We Need to Talk About Kevin* (2011) and *You Were Never Really Here* (2017) draw us into the vertiginous rhythmic qualities of traumatic experience, funneling the films' worlds

26 Suspense in Slow Time

Figure 1.1 *Le Samouraï*: Contract killer Jef, emotionally vacant, steals a car.

through their protagonists' psychic states, but this effect transpires without the use of traditional point-of-view devices and without much dialogue as expressivity is displaced onto sound, music, color, and texture. Even in a Hitchcock film, characters may remain objects of suspense. Do we ever learn all we need to know about Norman Bates (Anthony Perkins)? Can we ever reconcile his presence in the frame with the offscreen voice of Mrs. Bates? Although the psychiatrist delivers a temptingly neat *gothic explique* that dispels all irrational possibilities and returns the narrative to the realm of reason, blind spots remain—for him and for us. We have witnessed far more than this supposed expert has, and yet we have no way to account for the residually uncanny disconnect between the voice of Mrs. Bates and the vocal capabilities of Norman or, for that matter, of Anthony Perkins. That Mrs. Bates's voice has a factual, material status within the film's world is secured by the indication that Marion also hears it through her hotel room's open window, but Norman can't conceivably produce that voice. The film, in its final moments at the jail, responds to and undercuts the psychiatrist's smug explanation with a defiant close-up of Norman/Mrs. Bates returning our gaze, daring us to diagnose him/her/them in such simplified terms as the ones we have just been offered as the persistently strange voice of Mrs. Bates resurfaces. Contrary to what several scholars have written of the psychiatrist's report, the film's suspense regarding Norman doesn't quite end. Since when does Hitchcock's work urge us to trust in the experts, anyway?[17]

What we routinely brand "suspense" traffics in as many assurances as it does unknowns. In mainstream examples, there is often an unspoken guarantee that we will *eventually* come to know a primary character as much as we need to—that we will have access to their subjectivity when it most suits the plot. This contractual assurance combines with the guarantee of narrative closure, which moderates each unfilled gap, each loose end, along the way. For Roland Barthes, classical suspense walks a balance between, on the one hand, elongating a sequence in order to keep it thrillingly "open" and, on the other hand, holding out a "threat" that this same sequence may *never* find completion. This "game with structure" likes to "glorify" and "endanger" itself, while offering us pleasure *in* the anxiety, "all the more so because it is always made right in the end."[18] But Hitchcock's refusals of closure strand us in a fog of uncertainty. The avian attacks in *The Birds* (1963), for instance, are but instruments to enflame what Robin Wood calls the deeper, existential *horror of not knowing*—of not being able to explain a precarious, hostile, and possibly meaningless modern world.[19]

Plot-based and character-based suspense, when they hold out tacit promises regarding the future course of events, may operate as a kind of pseudo-suspense. This tendency, which upholds standards of good taste and caters to the viewer's desire for a positive outcome, has its origins in the last-minute rescue sequence. D. W. Griffith's films as well as Lois Weber's film *Suspense* (1913) employ a rhetoric of crosscutting that cleanly splits the world into "good" and "evil." The technique comes with a built-in assurance that the innocent, imperiled characters will be saved—that a heroic act will occur before it's too late.[20] Paradoxically, the crosscutting both quickens our anxiety and tells us that we and the characters have nothing to fret about. This isn't to say that we can't still *feel* legitimate suspense in the face of false uncertainty. When the covert field operations agent Ethan Hunt (Tom Cruise) scales a skyscraper in *Mission: Impossible—Rogue Nation* (Christopher McQuarrie, 2015), we *know* that he won't fall to his death (neither stardom nor the lightly humorous tone in this part of the film would allow it), but we may still feel a visceral attachment to his figure when he is framed against an infinite drop that takes our breath away. Or we may be in cognitive suspense as to exactly *how* Hunt will bring off his "high-risk" maneuver. But suspense is not properly suspense when it comes with guarantees of inevitable relief, completion, and closure. My case studies in this book avoid pseudo-suspense and practice what can be called "suspense without rescue."

Most descriptions of suspense stop after plot and character, but that only scratches the surface. There are also structural, generic, perceptual, and atmospheric levels that, far from being merely supportive, at times override the first two types. Let us recall that Barthes defines suspense as a "game with structure" that draws the audience into pleasurable anxieties. This game goes beyond the temporal protraction of an undecided narrative event. What I call *structural suspense* occurs when we find ourselves anxiously pressed to keep track of and sort out not just epistemic issues of plot but a governing logic of presentation, an unfolding process at the level of cinematic style and structure.[21] In structural suspense, the film invites us to contemplate the basis for mysterious formal patterns that repeat with nuanced variations in and across multiple segments, sometimes in excess of or oblique to the narrative. Even if this suspense variety, like plot-based suspense, calls attention to the telling or articulation of the story, it has more to do with the spectator's tracking of motifs and patterns whose relationships to the plot are unclear (and in fact there may be no relation to the plot whatsoever). Think of the systems of doubling that abound in thrillers of every possible stripe. If, for instance, we pick up on the pervasive and constantly modulated use of doubling in Hitchcock's *Shadow of a Doubt* (1943) and *The Wrong Man* (1956), then we start to wonder why the film builds up in this manner alongside its linear plot. Why should we notice and keep track of these doubled components—shots, scenes, gestures, lines of dialogue, camera movements, characters, and objects? Where is this doubling headed? Sensing that *every* screen moment potentially has its echo elsewhere in the film produces an extra layer of anxiety. We don't want to miss something crucial.[22] Many Hitchcockian styles of suspense play on our apprehensive attention.[23] Take the frantic zooms and dollies and focus pulls throughout Nicolas Roeg's *Don't Look Now* (1973) as well as its ubiquitous flecks of red somewhere in the mise-en-scène, which excessively signal importance by teasing us with the prospect of an omen. Martin Scorsese's *After Hours* (1985) also plays a game of "hyperbolic" suspense, as Lesley Stern calls it, through misleading punctuations in its manic style. For Stern, the referent for such suspense is nothing other than anxiety itself.[24]

Structural suspense may also emerge through understatement. In the muted, melancholic, and more gradually paced work of Jean-Pierre Melville, it follows from stylistic patterning that ties together multiple scenes through parallels and contrasts that an audience perhaps only half-gathers during a first watch. Cristina Álvarez López and Adrian Martin illustrate how Melville's *Le cercle rouge* (1970) weaves a nearly subliminal fabric of "fateful connections" among the lives of four taciturn men: a police detective and three criminals. Suspense imbues not only the heist plot but also the "strange magnetism" imparted by formal repetitions and by the exchange of objects and gestures within a "net of casual coincidences." The film is an "elaborate diagram" of crisscrossed relationships, but we grasp this only in hindsight, and the bonds remain stealthy.[25] The structural suspense that is part of Melville's "baroque minimalism," as Ginette Vincendeau calls it, fixes our attention on subtle yet sharply orchestrated details and processes, including the film's formal choices. Watching Melville's *Army of Shadows* (1969), we wonder if a given suspenseful moment will climax according to stylistic precedents already set. The escape scenes involving our protagonist Gerbier (Lino Ventura), a French Resistance leader on the run from the Gestapo, are styled as surprising versions of each other—that is, as slow, spare, slightly abstract, and oneiric games of delay. The surfacing patterns within a single scene may bring on structural suspense, as when Resistance members in *Army of Shadows* disguise themselves in German uniforms and try to rescue one of their own who is held captive but who, unbeknownst to them, is too weak to be transferred. For Vincendeau, suspense takes hold because of the scene's "agonizingly slow pace" and the quiet sound design as Melville's style "eschews emphasis but builds up tension."[26] More to my point, intense distress results from the structurally repetitive noises of the Nazi soldiers' footsteps and the clacking gates that open and shut when our protagonists pass from one checkpoint to another in the mazelike compound.

Minimalist varieties of structural suspense thrive in contemporary slow cinema. Consider the gently virtuosic doubling operations across the respective work of Apichatpong and Hong Sang-soo, both of whom embrace duplex narrative structures, wherein the second half of the film revisits, relocates, and restages the first half. The former's *Syndromes and a Century* (2006) and the latter's *Right Now, Wrong Then* (2015) offer two examples where suspense, while lined with low-key uneasiness, blends with tonal notes of wonder, sadness, and awkward social comedy. Indeed, structural suspense well suits humor. Roy Andersson's *You, the Living* (2007), which many critics have situated as slow cinema, advances as a series of comically grim tableaux with deadpan, zombielike characters shot in mostly static long takes. Through repetition, the film primes us to expect the emergence of a gag in each tableau, be it a subtle change or startling revelation: a person gawkily steps out from a behind a tree; a framed picture falls off the wall; two swastikas are exposed underneath a rich family's tablecloth after a working-class man's magic trick goes awry. The film's slow and darkly humorous toying with our anticipation bears out John Carpenter's concise description of suspense: "You know something is going to happen; the question is when."[27]

Structural suspense is *play*. Truffaut, in a line later taken up by Gilles Deleuze, writes that suspense casts the spectator as a participant in a "three-way game" with the film and its implied director.[28] But this is not to suggest we are granted the convenience of knowing that aesthetic gestures and motifs are at all structural points the expression of an auteur who serves as an *explanatory* presence.[29] Some of the films I study in this book (such as those of Kiyoshi Kurosawa) are suspenseful precisely where they obstruct this protocol of interpretation and open the game of suspense onto atmospheric agencies that are nonhuman. Not always "fun," this game may implicate the viewer in uncomfortable ways. Hitchcockian suspense not only makes us complicit in what we see but also revokes the safe barrier of the fourth wall. When Thorwald (Raymond Burr) gazes back at us in *Rear Window* (1954), when we confront "Mrs. Bates" at the threshold of the screen just as the shower curtain is ripped away, or when birds swoop toward us and seem to crack the screen itself in *The Birds*, the film's address is assaultive, "murderous"—a trope that William Rothman mines at length.[30] Suspense brings into play our side of the screen in ways that are quasi-corporeal, not just psychological.[31]

A related game unfolds through *generic suspense*, which may transpire whenever a film is noncommittal to genres it invokes. Either the film hints at certain genre elements that may or may not be active, leaving us in doubt, or it moves fluidly among multiple genres without quite settling resolutely into any. Let us not confuse this form of suspense with the overly reductive classification of "suspense" as a genre unto itself. What I call "generic suspense" has to do with slighter insinuations of genre identity and with fickle transformations between genres in the possible mix. I am not simply describing genre fusions. Hitchcock's suspense—apart from the shockingly violent turn in *Psycho*—often seamlessly blends the genres of romance, thriller, comedy, horror, and melodrama, all of which are readily apparent and mutually supportive. Generic suspense may more deeply mislead, puzzle, and astonish the viewer when a film morphs from one genre into another, not necessarily through an abrupt turnabout but through subtler, more graded transitions that lead us to wonder about the film's generic status and whether one of the possible genres in play will become predominant. One thinks of Bong Joon-ho's *Parasite* (2019) and its gradual slide from comedy/melodrama into thriller/horror. Closer to my province of slow art-house cinema, Mati Diop's *Atlantics* (2019) opens as a class-conscious coming-of-age drama/romance set against a realist backdrop of labor exploitation in Senegal, but little by little it turns into an atmospheric zombie movie about ghostly possession (fig. 1.2). Likewise, Kleber Mendonça Filho and Juliano Dornelles's *Bacurau* (2019) gradually and playfully mutates from a neorealist postcolonial drama into cult-cinema territory with ample borrowings from science fiction, spaghetti Westerns, and John Carpenter thrillers. These weirdly shapeshifting films use genre trappings to lure us into a false sense of security about the kind of experience on offer. They keep us guessing as they diverge from the expectations they initially set.[32] This form of suspense unleashes unnerving affects from their domestication at the hands of genre rules that tend to be steadfastly observed. Often eerier and more disorienting is the horror-adjacent film that slinks between many tones and registers (e.g., *Lost Highway*) rather than being an outright, to-the-letter genre exercise.

Theories that confine themselves to narrative suspense tend to ignore stylistic factors that raise problems for our perception. *Perceptual suspense* describes situations when a film creates tension by restricting or hindering our ability to read the onscreen world visually and sonically. Pascal Bonitzer astutely identifies this type of suspense, which departs from the ideal viewing positions afforded by classical crosscutting. For Bonitzer, genuine suspense always "implies a labyrinth" that characters or spectators must negotiate with merely "partial vision."[33] Whether the labyrinth is literalized like the hotel and the

Figure 1.2 While grounding itself in the art house, *Atlantics* shades into supernatural horror.

hedge maze in Stanley Kubrick's *The Shining* (1980) or effected through film form, it is a space of enigma and disorientation that requires us to deal with "blind spots" in our perception. The frame imposes an alarmingly constrained visual field, while cueing awareness of offscreen spaces fraught with ambiguity. For Bonitzer, even a seemingly boundless screen space, like the flat and bare expanse where Roger Thornhill awaits his fate in the crop-duster scene in *North by Northwest* (Hitchcock, 1959), can be a prison in disguise.[34] In my account, any device of mise-en-scène, cinematography, editing, or sound that perturbingly limits a film's visual or aural discernability may fall within this level of suspense. Think of the creepy, protrusive darkness in Jacques Tourneur's films or in Alan Pakula's *Klute* (1971): obscurity partners with silence so as to dovetail with the dark and quiet environment of the movie theater, enkindling a state of paranoiac attention.

Alejandro Amenábar's horror films *Thesis* (1996) and *The Others* (2001) specialize in low-threshold perceptual suspense, building tension with rather slight ambient noises around characters in tightly cramped frames. Or consider the spot blurring of characters' faces in the initial scene of Lynch's *Inland Empire*, whose use of fuzzy, low-definition video presents an anxious affront to clarity. In Kyle Edward Ball's horror film *Skinamarink* (2022), which takes inspiration from slow, durational experiments such as Michael Snow's *Wavelength* (1967) and Chantal Akerman's work,[35] the suspenseful situation of two children wandering through their inexplicably vacated house in the dead of night is exacerbated by obstacles to our vision, from the characters' hidden faces to grainy digital images that result from "bad" lighting. The film slowly induces us to read into its world a magnified feeling of danger beyond what we in fact detect. Suspense at this perceptual level also tends to relish the truncation and abstraction of bodies. In *The Headless Woman*, perceptual suspense correlates with and intensifies character-based suspense through framings (or what Bonitzer would call "deframings") wherein the heroine is obfuscated and decentered or subdivided in reflective surfaces, her face repeatedly turned away from us, her figure reduced to fragments.[36] This scenic unclarity makes the pace feel even slower by curbing the speed of our narrative uptake (fig. 1.3).

Perceptual suspense often conspires with another level of suspense that is particularly vital for my purposes: *atmospheric suspense*. As I observed in the introduction, the topic of atmosphere has recently attracted a number of film theorists, who, usually working from phenomenological approaches, have rethought cinema's capacity to spatialize moods and feelings that pervade the diegesis and attune the immersed spectator. These arguments have established how atmosphere is not simply limited to scenery in the image, assumed to be secondary to the narrative. Rather, its aesthetic mediations charge our space of virtual contact, providing an envelope within which our viewing experience happens. Indeed, it is chiefly on account of atmospheric stimuli that we feel suspense *in a present* that affectively outweighs a future narrative turn of events: something is astir and mediating our encounter *right now*.

But let us delve more deeply into how atmosphere may foster suspense, whether by itself, in concert with, or at variance with the other levels in our morphology. The mood-setting role of meteorological phenomena—rain, thunder, mist, clouds, wind—comes to mind right away when considering atmospheric suspense, as do gothic uses of architecture and landscape in examples ranging from popular films (*The Old Dark House* [James Whale, 1932]) to art cinema (*The Fall of the House of Usher* [Jean Epstein, 1928]) and through to contemporary films that robustly put forth their gothic moodiness (*A Girl Walks Home Alone at Night* [Ana Lily Amirpour, 2014] and *The Lighthouse* [Robert Eggers, 2019]). In popular narrative cinema, the time-honored use of atmosphere to signal foreboding still tends to privilege plot. Or, at the very least, ingrained ways of reading films, pervasive in criticism as well as in spectators' sensibilities, insist on seeing atmosphere as ornamental and auxiliary to what most matters and carries semantic weight. But another attitude, one that squares with aesthetic practices across all my case studies, is on display in Boris Pasternak's statement from 1913: "Let [the cinema] photograph not stories, but the atmospheres of stories."[37] Fittingly citing these words in a study of Andrei Tarkovsky's *Andrei Rublev* (1966), Robert Bird orients us toward an altered economy of relations between narrative and atmosphere where the latter may gain primacy, as it must if a film realizes the sensorial promise of its medium.[38]

Suspense in Slow Time 33

Figure 1.3 Our protagonist, Vero, is persistently "deframed" in *The Headless Woman*.

Certain French poetic realist productions of the 1930s work in registers of perceptual and atmospheric suspense that prefigure the slow and minimalist tendencies at the crux of my study. Jean Grémillon's earliest sync sound film, *La petite Lise* (1930), elevates mood above climactic narrative and visual clarity. A fatalistic crime story that revolves around social outcasts and the accidental murder of a pawnbroker, the film has long stretches of wordlessness, sparse diegetic sounds that obliquely relate to the events they accompany, extended takes, and shots that linger on characters' backs, suppressing the frontality of representation. Keenly attuned to the film's atmosphere, Dudley Andrew observes how suspense during the murder scene takes effect "less through cutting than through the reactions of characters to their milieu, largely a sound milieu" that adds tension to unforthcoming images.[39] One meaning of the word *suspense*—part of its etymology but lost in today's cultural uses of the term—is "deprivation." Suspense involves curiosity in the face of something desired being withheld. To take a metaphor from Pedro Costa, it is "a closed door that leaves us guessing."[40] *La petite Lise* hides the murder and its aftermath in abstraction by relegating details to the offscreen and depriving us of the grammar of orthodox thrillers, and yet precisely in doing so the film atmospherically grips us. A kindred aesthetic approach can be found in more contemporary slow films such as György Fehér's *Twilight* (1990), a barebones police procedural in which the clues surrounding the murder of a child are engulfed by a gloomy, rural, Béla Tarr–like atmosphere in marginally disclosive grayscale compositions—engulfed along with any hope of the aging inspector or the audience alighting on the truth.

Jonathan Glazer's *The Zone of Interest* (2023) is another stunning example of suspense as deprivation, with perceptual and atmospheric levels working in concert. The slow-progressing film restricts itself to the everyday life of a Nazi death camp commander and his family as they routinely ignore or accept the not quite ignorable signs of atrocity from beyond the wall to their house and lush garden: wafting smoke and ash, train whistles, occasional screams and gunfire. Ambient murmurs of activity behind the wall tune us into what the characters refuse to address, what is not shown directly—unspeakable pain and suffering with which the family is complicit. For the audience, there is little suspense about the events unfolding inside Auschwitz: what is suppressed for us perceptually, behind the barrier, is not a potentially threatening unknown, as in more orthodox suspense, so much as a horrifying known. But the family's bliss of dissociation stands at odds with the slow build of tension and dread we experience, not just the horror of the camp but the dread of seeing this potential for negligence and acceptance in ourselves—a notion we are pressed to consider when the film cuts to a black screen or in one moment dissolves from a close-up of a flower into a blood-red screen. In many examples of atmospheric suspense, the audience, at an earlier point than the characters, tunes into something that trespasses a boundary, as in the increasingly intrusive and noticeable blue light outside the main character's window in Akerman's *Jeanne Dielman, 23 quai du Commerce, 1080 Bruxelles* (1975).

As Robert Spadoni persuasively shows in his recent articles on the subject, atmosphere in cinema is everywhere *styled*, and *all* the stylistic resources at the filmmaker's disposal may have a shaping and texturing role.[41] In Epstein's *The Fall of the House of Usher*, what is atmospheric is not just, for example, the fog that sweeps across a field, the sunlight that reflects on a rippling lake, or the wind that moves through bare tree limbs outside the Usher manor. These events become atmospheric by undergoing qualitative amplifications through their cinematic treatment, taking on moods and sensations as "added values."[42] Film style, inextricably, *is part of the atmospheres it articulates*. In Epstein's adaptation of Edgar Allan Poe's gothic short story, camera movements, superimpositions, focus pulls, slow motion, and intercutting collectively render delicate, "filmy" atmospheric textures that uncannily fuse with the diaphanous materials and phenomena pictured in the mise-en-scène, and this convergence happens on the basis of a melancholic and eerie yet lyrical and hypnotic mood that arises where form and content intersect. The optical devices are not given to feel like ornamental markings *upon* the diegesis at a remove. They instead feel like *endogenous* expressions and tracings of animate forces *within* the diegesis, forces that somehow associate the inside of the in-ruins manor with its surroundings and intertwine the psychological interiority of the ailing, hypersensitive Roderick (Jean Debucourt) with his environment. Suspense of an atmospheric kind colors our not quite knowing the logic of these felt yet elusive interrelations—a logic unexplained by the film's end.

Like perceptual suspense, atmospheric suspense frequently gathers around the veiled and the indefinite, but this may play out in broad daylight without reliance upon a gothic vocabulary of darkness and shadows. Here again, Hitchcock's *The Birds* warrants mention—its eerily spare and unscored sequences amid sunshine and ordinary sounds, not counting the strangeness of the electronic bird squawks. The film avoids sonic clichés of suspense (creaking doors, thunder, and the like) and denies us the convenience of nondiegetic music to cue and govern our response.[43] Jerzy Skolimowski's *The Shout* (1978) also takes place mainly during the day and hides little of its dramatic action as it atmospherically orchestrates uncanny effects associated with a sorcerous and potentially lethal shout. The threat of this scream marks the film as a whole, altering scenes of seeming normalcy and infecting the audience with reverberations. In film criticism, use of the word *atmosphere* tends to suggest its prominence, but discreet uses of atmosphere can be equally effective when they instill quiet spaces and prosaic events with vague signs of mystery, as in the oneiric game of absences that builds toward a possibly subjunctive climax amid fog, wind, sleet, and fire in Lee Chang-dong's slow revenge thriller *Burning* (2018).

In some cases, this form of suspense wholly supersedes the narrative. Peter Weir's *Picnic at Hanging Rock* (1975) opens with onscreen text, a compact précis of the film ahead: in 1900, a group of Australian schoolgirls vanished while picnicking, never to be found. This giveaway has led some critics to argue that the film discards suspense entirely. However, *atmospheric* suspense remains in effect throughout, its powers channeled through a combination of devices: slow cross-dissolves, soft focus, slow motion, diffusions of sunlight, filters that lend warmth and radiance to the images, and aural murmurs that suggest a possibly supernatural entity. This "dreamy, lyrical atmosphere," as Kristen Thompson describes it, wavers between pensive and sinister tones, while enmeshing the girls' movements with the landscape. For Thompson, the film touches on horror through its evocations of a monstrous power that seems to mesmerize the girls, nowhere revealing itself except, possibly, in airborne shots gazing down from Hanging Rock.[44] This stylization doesn't represent a world so much as it embodies an extensive mediating force—one that is bound up with the film medium. There are innumerable examples in horror in which eerie atmospheric mediation becomes a primary source and object of suspense. Think, for instance, of the resonant, uninhabited spaces in Dario Argento's films.

Atmospheric suspense cultivates anxiety around all manner of boundaries and thresholds. It confounds the basic analytical terms film scholars use to sort out sound from image, onscreen from offscreen, diegetic from nondiegetic, foreground from background, center from periphery, subject from object, spectacle from spectator—any parameter neatly dividing certain expressive elements from others. It traffics in mysterious energies of manipulation that escape containment. Sometimes this form of suspense enlists a rhetoric of contagion that extends to the barrier of the screen as it is made to seem porous. From the hidden force that causes a town's inhabitants to lose consciousness at the outset of Wolf Rilla's *Village of the Damned* (1960) to *The Shout*'s fugitive rumblings, through to ecothrillers such as Todd Haynes's *Dark Waters* (2019), atmospheric suspense may draw us into feeling exposed to contaminants that leak from the displayed fictional world into our zone of virtual contact.

For reasons I am just beginning to expound, atmospheric qualities of cinema demand that we account for both "gnostic" and "pathic" elements of suspense, to borrow terms from Erwin Straus's treatise *The Primary World of Senses* (1963). Gnostic elements are those that pertain to knowledge as well as to a hermeneutic practice whereby sensory experience—at a distance—passes into the understanding of things and events as they become objects of our apperception—that is, as we assimilate them to the general body of ideas we already have. Pathic dimensions, however, have to do with our "sensing" in intimate contact with the world.[45] In film suspense, there are pathic operations that take hold of us *before* and that may *have priority over* gnostic concerns of story. Atmospheric suspense entails a pathic "firstness" of sensation that works on our nervous system before, during, and possibly in excess of narrative, though we might not be mindful of its effects until afterward.[46] And this is how atmospheric suspense may reorganize the temporal structure of suspense: instead of always directing us toward some future narrative result, it has us wonder about affective forces that have already lined our viewing experience in earlier moments without our conscious awareness.

Atmospheric suspense, then, is temporal as much as spatial—including the time required for the viewer to become attuned to atmospheric stirrings and moods. The affective qualities we gradually sense may be tangibly specific to the historical and political tensions of a given place. Filmed and set in the Northeast Brazilian city of Recife, Kleber Mendonça Filho's *Neighboring Sounds* (2012) mobilizes an atmosphere of creeping dread around the residents of a modern, upmarket neighborhood owned by a nouveau riche family that has acquired its fortune from a sugar cane plantation. The slow art-house film doesn't signal allegiance to a genre, but horror and thriller tones punctuate its panoramic study of class-based and race-based architectural divisions (in a cross of generic and atmospheric suspense, we intuit these genres without knowing for certain if they are afoot). In an interview, Mendonça professes that he wanted *Neighboring Sounds* to feel like the first third of Carpenter's *Halloween* (1978), in which a starkly defined neighborhood is infused with an air of menace that hovers around the edges of the widescreen frame and mingles with mundane environmental details in the middle of the day.[47] *The Shining* functions as another reference for how the opening of *Neighboring Sounds* draws the viewer into its world with a flowing camera movement that closely follows a child on roller skates, invoking the Steadicam shots of Danny Torrance (Danny Lloyd) on his tricycle in Kubrick's film.

But in *Neighboring Sounds*, unlike in those iconic American horror films, there is no eerie nondiegetic music that shapes our impression of events. Instead, ambient noises intrude on the onscreen world from all directions and undermine the central characters' attempts to distance themselves from a servant class they condescendingly admit into their district. This besieging aural atmosphere—car traffic, a barking dog, construction racket, and low murmurs that lack a clearly defined source—is keyed to the residents' paranoid fear of crime as well as to the main family's suppressed guilt over the source of their wealth.

In a sequence that blatantly summons the horror genre, a young couple—João (Gustavo Jahn) and Sofia (Irma Brown)—stroll through the grounds of the rural sugar plantation, now in ruins, on the estate owned by João's grandfather Francisco (W. J. Solha), the family's patriarch. Uncanny sounds disturb their exploration of broken-down buildings. When they look inside a movie theater, a woman's cries, sampled from an old horror film, echo through the empty and roofless space. Sofia and João then meet up with Francisco for a leisurely shower beneath a waterfall, as if to check off the next item on their daytrip itinerary. But the tone sharply shifts when the sound drops in pitch and the water turns blood red, saturating the widescreen frame. The film cuts to a shot of João in bed, having stirred awake from his dream, yet this transition does little to dispel the surreal features of the scene we just witnessed. Like the blood from the elevator shaft in *The Shining*, this crimson waterfall evokes the collective suffering and violent abuse at the foundation of abiding structures of wealth, power, and influence. This atmospheric adjustment pressures us to face up to the ghostly legacy of enslaved African and Afro-Brazilian subjects who lost their lives in the region. It recalls the fact that Recife was the first slave port in the Americas, and it folds the family's sugar estate into a deeper history of exploitation, harking back to the montage that opens the film—a series of photographs that portray farmworkers and their families, some of them former slaves now employed by former slave owners. In short, the film's atmosphere excavates Recife's present to disclose how modern economic oppression bears the stamp of colonialism from the sixteenth century on.[48]

The film thus exemplifies how atmosphere may work its effects not just in terms of space but also through the layering of time. Like Michael Haneke's slow thriller *Caché* (2005) but more deeply attentive to architecture and urban planning, *Neighboring Sounds* builds an atmosphere through which the specter of racialized colonial injustice renders a critical verdict on the present.[49] Its atmospheric suspense activates what Bliss Cua Lim, in the context of postcolonial cinema, has theorized as a "spectral logic" that unsettles the assumed homogeneity of time in modernity by staging the return of a traumatic history that was never really dormant to begin with.[50] It is apt that *Neighboring Sounds* comes down to a conflict over a fence on the plantation—an injustice from which Francisco, the patriarch, can no longer hide. The film conveys the impression of an outside world closing in, and this atmosphere in the end carries a tone not of guilt or paranoia but of retribution. This atmosphere accepts no fences real or symbolic—no social stratifications—and *it has the viewer in its sights, too*. The film, we realize belatedly, has been a violent revenge thriller all along, driven by the secret mission of two minor and socially marginalized characters whom the nouveau riche family have largely ignored (fig. 1.4). Suspense has deferred this disclosure in a twist on the Hitchcockian trope of audience vulnerability and comeuppance. We are made to feel as if we, too, have been surreptitiously encroached upon, caught off guard. Suspense by way of atmosphere, then, does not entirely afford us a safe distance.

Suspense and/as Suspension in Slow Art Cinema

In most of my examples thus far, whether mainstream or art house, the suspense we experience is conditioned by slowness. Each form of suspense, from plot based to atmospheric, may lend itself to varying speeds as a film progresses. Slowness only registers as such in a comparative sense. A scene comes across

Figure 1.4 Defensive barriers abound in *Neighboring Sounds*, but they succeed in keeping out neither the environmental noise nor the two security guards who covertly seek revenge.

as slow *relative to* other moments in the same film, *relative to* other films in the same genre, or *relative to* the speeds of narrative pacing and fulfillment that are more profuse across one's mediascape. A film is slow *relative to* the more general velocities that organize and determine everyday routines in capitalistic societies—the quick rhythms of the marketplace, the work calendar, the news cycle, and social media activity. Our idea of slowness is shaped by the habitual speeds that inform our use of screen-based devices to ingest and react to endless flows of information. How many of us feel the recurrent pull of our phones when viewing a film on a rival screen? Though the term leaves something to be desired for many critics,[51] the coinage *slow cinema* has gained traction in reference to a certain tendency of art-house cinema, by and large a product of the global festival circuit since the late 1990s, precisely because the practices and experiences in question so starkly distinguish themselves from popular cinema's concurrent push in the opposite direction, with breakneck action and rapid-fire cutting rates in the service of "intensified continuity."[52] If the films of Lav Diaz, Joanna Hogg, Albert Serra, Jia Zhangke, and other usual suspects in critical rosters of contemporary slow art cinema seem to belong to the same corpus, despite significant cultural and aesthetic differences, this is because they make use of slowness in relatively severe ways to solicit a generally more patient encounter with images and sounds. Viewing these films in sync with their slower rhythms allows for the exercise of thought, feeling, and perception in ways that deviate from the experiential norms imposed by more culturally dominant economies of attention, a point that many critics and scholars have made, sometimes with inflated or utopian claims about how slowness relieves and rehabilitates us as we relearn how to concentrate in an era of haste and distractedness.[53] But it needs to be borne in mind that several slow films, including those cited in my morphology of suspense (such as *Neighboring Sounds* and *The Headless Woman*), are shot through with negative affects that furnish the requisite anxieties of suspense.[54]

Slowness conditions suspense not just by moderating the pace of narrative disclosure but also by magnifying our impression of time—that is, of time as it accrues without being tautly coerced into plot mechanics. Slowness alters the receptivity of the ear and the eye as well as the oscillation of thought. In binding time to space, slowness enables even minor sensory details to assume a sharper texture in our consciousness as atmosphere vies with and possibly overtakes narrative in terms of saliency. Even a seemingly inert shot changes under the accumulating pressure of slow time and sustained duration, carrying us past initial boredom into what Andrei Tarkovsky once heralded as "a new intensity of attention," a statement that complements Chantal Akerman's similar thoughts on the metamorphic capabilities of the long take.[55] Slowness modifies not just the integral components of a shot but also the spectator's mindfulness of the shot's borders and what ambiguously lies beyond them. As Noël Burch observes of the films of Yasujirō Ozu, the longer a shot lingers, especially one that appears vacant of action, "the greater the resulting tension between screen space and offscreen space, and the greater the attention concentrated on offscreen space as against screen space."[56]

Slow cinema's manners and gradations of suspense make a satellite term unavoidable for us: *suspension*. This cognate better leaves intact the literal meaning of the word *suspend*, which is "to halt a proceeding," to hold it in a state of temporary or permanent disuse. In slow cinema, what becomes suspended is the teleological drive of narrative that legislates what matters and how long events may last onscreen without weakening or sacrificing a certain dramatic arc. In the writings of Jean Epstein from the 1920s, we find a precedent for an art-cinematic notion of suspense *as* suspension that has been obscured by the Hitchcockian tradition and the codification of suspense in the 1940s as a genre rooted in our psychological identification with imperiled protagonists.[57] In the hope of developing a more primarily poetic and atmospheric kind of cinema, Epstein both theorized and practiced slow *suspension*—a term he reserved for a changed modality of perception where plot-based suspense is loosened, deferred, or made to dissipate. As Christophe Wall-Romana explains,

> Suspension, as Epstein means it, is akin to dramatic suspense, but for a crucial difference. Both suspense and suspension evince in the viewer a pleasurable tension of uncertainty and delay. But, in suspense, that tension points narratively forward, by playing with answers to the question: "what will happen next?" How will Cary Grant escape the police waiting for him by the train station in Hitchcock's *North by Northwest*? By contrast, in Epsteinian suspension,

the build-up comes entirely from the virtuality generated by the filmic images in the present. The questions are thus: "what is happening now?" "what am I experiencing as the viewer?" "what am I discovering while seeing this?" It is this free, imaginative, and highly intensified state of possibilities produced by a certain slackness or delay within the action.[58]

Suspension at least temporarily disbands narrative causation so that a moment can breathe on its own terms. Details in the image—objects, gestures, environs, movements, and textures—take on mystery and fascination beyond their service to a plot. As Wall-Romana explains, "Rather than leading to the next narrative unit with continuity and efficiency, the situation draws attention to its awkward present tense, to its unclear roots in past situations, to its inextricability—that is to say, to where it will *not* lead."[59] This state of suspension still brings on anxious uncertainty but realigns the feeling with perceptual alertness and curiosity, prompting a contemplative mode of involvement that wavers between absorption and self-questioning about the viewing experience amid a drawn-out present. Wall-Romana's extrapolation of Epstein's idea of "suspension" or "drama in suspense" refuses to bracket it off entirely from popular cinema. He maintains that Hitchcock's *Marnie* (1964) brings traditional narrative suspense and Epsteinian suspension into convergence and allows the spectator to vacillate between experiential registers during the same scene. He extends this dynamic to other films and cites assorted heirs to Epstein's methods, from Maya Deren's and Philippe Grandrieux's avant-garde films to Bruno Dumont's slow cinema and even Tony Gilroy's more mainstream legal thriller *Michael Clayton* (2007).[60]

Epstein's own short film *Le tempestaire* (The storm tamer, 1947) walks an eccentric and deliberately uneven balance between orthodox narrative suspense (Will the young heroine's fiancé survive his fishing expedition during a squall?) and slow, durationally stretched moments of suspension that have us study minor details of atmospheric topography and weather on the coast of Brittany, the sea churning and spraying mist against the craggy shoreline at night, our anxiety crossing with a muted sense of hypnotic wonder. Anticipating as it does contemporary slow art cinema (one thinks of Abbas Kiarostami's habit of suspending narrative action, which likewise yields expressive power to landscapes), Epstein's approach squares with a rare valence of the term *suspension*, as reported in the *Oxford English Dictionary*, from the seventeenth century in a spiritual setting: "an ecstasy of contemplation."[61] I want to recover this meaning as a possible mood of cinematic engagement. The slow suspension of narrative momentum, far from simply neutralizing suspense, renders it more conducive to contemplation at the levels of rhythm, tone, and affect. Even as plot-based and character-based forms of suspense are placed on hold, other forms in our morphology, namely perceptual and atmospheric, may move into greater relevance. This recalibration holds out an ecstatic potential for the viewer, but not without some quotients of boredom and exasperation as the film hovers indefinitely between "diffuse" and "nil suspense," to recall Raymond Durgnat's gradient.[62]

Regarding suspense as a form of suspension allows us to look carefully beyond the usual precincts. Wall-Romana is not alone in finding suspense in art films that lack thriller and horror attributes. Vivian Sobchack ascribes "a grave form of *suspense*" to Krzysztof Kieslowski's *The Dekalog* (1988), where the world is covertly instilled with a metaphysical yet immanent presence that is always in retreat, forever in "postponement," and that "reminds us of what is outside sight (and beyond the heard)."[63] Robert Bird, who also singles out Kieslowski, alongside Tarkovsky, writes that both eastern European directors enlist a meditative aesthetics of suspense that, in a seeming paradox, combines a metaphysical "aura of mystery" with defiantly material mise-en-scène. Bird calls the term *suspense* into alignment with *suspension* to explain how these directors' films relinquish any obligation to represent known or assumed realities. They instead *present* a world to viewers who can take little for granted, including the very relation between form and content. Furthermore, each director, but Tarkovsky in particular, unleashes powers of time that decelerate and cloud the narrative. Their films slowly give rise to radical forms of suspense by commanding "attention less through narrative uncertainty than through a more basic anxiety about . . . the very possibility of meaning in a dangerously empty world." In another seeming paradox, their films inspire both reflective distance and visceral immediacy as these two spectatorial modes become "suspended together in (or *as*) the passage of time." Expanding on a point from Tarkovsky's writings, Bird makes the phenomenological claim that the "viewer's own life is another dimension that thickens the experience of time on the screen."[64]

Adrian Martin defines *suspension* in a similar light while writing about slow art films such as Victor Erice's *The Spirit of the Beehive* (1973). In his argument, the term refers to a structural process that suspends the onset of narrative clarity, the clicking into place of the "simple facts" on which the story is based.[65] Suspension does this by preserving the poetic ambiguities of the film's first moments, where atmosphere is primary and dramatic links are but dim suggestions. Yet Martin avoids consigning narrative and atmosphere to opposite poles. They work *together* "as equal and intertwined parts" of this poetic process. The narrative aspect figures insofar as the film wavers between multiple story threads whose point of intersection is long postponed and whose logic of interrelation is enchantingly obscured. This slow, suspenseful process primes the viewer to intuit poetic linkages within the narrative.[66]

Gilberto Perez's description of Antonioni's work further reveals how suspense manifests as suspension in slow cinema. "An Antonioni film," he writes, weaves a texture of incompleteness, partial views of arresting partiality, empty spaces, narrative pauses, spaces between imbued with heedful disquiet, pieces missing in the story and characterization and, image by image, sequence by sequence, in the camera's unfolding picture of appearances. "By a flawless and quite personal feeling for the *interval*," wrote Vernon Young of Antonioni, "he infuses his films with steadily mounting suspense. *Suspension* would be as apt a word: the moments hang, the passages of an hour are gravid with expectation; waves of emotion crest but never break; each image threatens to disclose a monstrous withheld truth or to discharge an act of violence forever hinted but always suppressed—heat lightning without thunder." Antonioni's missing pieces should be distinguished not only from the classical ellipsis but also from the withholding of information in conventional narratives of mystery and suspense, a withholding that bespeaks knowledge of the answer—as when the criminal's face is teasingly kept out of view—and merely postpones a resolving disclosure. Asked about what happened to the missing Anna in *L'Avventura*, Antonioni, no better able than his film to answer that question, replied that he didn't know. Mystery and suspense in his kind of cinema, which offers an idiosyncratic modernist variant of that genre, stem from the resonantly uncertain, the hauntingly unknown, not the knowingly withheld and in due time disclosed.[67]

Perez's estimation falls in line with that of other critics, from Bonitzer to Umberto Eco, who understand Antonioni as a master of suspense by peculiar means,[68] and it strongly tallies with the account I have been giving. Antonioni radicalizes the suspenseful operations of delay and suppression by making them primary and stripping away their pledge of eventual clarification. To some extent, Perez's description correlates with Wood's reading of *The Birds* and with Bird's assessment of Kieslowski's and Tarkovsky's approaches. It also accords with how Wall-Romana and Martin redefine the workings of suspense. All their arguments attest to how suspense in the hands of these directors casts into fundamental doubt the readability and knowability of a precarious modern world and the lives and relationships within it. What becomes suspended is meaning itself as this atmosphere of doubt unremittingly conditions our interface with the screen. For Perez, Antonioni's films are "suspensive" insofar as they resist our ingrained habits of spectatorship, forcing perception and thought to acclimate anew. Uncertainty figures not as a short-term contrivance for the needs of the plot but, rather, as a lasting medium in and through which the film's contemplative style maneuvers.[69]

And yet, while incarnating a "modernist variant" of suspense, Antonioni's slow cinema keeps one foot in thriller territory. *Story of a Love Affair* (1950), *L'avventura*, *Blow-Up* (1966), *The Passenger*, and *Identification of a Woman* (1982) incorporate thriller or thriller-melodrama components that they coolly subvert. Speaking of *The Passenger*, Antonioni states that he found it necessary "to reduce the suspense to a minimum, even though there had to be some left—and I do think there is some left, even if it is an element of indirect, filtered suspense."[70] This plan of reduction indeed retains each type of suspense I have enumerated (except for pseudo-suspense). Take the scene where our protagonist, the burned-out journalist David Locke (Jack Nicholson), exchanges identities with a British guest staying at the same North-central African hotel, a man named Robertson who has evidently died of a heart attack and who roughly resembles Locke, figuring as his double. As Locke switches clothes and belongings and then hauls Robertson's body into his own room, character-based suspense grows—not because we identify with Locke but because his motives are cloaked in secrecy. The slow-unfolding scene stages something of an epiphany, Locke's realization that he can possibly unbecome himself, but his reserved affect and behavior bar access to his reasoning. There is tension in the contrast between the character and the usually more energetic star performer who plays him.[71]

Generic suspense enters in as we detect, for the first time, a potential thriller narrative on the horizon, although the scene's reflective mood and measured pace do as much to slacken this feeling. Plot-based suspense emerges as we ask ourselves how far Locke will carry this switch and whether he will get away with faking his own death. Our questions stack up as he discovers more about Robertson in later scenes—namely, that he was dealing arms to a group of resistance fighters in Chad. Will Locke adhere to the international itinerary in the dead man's date book? Will he meet up with "Daisy," Robertson's contact? How will he improvise his way through the covert meetings and liaisons this new life entails? Throughout the film, Locke seems unruffled by these questions, which he never seems to be asking himself. He projects a vague curiosity rather than poise, commitment, or desperation.

In the initial identity-switch scene, the "indirect, filtered" suspense, as Antonioni puts it, evolves in a minimalist yet highly complex manner. Perceptual and atmospheric suspense lend the scene a fluctuating sense of ambiguity. As Locke swaps photographs in his and Robertson's passports, he listens to a recording of a friendly conversation he had with Robertson, but the sound *initially* seems anchored in the present, and a shot that reveals a tape player in the room is deferred for many minutes. Until then, the voices float indefinitely at the threshold of Locke's thought and memory. The slow-moving camera at times responds to his subtle gestures, as though to align with his subjectivity, but it has a mind of its own and is equally responsive to the ceiling fan to which it is curiously drawn. Unlike Hitchcock's dynamic camera, which accentuates things it already knows are salient (the money folded up in a newspaper on Marion Crane's hotel bed), Antonioni's camera more casually surveys the room. In a single take, the frame pans over to the terrace and presents an unexpected flashback: Robertson, as if revived, strolls into the shot and is soon trailed by

Locke, now in different attire. Without a cut or signaled transition—except for a shift in the acoustic pitch from the tape recorder to their dialogue and from the droning electric fan to the wind—we have receded in time.

The scene's atmosphere drifts between past and present timelines, between "subjective" and "objective" expression, between self and other, between the interior and the exterior, and between life and death. All along, there is something mysterious about the electric fan, whose constant whirring provides a score of sorts. Michel Chion singles out this part of the scene as an example of an "anempathetic effect"—that is, when a sound furnishes a backdrop of "cosmic indifference" to a pivotal dramatic event. Chion also refers to the hiss of the running shower in *Psycho*, which bookends Marion's murder with a matter-of-fact detail. The lack of congruence feels like a void. Chion relates this atmospheric indifference to the mechanical apparatus of cinema itself—the loudspeakers and the humming projection that generate only "simulacra of movement and life." For Chion, anempathetic effects "unveil this reality of cinema, its robotic face."[72] In *The Passenger*, whirring fans in the rooms of both men are a faintly hypnotic white noise. They accent the scene from the instant Robertson is found dead. Chion's point regarding the film apparatus, I must note, accords with my encounter with this film when a small, timeworn, and barely surviving art-house theater in Pittsburgh ran a 35-millimeter print of *The Passenger*. In quieter scenes like this one, the distinct sound of the projector supplemented the film's world—as an adjunct of its atmosphere. (It is no stretch to speculate that this uncanny correspondence between the electric fans onscreen and the projector in the viewing space has been a part of the experience for many audiences who have seen the film in art-house theaters, where this apparatus noise has historically come with the terrain.) If the fans visually and sonically inject mechanical indifference into this scene, they also confer automatism onto Locke as he becomes absorbed in the process of transformation: impervious to second thoughts and verging on self-destructiveness, he seals his fate. Even in our first viewing, we already have a premonition of his death scene.

Let one last observation describe Antonioni's reduced suspense. When Locke is about to drag his double's corpse into his room, he pauses at the edge of the hallway to see if the coast is clear. The framing of the lightly shadowed stucco walls assigns the image a sparse and abstract quality: minimalist chiaroscuro. The door to the lobby cracks open and casts a strip of daylight onto the adjacent wall, leading Locke to take cover—but the cause of this disturbance is only a draft of wind (fig. 1.5). A door ajar, edged in light, is stock thriller iconography, but Antonioni subtracts nearly all of its standard intensity. Atmospheric, perceptual, and plot-based suspense mark the scene at a magnitude just above the nothingness of dead time. The image has less in common with a Hitchcockian thriller than with the haunting tranquility of an Edward Hopper or a Vilhelm Hammershoi painting.

Figure 1.5 Checking the hallway, Locke perches on the threshold of a different identity in *The Passenger*.

Drifting Among Boredom, Wonder, and Anxiety

Antonioni's subtle approach prefigures more recent slow films that flirt with the thriller genre in one or more of its popular incarnations yet practice suspense by uncommon means at the levels of pacing, rhythm, and atmosphere. To end this chapter's discussion and prepare for analyses in the chapters ahead, I want to turn to two art-house films of the 2010s that assume a semblance of the traditional crime thriller but set about unraveling genre codes, one extremely measured step at time—not eliminating suspense but "filtering" it for the needs of an aesthetic approach whereby moments of suspension prompt viewers to drift among states of boredom, wonder, and anxiety. As customary plot-based suspense plateaus and scatters, other forms of suspense in my morphology become more principal. Ceylan's *Once Upon a Time in Anatolia* has the external attributes of a murder mystery and police-procedural thriller; however, the most conventionally thrilling events have already happened by the time the film's narrative begins. The police have already detained two suspects, and the suspects have already confessed to killing a person and burying the body in the grasslands outside the provincial Turkish town of Keskin. But the suspects cannot remember the burial site they chose. The first half of the film systematically deflates the genre's high-dramatic tension as a convoy of law enforcement and civic officers search the vast countryside in the middle of the night, plodding from one similar field to another while growing more impatient and exhausted.

The audience, to a degree, mirrors their frustration. We wait through a spell of boredom as we adjust to the film's slow pace and to its digressive and contemplative feel, which comes with mixed affective tones. On the one hand, the narrative suspension makes for droll comedy: the stalled investigation is funny, resulting as it does from incompetence on both sides of the law, and the authorities fill their downtime by debating irrelevant topics such as the taste and smell of unpasteurized buffalo yogurt. Ceylan repeatedly creates distance by staging scenes in extreme long shot against a landscape that miniaturizes the characters. But the mood becomes more meditative in and around conversations between two of the caravan's participants, Dr. Cemal (Muhammet Uzuner) and Prosecutor Nusret (Taner Birsel), who are shot in extended takes at close range and who have an ongoing dialogue about a woman's suicide and the possibility of knowing her motives (fig. 1.6). These wistful men seem to have wandered in from Tarkovsky's *Stalker* (1979), a film whose influence makes itself felt implicitly. Indeed, the rural Anatolian environment takes on a mystical presence as Ceylan's style accords primacy to the landscape and the elements, the wind in particular, which also figures crucially in Ceylan's earlier slow thriller *Three Monkeys* (2008). A German Shepherd appears out of nowhere and calls to mind the stray dog who haunts the Zone in Tarkovsky's film, a supposedly magical landscape. Is this the same dog we saw the victim feed in the film's opening shots or a different one? Is it the same animal whose distant bark accents the offscreen space now and then?

In periods of what Emre Çağlayan calls "descriptive pause," the atmosphere of *Once Upon a Time in Anatolia* comes to the fore and does as much to hinder our perception as to heighten it. As Çağlayan observes, multiple frame-within-frame compositions play on the "window" of the film screen while making it opaque. A car windshield in the police caravan, filmed in a long take from the

Figure 1.6 *Once Upon a Time in Anatolia*: Amid swirling leaves and a stagnant police search, the doctor and prosecutor engage in broody conversation.

inside, is incrementally and completely overtaken by rain (a reflexive flourish also on display in Kiarostami's films and gallery installations). The film's first shot performs a slow and absorbing rack focus through a grimy windowpane: we will only later come to realize that the people visible inside, laughing over a meal, are the two professed assailants and the man who will shortly die.[73] Between this shot and the preceding narrative there falls an ellipsis, a gap that will never be filled in for us. We cannot make out their conversation because it is overpowered by noises of wind, thunder, passing vehicles, and a barking dog—sounds that arise offscreen as if behind our backs. Such perceptual-and-atmospheric suspense has an odd cumulative effect: if initially it obscures plot information and highlights the environment, it gradually directs our thought *back around to the plot* as the mystery of the crime reopens. By the final scene, in which Dr. Cemal supervises an autopsy of the victim, a telling discrepancy brings on a plot twist, a change in the doctor's and our understanding of the murder and its impact on the family involved. The doctor cryptically chooses to ignore the revelation and falsify the report, leaving the plot to end in irresolution, albeit with the poignancy of a final beat in an Anton Chekov story.[74] While the doctor, with spattered blood from the victim's corpse on his cheek, stares out the hospital window (another embedded frame but notably clear) at the surviving wife and child in the distance, the film involves us in his wordless, fatigued contemplation through a point-of-view shot and the aural intimacy of his breathing. But this alignment with the doctor and the feeling of being privy to new information it grants us do not occasion the end of suspense.

Once Upon a Time in Anatolia illustrates that slow, minimalistic suspense doesn't simply indulge in atmosphere for the sake of formalism and a generalized pose of art-cinema ambiguity. Turning the boredom it induces to its advantage, it relies on suspension and rarefaction to set our perceptual sensitivity on edge as we vacillate between absorbed and detached modes of spectatorship. This style of suspense sustains a game of thresholds across different levels of our encounter. Anxious anticipation springs from the uncertain and fluctuant relationships between figure and environment, between the visible and invisible, between "subjective" and "objective," between action and inaction, between stillness and motion, between the film's articulated world and our orientation to it.[75]

Not all slow films translate boredom into wonder and perceptual alertness in the fashion of Ceylan's work. As Asbjørn Grønstad shows, the practice of slow suspension in twenty-first-century art cinema has as one of its gears a more "transgressive" foregrounding of bodies and landscapes that couples "unwatchable" mundaneness with equally challenging and affronting moments of brutal violence and graphic sexuality. Citing films such as Claire Denis's *Trouble Every Day* (2001) and Dumont's *Twentynine Palms* (2003), Grønstad charts a mode of *"slow seeing"* elicited by films that bore us with their persistent inaction and monotony only then to disturb us with their explicit and often hard-to-watch scenes of gore, sex, violence, and rape. For Grønstad, this trend positions art cinema as a "body genre" to be added to Linda Williams's well-known account of genres that center on corporealized spectacle and involvement (her main examples being horror, melodrama, and pornography).[76] Allison Taylor, who also writes about *Twentynine Palms* and its seeming apathy toward the violence that explodes within its narrative, comparably highlights the fluid relationship between banality and extremity in her study of the everyday in contemporary European art cinema.[77] For my last example in this chapter, I want to consider a slow art-house film that is germane to this more confrontational mode of suspension: Alain Guiraudie's *Stranger by the Lake*. This film partakes of a violence-inflected *"rhetoric of boredom"* but carries out a more delicate, still partly entrancing atmospheric project as it brings together horror, everydayness, explicit sexuality, and physical environment.[78]

As a queer and distantly Hitchcockian thriller, *Stranger by the Lake* takes place entirely at a placid lake and nude beach in southeastern France that, on one side of the water, serves as a cruising spot for gay men. The plot follows Franck (Pierre Deladonchamps) while he repeatedly visits this locale over a span of ten days, hooks up with partners in the surrounding woods, has platonic exchanges with a new friend, witnesses a murder, and falls in love with the handsome serial murderer, Michel (Christophe Paou). As Saige Walton shows, the film slowly enkindles our apprehension not so much through emotional and haptic sympathy with Franck as through the rhythmic patterns by which his daily routine is expressed. Our disquiet builds on account of low-key motifs of staging, editing, framing, lighting, and ambient sound as a choreography of bodies—its tone sensual yet impassive—synchronizes with the lakefront's natural rhythms (a dynamic I regard as structural suspense). Walton rightly insists that an aesthetics of suspension and distance tempers our alignment with Franck and neutralizes our anthropocentric concern for the very category of the human through an ecological use of ambience and landscape.[79] Yet there remains an element of film atmosphere that evokes a virtual intimacy between the viewer and the bodies onscreen, an element that, as I noted, figures in Ceylan's film as well: breath.

In his account of cinematic atmosphere, Spadoni makes the striking assertion, "Films and their audiences *breathe each other*."[80] Is this claim possibly more than metaphorical, despite the material differences that separate the film's world from ours? The history of screen suspense, to be sure, has habitually figured the breathing body as a motif that negotiates the threshold of the screen. Hanich has investigated how the spectacle of panicked characters breathing irregularly in mainstream horror films and thrillers can lead to "somatic empathy" in audience members who feel oxygen-deprived during the same scene.

He invokes Clarice Starling's trembling breath in the terrifying cellar climax of *The Silence of the Lambs* (Jonathan Demme, 1991) as one of his examples.[81] The films I am concerned with establish subtler versions of this experiential nexus between audience and screen, but I hesitate to ascribe to them a necessarily mimetic response on the spectator's part, remembering Walton's point that *Stranger by the Lake* rouses our uneasiness the more it imposes distance between ourselves and the characters. In *Stranger by the Lake*, Franck's low breathing stands out at key points—not in stark isolation in the manner of, say, the astronaut's respiration in Stanley Kubrick's *2001: A Space Odyssey* (1968) but as lightly stressed ambient noise. If this sound aligns us with Franck's point of view, it also blends in with the gentle, if at times ominous, swishing of wind: it forms a breathing motif that intermingles scenes of sex, swimming, and drowning and culminates in a chase sequence in the forest where Franck is viciously pursued by his knife-toting lover.

Plot-based, character-based, structural, atmospheric, and perceptual suspense all converge around Franck's quietly unsteady breath in the film's last seconds as he takes cover in the brush under a night sky that renders him obscure in a close-up. We are both close to and unbridgeably distanced from our protagonist, and by limiting our sensory field, this final scene magnifies our attention to the merest sign of disturbance and danger. As Franck turns and seems to stare back in our direction (fig. 1.7), we are likely to hear and be conscious of our own breath and perhaps of other spectators breathing in the theater. As slow-cinematic suspension combines with and eclipses conventional suspense, we find ourselves neither bored nor shocked nor relaxed nor under a spell of wonder. We linger in a mixed mood of anxious involvement among these extremes. The film subtly puts into place what Davina Quinlivan theorizes as a "locus of breath" between screen and viewer that stimulates embodied

Figure 1.7 *Stranger by the Lake*: In thick darkness, an intimacy of breath forms between Franck and the spectator.

sensitivity, albeit without our uneasiness having to mirror or be identical to the character's.[82]

As with *The Passenger*, *Neighboring Sounds*, and other films touched on in this chapter, both *Once Upon a Time in Anatolia* and *Stranger by the Lake* demonstrate that when the overly familiar, plot-driven kinds of suspense stall and evaporate, other less habitually acknowledged forms may realign and differently attune our engagement at the low end of Durgnat's suspense gradient. In slow, elongated time, suspense may morph in oddly mercurial ways between tonal signatures: now pensive, now fearful, now languid. At the end of *Stranger by the Lake*, Franck stands up in the brush to call out longingly in the dark for Michel, the killer he ran and hid from just moments earlier. Suspense stays in effect but ambiguously flows into a feeling of tenderness, and this turning point is no more possible to identify than it is to read the expression on Franck's face. As paired with slow art cinema, my expanded morphology has shown that we need a fuller and more sensitive account of the modulatory effects of suspense across all its interacting levels. The chapters ahead attempt to provide just that.

CHAPTER 2

MINIMAL THRILLS

We have already observed that slow-cinematic suspense sometimes straddles the art house and the mainstream, forming hybrids that challenge our categorical tendencies. More than a few incarnations adapt elements from the thriller genre. Rather than being bluntly negational "antithrillers," Antonioni's *The Passenger* (1975), Dumont's *Humanité* (1999), Loktev's *Day Night Day Night* (2006), Ceylan's *Once Upon a Time in Anatolia* (2011), and Guiraudie's *Stranger by the Lake* (2013) borrow and differently configure the thriller's sensory, affective, and cerebral dimensions. If these films, through their slowness and sparseness, strategically forsake some of the thriller's trappings, they also furnish "thrills" by alternative means within revised parameters of dramatic emphasis and spectator attention.

It would be false to assume that the thriller, across all its types (crime, action, espionage, erotic, and so forth), everywhere traffics in frantic, overwrought stimulation. With the genre's most popular examples chiefly in mind, Martin Rubin maintains that *excess* differentiates the thriller from other film genres: it excites "too much" suspense and atmosphere relative to the needs of the story. The thriller, he argues, distinguishes itself less through iconographic and narrative consistencies than through its sheer visceral power and "aggressive, sadomasochistic nature," whereby the spectator derives pleasure both from watching characters suffer and from sharing in that suffering vicariously. Rubin underscores an etymological link between *thrill* ("to pierce") and *thrall* ("a condition of bondage"), his claim being that the thriller more forcefully holds viewers captive than other genres.[1]

But what about less orthodox thrillers that seek to enthrall us by "go[ing] the other way," as Kelly Reichardt puts it in defense of her "thriller with a small t," *Night Moves* (2014)?[2] That is, what about unhurried, restrained thrillers that amplify suspense by thinning out, pulling back, and toning down? How must our generic definition of the thriller change when the films under discussion actively trouble the identificatory mechanisms at the basis of Rubin's concept of the viewer's sadomasochistic enjoyment? In addressing suspense as the thriller's aesthetic calling card, Rubin isolates the crucial operations of *"concealment* and *protraction"*: the former builds suspense by withholding information, while the latter does so by dragging out uncertainty for as long as the audience can endure.[3] I want to take up how this twofold process works in thrillers rooted in an aesthetics of radical reduction.

My chapter title, "Minimal Thrills," refers not to tedium but to a thrilling minimalism that holds out distinct pleasures and rewards—*if* the viewer adjusts to subtler patterns of emphasis. I want to tease out an approach to the thriller that takes cues from the stylistic austerity of Robert Bresson, a director frequently cited as a pioneer in accounts of slow cinema. Through a study of Bresson's *A Man Escaped* (1956), Chantal Akerman's *La captive* (2000), and Reichardt's *Night Moves*, I explore how this lineage recalibrates the thriller by changing the granularity of our attention. Each film in question does this while reconceiving a certain variety of thriller. *A Man Escaped* reworks the prison-escape drama, giving it a spiritual charge yet also focusing attention on immanent surfaces and objects. *La captive* dissects the erotic thriller and critically redesigns Hitchcock's *Vertigo* (1958). With a plot that concerns ecoterrorism, *Night Moves* refashions the 1970s-era paranoia thriller while also drawing on the heist genre. The plots of all three films transpire amid atmospheres of confinement, be it a literal prison camp, a romantic relationship beset with acute jealousy, or the pervasive grid of the surveillance state. Enfolding us within constricted arenas of suspense, these thrillers rivet attention to process and newly acclimate us to cinematic expression pitched just above naught.

Attending to Process: *A Man Escaped*

Bresson's critical supporters have tended to hold his work at a safe distance from popular genres and matters of suspense so as not to tarnish it by comparison. This protectionist stance—which traces back to long before slow cinema's categorical currency—results from Bresson's own rhetoric in interviews and writings as well as from prefatory gestures in the films.[4] Many have claimed that *A Man Escaped* rules out suspense through its main title (which gives away the story's outcome) and through its biblical subtitle, *The Wind Blows Where It Wishes* (which imparts a theological sense of inevitability). In an essay on Bresson's "spiritual style" published in 1964, a text that has profoundly informed Bresson's reception in Anglophone circles, Susan Sontag claims that Bresson removes suspense as a necessary step toward realizing a detached, "anti-dramatic" approach that adheres to a mode of "reflective art" espoused by Bertolt Brecht. She argues that while Bresson's work is cold in comparison to other films, it isn't *unemotional* so much as it refuses to be *immediately* emotional. It sternly "imposes a certain discipline on the audience—postponing easy gratification."[5]

In Sontag's wake, commentary on Bresson's work has been quick to relegate *all* suspense to the category of "easy gratification" his films deny us. The question of suspense is often deemed unbefitting, whether the scholar or critic insists on a religious framework for Bresson's cinema or, on the contrary, advances a thoroughly materialist reading. Paul Schrader's widely cited study of Bresson's transcendental style is diametrically opposed by Brian Price's take on Bresson's "erotic celebrations of surface," yet both assume suspense is wholly irrelevant.[6] Others, from Eric Rohmer and François Truffaut to more recent commentators such as Mirella Jona Affron, Jonathan Rosenbaum, Adrian Martin, Tony Pipolo, Gwendolyn Audrey Foster, and Darragh O'Donoghue, have found *A Man Escaped* agonizingly suspenseful, as have my students.[7] The notion that Bresson disavows suspense will sound amiss to those who have just experienced the film's absorbing power for the first time. It is not the film that removes all suspense, but critics who do so when they pivot too far away from the initial spectatorial encounter.[8]

In *Notes on the Cinematograph* (1975), his book of maxims, Bresson conveys how his reduced yet exacting approach to cinema attempts to "*draw* the attention of the public (as we say that a chimney draws)." He insists the attentional pull of his sounds and images increases in direct proportion to the extent that he strips away inessential detail, relying where possible on silence, stillness, blankness, slowness, and absence.[9] He hints at the suspense-building function of such subtractions in an interview in 1966:

> Art proceeds by way of suggestion. The great challenge for cinematography is, precisely, not to show. The ideal would be to show nothing at all, but that isn't possible. So we have to show things at an angle, a single angle that is capable of evoking all the other angles, without revealing them. You have to allow the viewer to guess, to want to guess, to be transfixed in a state of attention and expectation.... You have to preserve the mystery. We live in a state of mystery; that mystery has to manifest on the screen. Effects must always appear before their cause, as happens in life. The great majority of events that we witness are due to unknown causes. We watch their effects, and perhaps we discover their causes much later.[10]

A Man Escaped rigorously relies on such mysterious suggestion, but I should note that it is not strictly a slow film if by "slow" one refers to metrical shot length on par with the work of Tsai Ming-liang, Lav Diaz, Béla Tarr, and other directors who hyperbolically make use of real-time duration. Bresson isn't a long-take specialist to such an extreme degree, although there are lengthy takes that modify the rhythms of *A Man Escaped*. Some contemporary slow films clock in with an average shot length of around a minute or more, whereas *A Man Escaped* has an average shot length of 11.2 seconds, putting it close to the standard of French narrative films of the 1950s.[11] *A Man Escaped* rushes ahead at most junctures with briskly edited scenes that demand a quick eye, yet its pared-down scenography, its protracted wordlessness, its disinclination to psychologize, and its elliptical orchestration of time and perspective amount to a style that is slow (i.e., reluctant) to make the film's world and its characters fully legible.

Adapted from a memoir written by André Devigny in 1954 that reports his experience in a German prison camp, *A Man Escaped* takes place in occupied Lyon, France, during World War II. Like Devigny, the film's protagonist, Lieutenant Fontaine (François Leterrier), has been arrested for his Resistance activities. As he awaits execution—which might be imposed at any moment—he covertly plans his escape. More or less limited to his point of view, the film details the process whereby he communicates with other prisoners and converts utilitarian objects from his cell into the instruments of his liberation. He narrates events in retrospective voice-over passages, placing the film under the sign of memory. Bresson's handwritten statement at the outset assures us the account is grounded in historical truth and presented "without adornment," and a shot of a plaque honoring fallen Resistance fighters cements his claim.

This hindsight narrational perspective, the dedicatory tone, and the film's title might seem to repress uncertainty, but all six forms of suspense sketched out in chapter 1 are afoot. Narrative suspense emerges by virtue of pressing questions that belie—or at least push to the back of the spectator's consciousness—any promise of Fontaine's safety. *How* will his escape occur? Will he be punished or tortured *in the meantime*? Our concerns, after all, are not oriented just toward the ending and pinned on whether he will survive. As for the other inmates whom he befriends, will *they* be executed? Will their persistent warnings to him, which heighten a mood of urgency, have a bearing on his plans? When Fontaine is compelled to take in a cellmate, is the young man a spy? Can he be trusted? Will he become an accessory, or must he be strangled as the price of Fontaine's freedom? If we accept a spiritual reading, how and when does the metaphysical element cross with the physical details of Fontaine's quest? How, if at all, does the film convey this transaction? How can we be certain Fontaine's voice-over is sourced in a future space of survival? As Michel Chion asserts, that voice seems like "a dead soul speaking from a space–time where nothing happens anymore."[12]

As I have already pointed out in this book, countless films of suspense, in one rhetorical way or another, give away their outcomes in advance. In an action thriller, parallel editing tends to assure us that the bomb will be defused, that the crisis will be averted, and yet we experience suspense just the same: viscerality, *in the interim*, supersedes foreknowledge.[13] *A Man Escaped* provokes restless uncertainty by directing our attention away from any ordained ending—away from teleological narrative itself—and having us concentrate on spare physical actions displayed in the urgently unfolding present.[14]

P. Adams Sitney argues in his discussion of *A Man Escaped*, "It is a mark of Bresson's genius that he transferred an involvement with the suspense of escape to a fascination with *the means* of doing so." According to Sitney, this transference of attention decreases and almost eliminates suspense, which he implies is crassly commercial and beneath Bresson's genius. In a more traditional thriller, Sitney goes on, "details are supposed to accumulate before the climax to elongate the time of maximum tension. Therefore such details become negative spaces in the film, keeping the viewer from what he desires most to see, while he responds to the conditioning of what he has already seen. Conversely, in Bresson's film the details are even more fascinating than the situation, and the filmmaker dwells on them to the satisfaction of the viewer. If [*A Man Escaped*] can be called a suspense film, it is one of sensual fulfilment rather than postponed release."[15]

No doubt the film absorbingly accentuates the *means* of escape, but suspense remains in play on multiple levels. *Formulaic* thriller suspense may fade, but it gives way to a minimalistic style of suspense that has a grip and momentum of its own as the spectator's fascination with concrete detail is everywhere tinged with anxiety. Sitney's view of the thriller genre misses the fact that intermediary "sensual fulfillment" outweighs "postponed release" in mainstream examples, too, where dramatic closure is often obligatory and far less gratifying than the fetishistic emphasis on means and minutia leading up to it (think of almost any heist thriller, confidence-scheme thriller, Fred Zinnemann's *The Day of the Jackal* [1973] or Johnnie To's *The Mission* [1999]). Bresson's difference, while substantial, is still one of degree rather than of kind. I also eventually want to push back on Sitney's claim that our sensual encounter is fulfilled.

Let us consider the scenes inside Fontaine's prison cell and their levels of suspense more closely. The plot-based suspense I have already noted is further advanced by Bresson's elliptical presentation of events. Moving to a propulsive rhythm that alternately compresses and distends time, the film omits stages of Fontaine's planning. Dissolves and fades usher in his performance of tasks that are already underway, his voice-over often on hold or redundantly descriptive of actions in medias res. This subtractive method dovetails with character-based suspense: our protagonist is so sparingly limned as to be a cipher, a zero. We learn little about Fontaine beyond the fact that he is a Resistance fighter whom the Gestapo have detained for his role in the bombing of a bridge. Even as the film aligns us with him, not much in the way of backstory enforces psychological identification. In keeping with Bresson's doctrine of the film actor as "model," Leterrier plays Fontaine with dulled, flattened affect, his expressivity at neutral or just above it, his movements almost somnambulistic, and his speech virtually monotone. Although he cries at one point, his despair and condition of mortal danger are conveyed less strongly by his face than by his blood-splattered shirt. In the compacted scenes in his cell, the film at times synchronizes his look with ours, as when he gazes out the door's spyhole, but at other moments Bresson's style eludes subjective registers of framing and syntax.

When Fontaine first notices the wooden door to his cell is feebly constructed and able to be dismantled, a close-up of his hand caressing the oak surface couples with voice-over narration reporting his thoughts. Though the vocal interiority lends the image the impression of a point-of-view shot, the frame is oblique to Fontaine's eyeline: the separation is slight but significant. In ensuing scenes, he steals an iron spoon from his meal serving, grinds it into a chisel against his concrete floor, and gradually removes the planks in the door, resecuring them when footsteps approach. These close-ups of his labor tend to be described as clinging to his ocular perspective when in fact they veer from it, the camera position askew. When he grinds the spoon, the frame is low and slanted downward but removed from his sightline by 180 degrees. When he tests out this refunctioned instrument, using it to pry loose one slat, a close-up shows this gesture from a sidelong angle. The chisel dramatically glints in light under a viewpoint that does not belong to Fontaine. In such moments, the framing enters a register of description that is neither subjective nor objective but somewhere in between. They occasion what Gregory Flaxman, with Bresson's cinema in mind, theorizes as the "zerocular" image.[16]

"Zerocularity," for Flaxman, is a key practice in Bresson's "thoroughgoing commitment to askesis," the clearing away of ornament and excess to the point of "starving" our vision and the image field itself. Bresson's subtractions extend to the temporary sidelining or deletion of the protagonist as subject. "Zerocular" images effect this removal in that they *lack attribution to the vantage of a person or agent*. Neither internal nor external, such images inscribe a gaze that "belongs to no one," a look steeped in an "impersonalism" that cinema intrinsically affords as a mechanical, automatic medium.[17] Close-ups of Fontaine's slow and dexterous handiwork assert this zerocular quality. Although intermittent cuts, dissolves, camera movements, and first-person monologues in voice-over reinstate a narrative focalization around Fontaine and return us to his face, the views of his toiling hands are fragmentary and well-nigh autonomous. These scenes lock us into Fontaine's *aural* perspective, and yet, as Flaxman shows while channeling Gilles Deleuze, a system of free-indirect discourse makes for significant degrees of separation from Fontaine at the optical level.[18] The zerocular shots of his labor temporarily suspend the visual rhetoric of character subjectivity, and in this respect they are the polar opposite of Hitchcock's expressionistic prison scenes in *The Wrong Man* (1956), where we find ourselves immersed in the gaze of a more visibly distraught protagonist—a viewing position induced by an unsettling score, chiaroscuro lighting, and a vivid geometry of space built around point-of-view structures. Bresson's suspense deprives us of the psychological, emotional, perspectival, and spatial fullness of orientation on which Hitchcock's cinema relies.

Bresson's scenes of delicate labor in a confined space accord with what Salomé Aguilera Skvirsky has recently called "the process genre," a loose corpus of films and other audiovisual media that demonstratively stage activities of labor in sequential steps for the pleasure and curiosity of an absorbed audience. Skvirsky incorporates the art cinema of Bresson and Chantal Akerman as well as documentaries such as *Nanook of the North* (Robert Flaherty, 1922) and heist films such as *Rififi* (Jules Dassin, 1955). Skvirsky's notion of "processual representation"—its hypnotic pull, its fixation on materiality and ritualized labor—meshes with my concerns in this chapter. She generatively considers how suspense serves as a "curiosity structure" in process-based, instruction-oriented films, but she restricts her definition of suspense to situations in which the viewer's anticipation is directed toward a looming, yet-to-be-disclosed narrative event. Her analysis of *A Man Escaped* honors the received assumption that the film's title divulges the narrative outcome and thus waives suspense. Building on (and revising) Brian Price's explanation of the film as a subversive how-to-escape-from-prison manual, she contends that the viewer's curiosity is driven in the main by Fontaine's "repurposings of ordinary objects" as he maneuvers around the impediments to his escape. Inspiring elatedness, the film trains us to see, like Fontaine does, the multiuse potential in objects designed for singular purposes.[19]

As cogent as this reading is, it edits out the anxiety that lines our viewing experience, the visceral sensations that set us on edge, the aggressively sharp, percussive, reverberant offscreen sounds, from bootsteps and door bolts to machine-gun fire, that issue from anonymous Gestapos who lurk capriciously around the cramped frame. In voice-over, Fontaine stresses "the constant threat of being taken by surprise," noting that his "smallest error could prove fatal." We should bear in mind that he carries out his work under an indefinite yet menacing surveillance system. Neither the toning down of the drama nor the hypnotic effect of his gestures is enough to annul the tense atmosphere in which the slightest rasp from his actions can have tragic consequences for him or his neighbors. His scraping taxes our nerves, given that we cannot know how far the sound travels in the abstract labyrinth of the prison. As Chion notes, "Because of the *uncertain extent of the auditory field*," the viewer increasingly feels a "shared complicity" in the wordless silence required for Fontaine's escape activities, as if any noise, even from our side of the screen, could alert the guards (fig. 2.1).[20]

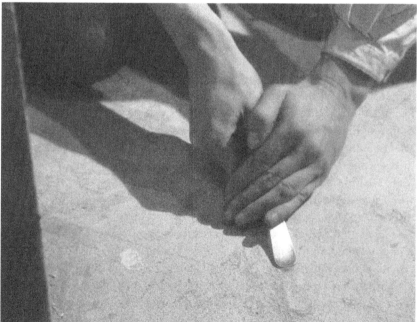

Figure 2.1 Tight framings capture Fontaine's theft and transformation of an iron spoon in *A Man Escaped*.

Figure 2.1 (Continued)

The processual element is indeed crucial, but it doesn't pull away from suspense so much as it differently calibrates it. Instructive here is Colin McArthur's earlier account of "the cinema of process," which he supplies in relation to Jean-Pierre Melville's comparably reductive style of suspense. McArthur's definition, roughly similar to Skvirsky's, emphasizes filmic structures that focus attention on multistep physical tasks presented "in a way significantly closer to 'real' time than was formerly the case in fictive, particularly Hollywood, cinema." He links this approach to a "stylized impassivity" that defines both Melville's gangster characters and the film's formal system, and he observes how this concern with physical detail and "the brute facticity of objects" evolves from the (partly conflicting) crosscurrents of existentialism, surrealism, and the *nouveau roman* (new novel) in postwar France. For McArthur, this cinema of process may commence without exposition, stoking our curiosity and testing our patience by having us study details that prove meaningful only in retrospect. Moreover, the staged processes reflect the fine-tuned skills of a given vocation in a world where proficiency is respected on both sides of the law. Invoking Melville's *Le Samouraï* (1967), McArthur discusses sparse, nonverbal, and inordinately prolonged scenes in which Jeff (Alain Delon), the affectless hitman protagonist, searches for microphones hidden by the police in his apartment, tends to his gunshot wound, and steals a car on the street by means of a suspenseful trial-and-error procedure involving his key ring.[21]

In McArthur's account, one finds a genetic connection between Melville and Bresson not just because of stylistic affinities but because Melville's cinema of process takes cues from Jacques Becker's *Le trou* (The hole, 1960), a Bresson-inspired prison-escape thriller. In an unforgettable scene that McArthur singles out, *Le trou* has us focus on the arduous labor of cellmates as they use an iron implement from a bedframe to smash through their concrete floor.[22] The long-held framing is zerocular, and the loud, repetitive process—as grating as it is riveting—takes up eight minutes of screen time. There is suspense, in part, in our wondering just how long this quasi-documentary observation can go on without derailing the fiction.

McArthur's concept of processual cinema invites us to situate *A Man Escaped* alongside other low-key thrillers at the nexus of art cinema and popular cinema—without placing suspense on the chopping block and without consigning all suspense to epistemic matters of plot. It also grants us purchase on the film's shifting tonal qualities, which circle between hypnotic fixation and an anxiety that never fully abates. Further, McArthur's stress on process, if we extend it to *A Man Escaped*, bears out what I have called "structural suspense," which arises when structural patterns repeat across multiple scenes and make us sensitive to—and curious about—their motive force. The scenes of Fontaine in his cell, reshaping his iron spoon, bed wires, and clothing into escape tools, ignite mysterious patterns of ritual. It isn't just his labor but the film's presentational logic, its "ritualized rhythm," that fuels our curiosity.[23] His labor process transpires within a regime of repeated *events* (his trips to the courtyard and washbasin, where he furtively interacts with other inmates; his glances out the barred window of his cell; his attempted dialogue with an adjacent prisoner; sounds such as trolley bells that recur like clockwork and the clearing of Fontaine's throat to muffle illicit noise); and repeated *techniques* (nondiegetic snippets of Mozart's "Kyrie"; voice-over passages; editing fades and dissolves that impart a propulsive yet elliptical pace; and cinematography that flattens space, truncates Fontaine's body, and renders the frame a compact cell in its own right). Whatever lull these cyclical patterns instill is undone when things go awry, as when Fontaine's spoon/chisel breaks off in his door, and he must find a replacement before his critical error is found out.

This structural suspense flirts with the possibility of spiritual grace but anchors itself on an immanent plane. The *iron* spoon—not the tin or aluminum ones Fontaine more often receives with his meals—is the essential tool that allows him to conceive of escape. His slow battle with the door (always a partly metaphysical object in Bresson's films) is at once spiritual, figurative, and intensely literal. Not long after the spoon breaks, he fortuitously discovers another iron one waiting for him on a ledge near the washbasin as he interacts with a fellow inmate, a pastor who is ecstatic to have recently acquired a Bible. These moments and others insinuate spiritual, possibly divine, agency into the film's material events and processes, reminding us of the film's subtitle, taken from a New Testament parable, its allusion to a shaping wind of obscure source and direction. Chance events have an unconfirmed air of the miraculous. Not unlike the spiritualized act of theft in Bresson's *Pickpocket* (1959), Fontaine's escape process is conveyed by means of structural suspense that intertwines the metaphysical with the material, corporeal, and earthly but that refuses to explain how, why, and to what extent this transaction happens. Such ambiguous structuring, which permits neither a strictly theological reading nor a strictly secular one, infuses the abiding legacy of the Bressonian thriller, as Dumont's *Humanité* and Paul Schrader's *First Reformed* (2017) attest.[24]

Compounding our unknowingness, perceptual suspense and atmospheric suspense accrue by means of the film's soundscape and use of offscreen space. This operation climaxes with the nocturnal rooftop sequence in which Fontaine attempts escape with an obligatory partner, Jost (Charles le Clainche), a cellmate who could betray him at any turn. Their climb onto the prison roof occurs simultaneously with the offscreen rattle of a passing train that covers their noise yet amplifies a mood of tension. The tight, depthless framing keeps us from seeing the surrounding space from which sounds surface with cyclical repetition: trains, vehicles, whistles, bells, and a high-pitched creak that turns out to be a sentinel making rounds on a bike. Delaying continuity and restricting vision even further, empty frames linger for several pensive seconds, both after Fontaine and Jost exit the current shot and before they enter the ensuing shot.[25]

In one of the film's most unbearably protracted moments of suspense, Fontaine—having learned that he must murder a pacing guard—hides at the corner of a building and waits for the most advantageous instant to strike. A long, immobile take dilates the interval of his decision as he presses his back against the wall, hidden in shadow as the camera tracks in and renders screen space even shallower. He has put aside a metal hook, opting to use his bare hands instead. The aural pitch and volume of the offscreen guard's footsteps on gravel imply his shifting position. By chance (destiny?), the passing of a train concurs with the guard's point of closest proximity. Again using the train's uproar to drown out his actions, Fontaine rounds the corner, yet there is no cut: the long take remains fixed on a vacant, impeded view. The decisive event unfolds in a space "behind the set," to use one of Noël Burch's categories of the offscreen.[26] Noise from the train stifles any sound of struggle. Only when Fontaine reenters the long take can we infer, with relief, that he has succeeded, though his face tells us nothing.

Chion points out that Fontaine's suspenseful, life-and-death trajectory comes down to his and the spectator's deferred discoveries of the source of acousmatic sounds—noises that initially emerge without their causal objects or entities in view. Keying on the sounds of the locomotive, Chion notes that its rhythmic presence haunts the ambiguous borderlands between onscreen and offscreen space. To escape, Fontaine must reach this "increasingly closer, more concrete, and more insistent" noise by, in effect, "de-acousmatizing it." Indeed, when Fontaine and Jost have negotiated their final obstacle to freedom, they walk past a swirl of steam rising from an invisible rail station, its billows eventually overtaking the shot as a "FIN" title appears. "The train we have finally gotten to is in the image," observes Chion, "but only in the form of a trail of smoke—and retains its mystery."[27]

As the escapees fade into the dim background and the steam, moving toward us, blankets the foreground, a swell of sacred choral music (nondiegetic) denotes triumph. However, there is something teasingly partial and unforthcoming about this cloud of steam. It is a kind of "quasi-thing,"[28] the pictorial equivalent of an acousmatic sound: an effect whose causal source is veiled. In a register between matter and spirit, it at once closes and reopens the film with another riff on the limits of visibility. The title has been fulfilled, yet suspense endures on account of unsettled questions that have gathered around the *how* as much as the *what*. Too much has been reduced, omitted, and obscured for us to gauge with confidence the degree to which spiritual grace, if at all, has inflected the dramatic situations we have only partially witnessed. Posing as it does an alternative to the Hitchcockian paradigm of suspense, Bresson's sparse and elliptical method of subtraction has subtler ways of stoking uncertainty, and yet the cumulative effect is excruciatingly and exhilaratingly suspenseful on its own terms.

Eye and Ear in the Labyrinth: *La captive*

Though it is no less of a genre endeavor than *Le trou* and *Escape from Alcatraz* (Don Siegel, 1979), *A Man Escaped* redefines what constitutes a "thrill." The film's thrillingly rhythmic, precisely articulated ambiguities at once test, occlude, strain, and reattune our absorbed perception in an atmosphere laced with uneasiness. Its aural sensations from out of frame not only raise ambient noise to primary expression but also undermine certainty of their origins, in keeping with Bresson's linkage of "mystery" to the separation of effects from their causes.[29] Bresson's privational style is a far cry from Rubin's quantitative and psychologistic criteria regarding the thriller, but *A Man Escaped* aggressively enthralls the viewer made to adjust to a more reserved distribution of affect, a more finely graded regime of attention.

This approach exemplifies an alternative *phasing* of suspense with affective and attentional ramifications for the spectator. The progression of suspense is typically defined on the basis of narrative information alone: clues amass and give rise to possible threads and outcomes about which characters and, by extension, the viewer fret. Concealment and protraction thus induce anxiety regarding the narrative's approaching end point.[30] But we have seen that with Bresson these operations—not just concealment and protraction but also cumulation, constriction, and deferral—have more to do with sensory, rhythmic stimuli and physical activities that fascinate us above and beyond questions of narrative eventuation.

Chantal Akerman's *La captive* is another case in point, an art-house spin on the erotic thriller that interrogates the very theme of captivation. Like Bresson's film (minus the spiritual undertones), it delivers suspense through an understated yet gripping atmosphere of confinement. Akerman's cinematic style, as many have remarked, begs comparison to Bresson's, and it tends to receive the same descriptive language: "austere," "ascetic," "restrained," "toned down," "processual," "deadpan," "frugal," "exacting," and so on. There are certainly grounds to situate Akerman within a line of Bressonian suspense, but I also want to give the aesthetic and political distinctiveness of her work its due. Akerman acknowledged her affinities with Bresson's cinema and voiced her admiration especially for *Diary of a Country Priest* (1951), *Pickpocket*, and *Mouchette* (1967).[31] The suspenseful aspects of her filmmaking, however, have additional influences and motivations at the level of technique. It was her encounter with contemporary North American experimental cinema at Anthology Film Archives while she was living in New York from 1971 to 1972 that introduced her to a radically minimalized form of suspense in the structural films of the Canadian artist Michael Snow. Recalling her response to Snow's *La région centrale* (1971), she explains to Nicole Brenez in 2011: "The sensory experience I underwent was extraordinarily powerful and physical. It was a revelation for me, that you could make a film without telling a story. And yet the tracking shots of <---> (*Back and Forth*, 1969) in the classroom, with movements that are purely spatial while nothing is happening, produce a state of suspense as tense as anything in Hitchcock. I learned from them that a camera movement, just a movement of the camera, could trigger an emotional response as strong as from any narrative."[32]

Akerman's films of the early 1970s reengineer this experience. Her approach, in her own words, is less "scientific" than Snow's—that is, less beholden to preprogrammed ideas and constructs.[33] Yet her films test out comparable modes of suspense amid seeming nothingness, driven by microformal processes at a remove from narrative teleology. Reworking the 360-degree pan of Snow's *Standard Time* (1967), Akerman's *La chambre* (1972) consists of a single, eleven-minute take that pans repeatedly around a New York apartment (Akerman's own).[34] Filmed by Babette Mangolte, who had introduced Akerman to Snow's work, this silent short elicits suspense through the slow reveal of domestic clutter and a series of modulations involving a woman (Akerman) as she returns the camera's gaze and eats an apple in bed. Akerman's *Hotel Monterey* (1972), which is also silent and filmed by Mangolte, explores the dark, labyrinthine interior of a Manhattan hotel that has fallen from its Art Deco grandeur and now bears the ravages of time as a low-rent housing complex for financially precarious senior citizens. A mood of suspense attends unoccupied shots of corridors, elevators, windows, and doorways—frames within frames that linger indefinitely on the edge of an event.

Three-quarters into *Hotel Monterey*, the camera, which has been stationary so far, begins to track down a symmetrically framed hallway. This change startles at first but the sensation of motion reinstates a hypnotic hold. While still channeling the structural avant-garde, these slow tracking shots add to an atmosphere that already verges on the gothic with its ghostly absences, vectorized architecture, games with color and shadow, and eerie conferrals of not-quite-human agency onto the camera and automated elevator doors. Because of their stretched-out durations, shots vacillate between the registers of documentary observation and purely graphic abstraction. In interviews, Akerman often theorizes that when time dilates to such a degree in the absence of a cut, the image circles between the literal and the abstract in the viewer's perception, conjuring memories and instilling unseen, possibly traumatic resonances.[35]

What Manny Farber praised in Snow's work in 1970—its prioritization of faintly variable rudiments of light, shade, movement, and texture in a drama of surface that affects an onlooker like a tense basketball game, albeit with "purposefully intolerable stretches"—also defines Akerman's enterprise whenever a sensitive viewer plays along.[36] Ivone Margulies, in her seminal book *Nothing Happens: Chantal Akerman's Hyperrealist Everyday* (1996), situates Akerman's "hyperbolic" minimalism alongside Bresson's practice and astutely considers the political stakes of spectatorial attention—all the while casting light on Akerman's style in ways that relate to my conception of slow, subtractive suspense. According to Margulies's account, Akerman developed a kinship with Bresson's approach instinctively, years before seeing his films. This happened as she transitioned—now equipped with sound—into feature-length drama with *Jeanne Dielman, 23 quai du Commerce, 1080 Bruxelles* (1975).[37]

Another landmark instance of confinement cinema, *Jeanne Dielman* has us scrutinize the mundane domestic rituals of the eponymous lead character (Delphine Seyrig), a sex worker who receives male clients in a Brussels apartment where she lives with her son. As Margulies notes, the film is Bresson-like in its unwavering fixation on concrete detail, with Seyrig's performance exhibiting the antinaturalist peculiarity of the Bressonian model, her flattened affect and strict gestures made to comport with the automatic, mechanical attributes of the film medium.[38] Further akin to Bresson's style, Akerman brings on mystery through a sparing sound ambience and the use of vacated frames that hold for several seconds after Jeanne exits, halting narrative continuity. Like

Bresson's delineation of Fontaine's tasks in *A Man Escaped* (except filmed frontally rather than from oblique angles), *Jeanne Dielman* presents a serialized formal process that little by little converts household chores into an entrancing spectacle. In Akerman's project, though, this serialization of form more robustly administers the long take and is geared precisely to the rhythms and anxieties of so-called woman's work enacted by a gendered body. The film famously recuperates such corporeal routines from banality, from marginality, and raises them to matters of rigorous "social attention."[39]

When discussing *Jeanne Dielman*, Akerman strongly insists that "suspense" creeps into the film's processual system, its repetitious display of routine tasks (cooking, cleaning, bathing, and so forth), bringing on anxiety—in both Jeanne and the spectator—instead of keeping it at bay. Speaking to how tension arises when slight disturbances break the rigid pattern, Akerman states that "suspense builds because I think that deep down, we know that something's going to happen. It's like a Greek tragedy, yet there's practically nothing there."[40] Suspense, then, enters the affective equation when a series of little disasters (overdone potatoes, a dropped shoe brush, a loose lock of hair) vaguely prefigure a large one as the chain leads to Jeanne's murder of a client after sex. The imminent cataclysm is, moreover, signaled through activations of offscreen space, such as a flashing blue-neon light that invades the living room from a window and dances across reflective glass tables and cabinets, its source invisible.

Scholars writing about *Jeanne Dielman* tend to ignore or devalue the role of suspense or to invoke it in a way that all but nullifies it. Mary Ann Doane's nuanced analysis compares the film to Sally Potter's *Thriller* (1979), a reflexive inquiry into the victimized roles in which women are cast in popular genres. She writes that both of these women-directed films "construct a suspense *without expectation*" as part of a new, defamiliarized "syntax" for the portrayal of female bodies onscreen—a syntax that avoids the gendered "codification of suspense" in classical narrative cinema.[41] *Jeanne Dielman*'s feminist radicality along syntactical lines is, no doubt, central to its power, but does the film indeed clear away *all* audience expectation as it strands us in the present? Can we have "suspense" when no expectation colors it? When Akerman, by contrast, attributes suspense to the film, her definition *hinges on our nervous expectation*, our attunement to a tragic turn that evolves out of "practically nothing" but a series of glitches in Jeanne's routine.

The film's temporal suspensions may dissolve traditional genre suspense, and Delphine Seyrig's performance may bar psychological identification, but these maneuvers also call forth suspense of a different order. As Ivone Margulies argues, building on Doane's claim,

> One adjusts very slowly to the fact that the irruption of differences holds the promise of some dramatic change. In *Jeanne Dielman*, the suspension of

expectation generates another kind of suspense: the film experiments with the possibility of an attention to silence, blankness, and minor events but not as either a sign of some form of asceticism (a moralistic standpoint against traditional narrative, for example) or the absolute precondition for or even announcement of drama (like the stillness that reinforces the suspense of a thriller). *Jeanne Dielman* constitutes a radical experiment with being undramatic and, paradoxically, with drama's absolute necessity.[42]

Expectation, if momentarily suspended, isn't altogether removed. We sense a looming turnabout of tragic proportions, but the film has us concentrate more fixedly on the present, its real-time actions and accidents that "are not to be read as forebodings," Margulies writes, "*although they eventually function that way.*"[43] Suspense—specifically what I have called "structural suspense"— therefore resides in the escalating conflict between divergent pulls of attention: one synchronic (focused on prolonged happenings at particular junctures) and the other diachronic (focused on serialized patterns that accumulate over time) (fig. 2.2).

Suspense also derives from the fact that even as we discern the incremental approach of disaster, no clear dramatic hierarchy distinguishes between "major" and "minor" events—that is, between "something" and "nothing."[44] The murder, which the film pushes toward with gradual, mechanical linearity, is both decisive and peripheral—a situation not unlike the mysterious death in Snow's durational apartment "thriller" *Wavelength* (1967). That said, Akerman's structural suspense, while indebted to the avant-garde, doesn't *entirely* depart from how thriller narratives juggle omens while disquieting the audience. Rather, it half-conceals its premonitions within a register of the quotidian that excessively spans time. If thrillers captivate through excess, this captivation may also come about at the low end of the spectrum when hyperbolic slowness and sparseness rouse uncertainty around too much of nothing.

La captive, a French/Belgian coproduction, returns to the enclosed architecture and constrictive forms of Akerman's earlier films. Set in a wealthy, rarefied Paris milieu that feels at once contemporary and lodged in the nineteenth century, the film is adapted from the fifth volume of Marcel Proust's *À la recherche du temps perdu* (*In Search of Lost Time*, 1913–1927). Proust's tale is told in the first person by a reclusive man whose extreme jealousy leads him to confine and investigate his partner, a young woman he suspects is having lesbian affairs. Intent on knowing every detail of her daily activities, no matter how trivial, he hires others to spy on her when she isn't cooped up in their fancy apartment. Akerman's dreamlike film also centers on a controlling male, Simon (Stanislas Merhar), and the dissolution of his relationship with his lover, Ariane (Sylvie Testud), but it forgoes the novel's first-person narration. In lieu of using voice-over, the film imparts an enclosed, paranoiac mood through

Figure 2.2 *Jeanne Dielman*: In moments of pause, Jeanne shows hints of anxiety, while our attention balances tensely between the current event and accumulated patterns thus far.

ambient sound, frames nested within frames, Bressonian performances that emote just above neutral, and mise-en-scène with noirish connotations. As Marion Schmid puts it, Akerman "adapts Proust's modernist novel of consciousness to the cinema of obsession, in particular the thriller and the *film noir*, which offers a visual corollary to Proust's exploration of extreme mental states." Observing that Akerman reimagines *Vertigo*, with Simon standing in for Hitchcock's detective, Schmid sums up *La captive*'s amalgamated nature:

"The Hitchcockian thriller, revered for its suspense, hypnotic camerawork, and astute character psychology, meets Akerman's more static film syntax in a bold synthesis of paralysis and movement, Akermanian duration and Hitchcockian tension."[45]

This hybridized film more specifically rethinks the erotic thriller. *Vertigo*, of course, has spawned numerous erotic thrillers, for which it supplies a template of voyeurism, enchantment, doubling, duplicity, recursive plot structures, and oneiric subjectivity. These later variations on Hitchcock's film, whether they emerge in mainstream, art-house, or exploitation markets, more vividly trade on sex, often though not always from the vantage of heterosexual male desire.[46] The poster for *La captive* advertises female nudity—a woman bathing behind semitransparent glass, vis-à-vis a man's look.[47] But the film starkly deviates from erotic thrillers in the style of the *Vertigo*-inspired *Basic Instinct* (Paul Verhoeven, 1992), several of which exultantly expand on the "vaguely pornographic impulse lurking at the edges" of Hitchcock's work.[48] Akerman's sensitivity to dynamics of gender and sexuality locates her erotic thriller somewhere between Jane Campion's *In the Cut* (2003) and French art-house ventures by the likes of François Ozon and Claude Chabrol. But unlike Campion's much grittier portrait of a woman's sexual desires, and unlike Christian Petzold's female-centric twists on *Vertigo* in *Phoenix* (2014) and *Undine* (2020), *La captive* hews close to the viewpoint of a male protagonist whose flaws echo those of *Vertigo*'s Scottie (James Stewart). Indeed, Akerman's allusions to *Vertigo* comport with recent feminist reappraisals of the rhetoric of the male gaze in Hitchcock's cinema, which illustrate how the gaze imprisons and undermines not only its object but its bearer (fig. 2.3).[49]

Figure 2.3 In *La captive*, Simon is held captive by his own insecurities and need to control.

It may seem ill-suited to consider Akerman's film in this generic context, but we should bear in mind that Akerman herself thought of *La captive* as something of a companion to *Eyes Wide Shut* (Stanley Kubrick, 1999), another slow, cryptic, dreamily anachronous film that takes shape around a crisis of masculinity and subjects the erotic thriller to a reflexive dismantling at the close of its most popular decade.[50] In *La captive*, erotic energies are toned down through a leveling of affect and channeled into the film's formal system: its sensuous play of color and texture, its ambient sound design, and, not least, its choreography of bodies. Eroticism bedevils Simon, ethically works as a kind of protective veil for Ariane, and yet remains in its sublimated form a suspenseful force for the viewer.

Hyperbolic slowness conditions three levels of suspense that work in concert in the film: perceptual, atmospheric, and structural. The *Vertigo*-like sequences of Simon following Ariane on the Paris streets and inside the Rodin Museum start by mimicking a Hitchcockian grammar of suspense with continuity cuts and psychological point-of-view structures, but then Akerman severely distends time through long takes that dwell on absences, diverting the narrative action into more ruminative suspensions (fig. 2.3). Simon's quest, foiled at each turn, leads him into a labyrinth of crisscrossing shadows and doubles, shot by the cinematographer Sabine Lancelin, who filmed Philippe Grandrieux's slow, bathed-in-darkness *Sombre* (1998), a horror/thriller exercise, just before working with Akerman.[51] Identifying a thrilling feat of inventive geography, Cristina Álvarez López and Adrian Martin observe how what appears to be a series of three different, vaguely interlocking spaces—across consecutive shots of Simon walking in pursuit of women who resemble Ariane—is, in fact, the same street corner presented sneakily from different angles and scales. Invoking Deleuze's conception of "any-space-whatever" in modern cinema, Álvarez López and Martin explicate how Akerman's minimalist games with architecture conjure up a "phantasmagorical and phantasmatic atmosphere," immersing us in a variable "labyrinth of streets that we cannot master. And we are, like Simon, tricked by optical illusions and false perceptions, lost in a city maze that gives rise to familiar but deceptive female figures, disembodied ghostly presences."[52] In the city scenes that track Simon's search, Akerman additionally doubles and divides her images internally through a striking, albeit low-key play of reflections in glass, from Simon's multiplied figure to abstract red scintillae from the lights of automobiles.

Such perceptual and atmospheric suspense is bound up with the film's thematic chipping away at Simon's possessive drive. Visual obscurity partners with entrancing ambient noise that charges the offscreen with an air of mystery related to Ariane's bisexuality. Richard Dyer notes how "erotic ambiguities" in the soundscape (e.g., the percussive clicking of Ariane's high heels as it blends in with other women's footsteps) resist and exasperate Simon's need to know her, his attempts to translate her otherness into his self-oriented meaning.[53]

Figure 2.4 A *Vertigo*-inspired scene of following in *La captive* results in possible evidence of Ariane's affair.

This reflective commentary on Simon's possessiveness and Ariane's endangered liberty is further on display in the structural suspense the film unfolds within and across ritualized sex scenes between Simon and Ariane, which persistently underscore through staging and mise-en-scène a boundary between their figures (fig. 2.5). In an interview by Dominique Païni in 2000, Akerman uses the term *dispositif* regarding the somnophiliac scenarios the lovers enact, the recurrent games in which Ariane (who is possibly fatigued from her trysts with other women) falls asleep for Simon's sexual gratification (though suspense and deadpan humor bear on the matter of whether she indeed sleeps or is feigning sleep).[54] We might extend this word *dispositif* (read as "arrangement") to encompass the varying formal setups and figurations that expand on this barrier motif, reconstituting it in different ways. This motif opens the film as Simon views lyrical Super 8 footage of Ariane on a beach with female companions. He watches from a cold, lifeless remove accented by an automatic projector hum, his shadowy figure distinct from the imagery on the screen before him. The scene summons the introduction of Devlin (Cary Grant) in Hitchcock's *Notorious* (1944): a dark, spectatorial entity at the boundary of our screen, eying a vibrant woman he intends to rein in (fig. 2.6).[55]

Álvarez López and Martin expertly call attention to Akerman's subtle repetitions with variations across multiple scenes, her "small moves" that install "currents of nervous tension" in a paranoiac atmosphere.[56] Added to these permutations is a no less suspenseful sound ambience that plays on discreet contrasts and echoes. In exterior scenes where Simon searches for Ariane, the purrs and swishes from passing cars become quasi-musical, at once lulling and portentous as they intermingle with Rachmaninov's "Isle of the Dead," with its slow, undulant sonorities that evoke a churning sea. Caught up in a network of

Figure 2.5 Physical barriers between Simon and Ariane proliferate in *La captive*.

Figure 2.6 Simon's shadowy, spectating presence in *La captive* resembles that of Devlin in Hitchcock's *Notorious*.

sensations, these wavelike drones hark back to the anempathetic whir of the projector from the film's opening. They also prefigure the plot's trajectory by mapping an ambient course to the film's tragic seaside finale.

Character-based suspense thickens around Ariane: not precisely traditional Hitchcockian suspense rooted in identification but a minimalist form of suspense that bars access to character interiority. This concealment of Ariane's inner life follows from Akerman's Emmanuel Levinas–influenced aesthetics and ethics of alterity, a reference that Akerman highlights in her interview with Brenez.[57] A Levinasian embrace of the irreducible mystery of the Other, whose well-being takes ethical priority over the self in a phenomenology of the interpersonal encounter, inflects Akerman's boundary motif, deliberately evasive portrait of Ariane, and persistent frustration of Simon's viewpoint.[58] These ethically inclined barriers, however, stay in effect only for so long. Late in *La captive*, worn down by Simon's prying, Ariane starts to communicate her inner life more openly through words and facial expressions. As with the final stretch of *Vertigo*, there is almost a hint of possibility for the couple, as though obstacles to acknowledging, mutually, the reality of their relationship are about to be removed, but this shift in *La captive* gives Ariane no increased deciding power, and it opens the door for Simon to resume his domineering once he declares their romance back on. If character suspense regarding Ariane momentarily abates, it is restored, coinciding with an upsurge of other suspense levels in the key of doom. The nocturnal waves that open the film return in the finale and now define the site where Ariane all but invisibly drowns outside a seaside hotel, a place Simon has taken them to celebrate their reunion (and to re-create, consciously or not, the jubilant beach scene caught in the 8-millimeter footage, swapping himself for the female revelers). But the ending asserts a gothic play of darkness and opacity that offsets their sunlit drive to the coast (fig. 2.7). Perceptual and atmospheric suspense keep us from knowing exactly what takes place once Ariane goes for a swim as Simon orders dinner. We have noted, even as Simon has not, that Ariane has been lured by the waves, but does she commit suicide, or is she drowned by Simon when he tries to save her? The last shot,

Figure 2.7 Heavy darkness descends on the "reunited" couple in the finale of *La captive*.

a long take in which he gradually approaches the foreground in a rescue boat at sunrise, amid a seascape of soft hues and spare lines, unfolds as a suspenseful reveal: after more than two unbearably stretched minutes, we see Ariane is missing from the boat. Our long wait leads us to contemplate how this incident has been prefigured. The boat's trolling motor echoes the projector hum from the start of the film, again stressing Simon's remove from an unknowable Other, and Ariane's sleeping game has anticipated her death. There is a dread-filled sense of this outcome having been inevitable—a terminal point toward which the film has marched from its first frames.[59]

Akerman's durational style transforms the thriller by magnifying small-scale details and sensations in the viewer's consciousness.[60] *La captive*, not unlike *Jeanne Dielman* in this sense, "excessively" takes what might seem to be ambient filler—outwardly nonsignificatory noise—and molds it into a carrier of crucial motifs. Although a late film in Akerman's corpus, it revives the spirit of a remark she made in 1977: "We follow stories because this is what we are trained to do; as spectators we habitually identify with characters. With my films, on the other hand, there are no protagonists and no familiar stories. What is happening lies elsewhere: in the rhythm, in the pulse, in the point of view. One image precedes another, like notes in music. Images are notes. You have only to look and listen—and that calls into question your role as spectator."[61] *La captive*, granted, is a familiar narrative about a dissolving couple, but it is also a structuralist experimental film in disguise—a work that suspensefully reattunes us to the rhythm, pulse, and music of its first-order atmospheric stimulation. For reasons bound up with its ethical themes, it fosters a fine-grained mode of attention that might even be called "nonneurotypical," given how differently it prioritizes the audiovisual field.

Environmental Dread: *Night Moves*

A stylistic heir to both Bresson and Akerman, Kelly Reichardt is a leading exemplar of minimalist, durational aesthetics in American independent cinema. Known for studies of adrift, dispossessed characters in films acutely sensitive to the environment, she is largely a regional artist who in frequent collaborations with the fiction writer Jonathan Raymond reflects on the ecological histories of the Oregon landscape.

Reichardt is yet another filmmaker in the ambit of my study whose enterprise calls for a nuanced appraisal of slow cinema's underexplored hybridity. Even as her films oppose hasty rhythms and overabundant stimuli, they invoke popular cinema of the past without necessarily negating it. She is more of a cinephile director than scholars have generally recognized, with a wide range of aesthetic references that bridge her creative output and her pedagogy at Bard

College, where she teaches as an artist in residence. Her sensibility revels in something for which she praises Barbara Loden's *Wanda* (1970): unexpected genre play.[62] Reichardt's games with the Western in *Meek's Cutoff* (2010), *Certain Women* (2016), and *First Cow* (2019) have been considered at length. However, her borrowings from crime genres—namely, the heist film and the paranoid thriller—have not met with the same level of attention despite being essential to her work on both formal and political grounds.

As with Bresson and Akerman, the matter of suspense comes up rarely in considerations of Reichardt's work. Isn't her style too sparse to offer much in the way of atmosphere? Aren't her films so toned down, decelerated, impassive, and immersed in the everyday as to reject suspense as a rule? My task here is to illustrate here how multiple manners of suspense, in fact, drive her practice. *Night Moves* entwines aesthetic and ecological senses of the word *atmosphere* as the film harnesses the negative affects of anxiety, dread, and paranoia that come with specific crime genres and their promise of suspense.

Reichardt's approach to suspense (like that of Bresson and Akerman, whose films figure prominently in her teaching) operates not only by way of subtractive, protractive, and restrictive measures but also through a focus on process—on the minutia of routine activities presented in their brute materiality. Her sensibility mines fictional and documentary practices that Skvirsky surveys under the name "process genre," where *Jeanne Dielman* and *Nanook of the North* share space with a heist film such as *Rififi*. Reichardt cites all three films as inspirations—*Rififi* for its famously tense and visceral sequence that, in the absence of dialogue and music, lingers for thirty minutes on the gestural and material details of a group robbery.[63] Reichardt's most astute critics, from Katherine Fusco and Nicole Seymour to Elena Gorfinkel, have sharply explained her thematic focus on the laboring body, relating it to the precarity of marginalized individuals under capitalism.[64] There is more to be said about how the heist film in particular bears on this concern with gesture and process. Reichardt, even with her Westerns in mind, has affirmed her debt to Jean-Pierre Melville's heist films, an understudied influence along the axes of minimalist suspense, social collaboration, and the dissection of masculinity.[65]

The plot of *Night Moves* concerns three radical environmentalists, not thieves, and yet its style deploys the grammar of the heist film when it fixates on the planning and execution of their extreme act: the bombing of a hydroelectric reservoir dam where a forest once flourished. As is typical of Reichardt's films, attention to process precedes and outweighs exposition. Before we are adequately introduced to our protagonists, whose backgrounds and motives are never more than thinly evident, the exact, immobile framing trains on specificities of their labor, tools, and materials. As Harmon (Peter Sarsgaard) and Dena (Dakota Fanning) make a fertilizer bomb in a concrete mixer, a close-up of the rotating mixer holds onscreen for several seconds, the camera entering a descriptive tenor removed from character subjectivity as well as from an omniscient viewpoint. The mixer's churning, repetitious drone reinforces the shot's impersonal nature. The extended take, moreover, sustains a circle motif that recurs throughout the film and "indicates the cycling of time."[66] Resumed in later images as a boat's steering wheel and a truck's tire visually rhyme with the mixer, this motif implies circular ironies at the level of ecological entanglement. The third conspirator, Josh (Jesse Eisenberg), works for a local organic-farming cooperative but "destroy[s] with the same material he uses to nourish," as Fusco and Seymour put it.[67] The shot of the mixer thus primes attention not only to the labor process rendered but also to the aesthetic gestures and processes of the film. Not unlike Akerman's suspensive and suspenseful style, Reichardt's lengthy durations allow for the image to shift between representational depiction and abstract, purely graphic expression capable of igniting motifs.

The film's opening moments likewise serve a purpose of attunement that supersedes plot exposition. The first shot patiently studies a rusty, circular release valve near the dam as it spurts out gallons of water (fig. 2.8). This stationary long take strongly recalls imagery of pollution from Bresson's *The Devil, Probably* (1977), a reference to which I return later. Denying spectators' hopes for a mainstream thriller's pace and sensory overload (which the trailer for *Night Moves*, against Reichardt's wishes, falsely advertises), this extended shot has us take in the landscape's painterly color and vibrancy as well as the loud, unnatural hiss of the water valve. With a cut to Josh and to his point of view from a bridge, this sound quietens. But now the birdsong—which Reichardt features

Figure 2.8 The static frame lingers on a spewing water valve in *Night Moves*.

with region-specific accuracy—is more sonically conspicuous than Josh and Dena's hushed conversation. It counters the valve's noise and points up the difference between natural and unnatural sounds. Ensuring we notice these musical chirps offscreen, Dena reacts to them: "Whoa, I think that was an oriole. Didn't know we had those." Environmental peculiarity, more than plot, claims attention in this in medias res opening. Only later do we surmise that Josh and Dena have been casing the dam.

Beyond having us dwell on processes enacted in the drama as the criminal conspiracy and material ecologies intersect, *Night Moves* initiates us into a *processual mode of attention*—a way of perceiving geared toward becoming sensitive to process-relational workings of environmental complexity. We are given to study each painstakingly composed sound-image not only for what it contains and directly captures but also for what it more allusively gestures toward: larger and enwrapping ecological relationships and processes that impinge on the narrative. Indeed, there is suspense of a perceptual and atmospheric variety at play in our attunement to these factors. They often go unspoken as nonlinguistic information and detail, *implicitly* embedded in the visual and acoustic field. In other words, a primary level of suspense, one that precedes and provides a filter for our understanding of the plot, revolves around figuring out how to parse the mise-en-scène in eco-conscious terms. Suspense, in part, forms around the uncommon ways in which the film's aesthetics fan our attention. To borrow apposite vocabulary from Adrian J. Ivakhiv's film theory of "perceptual ecology," *Night Moves* constantly and suspensefully encircles its anthropomorphic content (human agents, identities, constructions, political systems) with atmospheric assertions of both *biomorphic* (wildlife, plant life, nonhuman agency) and *geomorphic* (landscape, terrain, place) elements.[68] We are made aware of a chiefly environmental logic and its attendant play of forms and sensations. Sights and sounds of the reservoir, dam, and woods, whether they are central or peripheral to the staged human drama, serve as fragmentary indices of a greater, ongoing ecological history of change about which we are enticed to speculate. What makes this pull on our attention suspenseful—as opposed to just puzzling—is that its affective grip of unease and fascination is secured through what Ivakhiv calls the "firstness" of atmospheric expression— that is, the "immediate felt quality" of the film's world before it is given over to the "secondness" of narrative.[69] The film will soon evolve into a character-driven paranoia thriller configured around Josh, yet it does so without ever diminishing this wider, environmental range and onus of sensory address.

True to the formula of the heist film, the crew's meticulous plans go awry, and solidarity implodes due to pressure from without and distrust from within. Dread increasingly imbues our experience: we feel a gloomy disquiet that is distributed between our concern for the characters and our concern for the Oregon landscape and the slow process of ecological collapse that comes to our attention through atmospheric workings of style that spatialize affect and render the world onscreen textural and reverberant. Reichardt's atmospheres stand at odds with more customary ecothrillers that privilege the biomorphic dimension (e.g., the protagonists' altruistic deeds in *A Civil Action* [Steven Zaillian, 1998] and *Michael Clayton* [Tony Gilroy, 2007]) and invest all their commentary in the plot, while regarding atmosphere as a mere add-on to what matters most. As Reichardt explains in an interview in 2014, her style asks a patient observer to wrestle with "articulate" ambiguity in atmosphere-driven scenes that suppress dialogue and suspend the plot. For this to happen most effectively, she maintains, the film must not fully deliver on the genre's contract with the audience. "Once you rattle that," she says, "if you have an articulate frame, you have a place for the ambiguities to live without it all being a big mess. I think the filmmaking has to be really articulate, it has to have *lulls of ambiguity* in it."[70]

Night Moves lullingly alters the vocabulary of film suspense through a brooding tactics of delay and reduction that deprives the viewer of violent action and brings environmental crisis to the fore. Take the pivotal sequence where the protagonists, having loaded up a fishing boat with ammonium nitrate, haul it to the dam. The segment starts with a little tribute to Henri Clouzot's deliberately paced yet excruciatingly taut thriller *The Wages of Fear* (1953), a close-up of a tire spinning in mud. From there, Reichardt drags out their journey, keeping dialogue to a minimum but allowing for Dena's slightly hypocritical speech about dwindling biodiversity. Jeff Grace's ambient electronic score supplies an air of dread in wordless stretches when the images have us contemplate a wasteland of dead trees and clear-cuts (landscapes that are, in Ivakhiv's lexicon, "exoreferential" in that they attest to real-world ecological degradation).[71] Once the trio arrive at the dam, the scene has several markings of a formulaic thriller, including a countdown with a timed explosion, but Reichardt subtracts the event's spectacular nature: the acting is subdued, the pace is measured, and the blast is relegated to offscreen sound—a faint rumble in the background of a long take that holds on the trio's deadpan, unspeaking faces. This subtractive method does not eradicate tension, however: it *ratchets up* the suspense through minimal means, giving force to each small gesture and ambient sound. In a nod to the Bressonian roots of this style, Reichardt stages the approach of the trio's boat toward the dam in a way that re-creates the first shot in *The Devil, Probably*, which shows a boat somewhat eerily floating along the Seine at night.

The viewer of *Night Moves* is deprived in some ways and advantaged in others. Suspense, in its Hitchcockian formulation, tends to situate us ahead of the characters both perceptually and epistemically. In Reichardt's subtler take on this use of dramatic irony, the spectator's attention plays off against acts of negligence in the depicted narrative. In her earlier film *Old Joy* (2006), her approach to landscape directs the viewer's gaze in contrast to her self-absorbed characters' lack of ecological attentiveness. Shots from inside a moving car, aimed at topographies visible from the side windows, trace a deep history of environmental and economic changes between Portland and its outskirts (from gentrification to rusty industrial structures in decline), but the characters in the vehicle, two formerly close friends who delude themselves about their leftist political engagement, ignore—or rather "refuse"—the landscape as they look straight ahead.[72] For the spectator, the film's geomorphic firstness of atmosphere operates in stark tension with anthropomorphic secondness of narrative, and this is a "stark tension" only when the viewer is attuned accordingly; Reichardt's strategy will be missed if we latch onto the dialogue without simultaneously attending to the mise-en-scène. To some degree, the saboteurs in *Night Moves* are sympathetic filters for our attention, more sympathetic than the SUV-driving tourists and locals who regard the reservoir only as a playground for fishing and jet skis. Yet the film's ambiguities also critically comment on the trio, whose *swift* and symbolic deed falls under question as mere theater without real efficacy. A distant long take of the ecoradicals slinking up the river in their weaponized boat compares them to kids playing with water pistols in the deforested foreground (fig. 2.9). The slow history of devastation wrought upon the landscape appears indifferent to and unfazed by the trio's urgent and theatrical act.[73]

Although *Night Moves* is an ecothriller, it diverges from an activistic faith in the power of humanity to fix the situation. Shrewd on this score is Graig Uhlin's appraisal of how Reichardt's work articulates a link between ecological depletion and *feelings* of depletion embodied by her characters and by each film's mood. For Uhlin, this relationship arises through an atmospheric dispersion of negative affect that extends from the environments *in* the film to the spectator's apprehension *of* the film *as* an environment. Uhlin aligns *Old Joy* with a tendency that, instead of issuing a call for recuperative action, takes measure of the melancholy, exhaustion, grief, and hopelessness that stem from the *suspension* of political agency in the face of ecological crises.[74] *Night Moves*, while sharing something of its trio's fed-upness, suggests that misdirected agency is the flipside of political impotence.

Through recurring allusions to Bresson's portrait of environmental catastrophe and post-1968 revolutionary youth in *The Devil, Probably*, Reichardt distinguishes the trio, in particular Josh, from competing ideologies of political resistance. Earlier in the film, Josh and Dena attend a local screening of what they take to be a naive environmentalist documentary made by a preaching-to-the-choir underground artist. The assembly of countercultural youth at the screening echoes scenes in *The Devil, Probably*, as does some of the documentary's sights of ecological disasters. *Night Moves* then prompts us to weigh the hasty political recourse taken by our trio against the exceptionally *slow* and peaceful resistance mounted by the farming cooperative in which Josh works. But the film, adhering to Reichardt's embrace of ambiguity, doesn't take sides. Suspense in this way extends to the film's political perspective vis-à-vis that of

Figure 2.9 *Night Moves*: The saboteurs motor toward the hydraulic dam against a dying landscape.

the imperfect characters. As Josh emerges as the central protagonist (less flattened than Bresson's Fontaine and Akerman's Simon, though still emotionally taciturn), *Night Moves* neither upholds nor rejects his philosophy of radical political action. Although contrasts and contradictions cast his worldview into doubt, they do not condemn it.

This drama of differences across the milieux Josh haunts, with its affective combination of suspense, melancholy, and paranoia, is sustained in part by Reichardt's borrowings from the proto-environmentalist landscape paintings of Charles E. Burchfield (1893–1967). Reichardt kept artbooks of his work on hand during the production of *Night Moves* and considered them part of the script.[75] The American artist's watercolors of barren forests inform how the film not only presents the natural world in decline but renders it atmospherically emanative, infusing it with vibratory somberness through lighting, sound, and autumnal color. Reichardt's aesthetic reference to Burchfield's paintings is in part sonic, given their curious aural impressions from droning insects to buzzing telephone wires. Burchfield's more ecstatic and verdant landscapes influence the film's images of the Applegate Valley organic farm, with its energetic hues and undulant textures. This place and the temporalities of slow labor and cultivation that define it clash with Josh's impatient, purely spectacular method of political engagement. The painterly richness of the mise-en-scène in this milieu also stands in conflict with Josh's growing paranoia, as he is distracted from his work routine by rumbling noises from offscreen that possibly indicate the closing in of a criminal investigation (2.10).[76]

In the fallout of the accidental homicide that results when the dam explodes, *Night Moves* shifts more firmly into the paranoid thriller, an affiliation evoked in the film's title, which calls to mind Arthur Penn's film of the same name from 1975. Fusco and Seymour have remarked on how *Night Moves* reimagines the stylistic, emotional, and political strategies of New Hollywood paranoia thrillers from the 1970s, such as *The Conversation* (Francis Ford Coppola, 1974) and *Marathon Man* (John Schlesinger, 1976). Reichardt takes their defining aspects—antiheroic, usually male protagonists; justly cynical and fearful moods regarding

Figure 2.10 *Night Moves*: Josh anxiously looks out of frame as the slowness of organic farming contrasts with the swiftness of his act of sabotage and its consequences.

state power and neoliberal capitalism; and preoccupations with recording technologies, surveillance, and hidden networks of corruption—and transposes them onto the problem of ecological crisis. As a result, *Night Moves* has us anxiously reflect on all manner of webbed entanglements that intrude on and complicate the trio's activities.[77] As part of this riff on the paranoid thriller, the trio's gesture of protest is revealed to be inescapably part of the capitalistic conspiracy they defy, but the film refrains from identifying a particular agent, system, or organization that could be singled out as a targetable, comprehensible source of the problem.

As a politically conscious genre, the paranoid thriller revels in raising for its audience as well as for its characters the question of whether *paranoia* is the proper word for situations in which feelings of suspicion and anxiety respond to quite real causes. In her book *Ugly Feelings* (2005), Sianne Ngai views paranoia not as a pathology but as "a species of fear based on the dysphoric apprehension of a holistic and all-encompassing system." Referencing *The Conversation*, she explains how paranoia involves confusion regarding the objective or subjective status of the feeling: "Is the enemy *out there* or *in me*?" The felt "boundary between the psyche and the world" is "destabilize[d]," and yet the paranoiac, functioning as a sort of barometric registration device, may well be tuned into something real about the world.[78] Paranoia may thereby figure as a means of insight *from within* the holistic system. This goes for a paranoid thriller's audience, not just for its protagonist, insofar as the viewer's experience is paranoiac at one remove. Thomas Elsaesser notes how a certain nostalgia for paranoid thrillers of the 1970s has informed twenty-first-century generic explorations of paranoia in cinema, a return to a prior historical moment marked by comparable uncertainties and suspicions of forces of control, but this return has also sought to reclaim paranoia less as a bleakly embodied symptom than as a "productive pathology"—a rare means of intuiting "the big picture" of today's capitalistic world system.[79] With *Night Moves*, however, the film's mood of paranoia does not add up to a "productive" instrument of insight, knowledge acquisition, and criticism. Paranoia shades into irrepressible dread and confinement in the film's second half as Josh, on the lam from authorities who never appear in the diegesis, makes a doomed attempt to escape the grid. With our now main character serving as an affective and attentional filter, we are still made to feel encircled by abstract yet powerful forces, but the ecological factors attached to this feeling are now compounded by the alarming ubiquity of the surveillance state. Dread shares with paranoia the apprehension of a grand and potentially destructive scheme or entity in operation, but what fuels this feeling is more nebulous, and there is no hope of instrumentalizing dread to criticize or clarify the total state of things. Dread—unlike other forms of fear—allows no direct encounter with a causal agent but instead turns on obscurely menacing atmospheres, as Cynthia Freeland has shown. Dread resembles anxiety in that it is ongoing and anticipatory while lacking a distinct object, but dread more strongly entails the sensation of an outcome one is unable to forestall or negate.[80]

Across the structure of *Night Moves*, the vague profundity of dread is elicited and stoked by incremental stimuli at the very threshold of attention. Here, too, Reichardt follows Bresson's *The Devil, Probably*, where ambient sound—far from just filling in the diegesis for the sake of verisimilitude—contributes to a gradually building sense of atmospheric dread in relation to ecological crisis. Bresson orchestrates a series of anempathetic noises, associatively linking in our perception and memory the clatter of agricultural tools and machines, the blast of an atom bomb displayed on a television screen, and the outwardly less harmful drones of a 16-millimeter film projector, elevators, a record player, and auto traffic from the street. Bresson immerses us in a perceptual surround in which toxicity is widely distributed amid the everyday. We feel *infected* by this ambience in half-conscious ways at first, but through echoes it slides to the forefront of our attention. *Night Moves* deploys ambient noise in such a cumulative manner (the fertilizer mixer, rattling fans, a buzzing fly, the purring of the boat) and lends it a quality of dread. By the film's conclusion, mere car sounds on the highway carry a sense of menace, for Josh and for us, even if we are not thinking about carbon emissions or agents in pursuit.[81]

* * *

Through magnetic and magnifying forms that raise low-key sensation to a principal role, all three films examined in this chapter recalibrate the thrilling elements of suspense. *A Man Escaped*, *La captive*, and *Night Moves* tune us into elegantly withdrawn, durationally modulated patterns and processes of interconnection.[82] The latter two films do not just salute Bresson's practices but also make minimalist suspense their own for reasons as much political as aesthetic. Reichardt's lowercase thriller makes use of ecological knowledge not by fostering a way forward but rather by deftly articulating ambiguities that cast doubt on the surety of action. The film's atmosphere, although alluring, refuses to give a cathartic or epiphanic representation of the natural world. (There is no equivalent to *Old Joy*'s soothing, Tarkovskian hot-springs retreat in the wilderness.) What I have sketched as environmental dread instills feelings that verge on the negative sublime: the film is a dread-suffused reckoning with political powerlessness in the face of a worsening crisis that seems too immense to process, too widespread to attack, and possibly too entrenched to reverse. Instead of performing an intervention for us, then, Reichardt's minimalist thriller leaves us with unresolved suspense as we contemplate a disaster before which our faith in human agency is stalled, checked.

Notwithstanding the escape enacted in Bresson's prison thriller, the alternative styles of suspense I have studied in this chapter have entwined labyrinthine circumstances from which there is no outlet (except for Ariane's suicide at the close of *La captive*, if that is indeed what happens) with inevitable disasters before which we as viewers and listeners are made to feel powerless, even as an aesthetics of understatement curiously intensifies our attention instead of dulling it. This feeling of powerlessness to reverse a state of affairs modifies the more common type of helplessness we are enjoined to feel in popular narrative suspense. In the Hitchcockian tradition, our felt incapacity owes to our desire to see the characters (who are less apprised of the situation) evade misfortune and danger,[83] but with *Night Moves* our helplessness isn't strictly anthropological. Nor is it exclusively oriented toward plot and character, which are affectively outshone in some intervals by an all-pervasive ambience of unease that sets the mundane on a continuum with the potentially catastrophic. What we become acutely aware of in the waiting we're asked to do in suspense is that we have no control, not only over the course of events and their temporal sequence but also over the very disquietude we feel in large part because of the film's spatial-atmospheric qualities that envelop us and extend the labyrinth, beyond the drama's representation, to us.[84] In the chapters to follow, I illuminate this dimension of suspense through a fuller description of cinema as an ambient medium.

CHAPTER 3

THE AMBIENT LANDSCAPE

Far from being final and definitive, the morphology of suspense put forward in chapter 1 requires tweaks and enhancements as this book progresses. There is plenty more to discover about the sensory workings of suspense in slow-paced art films, and this chapter aims to further develop—not simply rehash—my conception of atmospheric suspense through a more pointed account of cinematic ambience. Here again, my chosen examples are unusual suspects for a study of suspense, but we will see that especially potent operations of suspense may arise under conditions of slowness and sparseness that cast ambience as a qualitative environmental force, an encircling and felt extension of the landscape.

Many of the questions voiced in contemporary debates about cinematic slowness come down to the preponderance of landscapes onscreen. Is the viewer bored, frustrated, entranced, finely attuned, or asleep when, for example, what seems to be an establishing shot of a foggy mountainside lake in Hou Hsiaohsien's *The Assassin* (2015) lingers to the point of primacy instead of leading to more plot, like a transition? What political, aesthetic, and philosophical possibilities open up (or disappear) with these experiments in duration and reduction? What counts as an event when action wanes to such a degree? What justifies all the waiting we are asked to endure as the film seems to overemphasize the environment? That slow cinema is a landscape art for meditative engagement is routinely noted. Critics have also considered how cinemas of slowness remediate the landscape practices of painting, photography, and gallery installation art for the purpose of encouraging or even forcing the spectator to adopt a patient look more suited to the fine arts.[1] What needs further probing, however, are the ways in which landscapes prime and foster low-key suspense.

From the mazelike steppe in *Once Upon a Time in Anatolia* (Ceylan, 2011) to the fading forest in *Night Moves* (Reichardt, 2014), my examples in this book have already shown the vital role of landscape, both visual and auditory. Indeed, suspense in slow cinema heavily depends on landscapes that restructure traditional hierarchies of the frame. If this use of landscape mingles slow art-house cinema with commercial genres, it also crosses with more radically experimental filmmaking. Consider Scott MacDonald's estimation of the durationally extended landscape films of James Benning. "Each shot in *small roads* [2011]," Benning's survey of forty-seven U.S. roads in as many long takes, "creates suspense." As MacDonald explains,

> At some point in most of the shots a car or truck . . . interrupts the relative quiet of the shot as it passes Benning's camera. Suspense is created as viewers wonder when a vehicle will pass; and after Benning first surprises viewers (in shot 7) by *not* including a passing vehicle, the suspense is doubled: *will* a vehicle pass—and when? Further, as in [Benning's] *13 Lakes* [2004] and *Ten Skies* [2004], the succession of shots creates a second kind of suspense: what will the next variation in landscape be; how will it add, visually and sonically, to the variety of what has already been seen and heard?[2]

This description of Benning's road movie of sorts embodies a manner of attention that in earlier chapters I have aligned with structural suspense—the tracking of patterned variations that may or may not pertain to a gradually surfacing arc, be it narrative or some other, perhaps purely formal pattern. Benning's waiting games, like those of Abbas Kiarostami in *Five Dedicated to Ozu* (2003) and *24 Frames* (2017), relish the tension between a static camera and gently dynamic landscapes that draw attention to inconspicuous change (e.g., stirrings of wildlife, fluctuations of weather and light), everywhere stoking curiosity as to where the lines fall between design and happenstance—between sleight of hand and fortuitous capture.

Kelly Reichardt's narrative cinema channels the experimental landscape tradition for the purpose of altering attentional habits. In a tribute to the landscape filmmaker Peter Hutton, the opening shot of *First Cow* (2019) has us watch from a distance a freight barge drift glacially across the immobile frame. In addition to its spare graphic scheme (the barge visually supplants a sun-streaked row of trees on the riverbank), the shot imposes a tempo of waiting that will soon "swell into quiet suspense" regarding the fates of two men in the Old West, more specifically Oregon County of the 1820s.[3] The plot has yet to announce itself, but the barge's low growl sets an ominous tone. The extended take acclimates us to the moderate rhythms, the environmental specifics, of the film ahead. For Reichardt, as for Hutton and Benning, landscape entails not just an aesthetic vista but also the process of attending to the materiality and history of place as well as to its ambient pulsations.

The prominence of landscape in slow cinema can be richly examined through recourse to Martin Lefebvre's accounts of pictorial space, both painterly and cinematic. Lefebvre contends that "setting" and "landscape" are inherently distinct: whereas "setting" relegates a space to the backdrop for more salient narrative actions, "landscape" in its proper sense is autonomous and expressive of itself. For Lefebvre, the possibility of the autonomous landscape "*haunts*" films even when it is inhibited by setting (that is, by the promoted mindset that sees space as setting). Any narrative film that features landscapes may prompt viewers to oscillate between different ways of regarding space. A "tug of war," writes Lefebvre, pits our narrative-based attention against a "landscape gaze" that sees the image primarily as "a space of aesthetic spectacle and contemplation." The landscape, then, is tenuous: "simultaneously like crystal and smoke," it passes in and out of the viewer's perception. However, Lefebvre turns to art-house films such as Michelangelo Antonioni's *Blow-Up* (1966) and Gus Van Sant's *Gerry* (2002) to illustrate how *temps morts* (dead time) may free up the landscape for sustained contemplation.[4]

Lefebvre's idea of landscape generally comports with arguments I have taken on board in earlier chapters—namely, Jean Epstein's poetics of suspension and Robert Spadoni's separation of atmosphere from mere scenery within a push-and-pull relationship to narrative.[5] That said, Lefebvre's framework doesn't reach far enough in accounting for sensorial matters beyond vision and thus for the tensions that landscapes (especially those of slow cinema) can heighten not only between narrative and spectacle but also between *the image seen as a picture plane* and *the audiovisual field sensed as an ambient surround*. But what does *ambience* mean where cinema is concerned—beyond being a textbook term for sounds (background noise) and illumination (light that already exists at a chosen location)? In earlier parts of this book, when describing films by Reichardt, Bresson, Akerman, and others, I have used the term as a cognate or synonym of *atmosphere*, but how, more precisely, should we associate the one word with the other? In this chapter, I want to pursue a specific definition of *cinematic ambience* that relates to suspenseful functions of landscape.

To argue for a clean-cut distinction between *ambience* and *atmosphere* would be unwise, given their etymological intimacy across cultures and disciplines, but one finds in Francophone and Anglophone research a tendency to construe *ambience* in terms of a "sensory point of view" bounded and influenced by the resonances of a force-filled space.[6] For a handful of authors in fields of geography, sociology, and urban planning, *ambience* defines an organism's *subjection to* the atmospheric effects of particular environments. In his book *Ambient Media* (2016), Paul Roquet contends that the word "always implies a more subjective element of mediation at work: some kind of agency behind the production of mood and a focus on the human body attuning to it." According to Roquet, atmospheres can be ambient insofar as they are "mediated by and for the human senses," and he invests ambience with a calming function in contexts of self-care, while being careful to call it a "*provisional* comfort that nonetheless registers the presence of external threats."[7] If today's commonplace uses of the term *ambient* convey relaxation, its scientific and philosophical meanings have swayed over time between "comfort" and "lack of comfort."

In his essay "*Milieu* and *Ambiance*" (1942), Leo Spitzer traces the word *ambience*'s evolutions from antiquity to modernity, observing how its "history . . . cannot be separated from that of *medium = milieu*." He points out that the Latin prefix *amb-* originally meant "on both sides (left and right)," hence the shared root of *ambience* with *ambidextrous*, *ambivalent*, and so on. Only later did the prefix indicate a "surround," similar to *circum-*. Ancient Greek precursors of the English term *ambience*, found in Plato, Aristotle, and physicists under their influence, allege a kinship between humans and a cosmic force in the air that affords warmth and security as it swirls "close to the bodily." For Cicero, the ambient air "is not only that by means of which we see and hear, but *that which sees and hears with us*." Spitzer finds in Sextus a comparable idea of "symphysis": the physical integration of humans with a circulatory, etherlike air that is both a medium for and an agent of perception. In the early-modern era, this harmonic ambience gives way to colder, less assuasive physical and metaphysical conceptions of the world, such as Descartes's "subtle matter," wherein the ambient air, instead of caressing bodies, invades them: "into every pore and crevice," writes Spitzer, "creeps this subtle ether, the same with which the celestial bodies are surrounded." With Newton's notion of "ambient medium," all "overtones of warmth and beneficence" disappear, leaving a "perfunctory phrase, used in the most trivial of references" to air and space. Ambience in its Newtonian form is banal contiguity and elemental diffusion in "an infinite chilly cosmos traversed by innumerable forces of attraction," a universe no longer casting humans as its measure.[8]

Spitzer's essay has been a touchstone for the atmospheric turn in film and media studies, with theorists invoking it to shore up their reconceptualizations of the term *medium* beyond its purely technical bases. In a Walter Benjamin–inspired account of the "*medium* of perception," Antonio Somaini glosses *ambience* as the *environment of* aesthetic engagement. He historically links the term to the *media diaphana*, "the various diaphanous substances—air, clouds, smoke, water, fluids, glass, crystals—that, with all their different states and their different degrees of transparency and consistency, condition our sensory perception."[9] Many directors tied to slow cinema (e.g., Hou, Akerman, Antonioni, Apichatpong Weerasethakul, Lav Diaz, Kiyoshi Kurosawa, and Alexander Sokurov) bring into play *media diaphana* for hypnotic or subtly perturbing aesthetic effects that implicate cinema itself as a medium embedded within myriad elemental media.[10] Giuliana Bruno cites Spitzer's study to ballast her genealogical history of the "ambience of projection" as it leads up to installations in museum space.[11] It must be said that in some of this contemporary scholarly work on ambience, sweeping comparisons across disciplines, histories, languages, cultures, and media leave us with overly general meanings of the word that are applicable to any instance of mediation and any sort of connection therein. In my use, the term *ambience* has to do with a specific shape of affective encounter and spatial situatedness. James J. Gibson's account of the "ambient array" in atmospheric perception is instructive here. The term *ambience*, for Gibson, refers to a situation where the observer is surrounded by sensations from all directions. Not to be confused with radiance, which is emanation *from* a single point, ambience *converges upon* a point from multiple reverberating sources and surfaces. It closes the circle around a position, rounding off the "spherical" part of atmosphere, yet it issues from a medium of air that extends well beyond the observer's locus and perspective.[12]

Gibson, I should acknowledge, refers mainly to real-world spatial immersion. He claims that a painted or photographic "picture," no matter how panoramic its reach, fails to be ambient, but he more favorably (if hypothetically) judges film's capacity to create conditions analogous to ambience.[13] I want to explore how cinema indeed renders ambiences in conflict with the merely pictorial. The films I study in this chapter—Lisandro Alonso's *Jauja* (2015), Lucrecia Martel's *Zama* (2017), and Jonathan Glazer's *Under the Skin* (2013)—all give rise to suspense through tensions between concretely portrayed visual landscapes and the pressure exerted by the more elusive ambient surround— tensions that become increasingly surreal. The offscreen remains a key concern in this chapter, but the generic and thematic contexts are notably different. As two Argentine quasi-Westerns and a British science fiction/horror hybrid, these art-house films diegetically involve a colonial quest (less overt in *Under the Skin*) that is stalled and drawn off course—a derailment that, in turn, suspensefully alters the established protocol of identification between viewer and protagonist. In each case, the relationship of ambience to point of view slips into radical doubt and prompts questions around what it means to perceive with and be affected by cinema as medium and apparatus. Although this is not a novel topic for us in this book, the examples ahead plunge into surrealism of an atmospheric kind that requires fresh analysis with respect to our broadened morphology of suspense. Further, these films demand even more focused attention to sound than I have offered so far, including cinema's incorporation of the ambient music genre.[14]

Desert Campaign Without a Compass: *Jauja*

Jauja opens with text defining the titular word as "a mythological land of abundance and happiness," a paradise that invariably leads astray its seekers. The film takes place in Patagonia in the early 1880s amid the last stretch of Argentina's military "Conquest of the Desert," which killed, enslaved, and displaced many thousands of Indigenous people, namely the Mapuche and Tehuelche. The plot, however, makes only glancing reference to this context, not effacing it but treating it elliptically. The opening shots of a coastal landscape suggest the aftermath of carnage: with a knife in his bloody hands (shown in Bressonian close-up), a soldier picks at the viscera of an animal he has already eaten, while on the horizon sea lions squirm and bellow as if in protest. A cut to the horizon introduces another soldier, masturbating in a watery ditch, his bare chest decorated with jewelry he has surely stolen from slain natives. As in a sparse landscape of the American West painted by Frederic Remington (e.g., *Fight for the Watering Hole*, 1903), we have a belated and manifestly partial image of genocidal history in which the "enemies," already decimated, are inscribed through haunting absence.[15]

The shot of the soldier pleasuring himself in a silvery tide pool is the first surreal jolt that nudges the film and its landscapes away from the traditional period epic. The spectator familiar with the region's terrain and climate will not fail to identify Patagonia as the location, but as the film advances, one might be excused for understanding the landscape—confined to a squarish 4:3 Academy ratio frame with rounded corners and unnaturally intensified colors—as more a metacinematic place that channels classical American Technicolor Westerns. Our protagonist, Captain Dinesen (Viggo Mortensen) is a Danish military engineer who, along with his teenage daughter, Ingeborg (Viilbjørk Malling Agger), has come to Argentina to assist with the settler task of digging irrigation networks. But, here again, details are so scant that the spectator must extrapolate, and the odd presence of a Danish officer in this environment plays fast and loose with history. When Ingeborg elopes with a soldier, stealing her father's compass, Dinesen sets out to find her, only to be overwhelmed by the desert as he loses his horse and telescope and is left with no choice but to follow a mysterious wolfhound who lures him and the film itself into a quiet vortex of spatiotemporal confusion.

Critics have made cosmetic, albeit inescapable comparisons to John Ford's *The Searchers* (1956) and have more soundly situated *Jauja* alongside Werner Herzog's *Aguirre, the Wrath of God* (1972), in which the European colonial gaze is powerfully disrupted by an all-too-physical landscape shown not to be the El Dorado of myth.[16] Yet Dinesen is much more restrained than Herzog's conquistador as played by Klaus Kinski, just as the style of *Jauja* is less pitched to an epic scale. Contemporary slow cinema—another invited avenue of comparison—has produced its share of films in which the aesthetics of pause and languorous suspension work to undermine colonial logics of linearity, progress, and efficiency, even as an element of Conradian exoticism regarding the rapturous landscape remains (e.g., in Chantal Akerman's *Almayer's Folly* [2011] and Miguel Gomes's *Tabu* [2012]). Lisandro Alonso is habitually named in roll calls of slow cinema, although *Jauja* departs from his earlier output while still relishing long takes of wilderness. The framing, courtesy of the Finnish cinematographer Timo Salminen, known for his many collaborations with Aki Kaurismäki, is generally more stationary and given to tableaux with a deadpan comic tone. Wordlessness, instead of marking the whole film, alternates with carefully scripted dialogue by the Argentine poet Fabián Casas. Instead of a nonprofessional lead actor, we have in Mortensen an international star who plays against type and contributes ideas as a coauthor.

Jauja is designed to flummox each of the interpretive lenses it invites. Much of the film's mystery and the suspenseful ambient feel has been neglected by readings that enlist explanatory frameworks of genre, transnational cinema, authorship, and postcolonialism *without* factoring in atmosphere because it is deemed irrelevant. Some have faulted *Jauja* for carelessly handling the memory of colonial violence; others have converted the film into a more plainspoken critique of empire (including Hollywood's global dominance) than it is.[17] Both positions tend to ignore the soundtrack. Take an odd moment that has gone unmentioned in every assessment of the film I have encountered. As Dinesen embarks on his quest to find Ingeborg, riding his horse into the background of an extended take at dawn, an echoic *ping* briefly cuts through the ambient sonic blend of wind, ocean, horse trots, and campfire, inciting a peculiar kind of suspense. As viewers, prone to trace sounds to their source, we survey the scene for the cause of this faint sonic disturbance. Is it a jingling sword? An insect's chirp? Spurs on Dinesen's or someone else's boots? Did we in fact hear this noise? Moments later, as the same long take pans over to a French administrator kneeling by the fire, this *ping* returns, confirming we heard it the first time and triggering a cut.

What is this carefully expressed sound doing in the film? Is it diegetic and therefore able to be heard by the characters? What creates it? Is it musical score, an extremely discreet cue that anticipates weighty events ahead? Suspense of a perceptual and atmospheric kind ramps up these questions over and against the plot-based suspense regarding the fates of Ingeborg and Dinesen and the ominous references to a defected military commander, Zuluaga, rumored to be hiding in the desert with Indigenous rebels. Untethered to the visual incident, this noise is fundamentally unlocatable, what Timothy Morton would call "Aeolian"—an indefinite "of the wind" sonority that is neither quite within nor quite without the world of the fiction.[18] The multichannel Dolby mix has it emerge evenly across the frontal loudspeakers and quickly reverb in the side and rear ones: it encircles us but lacks both a clear emanation point and a synchronization point with the image, unless we count the precise moment when Dinesen's dark figure graphically reaches the horizon. This ambient event softly destabilizes the onscreen world for us by evoking a beyond that is not adjacent to what the frame displays.[19]

This enigmatic *ping* is part of a host of formal operations that engender a slowly phased rupture in the film's spatiotemporal fabric. If the tableau style of composition *initially* seems to squeeze all the important information into the compact 4:3 frame, evoking order and mastery in step with the logic of colonial territorial conquest, we are increasingly invited to reflect on the folly of this view of space as it comes up against manifold tensions with an ambient field that cannot be neatly contained or navigated. Suspense mounts because of the felt conflict between the focus of a given shot and suggestions of a less scrutable environment beyond its margins. "Suspense exacerbates geography" by infusing the framed event with " 'background radiation' from all directions," writes Raymond Durgnat. Although Durgnat is referring to Hitchcock's *Psycho* (1960) and its stoking of uncertainty by means of the offscreen, this remark applies no less to *Jauja*'s ambient pressures and spatially disruptive forms.[20]

The 4:3 aspect ratio, which other slow films of the decade use with equal cleverness (e.g., Reichardt's *Meek's Cutoff* [2010], Pawel Pawlikowski's *Ida* [2013], Pedro Costa's *Horse Money* [2014], Hou's *The Assassin*, and Paul Schrader's *First Reformed* [2017]), is fundamental to the suspenseful exacerbation of geography throughout *Jauja*. Alonso has stated that he chose this aspect ratio to neutralize his star actor's association with heroic sword-swinging action and horsemanship.[21] The format also provokes anxious awareness of borders and limits— of the *partiality* of each view. From the outset, as Ingeborg looks out of frame and scans the desert, warmly professing that it "fills" her, there is an inborn strain between the boxy image and the vastness of the Patagonian surround.[22] Coupling surplus duration with maximum depth of field, Alonso's long takes often approach their end with the exits of characters on opposite planes of the shot, which divides the spectator's attention between the outer edges of the foreground and the background as the camera then holds on a vacated landscape. As Chelsea Birks observes, *Jauja* constructs space "backward" in relation to the audience. As opposed to the lateral staging in widescreen Westerns, in *Jauja* "actions tend to occur from back to front [and vice versa]."[23] Time and again we are made to wait as Dinesen trudges, shrinkingly, from the foreground toward a horizon behind which he disappears. More than once, he dips into a void in the middle planar range of the shot, as if swallowed by the landscape, never resurfacing before the cut finally arrives. These zones of disappearance within the frame are *not* quite spatially and temporally of a piece with the rest of the scene: they don't seem contiguous to the visual field in the sense that, say, the shark in *Jaws* (Spielberg, 1975) is implied to be just

Figure 3.1 *Jauja*: Reduced to a dark blip on the horizon, Dinesen's movement is unclear. Is he drawing closer or moving farther away?

under the water's surface when it momentarily disappears. Rather, Dinesen's vanishings open onto "a more radical Elsewhere, outside homogenous time and space," as Gilles Deleuze defines the offscreen in its modernist guise.[24] Even when Dinesen's movements on foot or horseback continue between shots with little to no lag, something feels off. Coming and going seem indistinguishable, uncannily mirrored (fig. 3.1).

The frames that linger on nothing but the weathered terrain break with Dinesen's point of view—a disruption that further comes across through games with sound perspective (he sings a nationalistic song that becomes *louder* the more he fades into the background) and through camera positions that are bluntly removed from his spyglass views of climactic action, such as a hilltop killing of a soldier at the hands of Zuluaga and a Mapuche rebel, an event we can barely make out because of its drastic scalar reduction. Though Dinesen manages to detect Ingeborg's trail, he is outpaced by a largely unseen Indigenous presence who also searches for the Danish young woman and more intimately knows the landscape. In a suspenseful scene where Dinesen finds Ingeborg's boyfriend left for dead (by Zuluaga, who seems to have kidnapped Ingeborg), the arm of a Mapuche insurgent reaches into the frame to steal

Dinesen's rifle and hat. In a dryly comic bit, this same character then seizes Dinesen's horse offscreen and is already riding into the distance by the time our chivalrous protagonist notices.

The convolution of linear, rational space–time that follows from this play with perspective in cramped frames is announced by the wolfhound's abrupt emergence in the mountains, sitting within an improbable pool of water (fig. 3.2) and thus evoking Tarkovsky's German Shepherd in *Stalker* (1979), a film whose folded, mercurial landscapes *Jauja* has on its mind. Dinesen, while trying ineffectually to give the dog commands, trails the animal, hoping to be taken to Ingeborg, and, indeed, he discovers on a rock a wooden toy soldier that she found earlier in the film, but at the same time the desert seems increasingly indifferent to his goal, as if the stonier topography and the colder, mistier climate no longer ground the original basis of the plot. Like in a fairy tale or, better, a fairy tale "for adults," as André Breton would have it,[25] the wolfhound escorts Dinesen to a cave and a water spring over which an elderly woman presides, a dressed-in-black, witchlike character (Ghita Nørby) whose dialogue in Danish confuses grammatical registers and morphs into riddles (fig. 3.2). Defined by liminality, she enters the film's world as a disincarnated voice anchored only by Dinesen's gaze out of frame. The countershot confirming her physical presence is suspensefully delayed, so that Dinesen at first seems to be talking to himself.

More uncanny business ensues when they enter the cave (blatantly a soundstage, the dark and sonorous conditions of which parallel those of the film theater). Conversation, with pronoun slippage, insinuates that this woman is somehow an aged and transformed version of Ingeborg, a feeling reinforced by the exchange of objects: she returns the stolen compass, and he returns to her the toy soldier, which brings a laugh of recognition. Chillingly, she says that all families are in time engulfed by the desert, "wiped off the face of the earth. I think it's for the best." The shot/countershot alternations, with long lags on either side of the cut, frame the woman and Dinesen against inky, abstract darkness. As they finish their dialogue, she vanishes into the offscreen again, while his back is turned. He restarts his quest under an imminent storm, yet her voice continues to haunt the landscape—a voice he hears, too, but cannot place. It comes from nowhere and everywhere at once. "What makes a life function and move forward?" the voice asks twice, bringing him to his knees in submission. "I don't know," he says before making his final, deathly disappearance into a furrow in the landscape near the horizon in another distantly offered long take.

But there is still more surrealist mischief. The film then cuts, with an ambient sound dissolve, to a chateau in the modern-day Danish countryside, where the same teenage actress who plays Ingeborg wakes from a night's sleep, leading us to wonder whether this character has dreamed the Patagonian affair. Has she stirred from or *passed into* a dream? The surreal oneiric mood is augmented

Figure 3.2 *Jauja*: In the desert, the wolfhound escorts Dinesen to a woman in a cave.

by the return of objects and motifs from the Argentine diegesis: the toy soldier and the girl's pet wolfhounds, one of whom has a "hot spot" on his side—a region he has scratched raw because of a nervous uncertainty he can't resolve. At least, this is how a houndsman explains the spot to the girl, alluding to her irresponsible absence. The film comes to an open end as the girl loses track of this dog in the forest and tosses the soldier figurine (to which the dog has just led her) into a pond. The rippling water dissolves back into the Patagonian shot that opened the film: sea lions on a horizon, stones blanketed with algae that chromatically matches the Danish green forest, but no humans in sight this time. This ending implies a loop, as if she returns the figurine, through the portal-like pond, to the Patagonian landscape where her double, Ingeborg, found it earlier. At the very least, this use of water imagery ties the Danish pond back to the cave spring and the irrigation ditch under Dinesen's supervision, suggesting forgotten links between modern European wealth and colonial plunder.

Critics have understandably taken up *Jauja*'s oneiric surrealism through comparisons to films by Raúl Ruiz (the set-in-Patagonia but filmed-in-Rotterdam *On Top of the Whale* [1982], with its mystical landscapes and send-up of colonialism), Luis Buñuel (barbed critiques of the ruling class in increasingly off-the-wall narratives offered up with matter-of-factness),[26] David Lynch (bifurcated worlds and identities beset with strange ambient powers), and Apichatpong (doublings and wilderness landscapes tinged with folkloric supernatural influences). Much of surrealist cinema, from the entomologist quirks of Buñuel and the scientific documentaries of Jean Painléve onward, playfully entangles humans with other species, as pertains to the wolfhounds and horses of *Jauja*. The film's mockery of assumed rational order and function is paradigmatic surrealist humor. And the linkage of the different diegeses through recurrent red accents (the wooden soldier, Dinesen's uniform, the hot spot on the wolfhound, and the blood-smeared soldier's hands in the first shot) exhibits a Nicolas Roeg–like logic of surreal iteration across subtle vertigoes of time and space. Tarkovsky's *Stalker* is part of this intertextual mix as well in that its German Shepherd is a material link between the numinous landscape of the Zone and the protagonist's return to his wearisome reality. Beyond being an appeal to our associative attention, Alonso's dog bears an arcane connection to the viewer through relays of red. Is there not a connection between the wolfhound's disquiet and that of the viewer, who is likewise left to confront a *feeling of* mystery that does not incline toward resolution?

To be sure, a resilient suspense grows out of the surrealism afoot in *Jauja*, suspense that is as much about the atmosphere as it is about hidden meanings. Surrealism, as regards the task of the spectator, is too frequently construed as parsing symbolism, deciphering codes. Let us not forget Buñuel's curt advice to the audience of his and Salvador Dalí's *Un chien andalou* (1929):

"NOTHING, in the film, SYMBOLIZES ANYTHING."[27] Putting aside what the toy soldier in *Jauja* means or whose dream the film might be, let us consider the ambient factors that actualize a key operation in surrealist cinema: what Breton, Jacques Brunius, and Ado Kyrou in their own ways call "crossing the bridge"—a phrase that, as Adam Lowenstein reminds us, Breton derives from an intertitle in F. W. Murnau's *Nosferatu* (1922) as the naive estates clerk enters an altered landscape: "When he had crossed the bridge the phantoms came to meet him."[28]

For Brunius, "crossing the bridge" refers to cinema's ability to objectify a mental process while also in the same moment converting external reality into subjective interiority.[29] For Kyrou, the phrase describes an orientation toward "surreality" as it exists in the earthly world, far from mere fantasy.[30] These writers apply the bridge metaphor to surrealist cinema's traversals of the gaps between binary oppositions: object versus subject, rational versus irrational, dream versus waking, intention versus accident, and so on. I am interested in the *spatial and affective* resonances of this process. In my sense, "crossing the bridge" has to do with an *aesthetic transition* that starts within a habituated, concretely established register of reality and then slides—piecemeal—into otherworldly impressions, but without sacrificing the foothold on the real, which is transformed under a different manner of perceiving. This phased, gradated "crossing" effect, which may span multiple scenes, slowly brings on a shockless shudder (close to how I conceptualize eeriness in chapter 5) and occasions a radical modulation of the film's world. Consider the atmospheric disruptions of the neorealist veneer of Buñuel's *Los olvidados* (1950) or the influx of gradually more apocalyptic weather in Peter Weir's *The Last Wave* (1977).[31] "Crossing the bridge," in this sense, newly calibrates all levels of suspense as it changes the viewer's, and perhaps an attendant character's, orientation to and grasp on the world.

Although *Jauja*'s desert cave warps the feel and the very status of the onscreen world, it comes into presence through a careful series of ambient shifts that soften its surprise (and there is delight in watching the film carry off this high-risk turnabout as it brazenly courts absurdity).[32] The suspense of not knowing our bearings is viscerally enhanced and extended by the vaporous environment, the closing in of a thunderstorm, the intensified winds with hints of microphone rumble, and the hypnotic, Tarkovskian dripping of water in the cave. When Dinesen exits the cave, the ambient charge of the world has a surplus value that doesn't *fully* conform to what the screen depicts. The vegetation is barely mussed by the stronger aeolian surges we hear. Despite this incongruity, it pays to recall that surrealist cinema, even when "crossing the bridge," tends to preserve an ontological rapport with physical reality (the word *surrealism* includes *realism*). There remains in *Jauja* a tangible commitment to the indexical properties of the image and to what André Bazin calls the "integrity" of the profilmic event.[33]

Yet there is also an impulse to bend these indexical traces toward ambient overflowings of the frame that involve an uncanny, less cooperative sound field. The *sur*-realism astir in *Jauja*'s landscapes is less the antithesis of a realist approach than its aberrant companion.

As the pomp of the colonial endeavor finds itself reduced to existential dust in the desert, the surrealist crossing, in turn, culminates the transition in *Jauja*'s presentational system from a geographical conception of space (as rationally navigable and compliant with racist attitudes of territorial requisition) toward an ambient sense of landscape as an uncontrollable and nebulous surround. Rather than being the ground against which more important action occurs, ambience becomes an environing force that ungrounds the action and asserts a less tractable, less chiefly visual landscape. Ceasing to be a basis for identification, Dinesen is dissolved into the ambience that encroachingly claims the viewer as its midpoint.

Stalled in Peripheral Disquiet: *Zama*

The eerily repeated question that stymies the military engineer in *Jauja*, "What makes a life function and move forward?," looms over all three films under discussion in this chapter. Suspense of a deeply existential kind imposes itself as the colonial soldier Dinesen's quest is slowed, impeded, sidetracked, and, in the end, dissolved by forces that are as much atmospheric as social and cultural. Taking place a century earlier than *Jauja*, in a remote, unglamorous colonial outpost of the Spanish Empire in what seems to be Paraguay, Lucrecia Martel's *Zama* concerns the darkly comic predicament of Don Diego de Zama (Daniel Giménez Cacho), a magistrate waiting—endlessly—for his transfer to Lerma, where he might reunite with his wife and children. Early in the film, Zama is defined through a parable of a fish whose lot in life is to swim eternally against a current that rejects him and holds him in place. Martel's sonic and visual style explores Zama's situation by setting forth a slow-timed and angsty atmosphere of congestion.[34] Though *Zama* has a widescreen aspect ratio of 1.78:1, it compares to *Jauja* in that it generates suspense through continual ambient conflict between the boundaries of the cinematic frame and the peripheral swirl of detail. The spectator's proxemic and perceptual relationship to Zama turns on the sensation of being converged upon, of being discordantly bounded within and by atmospheric space.

Against a black screen, *Zama* opens with a chorus of cicadas that lunges out toward the audience to establish 360 degrees of sonorous space. This rattling then withdraws, softens, and mingles with the pleasant trickling of water as the first shot introduces a uniformed Zama on a riverbank, looking marooned. From this serene expanse of river and sky, the film cuts to what becomes the prevailing compositional scheme: a claustrophobic frame in which upheaval and noise confound Zama's efforts to project a sense of dignity. Lost in the mazelike dunes, he is tugged in different directions by elusive laughter—sounds that bewilder the spectator as well. Split between the front-left and back-right channels of the Dolby mix, they divide our attention between the image and a region behind the camera. Or is the laughter perhaps in Zama's head? As he seeks the source, the chortling of birds also enters the sound mix: the environment itself seems to find our protagonist comically absurd. His bout of perceptual suspense leads him to a scene of naked African women bathing in mud and speaking of a mysterious "spider-wasp," an insect rumored to be plaguing the area. They catch him spying, poke fun at him, and one of them irreverently chases him until he turns and strikes her.

Akin to Alonso's approach in *Jauja*, Martel either deflates or discards conventions of the historical epic. The sweltering, pestilential world onscreen is devoid of romantic adventure and sensationalized cruelty, although the enslavement of Indigenous and Afro-Paraguayan peoples, who display defiance, constantly figures in the mise-en-scène, flanking the apparent focus of the shot and invalidating the pretense of European order and civility. *Zama* is loosely adapted from Antonio di Benedetto's existential novel of the same (1956), which he wrote, under the influence of Fyodor Dostoevsky and Franz Kafka, as the initial installment of what later became known as the "waiting trilogy" (including *El silenciero* [1964] and *Los suicidas* [1969]). Martel scraps the first-person narration of the literary source text but finds audiovisual forms for conveying a hell of stagnation amid nonsensical and hypocritical bureaucracy. Zama's hopes, in the eyes of the Crown, are tainted because he is a Spaniard born in South America rather than in Spain, which drastically reduces his stature regardless of his rank. Enduring perpetual humiliation, he does the bidding of each governor who passes through the outpost—officials who bait him with promises of writing a letter to the king on his behalf.

Suspense is the restive time of waiting, the time of the interim. In slow varieties, this waiting loses touch with a telos and becomes outright suspension to varying degrees, while maintaining an edge of uncertainty for the spectator. *Zama* is less metrically slow than *Jauja*, but a languor, filtered only partly through character subjectivity, weighs on each scene, no matter the cutting rate. Whether Zama will receive his transfer ceases to be a question of suspense as we sense that day is never coming.[35] Plot-based and atmospheric suspense are fueled more by the gossip that surrounds a bandit, Vicuña Porto (this film's counterpart to *Jauja*'s Zuluaga), who may or may not have been killed (severed ears, said to be his, change hands like currency) and who may or may not be sneaking into the outpost to have sex with a settler's daughters. *Zama*'s calculated refusals of narrative precision, a hallmark of Martel's practice, also perpetuate suspense from one half-intelligible scene to the next: we wonder if we are gleaning what we need to in the interest of a continuous plot.

The film's most fascinating perceptual and atmospheric suspense arises through ambient stylings of sound with an uncertain link to the cramped frame. In an early scene, Zama, making his rounds, visits an inn just as a man leaps from a loft in the background and scurries off before Zama can identify him. This man, we deduce, has been sexually involved with one or more of the innkeeper's complicit daughters, who whisper to each other and barely mask their delight in duping their father and Zama, the latter of whom seems to have taken liberties with one of the girls in the past. But Zama, suspecting theft, too, draws his sword, promises "there is nothing to fear," and searches ridiculously for an intruder at the darkened edges of the scene. While he does this, a chime repeats but is slightly differentiated from objects that could cause it, such as the coins (Are they coins? Is this inn a brothel?) that fall onto the floor and become hidden by the bed. One could say this sound accents or reflects the daughters' secrecy, but its emergence goes beyond this theme. Like the aeolian sound in *Jauja*, this chime insists on its separateness not only from the frame but also from the very order of the frameable.

According to Steven Connor, film sound is a body unto itself, ultimately distinct from the image and linked in a vibratory way to the spectator's body. It is "not primarily 'on' the screen, but *in the listener*." Connor more specifically argues that visual and aural perception operate through constitutively different corporeal dynamics. "Seeing," he explains, "is monoptic in the way it brings things to a point," whereas "hearing is panaural." The force of sound is "mapped across the whole body," head to feet, "rather than converging conelike on one organ of entry." The hearing body "become[s] a variably vibrating membrane," although our spectatorial habit, owing to convention, is to place sound within or near to the depictive screen. In suspenseful ways, *Zama* destabilizes what Connor calls the convention of the "*à voir*, the 'to-be-seen,'" by which sound's principal role is to funnel attention toward the visible.[36] The majority of sounds emanating from the atmosphere of *Zama* lack optical confirmation. Granted, there is a kind of *musique concrète* composed of the diegetic clanging of brandy glasses, the thwacking of straw boot cleaners, and so on. But diegetic sounds become oddly entangled with unseen resonances and with electrophonic Shepard tones that, in their slow and bottomless descent in sonic pitch, relate to Zama's plight. Basic uncertainties of orientation (exterior or interior? objective or subjective? diegetic or nondiegetic?) follow from the film's unleashing of a mutable sound field that goes only part of the way to correlate with the image and its perspectival structures.[37]

Let us consider the metamorphic trajectory of these Shepard tones, which technically are auditory deceptions that sound like endless fallings or escalations in pitch even though the pitch changes are cyclical. Named after Robert Shepard, the psychologist who discovered the phenomenon at Bell Labs in the mid-1960s, this effect greets the listener as a single tone, an infinite glissando; however, it consists of multiple tones of varying intensity, pitched an octave apart but moving in the same direction, the lower tones fading out as higher ones fade in or vice versa. What we perceive as an infinite vector is in fact a recursive pattern. Christopher Nolan's collaborations with Hans Zimmer—for example, Zimmer's panic-inducing score composed for *Dunkirk* (2017)—testify to the impact of ascending Shepard tones. In *Zama*, the descending Shepard scale comes into play as punctuation, initially nondiegetic: it surprisingly overtakes the sound field when others put Zama in his place as he listens in close-up, the rest of the frame a blur. In a long take that features this sonic device, an offscreen governor informs Zama that another man, whom Zama has street-fought with, is to be transferred to Lerma as punishment, a ruling that openly snubs Zama's request to be relocated there. As Zama receives this ridiculous news, a llama we spot in the background slowly winds its way forward into a pocket of focus right next to Zama's face, bearing a clear resemblance to him before clomping out of sight (fig. 3.3).

This funny if outlandish moment walks a tightrope between realist and surrealist manners of expression. The sinking feeling evoked by the Shepard scale perhaps invites us to apprehend the scene and its Buñuel-like gag with the creature in a figurative light: Zama's suspended and bureaucratically absurd situation has no chance of improving, and his stature within the system for which he is a functionary is equal to that of a domesticated llama. Although this

Figure 3.3 Zama and the llama figure as doubles in *Zama*.

reading is reasonably accurate, it understands the Shepard tone as a kind of musical stinger—cartoonish in its mockery. The shot *does* work this way up to a point, but the sinking tone more mysteriously introduces a woozy, dreamy state: its Dolby configuration enwraps us as the scene's grounding changes at our feet despite the shot's unbroken duration. In addition to its role as "to-be-seen" accompaniment rooted in character, this sound has a dizzying ambient function that becomes more and more intricate. In a later scene that takes place in a ramshackle hotel to which Zama relocates in a bid to prevent his furniture from being annexed by a governor, the Shepard tone returns but is more subdued, thinned out, and bewitching as it combines with insect stridulations and crackling fire in a deathly atmosphere oblique to Zama's point of view.[38]

Zama incessantly sensitizes the ear to minor ambient noise within which one can detect suspenseful echoes and permutations. In the last third of the film, as space opens out and Zama joins a posse of soldiers with the assignment of capturing Vicuña Porto (here the film flirts more generically with the Western), the Shepard tone returns in transmogrified forms at the unstable boundary between diegetic and nondiegetic. The long-held, brilliantly green landscape of palm trees that opens this section of the film marks a transition as the posse members move laterally across the shot on horseback in single file under a disproportionately low horizon line (fig. 3.4). Owing to scalar reduction, they look unwittingly at the mercy of the forest rather than in command of it. Ever so faintly, this slow, falsely serene shot brings back the Shepard tone but melds it into the din of insects and birds: the line between synthetic score and natural environmental sound can't be drawn, and the viewer-listener may puzzle over whether the tone has returned or not. Martel says in an interview that she and her crew accentuated the *least* organic-sounding noises of wildlife they ran across in the Chaco province of Argentina: "Before filming, we visited the Chaco region . . . to do field recordings. It's an unusual region that attracts an array of insects and wildlife because it has dramatic floods and droughts. We discovered that many of the frog and insect sounds had an unusual electronic quality. They sounded alien, almost like malfunctioning radios. So, we decided to avoid recording the most lyrical birds and focus on finding only the most mechanical sounds. Finding these natural sounds that didn't seem natural influenced our overall approach in the sound design."[39] These mechanical yet natural field-recorded sounds sneakily incorporate the Shepard tone. If the droning of wildlife indexes the region's actual environmental noise, those sounds are also fused with uncannily similar electrophonic timbres, resulting in a layered tremolo that—not unlike tremolos in orchestral film scores—"create[s] a feeling of dramatic tension, suspense, or alarm" by putting our senses on edge.[40] To this trembling the Shepard tone also contributes the feel of a glissando that moves between adjacent pitches.

Figure 3.4 *Zama*: Once the search party commences, Shepard tones sneakily return in the guise of insect and wildlife sounds.

In a climactic scene where Zama and the posse find themselves under attack by a stealth Indigenous brigade, a Shepard tone cues the suspense, but now the pitch modulation—so far as the ear can tell—is rendered wholly through cicada stridulations in a slow fall. To some extent, this drop in pitch can be said to signify Zama's bewilderment, but the scene's shot selections and cutting rhythms chaotically break away from his point of view. Indeed, this metamorphic trajectory through which the Shepard tone becomes something other than its initial function is concurrent with a shift in the film's presentational style (and here one can draw similarities to the surreal metamorphosis in *Jauja*). As the film has opened out from overcrowded frames to geographical expanses, and as the narrative texture has become more elliptical, the sound mix has pried us apart from the psychological and perspectival coordinates that the tone originally buoyed. The attack scene and the cryptic moments that follow, when surviving members of the posse are captured, taken to the Indigenous camp, stripped, and ritualistically covered in bright-red paint (How much time passes across these lacunary events?), decenter Zama as though he has ceased to be the protagonist.

The more the Shepard scale crosses over into the film's diegesis, the more it renounces its simple, almost risible role as a comment on Zama's hopeless existence and becomes much more unnervingly ubiquitous. The *sur*-realist shift in this late phase enacts the derailing not only of the search party (which is actually a quest for spoils) but also of the colonial project as Zama meets with alterity by force—a peripheralized presence that moves more to the center, albeit opaquely, in concert with the Shepard scale's morphing spread. Like this sonic tone, the tribes that pass by or enclose on the posse are entwined with the landscape, the fluctuant weather—everywhere and nowhere at once. The peripheral has become circumambient.[41]

Both *Jauja* and *Zama* rely on suspense to stage the comeuppance of imperious whiteness at the hands of an "alien" milieu it can't master. Zama is conspicuously less white than his pallid, "properly" Spaniard superiors—and this variance, together with the fact that he has indiscreetly fathered a child with an Indigenous woman, ensures his low status in the system. Martel states that she approached *Zama* as a riff on an abiding problem of identity in Argentina according to which middle- and upper-class citizens regard themselves as exiled Europeans, well removed from South American cultural diversity.[42] By atmospheric and darkly amusing means, the film associates whiteness of this attitude with disease: the wan cadaver of a European entrepreneur who has died from the plague (and who has been farcically portrayed) is doused with lime in a crypt as Zama, a mere shadow, watches the white dust hang in the air, an entrancing if eerie image that also alludes to the snowy winter for which Europeans in the film long (fig. 3.5).

From the forest-attack scene onward, Zama's forcedly immersive contact with otherness finds its complement in the film's multisensory address to and mystifying games of perception with the viewer. Significantly, the Indigenous communities do not become knowable to and for any preexisting, assumed capacity to understand them. Their speech goes untranslated, and the

Figure 3.5 Zama observes the quicklime-dusted burial of the European businessman in *Zama*.

meaning of their red-paint ritual goes unexplained. Their presence differently tunes cinematic space and reroutes the narrative, and yet no image or sound enters their point of view. It is clear that they *have* complex points of view (and superior defense methods), but their subjectivities are profoundly impassable from the vantage of colonial authority, which is now denuded of its signs and devices of domination. The suspense regarding Indigenous culture and subjectivity owes less to the occlusion of information than to a limit of the knowable for the "*imperial-spectacular gaze structure.*"[43] This suspense speaks to fissures in the historical archive on account of that gaze's limitations.[44] Yet the tribes do not become exotic pretexts for the wondrous or the dreadful—a risk that atmosphere-driven films about colonial histories frequently incur (from Herzog's work to Peter Weir's surreal rendering of Aboriginal cosmology in *The Last Wave*). In the late stretch of *Zama*, point of view *itself*, far from naively upholding such cultural asymmetries, loses its rhetorical purchase due to ambient upheavals. There is no stable point of audition, no place of localization, no scaffold of identification, and, ultimately, no "home," no landing ground, for the Shepard tone except for the listening body that its repetitions address.

The aural suspense of *Zama* moves toward immersion without suture: without a narrative and technical system that sweeps us into a firm subject position in the film's fiction.[45] The more the Shepard scale bleeds into the diegesis at the level of *effect*, the more it also emanates out in the opposite direction to enwrap the viewer-listener at the level of *affect*. Since the adoption of multi-track stereo in the 1950s, film sound has embraced this ubiquity while usually distracting from it through the steady pull of the "to-be-seen." Yet *Zama* has us feel and ponder the vertigo of aural tension with the image as the ubiquitous ambience is divided *expressively* on both sides of the screen. That is, *Zama*'s sonic style configures the screen as a porous boundary that opens onto the space in which we watch. The film reminds us that when we define ambience in cinema, the prefix *amb-* means "on both sides," which may refer to a breached boundary as well as to the spectator's encircled and besieged sensorium.

Interface of Uneasy Listening: *Under the Skin*

The "alien" environmental noise of which Martel speaks when discussing *Zama* carries a muted genre inflection: she made *Zama* in the aftermath of her planned science-fiction film that did not come to fruition, an adaptation of the Argentine serial comic *El eternauta* (1957–1959). The Shepard scale in *Zama* stands in distant but meaningful company with electronic scores that atmospherically convey the otherworldly in science fiction.[46] *Jauja* also remotely encompasses science fiction through references to *Stalker*. Let it come as no surprise, then, that our third case study of ambience and suspense in this chapter—another film about an out-of-place traveler's mission that goes awry—is an art-house amalgam of science fiction and horror.

Jonathan Glazer's *Under the Skin* is thinly adapted from Michel Faber's novel of the same title published in 2000. Viewers familiar with the literary source will know the protagonist, Isserley in the novel, is an extraterrestrial agent in female form, sent to Earth by a corporation on another planet to harvest humans for meat. The film, however, abandons all exposition of this colonial and capitalistic venture, and it would be wrong to assume its narrative lacunae are necessarily meant to be filled in by the novel's additional and more communicative content. In the novel, Isserley's humanlike consciousness is doled out through third-person limited narration, to the point where, as Mark Fisher argues, the unsettling ambiguity between alien and human life is quashed, but the film's anonymous, possibly extraterrestrial "woman" (Scarlett Johansson) is defined by a steely exterior that, while alluring and familiar, keeps us from accessing a subject underneath—her motivations and desires.[47] The physicality of this "English woman" disguises her actual body as she carries out serial murder with untiring focus, yet the film holds us in proximity to her, or its, perceptual apparatus, producing an ambience of dread that grows step by step to overwhelming proportions.

The score for *Under the Skin*, composed by the British experimental electro-pop musician Mica Levi (whose stage name is "Micachu"), can be classified as ambient in terms of music genre, but this genre, even when it lacks a supplementing image, is more than sonic: it is environmental. In the liner notes for his album *Music for Airports* (1978), Brian Eno famously defines *ambient* as an "atmosphere, or a surrounding influence: a tint" of the listening space that makes it conducive to thought and contemplation, not just workday productivity or benumbing calm (which would be the domains of Muzak). *Ambient*, for Eno, describes the confluence of listener, music, and the contingent acoustics of a given environment that might include, say, the purr of appliances, the sounds of auto traffic or birds, or, to use one of Eno's founding examples, rain from outside an open window. Because in today's parlance *ambience* has come to imply comfort, it tends to be forgotten that Eno preserves "doubt and uncertainty" as core qualitative tones in his definition of ambient music.[48] Aspiring to be landscape more than orthodox music, his ambient albums, up to and including *On Land* (1982), venture into uneasy mixes of synth instruments, animal/insect recordings, and noises that offset the impression of arcadian idyll with ulterior discordances. "Founded in slowness, receptivity, and the ambiguities of what is outside and what is inside,"[49] ambient music has attracted critical disputes akin to those about cinematic slowness. Does it enliven or deaden the listener? Does it withdraw from or engage the world and social concerns? In Eno's conception, ambience doesn't simply traffic in balmy delight. When this music isn't produced as barely varying electronica that pacifies, it shudders on the brink of anxious commotion.

From the outset of *Under the Skin*, Levi's ambient score assumes a mysterious processual function. We start with a protracted black screen that may lead the observer to suspect a problem with the projector. This surplus darkness and quiet as well as the abstract prelude that follows it overtly rework the commanding overture of Stanley Kubrick's *2001: A Space Odyssey* (1968). Against the darkness, there is an ominous build of music. Layered, recursive tremolos in Levi's score emulate avant-garde music that the cinephile will recognize, György Ligeti's *Lontano* (as used in Kubrick's *The Shining* [1980]) and *Atmosphères* (as used in *2001*). From the middle of the black screen a single white blip grows larger, resembling a little dot in a vision test until it morphs into an ocular globe: we gather by degrees that we're witnessing the manufacture of an eyeball, a black cylinder sliding into a pupil (fig. 3.6). Eerily entwining biological, cosmic, and technoindustrial forms, this process echoes the alignments of celestial bodies in *2001* (at the start and later, when the alien monolith appears). Glazer's opening climaxes with an extreme close-up of the eye, fully constructed and endowed with life. All the while, the looping score couples with a female voice (Johansson's) speaking a series of words in English, implying the acquisition or download of a human language by an alien intelligence. A sudden cut transports us to a white title screen that counterbalances the earlier blackness (one thinks of the stark contrasts in *2001* between the gleaming white ship and pitch-dark outer space). This cut is audial as well in that it sharply transitions—or, as Michel Chion words it, "commutes"—from one sonic ambience to another, a stylistic signature of *2001* that Glazer adopts.[50]

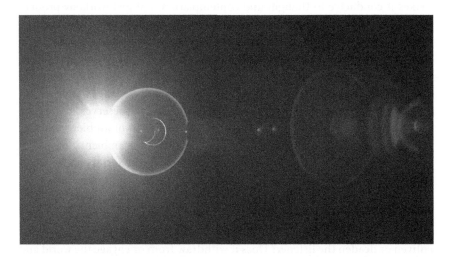

Figure 3.6 *Under the Skin* abstractly opens with the mechanical creation of an eyeball.

Beneath the score (a hollow drone fused with warped strings and a percussive mechanical clamor that sounds like a printer), do we hear *film* and *films* among the words the alien voice tests out for the first time? The first complete word stated is *feel*, but the subsequent series of words beginning with *f* is hard to differentiate, and the cinematic reflexivity of this scene is enough to bring *film* and *films* to mind, although the words could be *field* and *fields* or babble instead. To be sure, there are already other seminal "films" in the citational weft: in addition to Kubrick's work, the imagery here invokes the graphic forms and anonymous woman in the opening titles of Hitchcock's *Vertigo* (1958) as well as the strobing light amid pitch darkness at the start of Jean-Luc Godard's *Alphaville* (1965), and there is even a nod to the espresso cup reverie in Godard's *2 or 3 Things I Know About Her* (1967). In this way, Glazer's opening makes reflexive reference to other reflexive films, borrowing from their hypnotic and confrontational manners of spectator address. As *Under the Skin* unfolds, its breadth of allusion includes slow art-house films, from Chantal Akerman's *Jeanne Dielman* (1975) and Michelangelo Antonioni's *Identification of a Woman* (1982) to Abbas Kiarostami and Mania Akbari's *Ten* (2002), not to mention many science-fiction and gothic horror films in service of Glazer's ambition to invent "a new Frankenstein. A new Dracula. A new monster for our times."[51] The alien voicing of *film* (intuited correctly or not) is equally charged here as the technical apparatus of the medium finds resonances. What becomes the eye at first evokes the projector beam. The stuttering mechanical noise: Does it not resemble a droning *film* projector, despite the film's patently digital attributes? On seeing this film in a theater, I felt the distinct impression of its spare ambience meeting and texturally integrating the dark, air-conditioned ambience of the theater space, and a key passage from Jean-Louis Schefer entered my thoughts: "I don't believe we're in Plato's cave. We are, for an inconceivable eternity, suspended between a giant body and the object of its gaze. So I am not seated, but *suspended* beneath a beam of light. That light is alive. The slight anteriority of its movement in regards to the animation of the film's objects is visible like a scissor-effect, or as if these rays were kicking their legs, crossing and uncrossing them at irregular intervals."[52]

The salute to Kubrick's science-fiction film has weighty implications for *Under the Skin*'s uses of suspense. I say this not only because Glazer reworks a Kubrickian style of suspense but also because *2001* builds suspense around the film medium itself, a task to which *Under the Skin* aspires as well, while eliciting a spectator experience that is self-conscious and immersive at the same time.[53] The creation of the eye at once refers to the villainous HAL and the metamorphic Dave Bowman (Keir Dullea) in *2001*—the surveillance eye of a supercomputer and the bewildered eye of an astronaut. *2001* doesn't offer such extreme close-ups until late in the film, when Bowman soars through the stargate into another dimension of sight and bodily sensation over which, so it seems, a supernatural or alien force reigns. But Glazer—like Ridley Scott's tribute to Kubrick in *Blade Runner* (1982) and Steven Soderbergh in his re-edit of *2001, The Return of W. De Rijk* (2015)—*begins* with this enormous eye, suggesting a recalibration of perception necessary for our engagement with the film to follow. This address of the eye indicates both that we are being observed and that we find our gaze uncannily doubled by and processed through that of the woman, or alien imitation of a woman, just produced. It's as if the nameless Johansson character and the viewer are created simultaneously in each other's image.

As a reference standing in for cinema itself, *2001* imparts to *Under the Skin* the energy of rediscovery that Annette Michelson found in Kubrick's experiment upon its release: rebirth and rediscovery of the film medium as a vessel of bodily transport for a viewer made to acclimate anew to the darkness of the theater, the brilliance of the screen, the immersive forms displayed, with all this experiential disorientation and reorientation constituting, for Michelson, a radically reimagined mode of "suspense," a contention she ongoingly explores.[54]

Levi's ambient score, maintaining its suspenseful, process-based relationship to cinematic reflexivity, is ubiquitous during the first half of *Under the Skin*, where it pulses as "foreground music" even when its intensities become more subtle.[55] It provides a kind of vital, respiratory rhythm as the alien—in disguise as a low-income "woman on the prowl," disposable in the eyes of a misogynistic culture[56]—cruises Glasgow in a white van, stalking clueless men, whom she escorts to their doom in a black-liquid vault. She/it is a wandering spectator whose mechanized surveillance apparatus conspires with the film's formal system. Glazer constructs these glacially paced driving sequences around the alien's point of view, with the van's windshield serving as a mise en abyme of our film screen. As she scans the human passersby, our attention overlaps with and is unnervingly *mediated by* hers. Levi's score combines a Ligetian tone field with a cyclical noise that suggests breathing. Indeed, the score evokes the sound of Bowman breathing through his oxygen tank when he vies with HAL in *2001*, an aural ambience that is "both assuring and disturbing, as if our head were in the maw of a lion," as Chion describes it.[57] Likewise, in *Under the Skin* we are ensnared within, or "vehicularized" by, a nonhuman perceptual system that is built around an unreadable impostor who nonetheless figures as our hypnotic focal point and perspectival filter (fig. 3.7).[58]

Point of view and focalization are, for the spectator of this film, durational lures that pull us toward an absence of character subjectivity and an obliteration of the visual field. The more the film hints at the novel's meat-harvesting premise, the more the image track withdraws into opacity and abstraction. The alien crypt in which *Homo sapiens* are liquified into meat is a dread-inducing emblem of the unknowable. Its nocturnal, infinite environment opens onto an oven after the alien entrances its prey in a striptease recalling

Figure 3.7 While viewing and hearing *Under the Skin*, we are lured and possessed by an alien perceptual system, our impulse toward identification denied.

the protocinematic motion studies of Eadweard Muybridge. In Elena Gorfinkel's description of this oven apparatus, a bright-red "meat sludge" that resembles "molten lava" is transported "down a chute, turning over and converting into a depthless perspectival line of red at the center of the screen," along which the viewer is slowly drawn in turn. With a cut, this fiery glow fills the screen, as if to plunge us into this process of bodily "transvaluation."[59] A starburst, dislodged from spatial and temporal markers, emits light and returns us to the genesis of an eye, but what we see is the fact of our not seeing as the score encases us in a "beehive" of screechy microtones.[60] The film has lured us toward a discorrelating rupture from human perception.

At the midpoint of the film's running time, the alien swerves from its hunting mission by allowing a severely disfigured man to escape, but this event happens in an elliptical fashion that leaves the alien's motivation up in the air. Is this an act of kindness out of emergent respect for humanity? Has the alien empathically connected with this man, perhaps on physiognomic and psychological grounds? At best, we can surmise that the alien's volte-face sets it on a nomadic path of curiosity regarding the earthly environment and the pleasures and sensations of human life. In *Jauja* and *Zama*, the ambient and characterological transformations involve a slippage of identity and a subsumption into the landscape that neither the Danish military engineer nor the Spanish magistrate desires. Under duress, they confront otherness as their identities breakdown and expire. In *Under the Skin*, however, the alien already constitutes the film's most profound inscription of alterity (that is, from a human perspective), and its change in identity, as far as we can determine, stems from choice and curiosity or longing on its part.

The film's movement away from the alien's vehicular surveillance interface—and from Levi's entrapping ambient score that feels like an *endogenous* part of this system, part and parcel of the film's world instead of a nondiegetic component added to it—plays out in meteorological terms. After a long-held shot of a seascape (a beach where we earlier witnessed the alien kill a man and leave his infant child to die on the shore as well), we cut to a scene where the alien is overcome by a dense fog while driving. Invoking Antonioni's uses of fog (in *Red Desert* [1964] and *Identification of a Woman* in particular), this earthly phenomenon inspires the alien to step out of the van and take it in: wrapping and seeming to beguile it/her, vapor fills the screen and softens noises of an unseen bird and pedestrian. Caught between curiosity and a state of alarm, it/she is in suspense of an atmospheric and perceptual variety. The film cuts to an extreme long shot in which the alien, walking horizontally along the misty Highlands roadside, becomes a speck of hot pink, visible only by its/her shirt (fig. 3.8). The alien remains as enigmatic as ever, but it is clear enough that something about the fog exerts a seductive pull on a character who has drastically changed roles.

The Ambient Landscape 113

Figure 3.8 The alien is enwrapped by mist and engulfed by the landscape in *Under the Skin*.

As the alien attempts to acclimate to human life on Earth, the same classed and gendered disguise that aided its conquests in the film's first half now renders it a target in a world where violence against women is endemic. In the film's last section, the alien takes refuge in a boggy forest around Loch Eck—primeval, fairy-tale-like. Before this point, the terrestrial soundscape has replaced the Levi score, yet now the score returns as a low, breathy drone that mixes with a rainstorm as the alien, now a homeless and vulnerable immigrant, falls asleep in a shelter, showing signs of fatigue we didn't see earlier. A cross-dissolve ties her/its resting figure to the windswept trees outside. But the drone then rises to reestablish a mood of horror as the alien soon wakes up to be hunted and sexually attacked by an industrial woodsman who rips her/its false skin to expose blackness underneath, much to his—and to our—surprise. He douses the alien in gasoline, lights a match, and leaves her/it to burn away into the snowy sky. Coinciding with the assault, a winter storm has set in and covered the area.

Pervasive within the history of genres traditionally aligned with suspense, murder scenes, with their staged reductions of a subject to a lifeless object, pose ethical and aesthetic questions of social expendability.[61] When the character's death is more than just a plot necessity, we feel the draining away of the point of view with which we have been affiliated (as in Marion's death in *Psycho*), whether we have accessed an interiority and found it sympathetic or not.[62] Things and subjects, however, are irreducibly mysterious in *Under the Skin*. Gorfinkel observes how the alien, through an earlier-established trajectory that associates her/it with the natural environment, is tied to insects and various objects, among them a glowing space heater, that have a nonhuman vivacity of their own. At the same time, Gorfinkel argues, the alien's *unwilling* reduction to an object by the attack and murder speaks to violence historically visited upon subjects divested of subjecthood due to differences—gendered, sexual, racial, economic, or otherwise—that are seen as socially and ontologically disposable.[63]

Curiously, the mood here isn't *strictly* horrific: as we watch the decomposed matter of the alien dissipate into the winter landscape, the dreary cast of this ending takes on notes of wonder (fig. 3.9). Cueing the audience for this contemplative turn is an extreme long shot, moments earlier, of the alien's motorcyclist supervisor (a *human* male? perhaps henchman to the alien's boss?) looking into the white void of the surround, detecting no sign of his deserter employee. This shot mimics Caspar David Friedrich's iconic paintings of such figures who are pictured from behind and sublimely swallowed up by the landscapes they study as spectators inscribed within the painting. Wonder and dread interlace in the film's final seconds as the smoke from the alien's corpse vanishes and the falling snow glides past (and collides with) the upturned camera lens—a mechanical point of view associated with the alien's carbonized remains. The images spell death and evanescence but enticingly draw us toward their blankness.

This finale begs us to consider its ambient resonances and implications. In describing the alien's vector of "becoming weather," Gorfinkel notes that this parting imagery carefully adapts lines at the end of Faber's novel:

The atoms that had been herself would mingle with the oxygen and nitrogen in the air. Instead of ending up buried in the ground, she would become part of the sky: that was the way to look at it. Her invisible remains would combine, over time, with all the wonders under the sun. When it snowed, she would

Figure 3.9 The alien burns away into the atmosphere in/of *Under the Skin*.

be part of it, falling softly to earth, rising up again with the snow's evaporation. When it rained, she would be there in the spectral arch that spanned from firth to ground. She would help to wreathe the fields in the mist, and yet would always be transparent to the stars.[64]

These are Isserley's thoughts in third person following a car crash that obliges her to blow up the vehicle and herself. The sentences project an afterlife not realized in the novel, whereas the film quietly and tacitly conveys this atomic conversion, still insinuating the alien's *un*deadness as she/it *becomes* the dynamic atmosphere. In support of this motif, the snow flitting past the eye of the camera gives an inkling of the stargate sequence in *2001* and Bowman's passage—deathly alive—"beyond the infinite."[65] Although the score drops out again, its vital rhythm is converted into a music of ambient wind, wisping snowfall, and crackling cinder.

This ending suspensefully returns us to the tensions and concerns that inform the concept of ambience. Does it swaddle, menace, or indifferently displace humanity? What, moreover, do we make of the alien turning into *media diaphana*—the elemental ambient media of the earthly world (air, fog, water, etc.)? How does this event self-consciously describe *cinematic* ambience? Given the reflexivity *Under the Skin* exhibits through allusions not just to other films but also to the film medium and apparatus, how does "film itself," including spectatorial experience, factor into this dreadful yet peaceful and meditative finale? Does the generic mixture of science fiction and horror have a bearing on these matters?

The film's imagery tempts us to think through these questions according to the sublime, a well-trodden path in film studies when discussions turn to landscapes that bring on exalted if partly distressed or fearful emotional states in the spectator. *Under the Skin*'s expansive views of the wilderness, against which the "human" figure (imposter or no) becomes miniscule, at least flirt with an iconography of the sublime: faced with grand, mystifying events and forces, the subject feels outstripped, unable to fathom the environment as their faculties of sense and imagination are pushed to the absolute limits. Yet the sublime, in its Kantian formulation, is an experience in which the subject recovers through a reascension of the reasoning faculty once the unlimited capacity of *reflection upon our limits* is realized. This recovery enacts the triumph of cognition over mere sense perception and over the world's exteriority.[66] *Under the Skin* nowhere caters to this second, restorative step, and the film's momentum, paired with its focus on the nonhuman, has already made exceedingly strange the characterological and identificatory bases of such an idea of subjectivity. Notably, the cyclist who studies the landscape (returning the camera's stare for a moment as he turns 360 degrees) *sees nothing* in the white void of mist and snow, rather unlike Friedrich's shown-from-the-back observers. He is not engaged in awestruck contemplation, and his blocked vision and lack of knowledge stand at odds with our somber awareness of the alien's condition and whereabouts.

For the spectator, the ambient suspense of this finale is more in the vicinity of *photogénie* than of the Kantian sublime (although *photogénie*, at least as theorized and creatively practiced by Jean Epstein, taps into the "modern technological sublime").[67] Among all the potentials Epstein and other French theorists writing in the 1920s assign to the photogenic in cinema, what most pertains to our concerns here is cinema's kinship with the elemental rhythms and vibrations of the world as they are coaxed into *flowing* impressions for the fascinated spectator. Undulating liquids, slow-spreading mist, windblown landscapes, and diaphanous materials—these mobile visual textures strangely cooperate with and are enhanced by film's optical processes, such as altered motion, focus pulls, and superimpositions, and these stylistic devices, sometimes more demonstrably than in the original theorists' writings on *photogénie*, evince the poetic thrust and meaning of this multifaceted concept.[68] One of the basic defining impulses of *photogénie* is to synthesize film with *media diaphana* in a double display of atmospheric mediation that takes precedence over narrative and linguistic representation. In this avant-garde vocation of cinema that bloomed in the silent era, words and plot yield to ambience set in poetic motion. Glazer's work has shown affinities for this approach since the beginning of his career, as far back as his commercials and music videos of the 1990s.[69] When Glazer, in an interview for *Under the Skin* in 2014, voices a nostalgic view of cinema's power, linking it to suspense, there is a touch of longing for the photogenic: "I'm still obsessed by images.... How they sing, how they sync. And I wonder what cinema could have been *had it not gone down the word road*. But we always want to know what's going on. We hate to not know."[70]

Indeed, the evocations of *photogénie* that attend the alien's demise and transmutation are taciturn, uncommunicative. In contrast to the source novel, there is no impression of an interior, psychological state made legible as landscape. In terms of genre, horror and science fiction here frustrate any attempt to think of cinema as the anthropomorphic extension of our sight. At times, granted, these popular genres are inclined to absorb radically alien entities and phenomena into recognizably human frameworks of thought, feeling, and perception. The Faber novel does this, as already observed. Or take the red-filtered interface of blinking information that inscribes the nonhuman point of view of the titular character in James Cameron's *The Terminator* (1984).[71] Instead of temporarily signifying "alien perception" in this fashion, *Under the Skin* indefinitely and more profusely entwines the alien's perceptual system and vital, mediational energies with the film's baseline ambience. Glazer's more radically suspenseful film enlists its optical, graphic, and sonic devices as lower-keyed mediations that situate us in the grasp of an alien intelligence. This entwinement eerily describes cinema itself as a nonhuman, alien entity in command of and perhaps indifferent to our involvement. Glazer's nods to the metacinematic and atmospherically suspenseful techniques of *2001* lean in this direction.[72]

Talk of the sublime and *photogénie*, which emphasize visual perception, should not divert us from the point that the *sonic* alien ambience encircles and discomfits us most intensely—and persuades us that cinema is an oxygenated medium on both sides of the screen. The diaphanous medium of air, after all, is not in itself visual. In his book *Uncanny Cinema* (2022), Murray Pomerance defines film as a medium of space devoid of air: the viewer projects the presence of breathable air onto the film, but air isn't *really* there; we cannot share it with the characters. Air, he maintains, is a "logical construct" we apply to airless space: "Logic is not hapticity."[73] Does it follow from this argument that the impression of ambient air stirred by *Under the Skin* (and central to theories of atmosphere that declare "films and their audiences breathe each other") is an imagined supplement or a rhetorical ruse at best?[74] Not entirely. The *pictorial* space, from which we are removed by the screen's boundary, is airless apart from our imagination, but the film's sonorous body, which is more in the listener than on a screen and in the fiction, vibrates through the air immediately surrounding us. It burrows underneath the skin and rumbles in our bones—an aerial transmission, to be sure, that renders a direct impact, possibly a respiratory one should our breathing rate change in response to sound's pervading influence in conjunction with the image.

The suspense of this alien atmospheric invasion is geared toward destabilizing preformed notions of subjectivity and self in the embodied listener.[75] Some of the key images across *Jauja*, *Zama*, and *Under the Skin* that stage the dissolution or slippage of the stable, unitary subject are reflexive (and deathly) evocations of *the space of our encounter in the movie theater*, where the sonic field closes and amplifies the atmospheric circle. The leaky, capacious witch cave in *Jauja*, the powdery quicklime tomb in *Zama*, and the dark-liquid crypt in *Under the Skin*—these scenes distill how the films' ambient operations render our perceptual space boundless, airy, nocturnal, miasmic, "surfaceless," colloidal: a zone of becoming mingled with and emptied into something radically alien to oneself.

Germane here is the concept of "surfaceless space" put forward by Hermann Schmitz as a core feature of his neophenomenological account of atmosphere. For Schmitz, modern views of space are plagued by their biased fixation on surfaces, points, and intersecting geometrical lines, which leaves out qualitative, circulatory feelings, poured out in a space where they seize hold of the "perceiving felt body."[76] Schmitz doesn't single out *film* atmospheres, but his sense of space applies generously and suspensefully to the cinematic situations this chapter has analyzed across films that find ways to resurrect in us a sort of primal fascination for and anxious curiosity about the sensory experience of spectatorship. Through atmospheric suspense, these films render newly exhilarating, instead of pro forma, the theater's sealed-off orchestrations of light and obscurity, the impression of being suspended in a medium as atmosphere flows from the fictional world into the screening space, provoking virtual yet embodied contact. This feeling, again, is not far from the suspense Michelson ascribes to *2001*, not just the stargate sequence but even that film's unrushed intervals of plotlessness as well.[77]

* * *

Eventually, in chapter 6, it will be necessary to address how suspense has been affected by newer *dispositifs* in digital culture that have succeeded and imperiled theatrical viewing, but for now I conclude by insisting that slow cinema, especially when it harnesses its resources of suspense, can awaken a newfound bodily delight in and a reverence for the immersive experience that the theatrical encounter involves, doing so no less powerfully than those hyperspectacular studio blockbusters that, as we are told by journalists every summer, "save movie theaters." The slow films I consider don't have the commercial ability to keep afloat even the art-house exhibition network on which they rely. Their self-consciousness about the theatrical *dispositif* is most often elegiac. Yet through suspense slow films can rebuild a receptiveness that blockbusters have aggressively driven out of us, a sensitivity to ambient sensation that is keyed low. What slow cinema recuperates by means of suspense is something of the theatrical environment's matchless power to shape our anticipatory attention through understated stimuli as we submit to the pace and rhythm the film imposes. In this way, the slow art-house experience can be said to "save" the ambient subtlety of cinema.

CHAPTER 4

AILING BODIES ON THE THRESHOLD OF ACTION

Slow, durationally stretched cinema may ignite suspense without having to affiliate itself with a popular genre like the thriller. Its forms of restriction and rarefaction, its enforcement of extreme periods of waiting, have their own ways of generating suspense for a spectator whose experience may hover among anxiety, tedium, astonishment, irritation, and hypnotic calm. In this chapter, I want to continue to examine slow-paced art cinema's fundamentally mysterious relationships between character and environment, between the corporeal figures who inhabit the film frame in uncommon, often hard-to-grasp ways and the atmospheric motifs of light, shadow, texture, and sound that enfold them.

Recall that in chapter 1's morphology of suspense, I broadly distinguished between two forms of character-based suspense: one in which our anxieties mount through our involvement with a psychologically legible character in danger and another form in which suspense results from a sheer deficit of character information and psychological accessibility. My examples of slow, minimalist suspense in art-house cinema have concerned mainly the latter group: in their muted habits of gesture, speech, carriage, and emotion, the characters (and performances) we examined in chapters 2 and 3 recede from conventional dramatic intensities as well as from psychologistic vectors of spectator investment. As we have seen, these bodies are swathed in suspenseful ambiguity as they reconfigure dramatic expression along finer degrees of salience. Instead of bringing the film's aesthetic resonances to a dull standstill, their onscreen presences assist in a transference of expressive power and import onto the ambient landscape and sensorial patterns at the very brink of "drama."

This basic distinction within my morphology of character suspense, however, calls for a more careful calculus at this point. After all, hasn't each of our protagonists so far been in grave danger, and hasn't that narrative situation inflected our attachments to them—even when they elude emotional and psychological norms of legibility? From Kelly Reichardt's hopelessly on-the-run ecoterrorist to Jonathan Glazer's astray, equally doomed extraterrestrial, we might not have Hitchcockian suspense per se, but these protagonists are nonetheless vulnerable figures around which our affective and perceptual interests turn. In my earlier explanation, I allowed that character suspense may waver between these variations as a film advances: in one moment, we intuit a character's fears, motives, desires, and so forth, identifying with them on that basis, but then a moment later we don't, or can't, as that very foundation of identification dissolves. What separates the art-house films I have dealt with from the more familiar paradigm of identification is that the character we find ourselves attached to ceases to be an anchor point of focalization and meaning as atmospheric elements come forward, insisting on a sensory reorientation to the film's world, a reattunement that heightens, more than relieves, unknowingness.

This peculiar, resiliently suspenseful relationship between character and environment will be lost on those who fall back on what Benedict Morrison has called a "focalizing" tendency in critical responses to art-cinematic ambiguity. In the "character-centric" version of this protocol, the dramatis personae, once the critic endows them with far greater psychological cohesiveness and "articulacy" than they in fact manifest, are presented as the "key" to the film's formal and narrative difficulties—a center of meaning to which the film points as its "alibi." As Morrison shows, this protocol often dodges rather than confronts art cinema's complications (and regards as anathema the notion that a film could favor irresolution for any reason other than to summon the messianic intervention of a critic, who gives an explanation that "completes" the work, doing away with uncertainty or pretending to). For Morrison, the problem with focalizing criticism is that it regards character as a source of clarification that is divisible from the rest of the film and produces textual inscriptions of character contrary to their actual articulation. He argues that it isn't wrong to read an art film such as Terence Davies's *The Long Day Closes* (1992) through the prism of its protagonist's characterization as "a melancholic gay adolescent growing up in the stifling environment of 1950s Liverpool," but when the deliberate "contradictions" and "half-glimpses of unspoken complexities" are papered over so the film can be assumed to present a fixed and accessible identity, the interpretation grates against the film's aesthetic emphases on *in*articulacy and *in*congruity in relation to gay experience.[1] With the focalizing tendency of criticism, then, we find another ingrained perspective that takes its task to be the victorious exorcism of suspense.[2]

The art-house films under analysis in this book require a more holistic view of "character" that can encompass curious relationships between dramatis personae and environments without always weighing the former over the latter, as in the habit of claiming a landscape "externalizes" a person's inner thoughts and emotions. In film, no less than in life, *character* may serve as a synonym for *atmosphere*. Instead of parceling out the components of expression, we need to forge a critical vocabulary in touch with atmospheric processes of characterization that *resonate across* interwoven levels of figure and ground, person and milieu.

Slow cinema's dramatis personae tend to abide in states of being beneath the threshold of action or beneath what popular cinema trains us to *regard as* action.[3] But therein lie mysterious interplays with the atmospheric surroundings that raise suspense around the basic functions and capabilities of the corporeal gesturing figure as the film's world, in several cases, gently morphs between the ordinary and the fantastic. Take the revival of a dead woman in *Silent Light* (Carlos Reygadas, 2007), an event that circuitously fuses cosmic rhythms with sometimes mundane, sometimes dramatic gestures and moods embodied by a Mennonite farm community, portrayed by untrained actors whose presences are pitched between the neorealist nonprofessional and the Bressonian model.[4] From the homicide detective's levitation in *Humanité* (Dumont, 1999) to the ghostliness that underpins interactions in *Goodbye, Dragon Inn* (Tsai, 2003) and through to the surreal altering of the Patagonian quest in *Jauja* (Alonso, 2014), slow cinema's bodies—despite being static, hushed, or otherwise dialed back—are sometimes involved in atmospheric relays of force that border on or even explicitly introduce the supernatural.

This chapter turns specifically to ailing bodies and their suspenseful characteristics along these lines. My examples, Pedro Costa's *Horse Money* (2014) and Apichatpong Weerasethakul's *Cemetery of Splendor* (2015) and *Memoria* (2021), owe their slow-cinematic power to their strange configurations of the enfeebled body as a fulcrum around which aesthetic and political questions coalesce. In Costa's collaboration with José Tavares Borges, better known by the alias "Ventura," and in Apichatpong's respective collaborations with Jenjira Pongpas Widner and Tilda Swinton, main characters vexed by undiagnosed infirmities become enmeshed with uncanny atmospheres wherein past and present traumas overlay in an implied critique of state power and its inveterate abuses.[5] Despite their unobtrusive tonalities, these three films are quietly militant, and one of my goals is to illuminate and defend their suspenseful manners of political engagement. Much of the suspense arises from the unassumingly magnetic presences that Ventura, Pongpas Widner, and Swinton contribute as "actor-mediums," to borrow a term from Gilles Deleuze.[6] Not unlike the heroine of *Jeanne Dielman* (Akerman, 1975), they are particularized by time and physicality and place in observational character studies. But these screen figures are also enigmatic channelers of atmosphere, caught up in collective, multitemporal circuits of gestures, sensations, moods, and memories that reckon with historical traumas of a persistent and shared nature. If confinement and derailment were the situational factors driving the suspense in my earlier investigations, here the unwell body catalyzes and *becomes the conduit for* paranormal atmospheres of networked enmeshment.[7]

How are we to handle this suspenseful dynamic of characterization at the nexus between atmosphere and personage? How do these affective circuits factor in and perhaps factor out the embodied viewer? Are we immersed participants? More detached bystanders? Do we assume a mimetic or otherwise correspondent relationship to these infirm figures? Do we have a share in their therapeutic interactions? These questions on the table are not merely aesthetic: suspense of an ethical, political, and philosophical order encircles the boundaries of communal experience as these three films stake out our involvement in different ways.

Nightwork: *Horse Money*

The recondite plot of *Horse Money* unfolds around an aging Cape Verdean immigrant in Lisbon, a retired bricklayer now suffering from a mysterious nervous condition that causes his hands to shake uncontrollably. Ventura plays himself as the fatigued protagonist whose thoughts and perceptions become temporally unhinged in a hospital setting that morphs into a dark, subterranean maze of corridors, entranceways, elevators, stairwells, foyers, and canteens—a surreal blend of medieval and contemporary architecture stalked by apparitions from Ventura's past (fig. 4.1). It is unclear whether this shapeshifting location—which is thinly staffed by faceless health professionals and haunted by creaks, mutters, and whooshes from mostly offscreen activity—is indeed a hospital or psychiatric ward. Moreover, this nightmarish space seamlessly mingles with ruins of industrial capitalism in Lisbon. Multilevel suspense takes hold as we strain to gather frames of reference amid a loosely gothic delineation of space that defuses, more than endorses, the focalized reading that "it's all happening in Ventura's head."

Pedro Costa stages this vague narrative emplacement with austere formal precision. The Portuguese director's microbudgeted craft borrows evenly from Robert Bresson (modernist art cinema), Jean-Marie Straub and Danièle Huillet (Brechtian avant-garde), John Ford (classical Hollywood), and Jacques Tourneur (American B movies). His weft of influences also includes the roughly sympathetic styles of António Reis (his mentor), Roberto Rossellini, and Jean

Figure 4.1 Ventura roams the dark and convoluted hospital in *Horse Money*.

Rouch, thus allying realism with ethnography but flouting the documentary/fiction distinction. Costa's stylistic hybridity results in a method that limits our access to the psychological interiorities of characters. Yet *Horse Money* is authored by Ventura, too. The incidents come mostly from his personal remembrances, which he, through contributions to the screenplay, situates against the long aftermath of Portugal's Carnation Revolution of 1974.[8] Structured by the key motif of healing (a thread that weaves through all three films under discussion in this chapter), *Horse Money* tends to Ventura's physical and mental impairments in such a way as to counter official revolutionary history.[9] The film understatedly shoulders this mission by serving in the main as an experimental portrait for the satisfaction of Ventura and the Cape Verdean migrant community of Casal da Boba, a high-rise estate that houses (many would say detains) former residents of the Fontaínhas shantytown in Lisbon. Costa's methodical slowness, both the slow production schedule and the tempo of the finished film, ethically reflects the rhythms of life that define this dispossessed population.[10]

Horse Money begins with an oblique introduction of Ventura. A sound bridge of labored, echoing footsteps spans a series of black-and-white photographs of turn-of-the-twentieth-century slums. As the sounds continue, we are shown a painted portrait of a Black man in casual, turn-of-the-nineteenth-century dress, his gaze directed out of frame. The camera then pans over from the painting to depict Ventura from the back, half-nude as he steps down into a catacomb-like recess where a physician or, for all we know, mad scientist opens an iron gate. Nothing in the film identifies these artworks—indeed, there is suspense in the film's withholding of what appears to be critical information—but their origins matter. We find out only through research that the photos show multiethnic Lower Manhattan neighborhoods and were taken by the Dutch American journalist Jacob Riis for the purpose of promoting urban reform. The painting, Théodore Géricault's *Bust of a Black Man* (1812), hangs in Lisbon's Ajuda National Palace and is for the French Romantic painter an abolitionist gesture meant to affirm the subject's dignity.[11] If these references tie Ventura's predicament to global histories of slavery, urban-industrial labor exploitation, and racialized poverty, they also mutely sketch out Costa's project. While revealing injustice, Costa's task is less to lay bare mechanisms of abuse and demand urgent action than it is to foster a patient, exploratory collaboration with the Cape Verdean immigrants during the production. His practice is thus more in the spirit of Rouch's "shared anthropology," which insists on jointly creative interaction between filmmaker and subject.[12] Costa's approach, however, replaces Rouch's spontaneity with an exacting process of scripting, rehearsal, and multiple takes.

Horse Money repeatedly mulls an episode in the mid-1970s that turns over in Ventura's memory: his knife fight with a Cape Verdean work colleague named Joachim (Tito Furtado), which sent Ventura, escorted by militia soldiers, to a hospital, where he received ninety-three stitches. This event is bound up in the film's texture with the revolution that erupts in the city streets—a coup with popular support that removed the authoritarian Estado Novo regime and spurred the end of Portugal's colonial activities but also excluded and alarmed the Cape Verdean immigrants, who sought cover under night in a public garden. These historical details—which must be inferred because they are not directly depicted or clarified through exposition—strangely coincide with Ventura's visit to a hospital in the present (2014), where Joachim is still a patient and possibly a phantom. And yet the film doesn't flash back in time. Ventura's septuagenarian physicality stays the same throughout these replays of the past. As Jacques Rancière explains, his figure anchors a refractory present charged with a history of dishonor, anxiety, alienation, illness, and exhaustion—a history written onto not only his body but also "that of all those like him."[13]

It is hard to fathom these basic relations on a first watch. Low-key suspense takes effect through atmospheres at once opaque and mesmerizing, tinged with agitation and coupled with a defiant suppression of narrative context. *Horse Money* advances somewhat more quickly than Costa's earlier films but still boasts weighty durations and intervals of deferment. The film's suspensive slowness and obscurities allow Ventura's account to shade into a group testament. The struggles he restages in dilapidated offices and factories (stunningly shot in an adumbral, almost expressionistic style) have their uncanny echoes in frustrations to which several other people of Fontaínhas bear witness. A tissue of anxieties holds together this collective portrait, anxieties about all manner of documents (passports, travel tickets, permits, marriage licenses, visas, etc.), maladies, surgeries, troubles with the law, and the loss of loved ones destroyed by the same bureaucratic systems of relegation. Ventura's juddery neural condition, we learn, is a communally shared affliction the Cape Verdean laborers chalk up to a variety of causes, from mold growing in their walls to side effects of prescribed drugs. Adding indignation to chronic injury, this community is shaped by the experience of *waiting* endlessly in institutional spaces that confusingly blend together with a sense of menace: waiting for doctors, lab results, legal papers, paychecks, the arrival of family from abroad. . . .

Suspense names the apprehensive time of waiting, yet there is no direct parallel here, no mimetic correlation, between Ventura's plight and the spectator's waiting for the film to deliver itself. Suspended in a state of weariness, a purgatorial limbo between labor and sleep, Ventura's disposition resonates with what Elena Gorfinkel has defined as *enduration*. Gorfinkel coins this term, a composite of *endurance* and *duration*, to identify a certain mode of corporeality in films affiliated with the slow, contemplative style. Complicating the critical tendency to cite boredom, ennui, and inaction as the defining mood of this kind of cinema, Gorfinkel devises an alternative aesthetics of "exhaustion" linked directly to the quotidian body's capacities for labor under postindustrial logics of capitalism. She references, among other key examples, Akerman's *Jeanne Dielman*, Barbara Loden's *Wanda* (1970), Costa's *In Vanda's Room* (2000), Tsai Ming-liang's *I Don't Want to Sleep Alone* (2006), and especially Reichardt's *Wendy and Lucy* (2008) as films whose durational propensities are attuned to "the ordinary endurance of bodies on the margin." These examples enlist slowness as a tracing of fatigue, a measure of forces of economic dispossession as they bear on depleted and adrift beings in states of precariousness—characters in the process of confronting their own limits, outcasts who may be stripped of social and political agency.[14]

For Gorfinkel, however, enduration inclines toward *perseverance* instead of lingering defeatedly in weariness. Building on Jean Epstein's sense of fatigue as a condition charged with creative and perceptual potential, she argues: "The enduration of fatigue assigns a corporeal persistence, a certain resilience through and toward, a physical withstanding, a bearing of pressure, and a relation to something that passes through the flesh as well as a capacity to withstand the abrasion, the distress of the temporally and physically wearying. Enduration thus . . . can be a means of accounting for the processes of remaining, enduring, and persisting through forms of duress and despite them."[15]

This economically minded rethinking of slow cinema may be adapted to explain the fatigued yet resilient bodies who wait perpetually in and pace slowly through the derelict environments of *Horse Money*, bearing forth astonishing capacities of withstanding-ness despite their ailments and ruthless subordination. Although Costa's formal enterprise has been dismissed as "poverty porn" (a critique that usually fails to conceive of aesthetics beyond exploitative ornamentation), the community on view in *Horse Money* exudes a vibrant, indisputable dignity not unlike that of the American sharecropper families Walker Evans photographed for James Agee's book *Let Us Now Praise Famous Men* (1941)—a work Costa often references in interviews. The display of endurance is less for a voyeuristic, primed-for-outrage audience than it is for Ventura and his associates, whose participation begins to piece together a record of an entire citizenry left out of Portugal's self-congratulatory history of economic transition, democracy, and decolonization—a history for which Ventura and others like him provided infrastructural labor.

Horse Money is careful to divide the suspensions embodied *within* its diegetic world from our suspenseful encounter *before* that world. These anxious states are imbricated but not melded. We aren't quite meant to *know* Ventura and his occasional companion, Vitalina Varela, another author of the script who plays a version of herself—a middle-aged Cape Verdean woman who is still waiting to collect her widow's pension. An aesthetics of night, sustained by perceptual and atmospheric suspense, enshrouds these two imposing characters, warding off the invasive habits of conventional spectatorship.[16] To borrow Édouard Glissant's postcolonial poetics, these ailing figures mutually claim a "right to opacity."[17] If the film secures our interest and empathy in the characters' lives, it does so through guardedness and occlusion instead of through the pretense of universal psychological access.

In this regard, Costa's practice derives an ethics of suspense from Bresson's embrace of obliqueness, ellipsis, and abstraction. "Don't show all sides of things," writes Bresson in *Notes on the Cinematograph* (1975). Leave "a margin of indefiniteness." Further: "Displaying everything condemns CINEMA to cliché, obliges it to display things as everyone is in the habit of seeing them."[18] Margins of indefiniteness figure across all expressive and contextual levels of *Horse Money*. This principle, as Costa adopts it, results in pictorial tenebrism, images in which pitch darkness surrounds thinly highlighted details.[19] Half-hiddenness makes us struggle to see, to ascertain. This espousal of indefiniteness also sanctions the entrance into the film of materials, episodes, words, dialects, songs, and reminiscences over which Costa has little sway, contributions from the players that reflect *their* process of working through. As Costa states in interviews, *Horse Money* contains countless indefinite elements he can't explain, details he has not authored so much as curated and rearranged. As he words it, a vast "ocean" separates him from Ventura despite their long friendship and mutual interests in understanding each other.[20] Obscurities in the finished work are a corollary and index of this gap—this limit of shared knowledge and experience. Their trial-and-error collaboration has as its necessary condition an onscreen world of "shadow," "fragility," "doubt," and "a little bit of [the] unknown."[21]

Costa presents something like a theory of this ethics of suspense in "A Closed Door That Leaves Us Guessing," a transcription of his lectures at the Tokyo Film School in 2004. He argues that "the primary function of cinema"—regardless of the fiction/documentary divide, which he deems irrelevant—"is to make us feel that something isn't right." But there are qualifications. First, to "assert" social reality, a director (he cites Yasujirō Ozu) must also "hide things" at the same time, experimenting with "the idea of cinema as an art of absence" and thus letting some information stay secret. Second, a filmmaker must not "be in the business of selling feelings" by catering to popular delights of identification. The audience must be barred from entering and owning the fiction. The "door" to the film, as Costa metaphorically words it, must be closed or no more than slightly open:

> The spectator can see a film if something on the screen *resists* him. If he can recognize everything, he's going to project himself on the screen, he's not going to see things. If he sees a love story, he's going to see *his* love story. I'm not the only one to say that it's very difficult to see a film, but when I say "see" it's really seeing. It's not a joke, because you think that you see films, but you don't see films, you see yourself. It's very strange but I assure you, this is what happens. To see a film, that means *not crying with the character who cries*. If we don't understand that, then we don't understand anything. This is why I spoke of doors which close themselves. There are certain films, for me, which are like doors, even if there are no doors in them. They resemble doors that don't let you enter as the protagonist of the film. You are outside. You see a film, you are something else, and there are two distinct entities.

"Seeing," for Costa, involves more than just ocular verification. It is a process of critical vision, a nonnarcissistic perceptual act carried out with difficulty before an *unforthcoming* work. When a film pretends to treat its subject profusely, this treatment in fact assures us we will see very little. "A single gesture or glance of an actor," he argues, "can say a lot more about suffering, misery, or joy, than a documentary that shows everything."[22]

As this ethos of withholding pertains to *Horse Money*, it comes with potential pitfalls and grounds for objection. What is the point of this film, politically, if it is not to provoke awareness, identify culprits, and foster change? Are not Ventura and his colleagues all the more oppressed by this formal system that, in a cinephile-based process they have no stake in, subjects them to cinematographic schemes inspired by western European and American directors far removed from their subaltern scope of experience? Doesn't this method leave intact extreme imbalances between the vaunted auteur and the relegated group represented? Doesn't the film's obscurity in effect appoint Costa as the group's spokesperson since he must play the role, albeit reluctantly, of oracle to a mystified cultural elite in his promotional appearances on the global film festival circuit? And, not least, doesn't this aesthetics of night, what I have called Costa's "tenebrism," risk rehashing tropes of exoticization where the portrayal of racial Blackness is concerned, an artistic tendency that hews to legacies of colonialism?

In the light of these questions, we can gain a stronger foothold on the ethical and political ramifications of the film's suspensefulness by attending more closely to Ventura's and Vitalina's performances. It would be wrong to argue that their acting in *Horse Money* is entirely divested of emotional and psychological intensity. Although their words, postures, and gestures refuse to be *immediately* accessible in these respects (the "door" is shut, leaving us guessing), we are coaxed into a mode of empathic concern before a mournful atmosphere that conspires with the darkness of the movie theater. Indeed, the literal and figurative veils of night do not wholly remove signs of inner feeling from their performances, be it their vocal inflections or what Béla Balázs would call their "microphysiognomic" indicators of emotion and thought in facial close-ups.[23] Film actors, even nonprofessional ones in an art film such as *Horse Money*, not only inhabit aesthetic atmospheres but channel and add to them while projecting their own forces.[24] Both Ventura and Vitalina are atmospheric screen entities who bear a charisma somehow redoubled by reticence. And it is *their* embodied experiences—not Costa's allusions to other artists—that *authorize* this atmosphere and its subtle oscillations of feeling (fig. 4.2).

In their nightwork, Ventura and Vitalina stealthily deal with their own enduring traumas. They are turned inward, absorbed in thoughts and routines instead of theatrically playing to the viewer's observation. In lengthy takes, Vitalina reads documents aloud in a ritualized fashion, always in an elegiac whisper—her marriage license, her husband's birth and death certificates, and letters from the Cape Verde embassy concerning her husband's funeral, which a visa issue kept her from attending. These recitation scenes at times linger on her face in close-up as she resists our look and conveys indomitable poise, her layered interiority held largely in reserve. The tears that run down her face at one point aren't cues for the viewer's melancholy. Rather, they express dissonance, testifying to an inner life that far exceeds encapsulation by the blandly impersonal documents she recites.

Vitalina's and Ventura's pasts are uncannily entwined as her deceased husband becomes conflated with Joachim, the fellow Cape Verdean laborer with whom Ventura had the scuffle in his youth. Ventura's exchanges with Vitalina play out as therapeutic confrontations that in part address his guilt over the

Figure 4.2 *Horse Money*: Vitalina and Ventura cohabit a long-held, nocturnal frame.

knife fight, which left Joachim unable to work and his family without support. A circuit of simple gestures links these three characters. Vitalina places her hand atop Ventura's to calm his convulsion. Later, in the canteen, Ventura finds a solitary Joachim, who says he lacks feeling in his arm. Ventura gathers the force to steady his own hand so that he can raise a spoon and feed Joachim his soup (fig. 4.3). This modest, slowly repeated gesture of kindness, emphasized by a small pool of light in the frame, is the ultimate step in Ventura's recovery process, or what Vitalina calls his "road to perdition." Enacting this scene of shared humanity with his former rival brings a slender smile to Ventura's face just before the extended take ends. This action is also reciprocal insofar as it answers a kind gesture Joachim performs earlier in the film when he brings a houseplant to Ventura's bedside. For Ventura, feeding Joachim alters the setting's oppressive mood and at last constitutes a *new* event that breaks from the cycle of reenactment.

Ventura's triumph of endurance resides in his conversion of his hand movements from a spasm he cannot control into an action so subtle it barely registers as such—an act of penance and *hospitality*. This is also a way of appropriating the hospital space and its ostensive function, as there is no care to be found inside its walls except for the sanative acts the patients engage in with each other.

Figure 4.3 *Horse Money*: Ventura feeds Joachim soup in the otherwise empty cafeteria.

Ventura's gestures only gradually take on meaning and affective import, while in general remaining mysterious. Up until this point, his hand spasms—though they are constantly in play, sometimes as a rustling that disturbs the silence— don't quite signify in a manner conducive to interpretation. Are they phantom echoes of the labor he performed as a bricklayer, the physical counterpart to his mental fusion of past and present? Are they better understood as a Brechtian *Gestus* that weaves a pattern across the film's surface and opens out onto a larger social field of relations as his symptoms are shared by other immigrants? What we can say with confidence is that these ailing hands hold special significance *for Ventura* when he encounters others. Take the surreal climax in a stalled elevator, where he sustains a racist scolding from a talking statue of a militia soldier. Ventura attains a fleeting victory over this monument to the Carnation Revolution by crossing his own hands in a defensive, sorcerer-like pose that triggers a rush of organ music and brings the mobile statue to its knees.

Yet Ventura's gestural expressions do not, in the end, amount to signs of insurrection and newly acquired political agency. Granted, as he leaves the hospital, giving a doctor a handshake against a burnt-orange sky signaling dawn, he walks with a sense of purpose in his step. The next shot features a storefront display of knives as Ventura's feet are reflected in the glass. However, this shot, which ends the film, is inconclusive. Critics have attached to this image the prospect of political revolution, but its status is decidedly quotidian. Ventura is a man who carries a knife in the way one carries a handkerchief. Though his nightwork has been somewhat beneficial, the film has given us no indication he longs to revolt against the bureaucratic state or that he even holds this system accountable for his past and present misery.

Ventura's performance as himself haunts the threshold of legibility as well as the limit of shareability. Rancière, writing of Costa's earlier film *Colossal Youth* (2006), describes Ventura as a "sort of sublime errant, a figure of tragedy whose very existence interrupts communication and exchange." Neither exactly himself nor the auteur's model, he incarnates a "third figure . . . a character who is and is not foreign to our lives." For Rancière, the political basis and validity of Costa's portrayals of such figures lies not in a narrative of agentic transformation but in the film's negotiation of the space between "shareable" and "unshareable" experience vis-à-vis the viewer. Rancière concludes that Costa's mindfully paradoxical approach at once makes possible *and* impossible the sharing of experience where the people of Fontaínhas are concerned.[25]

If we were to base our reading of *Horse Money* strictly on Costa's remarks in interviews, we might be inclined to argue that the film achieves shareability by folding its characters into a universal sense of common humanity as enshrined in Western art and cinema. Seen in this light, Ventura is made familiar and intelligible once he is translated into a version of, say, Tom Joad (Henry Fonda) in John Ford's *The Grapes of Wrath* (1940). But *Horse Money* doesn't expunge alterity. On the contrary, Ventura's screen role reworks artistic forms and gestures of common humanity, rerouting them through the particularities of his existence. Suspense of a perceptual, atmospheric, and characterological nature mounts a durable *counterforce* to Costa's references by keeping the film's portrait guardedly specific to Ventura's lifeworld. What I have called an "aesthetics of night" demarcates the sphere in which his self-scripted exploration unfolds, its play of invisibility reflecting and responding to the relegated status he and Vitalina share with others like them in their community. What is suspense for the viewer, then, is a kind of social fabric for these two characters, who reclaim this nocturnal atmosphere for cathartic ends of their own as we receive less a share than a partial glimpse.[26]

Three-Way Dreaming: *Cemetery of Splendor*

By comparison, the door to Apichatpong Weerasethakul's slow cinema is more open, but not to the point of allowing orthodox identification with characters and an uncomplicated immersive relationship to a completely legible story world. Suspense negotiates a push and pull between spectator involvement and detachment, and the relationship between character and atmosphere here too abounds with inexhaustible mystery. *Cemetery of Splendor* revels in perceptual suspense as much as Costa's approach does, but instead of concealing and withholding things through nocturnal shadows, it puts forth a soft, well-lit ambience of everydayness within which centrally important events escape direct representation.

Apichatpong's *Cemetery of Splendor* comparably takes place in a hospital environment—a temporary clinic in northeastern Thailand—where the past and the present uncannily overlap. Though shot in a more naturalistic style than *Horse Money*, Apichatpong's film brings with it a supernatural plot that gradually insinuates a critique of political repression and control. Jenjira Pongpas Widner plays Jen, a protagonist inspired by the performer's actual biography. Jen is a new-on-the-scene volunteer nurse and physical therapist who tends to soldiers suffering from a strange sleeping malady. She herself suffers from a leg deformity that obliges her to walk at a slow pace with crutches. Suspense arises around not only the sleeping sickness, which doctors have been unable to explain and successfully treat, but also Jen's unassuming behavior, which refigures what counts as dramatic expressivity and action. The clinic occupies a former school she attended in her youth. Filled with memories that resound from the personal to the collective, this space slowly instigates a process of political awakening in Jen, but one that materializes only through communal dimensions of sleep.

Of all the twenty-first-century art cinema I sample in this book, Apichatpong's work most glaringly warrants an adjusted and expanded morphology of suspense. James Quandt asks in an interview with the queer Thai director in 2005, "Am I mistaken in finding a kind of Hitchcockian suspense in the long river sequence . . . in *Blissfully Yours* [2002]?" Apichatpong responds by affirming a roundabout connection to Hitchcock's *Psycho* (1960) that has to do with character vulnerability, no doubt a suspense component.[27] If not quite Hitchcockian, Apichatpong's work nevertheless exemplifies art-house suspense that more drastically apportions screen time for hypnotic yet uneasy suspensions of narrative drive. As with other slow cinema directors engaged in earlier chapters (Akerman, for instance), in these moments of suspension the subtlest gesture of style can marshal a suspenseful force. Discussing Apichatpong's video installation *Emerald* (2007), in particular its series of emptied-out, unpeopled hotel bedrooms, Adrian Martin writes: "Finally, the camera begins to move stealthily and ominously, like in a suspense thriller. . . . It is a very formal kind of suspense (comparable to Tsai's films), the type of eerie effect Apichatpong frequently achieves when he moves his camera in on some initially banal-looking window or air vent (as in his feature *Syndromes and a Century*, 2006)."[28] This moment Martin references in *Syndromes and a Century* is emblematic of suspense that entails the suspension of human-focused drama.

In the labyrinthine basement of a hospital, the camera tracks across an oddly mist-filled room with fluorescent lights and exposed ductwork, making its way toward a pipe that vacuums in the swirling vapor. Why does the film suddenly put the plot on idle like this? What, if anything, does the mist, which is drawn into the pipe with greater and greater speed, "represent"? Does the ductwork have something to do with the film's duplex structure, perhaps tying this space to the earlier rural hospital that anticipates it? Why is the camera attracted to the pipe and its dark recess, which suggest a surreal portal or a void, while also graphically echoing the solar eclipse in the film's first half? The scene fascinates but also unsettles in part because of the ambient score by Koichi Shimizu—a music of repeated, churning tones, almost-industrial noises, and spectral hints of conversation.

In *Cemetery of Splendor*, the suspense that develops between character and environment springs not just from Apichatpong's devices but also from performance. For those familiar with Apichatpong's work, Jenjira Pongpas Widner needs no introduction. Since her role in *Blissfully Yours*, the Thai actress has been a fixture of his films and installations. She initially appears as a supporting player who haunts the peripheries of loosely constructed narratives, strolling about with her distinctive hobble, the consequence of her real-life motorcycle accident and surgery that left one leg longer than the other. She has a more essential role in *Uncle Boonmee Who Can Recall His Past Lives* (2010), and in *Cemetery of Splendor* she finally graces the film as a primary collaborator. In addition to playing the lead, she contributed directly to the script and translated dialogue into the local Isan dialect. *Cemetery of Splendor* at one level carries out an ethnographic and autobiographical study of a specific location, the town of Khon Kaen, where Apichatpong grew up. Pongpas Widner is often referred to as a "nonprofessional" when in fact she trained as an actress well before meeting Apichatpong. Her ability to inhabit and enliven the aired-out ambiences of his work is a measure of skill.

Curious interplays between figure and environment greet Pongpas Widner's presence in the film. She most often appears in long or medium-long shots, her face at times de-emphasized in detail-rich environments that provoke a roaming and nondiscriminatory eye on the viewer's part. Despite the infrequency of close-ups, the informality of her gesturing, and the softness of her dialogue in the lyrical Isan dialect, Pongpas Widner *stands out*. Her vocal strikingness owes in part to the film's breaches of sound perspective relative to the camera's placement. When she speaks from the distant background, her voice hits our ears with a volume that denotes physical intimacy, even as it fuses with environmental sounds of wind, birds, and insects that constantly declare their force. No less significant is the pace of Jen's limp. The film's prolonged durations reflect less a director's preestablished affinity for slowness than an adaptive measure in step with her crutch-assisted movement (fig. 4.4).

Figure 4.4 *Cemetery of Splendor*: Jen dictates the film's leisurely pace and channels the low-key, mysterious atmosphere.

Distinguished by outwardly prosaic strolls, snacks, chats, and gestures of interaction that have a soothing quality, Jen is a kind of barometer—a figure who becomes attuned to invisible atmospheric stirrings. The stretched durations she inhabits are banal only in a deceptive sense, for the diegesis is gently imbued with spiritual energy, reincarnation, ghosts, and mediumistic contact between the present and an undead past. This hinted-at activity, precisely because it is played down and nearly hidden in the everyday, puts the real and the surreal on an enchanting continuum. This world is shaped by Isan Lao animist cosmology and Apichatpong's Buddhist outlook, which mixes with his fondness for science fiction, adventure, and horror genres.[29] To Jen's astonishment, two Buddhist goddesses in casual modern attire join her for a snack at an outdoor table, having nonchalantly come to life from mannequins in a shrine. Captured in one shot that exceeds four minutes, this "real-time" event opens onto uncanniness while remaining ordinary, urging us to adjust our perception. The nearby dinosaur statues—which evoke one of Apichatpong's favorite films, *The Lost World* (Harry O. Hoyt, 1925)—acquire a vital status, too, despite keeping their static, inorganic form.[30]

This ambiguous coexistence of the ordinary and the supernatural feeds into atmospheric suspense for the spectator as well as for Jen, who figures to some extent as a surrogate for our response. While pondering the strange sleeping illness and relating it to other occurrences in the vicinity that may have a conspiratorial role—namely, a government digging project with which the soldiers are unclearly associated and a fiber-optic company's plan to install cables under the clinic grounds—Jen undergoes a transformation that jolts her out of her naive patriotism. This change comes about through her intimate contact with two side characters: Itt (Banlop Lomnoi), a soldier patient with whom she forms a romantic bond (a man whose bed happens to be in the same position where she sat in her school desk years earlier), and Keng (Jarinpattra Rueangram), a psychic medium who may or may not work for the FBI and who interacts with the soldiers in their sleep, her power ignited by touch. Sharing words, gestures, sensations, moods, memories, and, most vitally, dreams, this inquisitive trio sets in motion a therapeutic, delicately eroticized drama of convergent bodies and histories. They discover that the present sits atop the past in a stratigraphic layering of time: beneath the hospital, an ancient battle is still being waged in the narrow interests of the Thai monarchy, a campaign that drags on through the forced enlistment of vulnerable twenty-first-century soldiers in their sleep.

When reduced to its synopsis, *Cemetery of Splendor* sounds blockbuster ready. Its dream-sharing premise, which brings to mind science-fiction thrillers such as *Paprika* (Satoshi Kon, 2006) and *Inception* (Christopher Nolan, 2010), lends itself to extravagant portrayal. We could easily imagine a more spectacular version of the film that relies on computer-generated imagery to stage the oneiric ancient battle. But Apichatpong attenuates and cloaks this thrilling content, never representing the dreamed events directly. We only learn about what happens in the dreams when characters describe their experiences through dialogue. The dream worlds are otherwise restricted to an unseen, extradimensional parameter of offscreen space. Perceptual suspense in broad daylight works by either denying us sonic and visual confirmation of the supernatural plot elements or by toning them down to such an extent that if we do see them, they appear as banal events within the fabric of the everyday. But this refusal is not exactly a refutation of the sensory affordances of perceptual and atmospheric suspense. As we are left to watch distended scenes of dream sharing that transport the trio to an unportrayed elsewhere, the film's aesthetic resources *still work to amplify our sensorium, too*, which factors us into the deeply suspenseful treatment of embodied perception. The dream-sharing motif, moreover, interweaves the sensorial and the political, offering as it does a critical allegory that links the contemporary Thai military junta, formed in the wake of a coup in 2014, to a long history of corruption and deceit that has hidden itself from a narcoleptic public through propaganda. As Jean Ma has shown, the question of sleep in the film is more intricate than it may seem. If sleep initially suggests acquiescence, the film reveals it to be a networked social endeavor, a means of escape or "line of flight" from the lack of options in waking life under authoritarian rule. Sleep becomes a potential avenue of survival for the Thai people.[31] Jen, Keng, and Itt reclaim sleep in a therapeutic environment, not unlike Ventura and Vitalina's appropriation of the hospital. The difference is that *Cemetery of Splendor* more openly includes the viewer in a phenomenological sense, albeit in a mystifying negotiation between distance and immersion, presence and absence, sleepiness and acuity, boredom and wonder, lulling tranquility and escalating dread.

In the film's climactic set piece, Keng, while operating as a vessel for Itt and transmitting his lucid dream, leads Jen on a stroll through a public grove that overlays a palace belonging to the ancient monarchy. The audience, like Jen, must take Itt/Keng's word for it that she is a vessel for the dreaming Itt. The film stays in the same descriptive register throughout this scene and leaves open the possibility that Keng isn't a legitimate medium. There are no modifications to Keng's voice and demeanor to indicate that she is possessed by Itt. At a hazy point, though, Jen's consciousness enters the dream as well and shares its sensorial dimensions, leaving us excluded. This jaunt leads up to a rather long take of Jen and Itt/Keng on a bench facing a lake, bordered by trees: Itt/Keng takes a medicinal tincture (a mix of goji berry and gingko biloba), pours it on Jen's disfigured leg, and slowly licks it off from a kneeling position, like a "little puppy," as Jen remarks. After a stint of nervous laughter, Jen is gradually and mysteriously brought to tears of release. She caresses Itt/Keng's cheek and shoulder, at once expressing gratitude and balancing herself (fig. 4.5).

Even as Keng substitutes for Itt in what is ostensibly a heterosexual date, this interaction between women still evokes same-sex intimacy and asserts a queer sensibility that is often part of Apichatpong's slow-cinema practice.[32] So many affectively charged motifs are layered into and consummated by this ménage à trois.[33] The "puppy" licking echoes a term of endearment, "little pup," that Jen uses toward Itt in earlier scenes. The tincture, which Jen has made to treat her husband's dementia, is repurposed into a double remedy for her leg and Itt's sleeping illness (since Keng ingests it on Itt's behalf). Moreover, the scene's sexualized emphasis on touch stirs our memory by harking back to Jen's application of lotion to Itt's chest, a gesture that pulls him out of his dream. The licking of Jen's leg thus reciprocates her care, and because Itt enacts this licking with Keng's tongue, Keng's mediumistic faculty of touch, in return, grants *him* access to *Jen's* thoughts and emotions. In this manner, the relatively simple event depicted is implied to carry out a highly complex and sensuous series of transformations where the diegetic world we see intersects with an ulterior, oneiric dimension we do not see.

This mutually therapeutic, dream-sharing "sex scene" endows all three participants with telepathic sensitivity. In the shot that follows, we are elliptically transferred back to Itt's bed in the clinic, the day having passed into dusk. The atmosphere is modulated by neon-light therapy tubes that vertically flank the soldiers' beds and shift in unison between gradients of blue, red, and green (fig. 4.5). Once Itt and Jen stir awake, we learn that Jen can now read *his mind* and experience *his dreams*, too. Keng is notably absent at this point, implying

Figure 4.5 *Cemetery of Splendor* hinges on sensual and cathartic dream sharing, with associated changes in atmospheric activity registered by light-therapy tubes (next to Itt's bed) and water turbines.

that this supernatural sharing of nervous systems no longer requires her role as a medium. The film then offers its only point-of-view shot, doing so from Jen's vantage as Itt stares into the camera and thus at the viewer, his face bathed in red-to-blue neon light from the machine. This selective use of point-of-view syntax is the film's rhetorical way of describing our share as viewers. Implicit here is the film's hope that we, too, will have been touched and transformed by the characters' subtly exchanged gestures of care—and by the call to political vigilance they issue. More than *Horse Money*, this film extends its rehabilitation exercise to the spectator.

Granted, perceptual suspense keeps us from entering the trio's dream world, but the film still makes a phenomenological appeal to our immersion by holding out sensory attractions and enigmas for our benefit without routing them through character subjectivity. The airiness of the film's aural and optical ambience makes the screen feel like an open window, a pleasing effect that may induce in us a soporific state. Images constantly embed open windows that—in a mise en abyme effect—demarcate the screen itself as an architectural fenestration through which the film's ambience filters into our viewing space. The neon tubes are for our trancelike experience as much as they are medical devices in the plot. Their varying colors seem to register uncanny environmental activity. Similarly, long-held shots of water turbines on the lake are folded into the film at various points, not as narrative cutaways so much as indices of atmospheric energy that eludes representation (fig. 4.5). In one instance, the film cuts from the turbines to a shot of clouds in the sky. As the lulling sibilation from the turbines continues, a gigantic amoeba floats into the frame, conflating the microscopic with the macroscopic in a surreal enlargement of life below the threshold of our unassisted sight. This playful moment thus acknowledges the mediational role of cinema as a partly scientific, partly magical tool that overcomes humanity's perceptual suspension between the infinitely small and the infinitely large. Further, in a motif of mise-en-scène strictly for our notice, the dreamers are color coded: Jen is defined by soft pink, Keng by cyan blue, and Itt by orange—colors in their attire that "rhyme" with environmental details such as the pink and blue tops that the two mannequin (yet sentient) Buddhist goddesses wear in their shrine and the orange mechanical excavators that dig into the soil.[34] In the film's color logic, the cool tones emitted by the neon-light therapy machines work to counterpoint the warm orange aligned with Itt's situation of being exploited by secret military entities.

No less than the neon-light tubes and hydraulic turbines, Jen is a registration device: she responds to atmospheric activity beyond what the film shows us. Her amplified perception, the upshot of contemplating her environment anew, relates implicitly to our sensorium before the film's world. During the climax, we feel a pull to engagement as Jen movingly exhibits how it feels to see, touch, and be touched in this way. The emphasis on the reciprocity and reversibility of touch doesn't pull *us* into dream but still heightens our tactile relation to the film. Illustrative here is Lesley Stern's concept of cinematic gesture as "a circuit of energy" that travels between the actor's body onscreen and the viewer's body in the theater.[35] In *Cemetery of Splendor*, this circuit implicates us somatically, even as the film's mystical content retreats from us. The film ends with a shot of Jen glaring wide-eyed at a soccer field where orange excavators go about their shady business. We're left to infer that she now sees to the stratigraphic core of this work and its ties to authoritarian control. Our vision and knowledge are surpassed by hers, but our experience absorbs the rapturous energy her awakening gives off.

This dynamic between viewer and film doesn't readily conform to some of the prevailing ways of defining slow cinema in scholarship. The film, no doubt, is something of a balm intent on reviving our aptitudes for patient thought, and its slowness nurtures a practice of "wondrous looking" and listening.[36] Yet there are also suspenseful ripples of dread—related to the abiding climate of political and economic despotism in Thailand—that vie with these palliative aspects and refuse to be fully quashed. Apichatpong has been discussed as an artist whose slow cinema carves out utopian possibilities of "communal viewing" by way of boredom—a shared embrace of "wasted" time that allows for queer intimacies at a remove from the accelerated tempos and efficiency-minded logics of "heterocentric" narrative.[37] This reading astutely speaks to some of Apichatpong's experiments and *Cemetery of Splendor*'s queering of time and romance, but the film's slow drift toward its gestural climax is not an exercise in boredom. Something profound (beyond an affront to the regulatory time schemes of popular cinema and neoliberal capitalism) happens here—something *ecstatic*. Let us recall that one of the ignored, now archaic meanings of *being in suspense* is "an ecstasy of contemplation."[38]

Mysteries of Contractile Sensation: *Memoria*

To be sure, Apichatpong's cinema gives us an auspicious occasion to confront a question that is central to this book but that has lurked mostly in the background of my chapters thus far: What exactly is the relationship of suspense to "contemplation" in the slow art-house films under discussion? I have delayed this key question for two reasons, the first being the need to distance my account of contemplation from the generic category of "contemplative cinema" that tends to be used synonymously with "slow cinema." Although it has become commonplace to attribute a "contemplative" agenda to Apichatpong's films, we need a less generalized understanding of contemplation if we are to give the sights, images, environments, and corporeal figures in his work their due. Second, the experiential, atmospheric, and perceptual valences of suspense (that is, suspense as parsed in chapter 1's morphology, which includes but also goes well beyond the Hitchcockian model) need to be understood first if we stand a chance of grasping how suspense, far from being opposed to contemplation, might work at the crux of it.

In criticism and theory, contemplation is usually construed as a quiet process of pensive observation, the act of reflecting on something—an artwork, a text, or a feature of the natural world—from which a subject doing the contemplation is removed. My claim, however, is that Apichatpong's style and its sensory address usher in a mode of cinematic contemplation that departs from the concept's dominant philosophical, theological, and critical legacies. In keeping with this chapter's main themes, Apichatpong's contemplative practice entails remarkably fluid relationships between ailing bodies and the atmospheric surroundings—relationships that charge the film's world in deeply suspenseful ways, leaving us to wonder about and feel anxious about our interface with the screen. Now bringing Apichatpong's follow-up feature, *Memoria*, into the discussion, I contend that its levels of suspense revolve around the slow, gradual constitution of the personal, impersonal, and atmospheric dimensions of a contemplative process that summons *as well as limits* our immersive role in the matter.

Let us begin with the suspense and work our way toward its merger with contemplation as enacted by and within the film. *Memoria*, more directly than either *Cemetery of Splendor* or *Horse Money*, inspires immediate associations with suspense through a sort of "detective film" premise. Indeed, trailers for the film suggest a somewhat conventional thriller. Our insomniac central character, Jessica (Tilda Swinton), is a recently widowed Scottish woman, an orchid farmer visiting her hospitalized sister in Bogotá.[39] Because she is unfamiliar with the culture and language, her social exchanges tend toward awkwardness. A plot synopsis that calls Jessica an "insomniac" misses some of the preliminary suspense that surrounds her condition. Only piecemeal do we learn this character is chronically unable to sleep, though we feel something of the exhaustion, the lugubrious anxiety, produced by this inability before we quite know their cause.[40] A middle-class white woman, she isn't a victim of state-organized exploitation like our other characters in this chapter, but because of her ailment she can be compared loosely to the restless Ventura in *Horse Money* and to the narcoleptic Itt in *Cemetery of Splendor* in that she is, from the outset, visibly out of sync with the "normal" rhythms of rest and wakefulness.

In connection with her insomnia—and here arises *Memoria*'s suspenseful detective-story aspect—Jessica periodically "hears" a piercing *thwack* that does not correspond to any apparent cause. The film's loosely spun plot concerns her partly apprehensive, partly therapeutic quest to trace this mysterious noise to its source. According to Apichatpong, the character's namesake is Jessica (Christine Gordon) from Jacques Tourneur's *I Walked with a Zombie* (1943), a catatonic woman lured by distant sounds of drums from the jungle. The Jessica of *Memoria* is comparably suspended in a trancelike state that results from her sleep disorder, grief, and alienation and that ultimately ties her sense perception to the Colombian wilderness.[41]

In the film's opening, Jessica "hears" this sound in her dark bedroom while attempting to sleep in bed. For the spectator, this jarringly loud noise feels nearby and located in the diegesis, but it accompanies images that are submerged in darkness, with Jessica reduced to a silhouette and the spatial geography of the scene kept uncertain.[42] Right away, questions swirl around the status of this noise. Is it objectively caused by an action offscreen? Is it internal and subjective, existing only in her consciousness? As the film progresses, Jessica, with increasing desperation, seeks to recapture and place this sound that suspensefully escapes distinctions between exterior and interior, objective and subjective, and so on. While she "hears" this bang periodically even during the day, we cannot quite fathom whether it is synchronous with its accompanying image. The film also teases us with ambient noises that approximate the thud—traffic sounds, musical chords, doors closing, and so on. These echoes underscore the vibratory force of everyday sounds that lack a significatory role in the narrative. Some of these ambient games with sound also have an uncanny quality even when Jessica is not present, as when the alarms of empty cars in a parking lot blare without an evident cause—shots that would be right at home in the eerie opening montage of John Carpenter's *The Fog* (1980). Once we hear this thud in *Memoria* for the first time (notably in a scene so flooded with darkness that we can't see much of anything) and then discover it is liable to reemerge at any second, our viewing experience becomes imbued with a persistent and evolving dread. Sonic repetition breeds sensitivity and pulls into alignment character-based, plot-based, structural, perceptual, and atmospheric suspense—not to mention generic suspense insofar as popular genres are potentially afoot.

With the assistance of a sound engineer, Hernán (Juan Pablo Urrego), in his studio, Jessica re-creates the bang from her memory: what she describes in faltering Spanish as a large concrete ball plummeting into a metal well surrounded by seawater (fig. 4.6). In a scene that reflexively integrates the technology of film production (with a muted reference to one of Apichatpong's favorite films, Francis Coppola's psychological thriller *The Conversation* [1974], and its scenes of audiotape manipulation),[43] Jessica and Hernán reconstitute this tone by altering the frequency of sounds culled from an effects library on Hernán's computer. Suspense mounts as we, too, wait for our memory of the sound to be matched. Jessica grips Hernán's forearm and braces herself when she at last hears the thud replicated (fig. 4.6). In the wake of this key scene, she adjusts to a mode of what Pierre Schaeffer would term "reduced listening": she learns to focus on and savor, instead of dread, the traits of the sound itself,

Ailing Bodies on the Threshold of Action 143

Figure 4.6 Jessica and Hernán re-create the enigmatic thump in *Memoria*.

without concern for their cause and context.[44] As our feelings about the thud shift in turn from trepidation to curiosity, its frequent repetitions from scene to scene absorb Jessica into a therapeutic process that leads her to the rural landscape, where cause and context progressively do become part of her attachment to the sound. Evoking science fiction, not unlike the supernatural dream-sharing conceit in *Cemetery of Splendor*, this steadily disclosed process of her transformation is mediated by touch—a tactile power to tap into the reverberations of the past. In her circuitous quest spurred by her ailment, Jessica comes to discover something about the world she inhabits that has long been in effect: namely, that its objects and bodies have the secret capacity to retain memories of both traumatic and mundane events—memories that can be aurally accessed *if* one has the perceptual gift of detection.

It is through this premise of tactile and aural sensitivity that *Memoria*'s style of suspense moves toward "an ecstasy of contemplation." In the film's climax, Jessica, having wandered to a secluded grassy brook in the township of Pijao, hears the bang again and interacts with a middle-aged Colombian man who is busy at work scaling fish. Over a series of extremely long takes, we learn this character is also named "Hernán" and is, possibly, an older version of the Hernán Jessica interacted with previously (before he vanished from his workplace). And yet this older Hernán is not precisely the same man in look, manner, class, and trade. As he explains for Jessica, he has a photographic memory as well as the power to extract from things, through touch, the memories they contain. This stretch of the film leads to a revelatory and emotionally gripping scene at Hernán's home since childhood, where Jessica drinks his homemade herbal alcohol, feels out the surroundings, and becomes inhabited by *his* memories of events that took place in the same locale. As Hernán, no less stunned by this turn of events and the relationship that forms between them, explains, "I'm a hard disk. And somehow . . . you are an antenna." She discovers in turn that he is in tune with "her" insomniac thud, which he hears upon touching her arm and then cryptically reports that this sound "was before our time." Apichatpong here draws on the quiet, suspenseful, alcohol-inflected scene in *Jaws* (Spielberg, 1975) when the bootlegging shark hunter recollects the horrible fate of soldiers aboard the USS *Indianapolis* in World War II, but the scene in *Memoria* is more mystical in tone.

Conducting a séance of sorts, Jessica and the older Hernán clutch hands and arms at his kitchen table and transmit memories to each other. Sounds of these recalled events ambiguously materialize (for them *and for us*) outside an open window with a gauzy curtain that nearly matches Jessica's shirt (as with *Cemetery of Splendor*, chromatic ties between characters and their surroundings suggest subtle relations of enmeshment). Calling back to her interaction in the sound studio with the younger Hernán, this therapeutic scene, the energy of which replaces Apichatpong's more overt use of eroticism in earlier films, requires slow time. Replete with visual stasis and extended pauses between lines of dialogue, slowness coaxes the event into existence while folding the present onto the past and allowing affects to move between character and environment. Jessica's tears, for instance, give way to and become a rainstorm. The sonic stream of memories "outside" the window hisses, squelches, and crackles like the ground noise of an old radio broadcast (fig. 4.7). Casting people as media, this shared transmission permits Jessica to overcome, in an ecstatic and contemplative way, her social alienation, but its thematic significance stretches well beyond the arc of an individual character.[45]

Figure 4.7 An older version of (the same?) Hernán and Jessica listen to the past in *Memoria*.

What sort of contemplation does this scene crystallize, not just within the film's world but where the viewer's potential share is concerned? I ask not merely out of scholarly interest. *The film itself* tacitly raises this question through its atmospherics of suspense, where character and environment mesh. The term *contemplation*, as I noted earlier, is typically understood to mean "attentive looking" or—more abstractly—the "process of thinking deeply or carefully about a person or thing."[46] Its Latin root refers to a circumscribed space, a *templum* demarcated by the staff of the augur who interprets nature for signs of divine support or censure of some planned action. Religious meanings of the word from the medieval era onward as well as its ancient and modern aesthetic formulations involve circumstances of pause and restriction before an object engaged at the appropriate distance needed for reflection. Most modern aesthetic meanings that emphasize spectatorial experience install a stable, Kantian subject removed from the artwork's world. By contrast, Mikel Dufrenne describes contemplation in more immersive terms whereby the observer—as in a dream state—merges with the sensuous world depicted in a painting. This merger happens through a partially submissive activity of perception.[47]

What, then, is *cinematic contemplation*? How might we define a contemplative mode that takes into account the specific capabilities and affordances of the film medium? In other words, how does cinema not only represent a profilmic event of contemplation but elementally factor into the contemplative process? The peculiar climax and underlying aesthetic basis of *Memoria* urge this question, and so a further detour into the meanings of the term *contemplation* is in order. By and large, film theory has not privileged the term. Its general disfavor owes to Walter Benjamin's immortal essay "The Work of Art in the Age of Its Technological Reproducibility" (1936), which denies cinema the very possibility of a contemplative observer, given the speed and fluctuation of the medium's inherently "distracting" techniques: nothing on the screen is still enough or lingers long enough for the contemplative eye.[48] Today's espousals of slow cinema, however, favorably emphasize the notions of stillness and reflective distance with which the term *contemplation* is freighted: rapidly paced action, chaotic movement, and the viewer's distraction are often seen as the *problems* that slowness combats. But there is no consensus as to what kind of state of spectatorship contemplation institutes in its cinematic forms. In his recent account of the long take in contemporary art cinema and screen-based installations, Lutz Koepnick theorizes "contemplative viewing" in contradistinction to reverie and absorption. In the latter two states, the observer, as if inebriated, loses awareness of the process of looking and acquiescently falls into a timeless obliviousness. But contemplation, per Koepnick, involves the deeply attentive scrutinization of an artwork over an extended duration of which the observer is mindful while alternating between distance and immersion.[49] Koepnick brings cinema into the picture through Raymond Bellour's conception of the "pensive spectator," a touchstone in debates about slow cinema. Indebted to Roland Barthes's writings on photography, Bellour's argument hinges on "effects of suspension" that intermittently halt the forward rush of the film, both its narrative momentum and its technical succession of images. These stoppages, such as the insertion of a lingering photograph, "uncouple" us from the film's rhythmic flow and grant us time to think, opening a parenthesis within which to contemplate not just the film before us but also the film medium, its foundation upon photographic stillness at the level of the filmstrip.[50] Bellour and Koepnick, in their definitions of contemplation, are averse to the idea of a spectator's sustained state of immersion vis-à-vis the film's world. Fixated on looking (just as Benjamin's "Work of Art" essay limits contemplation to "optical" activity),[51] neither account attends to multisensory atmosphere as a contemplative element or to the curious relationship between the spectator and the spectator-like figures who enact contemplation within the diegesis. For these reasons, neither formulation lends itself to the climax in *Memoria*.

A stranger and more appropriate description of the contemplative—and one that I believe helps us to cross the distance between contemplation and suspense—can be found in the thought of Gilles Deleuze. My point in turning to the French philosopher at this juncture is not to furnish an external, anterior framework according to which everything of interest happening in *Memoria* can be explained. That would effectively terminate the cinematic suspense I want to keep intact in my analysis. Rather, I take a brief detour through

Deleuze so that we can begin to understand contemplation in a new light that is pertinent to, not identical to, *Memoria*. In *Difference and Repetition* (1968), Deleuze dispenses with the subjectivist ground upon which prevailing models of contemplation are based. In his philosophy of time, contemplation is not a static and detached circumstance wherein a (necessarily human) subject actively takes the world or an artwork as an object for scrutiny. Neither conscious nor active nor bounded within homogenous blocks of time, contemplation is a form of "passive synthesis" that has as its operative dynamic what Deleuze calls "contraction," in the sense that one contracts an infection through exposure to a pathogen or contracts a habit through repetition.[52] To contemplate is to *contract something* from the world and the vibrational flux of elements into which we are thrust, to take something in porously as well as passively. In temporal terms, to contemplate is *to preserve something of the before in the after*, hence its link to repetition and duration. For Deleuze, this contractile process doesn't yet amount to "memory." It is a more passive acquisition of something (a characteristic, a rhythmic pattern) from the flux of the outside world—something the "contemplative soul," be it a person or even a thing, becomes shaped and inhabited by in turn. A pebble on the beach, for instance, is a "contemplative soul" in Deleuze's sense. This pebble *is* the series of elemental contemplations that it endures in its environment, affected intensely by actions of the sea, wind, and weather on its composition.[53] This series of contractions extends from the past into the "living present," and bodes futures for which the pebble, primed as it is by habit and expectation, *waits*—albeit before and below the register of conscious activity.[54]

Deleuze's eccentric theory of contemplation holds that we, too, at a primary level of life *are* the variable adaptation of what we synthetically contract: "All our rhythms, our reserves, our reaction times, the thousand intertwinings, the presents and fatigues of which we are composed, are defined on the basis of our contemplations." In Deleuze's words, "We do not contemplate ourselves, but we exist only in contemplating—that is to say, in *contracting that from which we come*." Furthermore, contemplation itself *does* nothing, and yet "something *is done through it*, something completely novel." It is not administered by the mind "but occurs *in* the mind which contemplates prior to all memory and all reflection."[55]

What makes this theory of contemplation more conducive to the atmospheric, temporal, and perceptual situation we have before us in *Memoria* is precisely Deleuze's use of the term to describe worldly entanglements instead of just distant acts of reflection. Additionally instructive is Deleuze's text *What Is Philosophy?* (1991), coauthored with Félix Guattari, which tries to understand just how we are affected by the elements we come into contact with, how things are contemplated—that is, contracted into thought—through the workings of sensation. But, again, *contemplation* is recast along *a-subjective*, impersonal lines. More so than in Deleuze's earlier account, the term defines a *cosmological* process that ubiquitously reaches beyond humans to include plants, animals, and inorganic life. Further, this process is generative: "Contemplating is creating, the mystery of passive creation," inasmuch as something new—previously undisclosed at the most basic ontological level—paradoxically emerges in repetition. The self, at once formed by and dissolved into this process, is not a stable subject but rather what Deleuze and Guattari call an "inject," or "superject," adopting a term from the process philosophy of Alfred North Whitehead. This way of thinking has deep implications for aesthetics (and implicitly for cinema). In their chapter on the capacities of art, Deleuze and Guattari quote Paul Cézanne on the need, presumably of the artist and the spectator alike, to "become" each "minute" of the world viewed, and this leads them to pronounce an aphorism of their own: "We are not in the world, we become with the world; we become by contemplating it. Everything is vision, becoming. We become universes."[56]

In the transformative climax of *Memoria*, do not Jessica and Hernán "become with the world" in a manner akin to this formulation? One must be careful not to apply Deleuze's view of the contemplative so heftily that it does away with the durable suspense that suffuses this scene and the aesthetic logic of the entire film. But this recourse to Deleuze allows us better purchase on the scene's animation of time, world, and multisensory feeling. Each aspect of mise-en-scène functions as an elemental medium that "contemplates"—that is, absorbs, contains, and retransmits—prior events. In touching one another and the objects in Hernán's home, from the wooden floor to the furniture, Jessica and Hernán release into the atmosphere residues from the past in the form of sounds that they detect. And the herbal moonshine they sip, like the tincture in *Cemetery of Splendor*'s climax, enhances this ecstatic event, its impact going beyond inebriation. We infer from the film's conception of world that because Hernán has held in his hands the herbs (which are already vested with contemplative retentions of their own) while making the liquor, his memories, some of which are distressing (a raid of this same space during his youth), instill the liquid. After imbibing, Jessica cries less her tears than Hernán's, tears that both remediate the moonshine and anticipate the rainstorm outside. But let me again stress that the film is far less forthcoming than my description of it: suspense accumulates in and across the disclosure of this contemplative dynamic between character and atmosphere—and once we intuit this dynamic as it operates socially, suspense endures and blends with astonishment.

Deleuze's theory is relevant in offering a view of contemplation that isn't subject-centric. After all, Jessica is less the agent of this contemplative relay than its conduit, and her relation to the larger environment of Pijao—which has seen and absorbed all manner of catastrophes and upheavals, from the colonial subjugation of now-displaced Indigenous peoples to earthquakes, guerilla occupations, economic coffee crises, drug wars, and the widespread killings of leftists during Colombia's civil war in the 1940s and 1950s, the likely context of Hernán's memory from childhood—is not expressly about her. Exerting an affective force in the scene, these traumatic histories still pulse below the threshold of ordinary human perception, through the atmosphere and up from the ground, making themselves felt if not consciously heard unless one has Hernán's extrasensory gift.

By a similar structural logic, motifs that have suspensefully accrued across the film now converge around Jessica and Hernán's interaction: references to an elusive tribe somewhere in the Amazon; remains, examined by Jessica in a laboratory, of a woman with a hole in her skull, supposedly the result of a tribal exorcism; a stray dog that crosses Jessica's path in Bogotá and evokes her anthropologist sister's illness, which is guessed to have been triggered either by her dream of a dog or by a spell cast by an Indigenous group who doesn't wish its ways of living to be made known; and an excavation site, a tunnel where human remains are found. Inquisitively drawn by the mystery of her malady, Jessica, through her exploration of the environment and her encounters with the two Hernáns, is contracted into syntheses of time that interweave these motifs and events, shedding her sense of self in the process.

In interviews, both Apichatpong and Swinton have characterized Jessica as a stand-in, or "portal," for the spectator.[57] This holds to an extent, but, as with *Cemetery of Splendor*, there are barriers that reduce and *suspend* our share, even as we absorb the energy of her experience. We hear the radio-like transmission "outside," yet Hernán's impact on her perception doesn't fully manifest in the film's sensible content. The depth of her attunement leaves us in the dust. At the table, she lets go of his forearm, prompting the film's audio track to drop into total silence. The film then cuts elliptically to another room of Hernán's home, where Jessica listens to the world beyond the window. She appears more emaciated than before, as if a double of the skeleton she studied earlier, though she has a faint smile on her face, imparting relief and curiosity. The thud she has learned to embrace resurfaces as a sound bridge to a view of a tropical forest—but time and space are made uncertain in this dis/continuous transition. For all we know, this landscape is prehistoric. As the bang repeats, mixing with wind and technological ground noise, we trace it to a peculiar object or life-form in the frame that slowly turns out to be a fishlike alien aircraft, rendered as computer-generated imagery.[58] It floats upward and then takes off into the distance with a deep, powerful thud that leaves a circle of exhaust. We cannot say for certain if Jessica sees this event with us, but we gather she has finally traced the bang to this alien source. This surprising reveal implicitly affirms, or makes more plausible, a suspicion we have perhaps already formed— that Hernán is not of our Earth but possibly a descendent of extraterrestrials. This question hangs as we take in the tranquil landscapes that end the film by announcing another rainstorm in the present, the weather mixing with a radio broadcast in a final emphasis on ordinary atmospheric and technological mediation, now made to feel unordinary in the wake of the spaceship revelation.

The slow, atmospheric suspense that leavens *Memoria*'s enactment of contemplation also bears on and tempers the film's political content. Some critics have faulted the film for not more openly addressing the political contexts and histories of Colombia. One reviewer, bristling at the film's dreamlike elusiveness, complains that "to even graze the tip of Hernán's finger would be electrifying, enlightening. But sadly, he takes Jessica's hand, not ours."[59] Criticisms like this one, which assume that political cinema must always adopt the posture of frank and edifying representation, have in fact been aimed at all three of our main examples in this chapter, but these films take a different path. Certain political strategies of contemporary slow cinema may sometimes appear disengaged because of their demotion of the spoken word in favor of more atmosphere-driven expression, which puts these films at variance with methods such as the recent penchant on the film festival circuit for staging politically charged monologues in long takes where characters powerfully and affectingly vocalize their trauma-shaped points of view (e.g., Alice Diop's *Saint Omer* [2022] and Sarah Polley's *Women Talking* [2022]). Monologues abound in *Horse Money*, and speech has a key political role in both *Memoria* and *Cemetery of Splendor*, but the words in these cases are part of a style that also involves breakdowns in mutual comprehension and transmissible experience between film and viewer, from the opacity that blocks a universalizing will to know as we view *Horse Money* to the thoroughgoing reliance on offscreen space in Apichatpong's two films. In negotiating the very limits of communication, these slow films confront political, ethical, and historical issues in more radically suspenseful ways.[60] As an "alien" in the Colombian environment, Apichatpong, not unlike Costa with *Horse Money*, regards his outsider status as a reason to avoid offering a neatly accessible and didactic exercise in ethnography.[61] Leaving a "margin of indefiniteness," *Memoria* stakes itself on the altered sensorium of the spectator in accordance with a contemplative dynamic that asserts that any space in which we might find—and lose—ourselves vibrates with undead histories. We're encouraged to feel this possibility that the film realizes only incompletely. And if Apichatpong refuses to make these histories into objects for our detached, subjective reflection, he does so because those histories touch, resound through, and contemplate *us*, whether we know it or not.

Memoria's commitment to atmospheric suspense also underpins its reflexive treatment of film and its relationship to human (and nonhuman) thought, feeling, and remembrance. *Memoria* partakes of a certain form of "medium suspense" (a notion I return to in chapter 6) in which the ontological and experiential features of cinema are cast as a partly anxious and partly wondrous matter of speculation. Swinton reports that during the film's production

Apichatpong remarked half-jokingly, "Well, Jessica is cinema!"[62] To a great extent, *Memoria* has cinema on its mind, beginning with its choice to use photochemical film (a change from *Cemetery of Splendor*'s digital format) with palpable grain in the image.[63] But "film" takes on an aura of suspense not just as a medium of capture, retention, and reanimation but also as an environment—namely, the theatrical circumstance. In 2021, *Memoria*'s release in the United States was limited to an unusual roadshow pattern that had it "exclusively playing [in] no more than one theater at any given time. The only means of experiencing *Memoria* will be in theaters . . . forever."[64] By restricting itself in this fashion, the film subtly *plays to* the theater space. The silence during the climax activates, brings into account, the environmental noises of the theater: chairs creaking, patrons breathing and whispering, the hum of the projector, and so forth. The cave where the mysterious excavation occurs within the film's world is a kind of analogue to the dark and reverberant theater space. An early scene in which Jessica visits her sister at the hospital concludes with a lightly asserted creak of her chair—a sound that has its echo in the ambient spectatorial noises of the theater. Jessica's sleeplessness bears a correspondent link to the soporific state of the viewer insofar as it has been induced in part by the theatrical viewing *dispositif,* the technical and spatial arrangement that institutionally primes us for and holds our attention to the spectacle. Some critics have maintained that the actionless durations of slow cinema prompt us to change gears and swivel attention away from the film to the viewing space so as to participate in a mutually felt sense of nonproductivity with other attendees.[65] In the case of *Memoria*, however, a more complex atmospheric attunement offers itself as we are urged to see, hear, and feel the auditorium as an integral feature of the film.

Dufrenne writes of the "tentacular" connection between the work of art and its designated environment of contemplation. To paraphrase this claim and extend it to cinema, the film aestheticizes the physical surroundings in which it is displayed and integrates them into its world.[66] In the case of Apichatpong's film, to move our attention from the screen to the theater space (and back again) is *not* to disregard the film's effects. The slow-developing suspense of *Memoria* is such that the spatial, affective, and temporal possibilities in its diegetic world implicitly include the space of our encounter. There is an unspoken logic to this transference of atmosphere from one side of the screen to the other. The medium of cinema is to our sensitivity what Hernán is to Jessica's: an alien intelligence whose perceptions, memories, and retransmissions we become suspensefully synchronized with, not knowing where we will be led. It is precisely because we are not given a full share in Jessica's sensory journey that cinema has a space to wield an alien prosthetic potential for us (fig. 4.8).

Let me make one final point by way of conclusion. We have seen across our case studies in this chapter that character suspense—that is, the variant of

Figure 4.8 Jessica perceives sounds in the landscape that we do not, even as *Memoria* addresses itself to our theater space through images that invoke its sonorous darkness.

character suspense that disallows us convenient and thorough access to a psychological interiority associated with the bodies on the screen, closing the door in order to keep us guessing, as Costa would have it—can interact with other types of suspense in highly unusual ways that surpass the limitations of traditional narrative suspense. In no way deficient in character development, the slow art-house films we have investigated create new forms in and through which character suspense fluidly combines with atmospheric, perceptual, structural, and generic levels of suspense. In forging uncommon relations between figure and environment as well as between screen and viewer, the compound suspense on offer enlarges the meaning of "characterization" to include atmospheric dimensions of film style and spectator address.

CHAPTER 5

GOTHIC UNCERTAINTY, BORDERING ON HORROR

D

o you know this theater is haunted?" asks one cruising patron of another as they smoke cigarettes in a dark hallway somewhere in the recesses of the dilapidated Fu Ho Grand Theater on its final night of business in Tsai Ming-liang's *Goodbye, Dragon Inn* (2003). The same man, as if to affirm his own spectrality, goes on: "This theater is haunted. Ghosts." Deferred until the film's forty-five-minute mark, these first lines of dialogue spoken by Tsai's characters occur in an exceptionally long, quiet take, the only other sounds being the smokers' exhalations and the whir of a fan that echoes the theater's projector, as heard in the preceding shot. This fan resides at the frame's upper boundary and is only partially visible, but its rotary blades throw shadows on the wall below and delimit a zone of visual obscurity through which the two "zombie-like" men walk as they enter and exit the shot.[1] Back inside the theater, one of these men, a Japanese tourist, is soon scared away by a melon-seed-eating woman who may be a ghost and who slowly closes in behind his seat in sync with foreboding music from King Hu's *Dragon Inn* (1967), the film projected on the intradiegetic screen.

Several critics have noted how *Goodbye, Dragon Inn*—while working as a paradigmatic case of slow cinema—lightly borrows from popular idioms a sense of ghostliness that marks the Taipei theater's fading "milieu of same-sex desire" as well as the aging, deteriorating medium of film itself in an emergent digital media climate.[2] Indeed, Tsai's tonal conjunction of eeriness, nostalgia, and humor, set in a leaky, cavernous building amid a rainstorm at night, offers a slow and playfully reflexive variation on "old dark house" horror. Far from being an outlier, however, *Goodbye, Dragon Inn* is part of a larger gothic direction of contemporary cinematic slowness that has not been charted extensively enough, given its lack of fit with accounts that too rigidly stress realism and a polar opposition to the popular.

Gothic accents understatedly materialize in a number of films that are either firmly within the slow cinema category or on the margins of it. The tenebrous hospital maze in which Ventura labors in *Horse Money* (Costa, 2014); the witchy cave into which the protagonist wanders in search of his runaway daughter in *Jauja* (Alonso, 2015); the haunted remains of a rural movie theater tied to the colonial past in *Neighboring Sounds* (Mendonça Filho, 2012); the ghostliness that infuses Lav Diaz's dissections of traumatic Filipino history in *Death in the Land of Encantos* (2007) and *Melancholia* (2008)—all these examples partake of gothic and uncanny forms that harbor some relationship, however tenuous, to popular genres. They complicate descriptions of slow cinema as a realist enterprise that dutifully preserves the temporal and spatial unities of profilmic events.[3] As we saw in our encounter with Apichatpong's films in chapter 4, long durations can bend and perforate the real time of the present by bringing into play hidden realms and persistent pasts. Victor Erice's no less mercurial uses of slowness in *The Spirit of the Beehive* (1973) and *El Sur* (1983) overtly cite gothic sources: the former through its reflexive integration of James Whale's *Frankenstein* (1932) and the latter through its reference not just to Adelaida García Morales's source novel but also to Alfred Hitchcock's *Shadow of a Doubt* (1943).[4] Earlier in this book, I have also had occasion to find gothic notes in *Under the Skin* (Glazer, 2014) as well as in some of Chantal Akerman's films, where they are more attenuated.

In speaking of the gothic as it creeps into these art-house films, I have in mind something more categorically flexible and aesthetically nuanced than the standard genre-based account of how gothic literature of the eighteenth and nineteenth centuries lays the foundation for what is codified as the horror film in the 1930s. Although the gothic consistently imparts uneasy affects in the vicinity of fear, it comprises less a genre, bound to a certain iconography, than a protean and migratory *mode*,[5] one that may infiltrate any number of genres while imposing itself with differing levels of visibility and stress. If a gothic sensibility carries something of the counter-Enlightenment spirit of many of its literary forebears, retaining a staunch fascination with the irrational, the uncanny, and unhinged psychological states, it need not come with cobwebbed castles and grotesque monsters. Some of the slow art films at the core of this book restyle the gothic's atmospheric affordances in more hushed ways. The gothic requires a relatively slow narrative pace for its prioritization of atmosphere, its thickening of eeriness around hazardous locales. As such, it lends itself more readily than one might expect to the temporal and spatial quirks of today's slow cinema, but this affinity also comes down to the film medium. It is no coincidence that cinematic reflexivity marks almost all the gothic inscriptions in slow cinema that I have identified so far. For some theorists of the gothic, cinema is *the* gothic medium par excellence, from its animations of ghostly bodies to its elemental intertwining of absence and presence, death and life, darkness and light.[6] If some examples of slow cinema slip into gothic territory on occasion, it is in part because the film medium, once it is dialed down to such an extent, is made to confess its innately gothic qualities—a reflexive situation that puts *Goodbye, Dragon Inn* and *Under the Skin* at least distantly in touch with F. W. Murnau's *Nosferatu* (1922) and Todd Browning's *Dracula* (1931).[7]

The gothic, as I explain in detail in this chapter, cultivates all manner of suspenseful ambiguities that chiefly concern mood and atmosphere. These uncertainties extend to the question of genre and trouble the impulse to classify. Some artists associated with slow cinema, such as the London-based experimental filmmaker Ben Rivers, flirt with gothic forms precisely where the lines between genres, between institutional frameworks of film exhibition, and between fiction and documentary become unclear. His early, 16-millimeter short films, such as *Old Dark House* (2003) and *House* (2005–2007), adapt a gothic sense of space to their studies of vacated dwellings in states of decay, the textures of which complement the graininess of the black-and-white film stock. In *House*, a study of decrepit rooms streaked by a flashlight from out of frame, a lit candle hovers of its own accord across a shot, the first in a series of increasingly obscure ghostly disturbances that are pitched somewhere between anachronistic film trickery and forensic evidence of rotting architecture. Rivers's short film *Terror!* (2007) is a compilation of moody mise-en-scène culled from VHS tapes of both mainstream and exploitation horror films. Though the video slowly culminates in gore, the bulk of the montage shows quiet-before-the-storm moments—from misty establishing shots to scenes of characters carrying out everyday actions in and around their homes—that are made to feel suspenseful *apart from* their foretokening role in their original narrative contexts, *apart from* their lead-up to a jump scare or assault.[8] Rivers confirms that he endeavors to channel this vaguely unsettling quality in his films: "That sense of dread, the uncertainty that you get from great genre cinema, *before* the big shocks come. It isn't so far from some of my slow films."[9]

In turning more concertedly to this gothic direction in slow cinema, I want to investigate how the gothic mode engenders curious and especially resourceful variants of atmospheric and perceptual suspense—variants that crucially implicate the film medium itself. Japan's Kiyoshi Kurosawa serves as my main example, a filmmaker who is often too neatly pegged a J-horror specialist in reference to a particular strand of Japanese horror cinema in the 1990s and early 2000s, a phenomenon sparked by Hideo Nakata's *Ring* (1998) and its premise of a haunted videotape. Kurosawa's work over the past five decades has certainly orbited around the horror genre, and his gradually paced atmospheric approach would be well suited to the "slow horror" lineage that Glyn Davis has sketched.[10] But for my purposes I am less invested in Kurosawa's horror films proper than in some of his horror-adjacent projects—*Charisma* (1999), *Journey to the Shore* (2015), and *Creepy* (2016)—and the strangely gothicized registers in which they work. These films have a fringe relationship not only to horror but also to the canon of slow cinema, and they share with my other examples in this book a gravitation toward profoundly unsettled suspense at the crossroads of popular and art-house practices, where they bring to bear affective resonances that cannot be easily named and placed. Their screen worlds call for a more refined engagement with the uncanny and environmental dread. Reviving my earlier chapters' concerns with the interplays of absence and presence as regards the contents of the frame, I inspect how these three gothic-tinged films sabotage our best efforts to gather a full, legible picture of their events. In a playful dialogue with multiple suspense traditions, both Eastern and Western, they put into service the veiling and unveiling capacities of the frame in ways that hinder perception and mobilize the unseeable. A monster film of sorts, a ghost romance, and an equally odd serial killer/police procedural exercise, these films *border on* horror, and I dwell on them for that very reason: their generic liminality is a crucial wellspring of the slow, atmospheric suspense at the heart of this book's arguments.

Adrift in the Gothic Forest: *Charisma*

Despite his intriguing directorial affinities with Yasujirō Ozu, Andrei Tarkovsky, Edward Yang, and Theo Angelopoulos, Kiyoshi Kurosawa is rarely invoked in discussions of the slow, contemplative style. His films *Charisma* and *Barren Illusion* (1999) clock in with average shot lengths of twenty-two and eighteen seconds, respectively, landing them in company with East Asian long-take specialists such as Hirokazu Kore-eda and Hou Hsiao-hsien, but few besides David Bordwell have situated Kurosawa in the environs of slow cinema.[11] He tends to be branded a J-horror director on the basis of his films *Cure* (1997), *Séance* (2000), *Pulse* (2001), and *Retribution* (2006), and this proximity to horror, in the eyes of most critics, places him at odds with the slow cinema corpus, even as J-horror is known for its sedate rhythms and privileging of mood over narrative action. But much of Kurosawa's output, whatever the genre, is distinguished by slowly wrought and perturbing atmospherics: shadowy frames embedded within frames; distantly shot landscapes that diminish the human figure; wind-rustled draperies and plants; impersonal architecture in ambiguous institutional settings, or what Chika Kinoshita has called "space[s] with no name";[12] and eerie activations of the offscreen through lighting, camera movement, and auditory drones. Some of his films fit the "slow horror" criteria Davis proposes, and others, while keeping a slow-paced gothic disposition, foray into romance, melodrama, science-fiction, comedy, and art-house projects almost shorn of popular-genre ingredients.

As a former pupil of the film scholar Shigehiko Hasumi, and as a film professor and historian in his own right, Kurosawa is a more versatile director than his J-horror reputation indicates. In addition to tinkering within and across established genres, he tests out forms of hybridity that leave us guessing whether genre conventions apply and, if so, which genre in the mix is the most dominant (a practice I term "generic suspense" in chapter 1).[13] We may also feel suspense regarding the uncertain *extent to which* a genre bears on a film's narrative and affective contours. In an interview about *Before We Vanish* (2017), his alien-invasion film with shadings of romance and absurdist comedy, Kurosawa stresses his need to suppress expected genre payoffs: "I prefer to tone down. Something I often wrack my brains over is to what degree I should add elements that hint at what the film's genre is."[14] This tentative approach also results in vaguely generic art-house productions. The mise-en-scène of *Barren Illusion* only scarcely evokes dystopic science fiction as it articulates a future world of disaffected youth troubled by an epidemic of viral allergens. The film lingers on banal events into which a generalized and elusive eeriness seeps. For instance, as a long take shuttles back and forth on a horizontal path in a dark basement, we watch a postal worker fumble with a faulty Xerox machine until a ghostlike woman appears from the offscreen, bringing a jump scare of sorts into the mobile frame. Another scene riffs on Herk Harvey's oneiric ghost film *Carnival of Souls* (1962),[15] but Kurosawa here never settles into horror or science fiction outright. Aaron Gerow treats *Barren Illusion* as a companion to *Pulse*, in which Japan is plagued by a wave of lethal hauntings through the internet. "Both are essentially apocalyptic films . . . that make the fading out of the self a central issue."[16] *Barren Illusion* literalizes this metaphysical motif when the main character, in the middle of a lengthy take, fades in and out of corporeality in his daylit apartment, hovering at a threshold of existence amid a breezy, mundane ambience. "It is as if in Kurosawa's cinema," observes Gerow, "the world and the people that inhabit it are themselves ghostly from the start."[17] The character's initial fade-out triggers a cut (editing, not just the lack thereof, is pivotal in Kurosawa's use of slowness), and then he reappears in a changed position in a second long take. Between one shot and the next, he has mysteriously moved in a dimension not shown to us. Low-level suspense builds as Kurosawa here strips the uncanny of its customary trappings and locates it *within the everyday*.

And yet a gothic sensibility stays in effect in Kurosawa's modulations. As he has pointed out several times in public statements, his slowly rendered film atmospheres take cues, in part, from the Japanese *kaiki* genre—critically maligned B films with fantastical themes and highly artificial interior sets (spooky woodlands, castles, and temples). A staple of popular Japanese cinema from the silent era through the 1960s, these films predate the entry of the term *hōra*, "horror," into Japan's film-critical lexicon in the 1980s.[18] Since the term *gothic* calls to mind Western literary tropes imported into cinema (grotesque monsters; precarious, possibly sentient spaces beset with menace; events that test the limits of rationality), we should proceed with care when applying the term to Asian cinema. That said, Charles Shirō Inouye has shown how the gothic developed in Japan as an outgrowth of ancient animistic beliefs long before the culture's modern adoption of the transliterated word *goshikku*.[19] Kurosawa freely enlists the term *gothic* when reflecting on *kaiki* cinema:

> *Kaiki*'s nuance might be termed "gothic horror" in English. It's things like Hammer movies and *The Ghost Story of Yotsuya* [Nobuo Nakagawa, 1959], period pieces in which ghosts or mysterious figures like Dracula appear, and the whole movie has a sense of taking place "not now," but "long long ago." I suppose that's very similar to gothic horror. Those films aren't mainly about horror, the ones I want to call *kaiki*. They're atmospheric, moody. Even if they're provisionally set in the modern day, the action will take place in some old mansion, like in *Eyes Without a Face* [George Franju, 1960]. It's actually "the present" yet it has a very old, period feel to it.... I would say fear isn't even a necessary element of *kaiki* cinema.[20]

Kurosawa's reference to the French surrealist example *Eyes Without a Face* makes clear that in Japan the *kaiki* classification is broadly transnational. In *My Horrifying History of Cinema* (2008), a collection of interviews of him by Makato Shinozaki, Kurosawa discusses films such as Giorgio Ferroni's *Mill of the Stone Women* (1960, Italy/France), Jack Clayton's *The Innocents* (1961, United Kingdom), Mario Bava's *The Whip and the Body* (1963, Italy/France), and Terence Fisher's *The Gorgon* (1964, United Kingdom) as *kaiki* that fall on a gothic spectrum between horror and melodrama.[21] Although his claim that "fear" isn't essential to *kaiki* is perhaps a slight overstatement, it speaks to his own creative probing of subtly unnerving effects in lieu of violent shocks.[22]

Kaiki nuances, especially where the cinematic rendering of ghostliness is concerned, are readily identifiable within and across *Pulse*, *Retribution*, *Séance*, and Kurosawa's other horror outings. But I am more interested in his transpositions of gothic eeriness into cinematic worlds that only obliquely summon popular cinema. The gothic, in my account, is not a self-enclosed genre restricted to certain iconographies. Rather, it names a *spatial-perceptual regime of mood* that inflects Kurosawa's play with multiple genres. His feel for the gothic, we will see, thrives when generic liminality aligns with "ontological liminality," to use Gerow's term.[23] Films that slide between genres or that arcanely fuse them are for Kurosawa vehicles for exploring fragile, disoriented states of being in the world. They stage reckonings—some dreadful and some droll—with the elemental uncanniness of lived experience.

Let us take *Charisma* as our first provocation to sort out the gothic in Kurosawa's horror-adjacent slow cinema. The film opens, like his later *Bright Future* (2002), at a blurred threshold between sleep and waking. Offscreen clatter from a typewriter minimally establishes a police station foyer where a detective lying prostrate, Yabuike (Kurosawa regular Kōji Yakusho), is stirred awake by a supervisor. Ignoring advice to go home and relax with his family, Yabuike disastrously fails to negotiate a hostage situation after the assailant, who holds a politician at gunpoint, hands him a bizarre ransom note: "Restore the Rules of the World." Forced to take a vacation and then fired soon after, Yabuike, alone, travels to a mountain forest on the city's outskirts. Almost like a drifter in a Western (he wears a duster instead of a detective's trench coat), he wanders into a small-community dispute and is courted by each side,[24] but, unlike a gunfighting hero, Yabuike is a borderline narcoleptic who lacks a consistent sense of purpose and who farcically becomes addicted to psychedelic mushrooms. By turns ludic and ominous, the film also invites consideration as ecohorror because the conflict in the plot concerns a rare tree the community has named "Charisma," a "monstrous" entity that, despite being feeble, is slowly killing the forest through toxic root secretions.[25]

Yabuike strays into this forest after waiting at an abandoned bus stop. The film portrays his aimless actions in elliptical fragments that leave the plot unreadable—until he is pressed to weigh the conflicting positions of each party with an investment in Charisma's fate: a botanist who hopes to destroy it and thus revive the forest; a lodger of a derelict sanitorium who guards and nurses the rare tree; and militia troops who wish to obtain it for a collector. "What are you going to do?" Yabuike is asked repeatedly, an existential question, like those that economically distill Kurosawa's horror films: "Would you like to meet a ghost?" in *Pulse*; "Who are you?" in *Cure*. In *Charisma*, the underlying questions of identity and action are still more suspenseful. We can know neither Yabuike nor the genre into which he has meandered. An atmosphere of radical uncanniness denies us a foothold.

But what exactly produces uncanny effects in *Charisma*? How best to define the uncanny in a manner appropriate to our Kurosawa-directed case studies? Film scholars typically turn to Freud's seminal text on the uncanny from 1919, even though all its examples are lifted from literary narrative, and Freud nowhere references the film medium. His thorough inventory of things and situations that uncannily reawaken the repressed past (doublings, doppelgängers, mirrors, in/animate objects, etc.) of course pertains to cinema, too, but it pays to remember that form—not just content—brings about uncanniness. The basic disparity in medium matters along these lines. A film is a luminous, spatially radiant world as well as a *reverberant* world since the advent of sound.[26] The technical devices and registers that (always incompletely) deliver the multisensory spectacle to us are inherently uncanny in ways that gothic cinema has readily exploited.[27] Think of how the filmic apparatus itself is evoked by ghostly mechanisms in the mise-en-scène of Carl Th. Dreyer's *Vampyr* (1932) and by the abstract sounds and images that manufacture the alien and set in motion *Under the Skin*.[28]

It also pays to recall that the uncanny, even for Freud, describes an embodied response as opposed to mere cognitive puzzlement. It is foremost a *feeling* triggered by the copresence of the strange and familiar, the "unhomely" (*unheimlich*) and "homely" (*heimlich*).[29] Conventional accounts of uncanniness in cinema tend to fixate on objects and themes while glossing over the viewer's experience, the dizzy sensation of one's routine existence being "undercut by a subtle atmosphere of disquiet."[30] Stanley Kubrick, discussing what he gleaned from Freud's essay (as well as from H. P. Lovecraft's writings) as he prepared *The Shining* (1980), defines the uncanny as an "arena of feeling" conjured up where explanation fails.[31]

The Freudian psychoanalytic uncanny goes some way to illuminate the arenas of feeling in Kurosawa's gothic cinema, but not far enough. In *Charisma*, the traumatic past is reopened in a Freudian sense when the titular tree, in what seems to be a hallucination for Yabuike, looms as a colossal mushroom in the shape of an atomic cloud, at once recalling Japan's nuclear traumas and graphically resembling Godzilla, a monster already linked through its radioactive breath to the atmospheric ramifications of the blasts. Freud's model, however, has shortcomings in the face of Kurosawa's style. The Freudian uncanny, although it sheds light on the layering of present and past in *Charisma*, does little to describe the film's relationships between human subject and world, between character and environment, and between spectator and screen.

What we need, then, is a more particularized notion of the uncanny that can be detached from a psychoanalytic approach and plied more carefully in relation to the affective capabilities of film. Useful for our purposes, Mark Fisher's book *The Weird and the Eerie* (2016) investigates two affective modes that fall through the cracks of the Freudian uncanny, a paradigm that Fisher finds limiting because of its focus on processes *internal to* the individual subject vis-à-vis the nuclear family. He argues that Freud's psychic framework makes a "compensatory move" whereby external strangeness is ultimately folded back into the familiar and the homely—a move that fortifies the subject and "retreat[s] from the outside." By contrast, "the weird and the eerie make the opposite move: they allow us to see the inside *from the perspective of the outside*." Citing films by Tarkovsky, Kubrick, R. W. Fassbinder, David Lynch, Jonathan Glazer, and others, Fisher regards the weird and the eerie as two manners of the residually strange that stop short of "the horrific."[32] *Low*-key sensations have jurisdiction in the affective realms of eeriness and weirdness, much as they do in Kurosawa's *kaiki*-informed art-house films.

Weirdness, explains Fisher, "is constituted by . . . the presence of *that which does not belong*," at least from the vantage of our ingrained ways of knowing, our presumed ability to make sense of the human and nonhuman world. Weirdness can be "marked by an exorbitant presence, a teeming which exceeds our capacity to represent it." It issues from a brute exteriority for which humanity has little or no explanatory resort (this exteriority is what constitutes "the outside" for Fisher, "that which lies beyond standard perception, cognition, and experience"). Traditional monsters such as vampires, Fisher claims, are not weird because they can be absorbed into the familiar. A black hole occurring in nature or a monster in the tales of Lovecraft are far weirder than a werewolf, whose presence generically brings in tow a "preexisting lore" that aids interpretation. In contrast, eeriness, for its part, involves either a "*failure of absence*" or a "*failure of presence*": in the first case, "there is something present where there should be nothing"; in the latter, "there is nothing present when there should be something." The cry of an unseen bird is a "failure of absence" insofar as it evokes a mysterious quality of intent "that we do not usually associate with a bird." As to what constitutes a "failure of presence," Fisher points to ruined landscapes and deserted buildings that have lost traces of their original purposes—signs conveying why and for whom these structures were built. He cites the postapocalyptic landscape of unrevealed origins and mystical powers in Tarkovsky's *Stalker* (1979), a film Kurosawa channels throughout *Charisma*. Although general similarities bridge weirdness and eeriness, Fisher contends that "the eerie necessarily involves forms of speculation and *suspense* that are not an essential feature of the weird." He goes on to explain, in terms befitting Kurosawa's films,

> Is there something anomalous about this bird's cry? What exactly is strange about it? Is, perhaps, the bird possessed—and if it is, by what kind of entity? Such speculations are intrinsic to the eerie, and once the questions and enigmas are resolved, the eerie immediately dissipates. The eerie concerns the unknown; when knowledge is achieved, the eerie disappears. It must be stressed at this point that not all mysteries generate the eerie. There must also be a sense of alterity, a feeling that the enigma might involve forms of knowledge, subjectivity and sensation that lie beyond common experience.[33]

In *Charisma*, the tree (Is it indeed a tree?) is both a weird and an eerie phenomenon. On the one hand, it is an irreducibly strange physical presence that does not belong. Marking it off from the rest of the forest is a barren swath of land (it has killed its immediate neighbors) and a protective metal armature placed around its trunk by the former sanitorium resident, the tree's zealous guardian, who has also attached tubes and bandages to its limbs. And yet the weird mise-en-scène gives way to an eerie failure of presence: the tree looks weak, innocuous, but we sense the invisible atmospheric circuitry, both below and above ground, through which its intoxicating and lethal forces operate. Its static appearance is but a distraction from what it atmospherically does through its roots and perhaps the air. Through irrational sonic tones and a motif of undulant, metallic light from an offscreen source that has no concrete status in the narrative, each shot of the tree eerily reminds us of what eludes our vision: an enigmatic agency about which we are left to speculate as to its mechanisms and magnitudes. The very name "Charisma" designates less a definite object than a spirit of magnetism imposed on its surroundings. The botanist tells Yabuike that other plants in the forest are mysteriously attracted to the tree, as if embracing their death. Like the venomous mutant jellyfish in *Bright Future*, the anonymous hypnotist in *Cure*, and the internet phantoms in *Pulse*, the tree is fatally seductive.

Fisher's concept of the eerie dovetails with what I called "environmental dread" in chapter 2. Eeriness and dread overlap in their difference from sheer fright: both have to do with potentially malign forces that are sensed *indirectly* in lieu of an encounter with a causal entity. According to Cynthia Freeland in her study of gothic horror films that are "a matter of mood more than monsters," dread takes hold when one discerns an "obscure" yet "profound" threat.[34] Tracing M. Night Shyamalan's *The Sixth Sense* (1999) and Alejandro Amenábar's *The Others* (2001) back to Jacques Tourneur's oblique "fog and shadows" aesthetic in *Cat People* (1942) and *I Walked with a Zombie* (1943), Freeland argues that dread builds up through anticipation but without periodic shocks before identifiable agents that are the cause of such negative feelings. Dread is a more "ongoing" apprehension amid something vaguely evident and "abhorrent to reason." It elicits from the viewer "an exercise of imaginative conceptualization," a strained effort to surmise causal factors, because there is no clear basis for why the film's world and its events unnerve us. For Freeland, duration matters in that dread is chronic, having deeper and more lasting roots than anxiety, nourished as it is by one's existential impression of an unalterably "unjust cosmos." Dread, furthermore, harbors sensations of a future outcome one is powerless to reverse.[35]

The eerie is likewise a sphere of absently present agencies that unsettle us without quite delivering a shock, yet eeriness, in my understanding, is more an incipient impression that may or may not escalate into dread. Eerie and dreadful experiences ignite suspense and the urge to speculate about likely cause-and-effect mechanisms, but eeriness doesn't necessarily endure for a lengthy period and include the aspects of *profundity* and *inexorability*. As Fisher notes, the eerie may occasion calm detachment instead of distress.[36] Whether an initial sensation of eeriness will phase into dread is a point of suspense. As part of its puzzling tonal mishmash, *Charisma* advances from eeriness to dread along a spectrum. The film slowly maneuvers within and along a restrained eeriness-to-dread gradient, moving us from mere impressions into gradually stronger proof of an unstoppable disaster.

This trajectory unfolds by way of atmosphere across initially distinct spaces that start to strangely echo each other. First, there is the makeshift canteen at the forest's edge—a wrecked, prisonlike space in which eeriness is generated by Kurosawa's "deframing" of imagery in long takes that refuse us a clear, advantageous view of narrative events. As Pascal Bonitzer theorizes the technique, deframing forgoes customary uses of compositional space that offer the viewer opportune views and continually confirm relevant story information, this being a convention cinema has inherited from Renaissance painting and the science of perspective that underpins it, a pictorial system catering to the desire for control. Disrupting this practice, deframing transforms the visual field into a zone of obscurity that disorients the observer, confounds point of view, and ushers in "non-narrative suspense" as the action halts. Steeped in a tension between presence and absence, the voided-out image cedes priority to the offscreen: a *beyond* that is not necessarily adjacent to or simultaneous with the space on view. Images, then, become "solicitations of the hidden and the invisible." Bonitzer has in mind the films of Robert Bresson and Michelangelo Antonioni, but he invokes gothic horror when he describes how deframing plays a "sadistic" and "perverse" game with the viewer that kindles sensations of "mystery, of fear, of semi-nightmare."[37]

In the long take that introduces the canteen in *Charisma*, Yabuike sits inertly in darkness, unreadable behind rusty bars of a broken window (fig. 5.1). The camera tracks horizontally, as if to seek a better vantage, but is again obstructed, this time by fibrous tree limbs. The mystery of the greater forest offscreen haunts this image, amplifying a tension between the interior and the exterior in both architectural and psychological terms. This kind of spatialized tension abounds in the gothic mode. Consider Jack Clayton's *The Innocents*, a film Kurosawa has frequently praised.[38] Adapted from Henry James's novella *The Turn of the Screw* (1898), its perceptual games revolve around the thin-to-undecidable lines between the supernatural (there are ghostly entities afoot in the manor) and the psychological (our distressed heroine is hallucinating). This perceptual quandary is presented to us architecturally as the inside/outside of the manor and the inside/outside of character subjectivity are correlated. In a reflexive sense, the motif also extends to the disclosive and omitting operations of the film frame—which, after all, is an architectural unit in its own right, no less gothic than the windows that serve as its double in frame-within-the-frame compositions. Offscreen sounds, such as the trilling of doves, provoke *endless* doubt and suspicion in the viewer, with eeriness shading steadily into dread. *Charisma*'s Yabuike is less knowable, and less interpretable, than the

Figure 5.1 *Charisma*: Our detective, Yabuike, is concealed by shadows and obstacles across gothic spaces that are atmospherically interlinked.

protagonist in *The Innocents*, but Kurosawa marshals a similar gothic disposition of the frame and the out of frame, making the difference between mental space and environmental space at times impossible to determine, not least during Yabuike's hallucinatory fits.

Eerier than the canteen, which it echoes, is the "hotel" where Yabuike lodges—a former sanitorium presided over by Kiriyama (Hiroyuki Ikeuchi), who is also the fanatical protector of Charisma. Located deeper within the forest, this partly flooded space is acutely gothic, with its obfuscating darkness and shadows cast in filigreed patterns by vegetation from outside and by

Figure 5.2 *Charisma*: Kiriyama (*rear*) and Yabuike (*front*) are mutually infected by the forest spilling into the space of the "hotel."

architectural viscera in ruins. Forest overgrowth creeps in through imploded walls and broken windows. Billowy reflected light, like that which surrounds Charisma, textures events in the "hotel" from an abstract offscreen source. Reminiscent of the dilapidated spaces within the Zone in *Stalker*, this "hotel" is also defined sonically by low-frequency rumbles and echoic drips that do not quite conform to the puddles and reflections of water onscreen. Yabuike's interactions with Kiriyama unfurl, often in lengthy takes, as deframed dialogues between spectral beings who fade into shadow, switch places in the frame, and increasingly seem like extensions of each other (fig. 5.2). This works in the vein of coupled figures on the Noh stage who occupy the same psyche (the *shite* protagonist and *waki* deuteragonist in a *mugen* play, wherein the supernatural and the natural fall on a continuum).[39] Just as the poisoned forest encroaches on this space, both of these men are marked by Charisma's invasive force: Kiriyama in his zealotry and Yabuike in his ingestion of foraged mushrooms. *The outside is charismatically inside.* Near the film's end, when Kiriyama confers his caretaker role onto Yabuike and says, "*You're* Charisma," the point is literal: Yabuike has consumed and absorbed the tree's chemical properties.[40]

Editing, no less than durationally presented mise-en-scène, puts forward an eerie feeling of atmospheric contamination—and distributes this feeling across disparate spaces that collapse into one another. Gerow identifies in Kurosawa's cinema a system of "dis/continuity" that uses elliptical cuts in combination with long takes, introducing syntactical ambiguities that flummox interpretation. Asserted in transitions between and within scenes, "dis/continuity" is a register "between showing and not showing, between explaining and not explaining."⁴¹ This structural procedure is disruptive in certain respects and at the same time connective in others. *Charisma* dis/continuously offsets its long takes with sporadic cuts that emphasize changes in sound tone. One shot of *Charisma* sonically morphs from wind into a drone whose volume builds up to the edge of the oncoming cut. The next shot of Yabuike foraging in the woods is silent, wiped of sound entirely, but the film cuts again to a shot of a flowing creek, the sound now back in full effect. In another odd moment of sonic discordance and suspension, the film cuts abruptly to a mute, nocturnal shot of a smoke-enshrouded tree—a hallucinatory vision of what turns out to be a new, larger, and more gothic-looking Charisma.⁴²

By attuning us to timbral contrasts between spaces, this elliptical editing system sees to it that we notice when, for instance, the lakeside well near the forest begins to emit *the same* sonic ambience as the sanitorium, hinting at their interconnectedness, both geographical and aesthetic. By the same token, we become sensitive to the fact that the house of the botanist, Jinbo (Yoriko Dōguchi), Kiriyama's archrival, takes on eerie parallels to the sanitorium despite seeming to be its architectural opposite: orderly, efficient. Oscillating between a greenhouse/kitchen/laboratory space and a darker adjacent room where an antique stove (a gothic touch) constantly burns wood, the dialogues presented between Jinbo and Yabuike echo the latter's interactions with Kiriyama. Dis/continuous cuts from the exterior to this interior assert subtle atmospheric links. The mute shot of the Godzilla-size mushroom cloud (formed of smoke from Charisma, which Jinbo has set ablaze) cuts to a high-angle shot of Jinbo relaxing in her home as she decants hot water for tea. This wordless long take accentuates the water, the wood-burning stove and heated air, and the wind lashing gossamer curtains—basic earthly elements that breach the boundaries of the house and figure as *media* of entwinement. Indeed, in Kurosawa's cinema, what ostensibly looks and sounds like "nothing" in terms of the narrative can be part of an atmospheric matrix of delicately mobile and interacting forces.

The well, sanitorium, and forest additionally connect to Jinbo's house by dint of the fact that she has been secretly poisoning the water well in an effort to destroy the entire forest and resuscitate its original ecosystem. Her sister calls her "crazy," as though she is a mad scientist instead of an environmentalist. Moreover, because *Charisma* nowhere draws a line along the axis of causality between Jinbo's killing of the forest and the tree's lethal toxicity, we cannot know if her scientific perspective on the situation is any more valid than Kiriyama's mystical one—just as we can't know the extent to which Charisma is responsible. The fiery stove in Jinbo's house visually and aurally rhymes with various other sites in the film, and these links testify to what I earlier called the atmospheric circuitry through which Charisma indistinctly exerts its influence. The film's system of deframing and dis/continuity doesn't "represent" these relationships; rather, it obliquely alludes to this circuity and mediates its infective energies.

After Jinbo burns the original Charisma and Yabuike finds the tree's bigger, older gothic double in another part of the forest, he reluctantly agrees, after much debate, to help destroy the emergent monster, if this tree can be described as such. Jinbo and Yabuike's conversations uncannily echo the hostage negotiation at the film's outset, and here again Yabuike wonders whether *both* the tree and the forest can be saved, just as he hoped to save *both* the radical criminal/protestor and the politician hostage. Although he delivers a monologue espousing something like an embrace of chaos, it is not clear how his actions follow from this credo. In a scene that recalls the killing of the shark in *Jaws* (Spielberg, 1975), he and Jinbo blow up the tree, but this act reveals a green sapling inside the trunk's remains, suggesting Charisma is indestructibly multiple. In turn, this event somehow triggers a major catastrophe miles away in the city, now ablaze under a night sky in the closing shot as helicopters fly overhead.

How are we to take this finale? Eeriness has escalated to dread, but a spirit of playfulness remains, and the mood isn't dystopian so much as quizzical. Although the film has bordered on ecohorror and has keyed its atmospheric style to an ecosystem that escapes perceptibility, this ending doesn't exactly spell out a parable about climate catastrophe. Gerow cautions against too strict an ecocritical reading: "The long takes in *Charisma* . . . , dizzyingly moving between one camp and another, emphasize less spatial unity than disunity; they underline that the forest itself was from the start only established through Kurosawa's ambiguous cuts, making it impossible to determine, in this supposedly ecocritical film, whether there is even a forest here, or whether, in a story where debates about cutting down a tree are founded on tendentious assertions of cause and effect, cutting/editing is itself the only causality, juxtaposition the only forest."[43] I would add here that comic absurdities, as much as ecoconsciousness, make their way into the film's literalization of the clichéd "forest for the trees" quandary of perception.[44] Moreover, although *Charisma* engages this quandary by mapping atmospheric circuits between specific details and overarching systems, the film pulls ecological thought toward the gothic. Its forest evokes less a real and precise landscape than the spirit-infested woodlands of *kaiki*, shot through with ambient forces that outstrip our control and confront us with our own transience.

In its etymological history, before it came to define personal charm, the term *charisma* referred to a divine gift, a godsend.[45] The deadly tree, we are asked to consider, is a *blessing* in that it forces a drastic reevaluation of our entrenched notions of subjectivity in relation to the environment. In interviews, Kurosawa states that he approached *Charisma* with acute awareness of the fact that a new century and perhaps new forms of being were on the horizon.[46] The film's ending, in another peculiar reference to popular cinema, channels that of John Carpenter's *Escape from L.A.* (1996), where the antiheroic Snake Plissken (Kurt Russell) gleefully triggers a wave of electrical power failures that returns the world to the Dark Ages.[47] *Charisma* thereby suggests less a total planetary apocalypse than a restart of civilization from zero. Kurosawa's film flirts with a tonal mix comparable to that of Alex Garland's *Annihilation* (2018), which embraces—with a synthesis of dread and wonder—the loss of humanity as we know it for the sake of adapting to an unstoppably mutating world. If *Charisma* fosters an ecocritical attitude, it does so through a gothic mode, urging us to become at home with eerie atmospheric forces that cannot be confined, curtailed, or defeated.

Fatal Mechanisms: *Journey to the Shore*

In *Charisma*, the tree is less reverberantly eerie than the scenes within the former sanitorium, where personal subjectivity is evacuated. For Bonitzer—who ventures comparisons to paintings by Francis Bacon (1909–1992) and Leonardo Cremonini (1925–2010)—deframing also decenters and *disfigures* the body. Bresson's deframed images, he notes, "mutilate the body" through truncations that sever hands and feet.[48] In *Charisma*, Kurosawa's compositions disfigure through intense darkness that voids out the face and other distinguishing features. A form of perceptual suspense, this technique not only allows for spectral doublings between Yabuike and Kiriyama, who seem interchangeable at times, but also underscores a certain emptiness or deathliness at the core of being—a theme that goes beyond the characters to describe humanity more broadly (not least the film's spectators). The "frame" of the self is intruded on by a ghostly otherness that isn't supernatural so much as ontological. In *Charisma*, this fact of being is disclosed to Yabuike when, after eating mushrooms in the forest, he has a vision of a corpse hanging from a tree, the desiccated body of a man in clothing that uncannily resembles his own (fig. 5.3).

In *My Horrifying History of Cinema*, Kurosawa again associates this proximity to death with the *kaiki* tradition and the sense of deathly entrapment that imbues its worlds. In a move that furnishes insight into his own horror and horror-adjacent practice of filmmaking, he attributes to international *kaiki* the aesthetic logic of the *unmei no kikai*, "machine of fate" or, depending on translation, "fatal mechanism."[49] Invoking Giorgio Feroni's *Mill of the Stone Women*, Roger Corman's Edgar Allan Poe adaptations, Hammer films such as Terence Fisher's *The Mummy* (1959) and *The Gorgon* (1964), and virtually all of Tobe Hooper's horror films as examples of this doom-laden logic, Kurosawa defines the fatal mechanism as a situation geared toward an inevitable confrontation with "Death itself."[50] This trajectory may or may not bring characters face to

Figure 5.3 *Charisma*: In a hallucinatory vision, Yabuike confronts his deathly double.

face with lethal agents, but it compels them to reckon with the brute fact of their mortality—that is, with death's every-instant-of-the-day entwinement with life. Fatal mechanisms may be literal spaces and contraptions in which the film's characters are caught, such as the slow-descending apparatus of torture and execution in Corman's *The Pit and the Pendulum* (1961) or the amusement-park ride where teenage victims are trapped, stalked, and murdered in Hooper's *The Funhouse* (1981). As Mayumi Matsuo and David Matarasso point out, "Kurosawa is less interested in the [deadly] figure than in the devices and forms used—in death as a *cinematographic trap*, the articulation of spaces, objects and shots."[51] Hence, the workings of the film medium itself, to varying degrees of reflexivity, may be considered a fatal mechanism when we are prompted to think of a film's formal system as an ensnarement device with respect to the characters and, by extension, the viewer. At this level, Kurosawa reads a film such as *The Funhouse* with a director's eye toward the planning and precise construction of a set piece of murder or a near-death encounter: the way the framing and editing diagram an event structurally, enforcing a certain vector of action and restricting the position and movement of the characters in a space where menace lurks, as the viewer, too, is led into a precisely orchestrated trap. But Kurosawa doesn't limit this level of fatal mechanics to elaborate murder scenes. A film may invoke and implicate its own formal procedures in quieter ways that are in the tonal range of eeriness more than of terror, while still turning on a closeness to death.[52]

This metacinematic feature of fatal machinery informs not only Kurosawa's horror films but also his art-house gothic melodramas. His underseen, made-in-France film *Daguerrotype* (also known as *The Woman in the Silver Plate*, 2016) reworks themes from *Eyes Without a Face* and *Mill of the Stone Women*. A renowned, egotistical photographer practices the old art of daguerreotype portraiture and forces his daughter, who would rather tend to the rare plants in their greenhouse, to be his model (she is also a double for the deceased wife who periodically visits him). He creates large-format, life-size images in the gothic basement of his manor on the edge of Paris, using a massive camera and a metal armature, a kind of torture device, that fastens his daughter into place for extremely long exposure periods during which she must remain deathly still. This diegetic machine of fate nods to and implicates the film medium. The film's long-held frames eerily interlace with images produced by the photographer as the daguerreotype format alludes to the photochemical base of twentieth-century filmmaking, a bygone process that haunts Kurosawa's digital images within a *kaiki* temporality that blurs the difference between past and present. In this way, the daughter's fate is sealed through gothicized tensions innate to cinema as a medium: between stillness and movement, presence and absence, life and death.

In addition to staging close encounters with death in the onscreen world and implicating the operations of film style and technology as constituting a sort of deathtrap in their own right, *kaiki* fatal mechanisms, for Kurosawa, conceptually lay bare intermediary states between the living and the (not quite) dead, as when the carousel of statues in *Mill of the Stone Women* catches fire and grotesquely reveals several dead women preserved underneath wax casings.[53] Kurosawa sees another example in Kurt Neumann's *The Fly* (1958), the scene in which a cat, in a teleportation experiment gone wrong, is converted into a bodiless cry confined to the offscreen: an eerie liminal existence that, more than anything to be found in Nakata's J-horror ghost film sensation *Ring*, inspired Kurosawa's apparitions in *Pulse*.[54] Circling his discussion back to Japanese *kaiki* examples, Kurosawa points to *The Ghost Story of Yotsuya* (Nobuo Nakagawa, 1959), to which his practice is strongly indebted. He discusses the scene in which the poisoned and badly scarred Oiwa (Katsuko Wakasugi) ever so slowly transitions into ghostliness, brushing her hair yet tearing away her scalp.[55]

While this logic of the fatal mechanism encompasses a cross-cultural range of references that feed into Kurosawa's films, it also reaches back into Japanese animism and its conception of the "porous barrier" between the living and the dead—a worldview that sees ghostly revenants as commonplace. As Katarzyna Ancuta explains,

> Spiritual encounters are part of routine daily existence, since the earthly and spiritual worlds are seen as coexistent. And while there is no denying that some spirits are to be feared, as this response to the supernatural seems to disregard cultural differences, many Asian spirits are seen as arousing reverence instead,

172 Gothic Uncertainty, Bordering on Horror

and the rules of engagement are negotiated through a combination of bribes and offerings. If the spirits are understood in terms of the ancestors, they are, in fact, expected to meddle with the affairs of the living, and even the malicious ones merit obedience and respect rather than a hasty exorcism.[56]

Along similar lines, Kurosawa separates his work from "the standard American horror canon" in which ghosts violently attack and characters are afforded the chance to fend them off. "There is this idea in that genre that you can beat the bad thing and return to the good days of peace and happiness as a resolution," whereas in Japanese cinema "the best you can do is figure out a way to co-exist with the dead."[57]

Kurosawa's *Journey to the Shore*, an art-house ghost romance, reimagines the concept of the fatal mechanism in subdued ways that cross a range of affects. The plot concerns a grieving piano teacher, Mizuki (Eri Fukatsu), whose husband, Yusuke (Tadanobu Asano), returns home three years after his disappearance and suicide at sea, which followed the news of his terminal illness. He is conjured out of the offscreen into the domestic space by Mizuki's preparation of Shiratama rice cakes. Reconnecting and addressing their marital conflicts, Mizuki and Yusuke take an episodic voyage through the countryside, visiting places where he has spent time after dying. The film is a series of ordinary hauntings as each stop along the way features both ghosts and still-alive terrestrials who are wrestling with unsettled pasts. Only Yusuke can differentiate, for Mizuki and the viewer, the ghosts from the living since the spirits still go about their earthly routines, their gothic qualities minimized. Mizuki, with her ashen look and clothing, seems far ghostlier than Yusuke does. If eeriness textures the film in fits and starts, the predominant mood is one of tenderness crossed with wonder. There is no small measure of generic suspense as the viewer, perhaps waiting for a J-horror turn, wonders about the disarticulation of more frightening affective strategies that usually come with gothic hauntings.

The film pivots on interactions between the living and the dead that incite modulations of lighting, sound, and tempo. For instance, while revisiting a gyoza restaurant where Yusuke had worked for a stint, Mizuki finds an old piano in a banquet hall and plays the sheet music resting above the keys. The atmosphere changes as sunlight dims and wind disturbs the gauzy curtains. A young girl, who turns out to be the manager's deceased sister, shows up matter-of-factly, and Mizuki teaches her to play the piece, which the girl had struggled with in life. This slowed scene, in which long takes interact with elliptical cuts, allows a mutual, fleeting reconciliation to transpire, a working-through of sadness and guilt (fig. 5.4).

Smuggled-in *kaiki* aesthetic devices are put in touch with the Japanese concept of *mitoru*, which means the close accompaniment of someone on their deathbed, a situation that Kurosawa reimagines as an elongated trip.[58] *Mitoru*

Gothic Uncertainty, Bordering on Horror 173

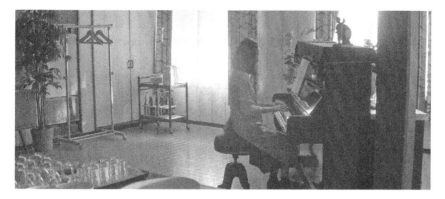

Figure 5.4 *Journey to the Shore*: A shift from daylight to darkness marks the arrival of a young girl's ghost. Notice the uncanny, unsourced pool of light on the sheet music.

(as "perception" plus "understanding") also means "close observation." Igniting suspense of a more contemplative than apprehensive order, *Journey to the Shore* activates this perceptual valence of *mitoru* in a scene where Yusuke, resuming duties as teacher in a rural community, delivers an absorbing lecture—to both an audience *in* the film and the audience *of* the film—on the physics of light. Riffing on a reflexive lecture scene in Jean-Luc Godard's *Notre musique* (2004),[59] this cosmic physics lesson is staged with tracking shots and a slow modulation of offscreen light that asks us to factor in the mediating physics of film—just as our phantom teacher eloquently describes a weightless, luminous nothingness that pervades all things, fusing matter and spirit. "Zero is the basis of everything," he states, but he assures his audience that "nothingness isn't the same as meaningless." This particulate- and wave-formed infinitude of zeroes is not negational but constitutive. "Mountains and rivers, the earth and human beings. Everything is made up of combinations of this nothingness. This would seem to be a true representation of the world."

Neither eerie nor dreadful—but suspenseful in perceptual and atmospheric terms that are aesthetic and cosmological—this lecture feels intent on delivering us *out of* nihilism instead of the reverse. In rhythm with the sunlight that pours into the space and weighs zero at its source, a soft electronic ambient chime (heard cyclically across the film) punctuates the lesson. It morphs out of the chirping of birds offscreen, but the chime is neither internal nor external to the story space, neither within the frame nor without it: we cannot tell whether it is filtered through character subjectivity, reserved for the viewer alone, or a material thing in the fictional world. This sound will later stand in for the eerie call of an offscreen bird that casts a silhouette as it swoops overhead, but this never-shown animal is another ghostly imposition of exteriority, a shadow that allows "communication between what is visible and the invisibility haunting it."[60] This chime rhetorically disregards the boundary between ourselves and the screen. It bears a close if cryptic connection to the physics lesson in that it lures us toward a diffuse, elemental zeroness constituting the entire world: a presence-absence close in spirit to what the Kyoto School philosophers call "absolute nothingness."[61] At the conclusion of the lesson, Yusuke, in medium close-up, scans the audience within the scene (fig. 5.5). At the exact moment his eyes meet the look of the camera and thus of the viewer, the film cuts, somewhat jarringly, to a new location. Our millisecond of eye contact with the ghost is displaced by a lacunary, discontinuous edit. (The space *between* two shots, Bonitzer reminds us, is twinned with the offscreen by virtue of "a double register of lack.")[62] The film, addressing us at the limit of its own expressive capacities, hints that this nothingness at the source of its world touches us, too—not only in the actual world outside but also before the film's virtual world. But we are deliberately left in suspense—lightly anxious, verging on an epiphany but not getting there—regarding how this filmic ambient play of nothingness touches and affects us.

Figure 5.5 *Journey to the Shore*: The philosopher ghost delivers his lecture.

Contagions Vaguely Hypnotic: *Creepy*

When being-in-the-world becomes an eerie condition in Kurosawa's cinema, ghostliness often goes hand in hand with another motif that questions the self and the limits of subjectivity: hypnosis. *Cure* turns on a wave of murders committed by citizens who, without being able to recall their crimes, carve an X into their targets' bodies. Triggered by hypnosis involving fire, water, air, and other everyday earthly elements, this epidemic also eerily partners with—and is partially *transmitted through*—the hypnotic style of the film. Audiovisual devices spread the contagion to our interface with the screen, and the effects of this atmosphere eerily precede the causes. By the time we catch up with the film's (possibly apocalyptic) plot-level ramifications, its visceral energies have already claimed us. This suspenseful investment in the precedence of atmospheric stimuli over narrative exposition runs through Kurosawa's cinema. Think of *Pulse*, where the opening noise of a modem (a twist on the televisual static that opens *Ring*) dials us into a ghostly, viral atmospheric network before there is any plot to speak of.

Full-blown dread springs from the obscurity surrounding the mechanisms of hypnosis in *Cure*. In the final scene, a server at a café may or may not stab her manager while under a spell that may or may not have been triggered by our detective protagonist (Kōji Yakusho), who in earlier scenes has been intimately preyed upon by the arch villain, a mesmerist equipped only with a Zippo lighter. The detective has also been exposed to an old phonograph recording of a Franz Mesmer–inspired incantation. It appears that instead of being at the mercy of the villain's powers of suggestion to commit murder, the detective has *acquired* those mysterious powers, perhaps unwittingly. His ordinary gestures (smoking a cigarette, sipping coffee) now carry an entrancing vibe. In this café scene, the clouding of causation and the denial of closure are such that hypnosis and homicide are but alluded to in a banal ambience filmed at a distance through the detective's dissolving cigarette smoke. Once the affectless server (whose apron straps form an X shape) grabs a kitchen knife, gripping it slasher-style at her waist, the film abruptly cuts to the end-credits screen, where, in place of the anticipated stabbing, the frame itself is graphically slashed, as if to breach the screen's barrier and suggest once more the seepage of a mesmerizing force—no more visible than air—into our viewing space.

Frame by frame, Kurosawa's practice lends credence to Raymond Bellour's conception of cinema as a hypnotic medium. For Bellour, hypnosis and cinema belong to a shared cultural history of emergence that bridges the late 1700s and late 1800s, with the scientific-therapeutic apparatus of hypnosis prefiguring film's power to induce and sustain states of fascination to a degree unrivaled by the neighboring arts. The *dispositif* of the cinematic viewing situation provokes a hypnotic condition of fusion between the body of the spectator and the material body of the film. What begins with a seizing of the gaze (which is analogous to the effect achieved by a hypnotist's pendulating object) becomes a full-bodied affair: the film's somatic events and rhythms are substituted for our own, prompting emotional responses that come before (and may well eclipse) our cognitive ones.[63] For Bellour, what makes hypnosis preferable to the dream as a general metaphor for the film experience is the fact that both hypnosis and film spectatorship involve "a determining cause that comes *from outside* the subject . . . , whereas the production of a dream is completely endogenous, without any exteriority."[64] In addition, according to Bellour, who repeatedly turns to Fritz Lang's *Dr. Mabuse the Gambler* (1922) to uphold this point, when hypnosis serves as a premise within a film's narrative, it inevitably becomes a mise en abyme of the overarching cinematic *dispositif* itself and its captivation of a spectator, who is lulled yet kept impressionably awake.[65]

Kurosawa's *Creepy* merits careful analysis in this regard. A companion piece to *Cure* that revisits the motif of obscure hypnotic suggestion, this film, which is vaguely positioned between art cinema and horror/psychological thriller in a popular, Hitchcockian mode, is a consummate example of how Kurosawa's atmospheric suspense extends the forces of hypnotic influence in the diegesis to the viewer's interface with the screen. The plot follows a recently retired police psychologist named Koichi (Hidetoshi Nishijima), who, like the detective in *Charisma*, fails to deescalate a hostage situation in the opening scene. In the fallout of a tragedy for which he is blamed, he takes a job as an academic criminologist and relocates with his wife, Yasuko (Yūko Takeuchi), to the serene, leafy suburbs of Tokyo. He soon becomes obsessed with a cold case about disappeared families. As he investigates and goes well beyond the scope of his new job, Yasuko, at home, has rather strange interactions with a neighbor, Nishino (Teruyuki Kagawa), who exerts a spellbinding sway over her despite his rudeness. We discover, long before Koichi does, that this neighbor is the serial offender he is searching for, a man who uses hypnosis, both in person and over the telephone, to turn families who are financially desperate into victims and abettors of his sinister schemes.[66] Like the villain in *Cure*, Nishino induces others to commit murder on his behalf, a well-trodden premise in gothic cinema's depictions of hypnosis.

Also like the villain in *Cure*, Nishino's creepy aura stems from his spare characterization, his affront to the very concept of personal identity. Because the film never reveals the *complete* mechanism by which his hypnosis works, we can't know the magnitude and range of that power, where it starts and ends. We do eventually learn that Nishino injects his victim-accomplices with an unspecified drug and that he has preyed on neighbors in different locations through a certain architectural setup (a subtle fatal mechanism, a vaguely hypnotic death trap) whose contiguous structural design eludes an earthbound gaze and is detectible only from a great height through the use of photography (and thus the imposition of a frame). But these details can explain only so much. In concert with the film's gradient climb from eeriness to dread, a feeling of mesmeric attraction reaches far beyond Nishino's monstrous actions and becomes indefinitely bound up with the film's atmosphere. As in *Charisma*, elegantly deframed compositions weave patterns of ensnarement across domestic and institutional spaces. Sonic rumblings and slow, autonomous camera movements survey architectural thresholds and imply the ingress of possibly hypnotic mediations from the outside and the offscreen.[67] Although the film is less metrically slow than *Charisma*, its rhythms of disclosure nevertheless suspend narrative momentum in stretches that prioritize the feel of the onscreen world.

The interior of the middle-class home (everywhere in Kurosawa's work as it gauges the financial pressures of post-Bubble Japan as well as gendered problems of communication that stem from patriarchal values) is a fortress easily breached by atmospheric externalities.[68] In an early scene, as our couple convey their sense of relief and satisfaction with having relocated to suburbia, the camera gradually pushes toward the frosted-glass kitchen window behind them, dividing our attention from theirs and contradicting their naïveté with a more foreboding tone. This is an almost disguised version of a Hitchcockian camera gesture that directs the viewer's attention, alights on important mise-en-scène, and puts us ahead of the character's knowledge. The window faces the adjacent house inhabited by Nishino, whom they have yet to meet, but the orange gift bag on the countertop is courteously meant for him. For the attentive spectator, the hue of this gift bag is subtly but immensely significant: it recalls the orange shirt worn by the escaped murderer in the film's initial scene, in which Koichi's overconfidence in his power to resolve a standoff causes a woman's death. The orange gift bag, *as the camera seems to know*, anticipates a traumatic repetition amid the outwardly pleasant milieu of sunshine, foliage, and wind through diaphanous curtains. That a mesmerizing force will atmospherically invade their abode is further implied by a tier of green houseplants stretching toward the soft light that filters in through the fogged kitchen window (the process of photosynthesis is implicitly gothicized in this film, too).[69] Eerie sensations deepen when Koichi and Yasuko first visit Nishino's gated home: after no one answers the bell, they exit the frame, and the camera recedes, holding for a prolonged moment on the bolted gate, the swaying trees, the flapping plastic industrial drape, a sibilant flourish of wind pitched between the quotidian and the ominous.[70] These atmospheric stimuli are already hints of hypnotic suggestion that play on our impressionability, too, where the placid and the cozy are but gateways to the horrific (fig. 5.6).[71]

Kurosawa's positioning of figures in the frame also suggests relays of hypnotic influence and vulnerability across multiple interpersonal conflicts. Beyond their being naive, what makes Koichi and Yasuko easy prey to Nishino

178 Gothic Uncertainty, Bordering on Horror

Figure 5.6 *Creepy* maps indefinite hypnotic forces through a running play on thresholds, as seen here in Yasuko's neighborly interactions with Nishino outside his home.

is their inability to be candid with one another. An air of the unsayable—what cannot be acknowledged and talked about—increasingly characterizes their scenes together in their home. The steady deterioration of their marriage is charted through blocking patterns that highlight graphic interferences in the compositional space between them: obstacles in the décor that signal their emotional and communicative rift, which is a common staging device in domestic melodrama. In a related motif also lifted from melodrama, the film stages conversation scenes by having two figures face in the same direction—one directly behind the other. Similar setups define Koichi's interactions with Saki (Haruna Kawaguchi), the young woman he interrogates regarding the cold case, who, we are given to notice, physically resembles Yasuko. Indeed, the film's repeated use of one-behind-the-other figural arrangements *asserts a scheme of doubles*, effecting structural suspense that augments both narrative and atmospheric suspense. The doubling occurs over three different recurring conversations that are paralleled and that gradually become commingled: those between Koichi and Yasuko, those between Nishino and Yasuko, and those between

Koichi and Saki. The doubling works partly in gendered terms to comment on how Koichi, not unlike Nishino, resorts to sadistic coercion. The bodies within each pairing also seem uncannily tethered by an unseeable cord.

If this staging technique borrows the melodramatic convention of granting the spectator privileged access to facial expressions that the character in the foreground conceals from the character in the background, Kurosawa does something eerier. A closer gothic reference here again is *The Innocents*, which repeatedly presents one-behind-the-other figural arrangements across scenes that, in effect, double several characters in relation to an ambiguous possibility of ghostly possession: namely, whether ghosts have taken control of two children and whether the governess heroine is a ghostly presence in her own right. The one-behind-the-other positioning of bodies is eerily given to evoke control and manipulation. The spatial gap between figures is made to feel like a charged zone of spectral possession—commanded by the character in back and invisibly informed by ghostly contagions associated with the offscreen and the architectural outside.[72] In *Creepy* and other recent Kurosawa films (most strikingly *Before We Vanish*), such positioning serves in part as spectator address. Bodies figure within choreographies that *mirror our own position when we view characters from the back*. Looking at someone from behind and being looked at from behind become intertwined *spectatorial* motifs that bear on our relationship to the screen. The characters aren't psychological sources of identification so much as doubles for our somatic apprehension. Indeed, at one remove, we are folded into this corporeal tethering motif from our side of the spectacle (fig. 5.7).[73]

In other words, the spatial, intercorporeal gap between ourselves and the screen is one of the thresholds tied to and infected by Nishino's hypnotic influence. In a scene that presses home this effect, Nishino, in a liminal space in their neighborhood, closes in on Yasuko and somehow sends her into a trance as their figures onscreen conform to the blocking technique I have just described. She attempts to flee but makes it only so far before he again collapses the interval between them. As if caught in a force field, she stops in a dark tunnel beneath an overpass for trains (Nishino's hypnotic aura has been affiliated with offscreen train sounds in prior scenes). Now entirely in silhouette, she flouts the fourth wall as she returns the camera's look and thus confronts the viewer. Kurosawa is fond of alterations of light and shadow on the frontal plane ("closer to" the audience) in a bid to synthesize onscreen conditions with the movie theater's darkness. Here the atmospheric effect is to suggest that Yasuko's figure has trespassed onto our side of the screen, crossing a frontier where the theater's no-longer-safe darkness begins. This uncanny play on thresholds is reminiscent of the shower murder in Hitchcock's *Psycho* (1960), which rhetorically removes the barrier between film and viewer when the curtain, flush with the screen, is pulled away in the immediate foreground, bringing us into

Figure 5.7 *Creepy* borrows its one-behind-the-other staging motif from gothic melodramas such as *The Innocents* (*top*), extending it over multiple relationships, including our interface with the screen and its displayed figures.

direct contact, as it were, with the dark, knife-wielding figure whose face is obscured in shadow. In *Creepy*, once Yasuko wrestles free again and exits the shot, *we* meet the inscrutable Nishino, a shadow of death, at the frontal plane, as if exposed to his menace. What Kurosawa would describe as the scene's "fatal mechanics" has entrapped *us*.[74] Whereas Hitchcock's scene stages such a switch-out between the endangered character and the spectator *before* the assault, Kurosawa's does so after it, delivering a shockless shudder (fig. 5.8).[75]

Be it through conceits of ghostliness, hypnosis, or both, Kurosawa's bordering-on-horror cinema enfolds the spectator within its offscreen space such that the liminal modes of being and the ambient contagions in the diegesis also pertain to us.[76] The filmic reflexivity that inheres in this gesture is not of the Brechtian variety that presumes to shake viewers out of their charmed passivity in relation to the image. Kurosawa's atmospheric style brooks no such all-or-nothing leap from passive (immersed) to active (distanced) viewing, as if these modes of spectatorship could be efficiently decoupled.[77] Hypnosis of necessity suspends the conscious will. For this reason, since its early-twentieth-century decline as a widespread clinical method and topic

Figure 5.8 *Creepy*: Nishino descends on Yasuko in a tunnel whose echoic darkness opens onto that of the theater in which we observe.

of scientific research, hypnosis has often been seen as worryingly "incompatible with humanist assumptions about the autonomous and voluntaristic character of human subjectivity."[78] The promise of therapeutic gains that could not be reached otherwise comes at a risky cost of the patient's surrender. If we frame *Creepy*'s address to the spectator in this light, a basic ethical distinction arises between Nishino's hypnotic influence and that of the film's stylistic system, which hardly seeks to induce violence. Moreover, perhaps we are not clinically hypnotized so much as hypnosis functions as an allegory for our attachment to the film's world. Then again, there remains no consensus in scientific and intellectual debates as to what exactly constitutes hypnotic suggestion and where the line falls between it and ordinary attentiveness. *Creepy* and *Cure* exploit this vaguely fluid affective domain.

If Kurosawa's cinema holds out something of the therapeutic potential of hypnosis, what "treatment" is on offer? What are we meant to be "cured" of amid the eeriness and dread mixed with cinematic reflexivity? With its agile evocations of the auditorium space and the hypnotic command of attention (per Bellour) that distinguish the *dispositif* of cinema, *Creepy* surprisingly has a good deal in common with the atmospheric aesthetics of *Memoria* examined in chapter 4. In both examples, reflexivity enhances our immersive, at least quasi-hypnotic experience. Might Kurosawa's cinema—as an additional point of comparison—dispense *remedial* effects in company with those of Apichatpong's therapy-oriented films, which display gothic touches of their own?

Part of the "cure" at stake in Kurosawa's recourse to hypnosis is our forced attunement to the feeble grounds of what we like to call "subjectivity." What falls into suspense beyond matters of the story is our faith in the principle of subjecthood. Atmospheric relays between the outside and the inside sweep us into partially undetectable circuitries that assail the integrity of the self and disclose a certain hollowness at the very seat of agential thought and behavior. As we have seen, eeriness and dread in Kurosawa's films are vectors that move us toward and immerse us in the feel of this ontological situation that we are ultimately urged to accept, given that, like it or not, we cannot dodge or defeat it. In *Before We Vanish*, an alien spellbinds humans from behind and divests them of ingrained concepts ("work," "family," "ownership," "love," and, not least, "self"), leaving them "cured" in some cases and tragicomically rudderless in others. The spectral and hypnotic effects of *Charisma*, *Journey to the Shore*, and *Creepy* perform a similar therapy on a tonal range from delight to dread. The uncanniness we are given to feel doesn't stem primarily from *intra*psychic mechanisms, like those unearthed in Freud's famous argument. We undergo something closer to Dylan Trigg's "phenomenological uncanny," which involves a loosening or even a dissipation of subjectivity as one must—in an atmosphere thick with dread—concede that one's body is *nonpossessable by oneself* and is instead possessed by inscrutable forces from the outside.[79] Kurosawa's work strongly resonates with Trigg's notion of "the radical spectrality of everydayness," wherein "the occult sits side by side with the banal," and the subject opens onto anonymous, "prepersonal" being.[80]

By rendering everydayness uncanny and tapping into a shadowy, ulterior layer of being that precedes the formation of subjectivity, this experience profoundly revises what it means to be "in suspense," as the parlance goes. Plot-level suspense has us wait for a critical turn of events, pointing us toward an uncertain but imminent future. In the gothic traditions Kurosawa reworks, our waiting is menaced by a force of otherness imposed from the outside, something obscure to be dreaded. In Kurosawa's cinema, this sort of suspense still crucially guides our attention, our emotional attachment, but when *atmospheric* suspense enfolds us within the film's liminal states of being, the source of dread is transferred from an event on the horizon to an underlying condition of spectrality and automatism *that seems to have already marked us*. Suspense thus not only augurs a future but unveils, slowly and belatedly, how the dreaded external force has already invaded us from the start, circulating through us, enabling our very relationship to the film's world. After the fact, then, we are pressed to negotiate with, rather than hopelessly resist, the "rise of a ghostly existence" attached to and born partially within ourselves, as in Jean Louis Schefer's at least quasi-gothic notion of the impersonal spectator "irradiated" in the presence of cinema's projected images, a ghostly yet embodied spectator "without qualities" or qualifications whose bent is not to interpret but to abide, anonymously, within a state of radical uncertainty.[81]

Kurosawa's manner of suspense lends itself to a certain nexus of French film theory and philosophy that links Schefer's *The Ordinary Man of Cinema* (1980) to Gilles Deleuze's cinema books and Maurice Blanchot's related ideas of the outside and the "neutral."[82] My adoption of Fisher's notion of the eerie could be given stronger philosophical bearings by bringing in these kindred thinkers of thresholds and limits that unground the subject and confront thought with outsides that escape, neutralize, or stymie phenomenal experience. But I want to conclude this chapter with a brief gloss on a theorist and critic much closer to home for Kurosawa, albeit one whose ideas are deeply inspired by French poststructuralist thought: Shigehiko Hasumi, under whom Kurosawa studied at Rikkyō University in the 1970s.[83]

The suspense described in this chapter is genetically tied to one of the tenets of Hasumi's approach to cinema—namely, that systems of knowledge, including theories of film, are founded upon layers of "stupidity" that they mask and forget, becoming "oblivious to their own lack of ultimate foundations for knowing."[84] Theorists too quickly and self-assuredly take cinema's resources for granted as they go about building epistemic frameworks and honoring protocols of interpretation. For Hasumi, cinema itself vanishes in this process. The only way to preserve a legitimate foothold on cinema is to acknowledge and remember one's "lack of qualifications" before the moving image and to affirm that cinema can be defined only in terms of its basic *incapacities*. For Hasumi, it must be recognized that films cannot in fact carry out some of the technical and expressive functions we ascribe to them. Continuity editing in popular cinema is one example: it falsifies continuous action through what are in fact disjunctive, highly abstract sound-image relationships, devices that Ozu's work openly reveals to be *"unnatural."* Beyond rebuffing any extant theory, Hasumi looks to *avow* "stupidity" as the "groundless ground" upon which we inescapably stand before cinema—before films whose forms and stylistic grammars are "absurd" insofar as they translate impossibilities into accepted conventions.[85] Hasumi's response to this problem is to theorize cinema—and critically investigate individual films—not according to exaggerated capabilities but in open acknowledgment of the medium's elemental "limitations" and "impairments."[86] For the viewer and the critic, this also means renouncing assumed knowledge *and identity*, including the "absurd" fiction of identification with characters and the pretext of mastering a film through a well-trained, discriminating eye. "Indeed," writes Hasumi, "to become buried through this movement in complete anonymity, and to lose one's face, memory, and name, is far more difficult work than to equate oneself with a fictional being, and thus create the illusion of maintaining one's subjectivity."[87]

This embrace of *in*capacities, this plunge into *a*-subjective being, becomes a fascinating affair in Kurosawa's work. We stretch toward this anonymity, this impairment of our habits of knowing, like the plants that surround the tree in *Charisma*. Suspense, in Hitchcock's wake, is routinely conceived as an operation of mastery, a notion that Kurosawa's recourse to hypnosis might seem to uphold. Kurosawa's films, however, for all their careful and adept calibrations, leave suspense *unmastered*. Deframing, as Bonitzer insists in words that complement Hasumi's ideas, flirts with arbitrariness and radically foils even the "directorial gaze" by reveling in "the *sterility* of its point of view." The director's "control-fixation" is held in check amid "a space lacking control."[88] Seen in this light, Kurosawa isn't a Mabuse-like hypnotist in total command of the cinematic machine and its powers, but—nearer to Apichatpong—a trial-and-error conjurer of unknown forces that neutralize mastery.

To be sure, the films investigated in this chapter have shown us that suspense—a durable suspense that doesn't guarantee its own resolution—emerges to fullest effect where our habitual, explanatory resort to masterful design falls short. This book, make no mistake, carefully attends to and celebrates the virtuosic craft of filmmakers who generate suspense through both traditional and unorthodox means. My next and final case study, a work authored mainly by David Lynch, is no exception. But in all the films in question, the sensory event of suspense cannot be stabilized or definitively cleared up by invoking an individual personage—whether a character or a director—as a source and center of meaning.

CHAPTER 6

STREAMING THE UNDEAD ENERGIES OF "FILM"

Any study of suspense in contemporary cinema must eventually reconcile itself with the sweeping technical and cultural changes that have redefined the viewing experience. In light of cinema's digital mutations and migrations in the twenty-first century, it would be wrong to assume that spectatorship and aesthetic forms have not been affected enough to demand a new appraisal of the suspenseful encounter. Without descending into the language of "death," "rupture," or "revolution" that has too frequently characterized debates around the shifts "film" has undergone over the past three decades, one is pressed to concede that neither spectatorship nor the medium, at present, is operationally the same as it was when, say, raptly attentive audiences were ensnared within the seductive narrative and atmospheric clutches of Hitchcock's *Psycho* during its theatrical run in 1960.

Given that home video and digital streaming have surpassed the theatrical situation as the culturally dominant forms of movie watching, shouldn't theories of spectator immersion face up to this fact? How might we reevaluate the phenomenon of suspense in an era where attention is less a given than it once was, where *film* increasingly seems an unfit designation, and where the too shiny, possibly handheld surface on which the "film" materializes is less a screen than a multiuse display on which algorithmic feeds of information may at any point assail the possibly mobile viewer who watches the film in fits and starts, if they make it all the way through, a task that can be assisted by upping the playback speed?[1] Amid this experience (the default fostered by smartphone and computer interfaces), how does suspense, especially of the slow and atmospheric kind, stand a fighting chance?

I address my remarks in this chapter mainly to changes ignited by digital streaming, but it must be recognized that the partly conflictual, partly cooperative aesthetic relationship between large (theatrical) and small (domestic) screens has been a determining factor on the forms and spectatorial dynamics of suspense since the arrival of television in the 1950s, of home-viewing technologies such as the VCR, cable networks, and satellite dishes in the 1970s and 1980s, and then of LaserDiscs and subsequently DVDs in the 1980s and 1990s. A deeper historical survey than the one I offer here would need to probe the interdependencies, cross-pollinations, and attentional differences that Caetlin Benson-Allott, Glen Creeber, John Ellis, and others have expertly charted in relation to these changes.[2] And this deeper history would be wholly relevant to my case study in this chapter in that *Twin Peaks*, already in its earliest version on network TV in 1990, stands out as a hybrid creation, a show that presents its lush 35-millimeter images as "cinematic" in a most alluring sense, addressed to an intently focused gaze, not to the more casual, semidistracted glance of traditional TV viewing.[3]

If these technical and spectatorial circumstances long predate digital streaming, cinema scholars, on average, have been disinclined to factor into their analyses the ways in which one's reading of a film may differ fundamentally depending on the specific technological manner of access. In a recent essay, Julian Hanich argues that "more than ever it is necessary to become dispositive conscious—even *dispositive conscientious*."[4] Film scholars must openly account for how competing *dispositifs* (conditions of engagement) that distinguish theatrical spectatorship from the experience of streaming may elicit different responses. Keying on the theatrical context and its "social affordances," Hanich asserts that "challenging films" (i.e., "modernist art films, slow cinema, avant-garde films") benefit from being viewed with anonymous others in public insofar as the theater space cultivates modes of "*joint deep attention*" or, possibly, "*heightened tranquility*."[5] This emphasis on the phenomenological importance of theatrical film exhibition squares with the reflexive tendency I have identified across multiple slow films studied in this book—a tendency whereby the film rhetorically fuses with or otherwise evokes the theatrical setting and *dispositif*. In the case of Apichatpong's *Memoria* (2021), the meditative film attempts to restrict itself to the theatrical situation exclusively, piracy notwithstanding.[6]

While embracing this call for "dispositive consciousness," in this final chapter I want to consider the dynamics of slow, atmospheric suspense with digital streaming chiefly in mind. I turn to an audiovisual object weirdly suspended between film and television, between popular and art-house proclivities, and between a follow-the-clues procedural crime thriller and a more metaphysical mystery without resolution: David Lynch's *Twin Peaks: The Return* (2017), an eighteen-part limited series for Showtime. Billed as a long-delayed third season of the *Twin Peaks* (1990–1991) series that aired on ABC, *The Return* follows up the Lynch-directed prequel feature film *Twin Peaks: Fire Walk with Me* (1992) as well as the compilation of previously unused material, *Twin Peaks: The Missing Pieces* (2014), which was released on home video. The scrolling credits that conclude each part of *The Return* refer to the undertaking as a "film." Parts 1 and 2 premiered at the Cannes Film Festival, and *Cahiers du Cinéma* later labeled it the best "film" of 2017. The series screened in its entirety at New York's Museum of Modern Art in a showcase of the year's standout "films." Is this culturally ratified designation as "film" just a bid for prestige that separates an auteur's experiment from the dross of formulaic television, or is something more important at stake?[7]

The Return is one of several slow-paced mystery/crime series that have recently flouted boundaries between film and television, relocating the arthouse theater on a digital frontier. To cite just a few, each of which exhibits Lynchian motifs, these series include Jane Campion's *Top of the Lake* (2013, 2017); Bruno Dumont's *Li'l Quinquin* (2014) and its sequel, *Coincoin and the Extra-humans* (2018); and Nicolas Winding Refn's *Too Old to Die Young* (2019). Wading into this digital stream, I want to illustrate how the suspensefulness of *The Return* revolves around the work's liminal, uncertain position in terms of medium. The "film" ruminates on this very matter with multiple senses of "medium" in play. And yet this reflexive theme isn't purely conceptual but also, as I will show, *energetic*, something to be sensed in and through the film's conveyance of atmosphere. If *The Return*'s massive fanbase and many of its scholars have been consumed by the task of decoding signs and symbols,[8] I remain chiefly invested in how things feel—how the sensory world is rhythmically textured as suspense arises little by little.

Of course, this rhythm is what comes under threat with the streaming *dispositif*, much to the dismay of Lynch, who has often taken severe measures to uphold the intended rhythm of his "pictures and sounds flowing together in time and in sequence" on DVD and Blu-ray editions of his films.[9] He forbids chapter breaks on the disc and digital copy. As the sound designer of his films, he also tries to preserve their auditory "power":

> If you're playing the [film's] music on a telephone or on your computer, you will never in a trillion years experience the film. You'll think you have experienced it, but you'll be . . . experiencing weakness, an extreme putrification of a potential experience in another world. So don't let your friends or some television advertisement trick you into accepting weakness. . . . *Power* in that world is critical. Everything has been worked on to be a certain way, and if you don't

have a setup for your films, it's . . . a sickening, horrifying joke, and this world is so troubled, and it's such a sadness that you think you've seen a film on your fucking telephone. Get real.[10]

Lynch's complaints, which date from the theatrical release of his film *Inland Empire* (2006), are not simply about directorial control but about what he sees as the atmospheric magic of cinema when viewers, on being lulled into contact with the film's partly abstract world, are allowed to exercise their "intuition"—spontaneous "feeling and thought together"—in step with the film's progression, without having too much explained for them and without being encouraged to fall back on "common sense."[11] At stake is the integrity of what Lynch calls the "circle" between audience and film, the feedback loop through which spectatorial intuition, he insists, will change the film's resonances each time it is shown.[12]

A decade later, in making *The Return*, Lynch resigned himself to the fact that computer screens would be a principal site of reception—a necessary trade-off for the creative leeway he received from Showtime. Dean Hurley, the sound supervisor and re-recording mixer for *The Return*, recalls that many times during the soundtrack's fine-tuning in Lynch's private, THX-certified sound facility, Lynch lamented that "no one's ever going to *hear* it like this," despite Hurley's assurance that the sonic detail would at least be "there in the DNA" of the final mix, whatever the capabilities of the viewer's home-speaker situation to bring it out.[13] In interviews to promote *The Return* in 2017, Lynch steadfastly holds that the serial "film" should be watched with headphones. Pointing out the musical importance of subtle volume fluctuations and of the entrances and exits of specific timbres, Lynch advises: "People should watch these parts of the film with headphones and get as close to the [computer or smartphone] screen as they can, and then they have a chance of getting into that world."[14]

How might wearing headphones indeed counterweigh the aesthetic world's diminution in the streaming situation? How does headphonic listening affect the "circle," as Lynch construes it, between viewer and screen? Does this option perhaps afford the spectator certain advantages over the theatrical *dispositif*? Studies of film sound have been hesitant to confront this issue. In a rare theorization of headphonic cinema's "intracranial aesthetics," Kyle Stevens elucidates how this way of listening reorients the parameters of frame, space, body, and implied subjectivity. As he explains, "The sound occurs inside the listener, rather than the listener occurring in the space of the sound." We are not immersed in the film's world by means of a resonance chamber for the chest, stomach, feet, and ears. Rather, the film sonically invades *us*, flooding "the resonators and cavities of the skull."[15] I have already argued in this book that sound locates itself in the embodied spectator, but the experiential differences presented by headphones now call for revisions. The conceptions of cinematic ambience I put forward in preceding chapters need to be rethought accordingly.

The Return is "dispositive conscious" insofar as it inscribes and compares different media forms and their systems of address: antiquated and new media, analog and digital media, pictorial and acoustic media, extant and invented science-fictional media. How, as part of this reflexivity regarding media, does the series ruminate on spectatorship in general and, possibly, the headphonic encounter in particular? By investigating these questions alongside Lynch's extraordinary use of atmospheric suspense, I aim to shed light on how and why *The Return* rather demandingly foregrounds *the atmospheric feel of mediation* through relays of force and energy that connect the present to unresolved pasts and uncanny futures. My contention is that streaming this episodic "film" with headphones on a laptop computer is not an unfortunate compromise but an advantageous way to experience what I define as *The Return*'s serial energetics of suspense.[16]

Medium Suspense: *Twin Peaks: The Return*

To prepare ourselves for *The Return*, let us spend a moment with *Twin Peaks: Fire Walk with Me*, which crucially sets the stage for the Showtime revival by way of atmosphere as much as plot. Upon its disastrous theatrical release, *Fire Walk with Me* irritated audiences by deforming and reimagining the original show, with tonal shifts away from quaint, pie-and-coffee charms into convulsive horror and melancholy. While detailing the last days of Laura Palmer (Sheryl Lee), the homecoming queen whose murder attracts an endless FBI investigation in the small Pacific Northwest U.S. town of Twin Peaks, the film's experimentation with atmosphere overrides the plot at several turns and opens onto labyrinthine passages between parallel worlds, teasing the audience with clues and esoteric events that do not quite add up—at least not on a first watch. *Fire Walk with Me* brings to a head the conflict, already there in the ABC series, between two related sources of suspense: (1) the *narrative trail of evidence* that corresponds to murder-mystery and procedural genres and (2) the metaphysical, oneiric, and electric *orchestration of atmosphere* that confounds our sense-making habits.[17] Alluding to the viewer's task of decryption, a droll scene spoofs the very activity of interpretation when FBI regional bureau chief Gordon Cole (David Lynch) shares with an agent classified information about a "Blue Rose" case through a coded pantomime. This symbolic language, which the agent deciphers, protects FBI clearance levels but does nothing to penetrate the infinitely more complicated mysteries toward which it gestures—mysteries that reach far beyond the rational manners of detection applied by the film's stumped law enforcement officers.

When we play the game of suspense that is *Fire Walk with Me*, the decoding of signs and symbols—the translation of events into manageable narrative meaning—isn't enough. Sensation counts in its own right.[18] What antagonistic reviews failed to appreciate and invest in when *Fire Walk with Me* had its theatrical run is that its brazen atmospherics do not simply obfuscate events and create confusion; they offer guidance that the plot alone does not provide. The film tutors us in the skill of atmospheric intuition—partially in stride with Laura's intuitive and risky detective work as she seeks a way out of her horrendous situation at home, where her father, ambiguously possessed by a demonic entity known as BOB (Henry Silva), has been violating her for years.[19] Far from being gratuitous, the formal pyrotechnics of light, color, energy, motion, noise, texture, and montage is what chiefly steers the drama, drives suspense, and puts us on Laura's emotional wavelength, even as she, too, remains opaque.[20] The film's atmosphere reattunes our perception and thereby makes analysis possible amid narrative incoherence.

We are lured into an atmospheric way of connecting motifs and resonances, yet we must acquire this perceptual skill as we go, without having our intuitions confirmed. We receive our first clue along these lines as early as the opening credits. Angelo Badalamenti's slow, somber musical combo of synth strings and a muted trumpet accompanies the titles on an abstract field of blue (a color Lynch limited in the ABC show's décor, where it marks liminal zones between parallel worlds).[21] The camera slowly withdraws, revealing this volatile blue texture to be static on a TV set that is soon destroyed by a shadowy figure wielding an axe. Offscreen, as though behind the audience, a woman screams, "No!" With a cut to black, we hear a dull thump and then silence or, rather, an ominous room tone.

This obscure event (Who are these people? Where is the scene located?) stages a contrast between the square television set and the wider dimensions of Lynch's 1:85:1 film frame. Many have taken the destruction of the TV to indicate Lynch's hostility toward the televisual medium and what the ABC series had become in its second season as it fell off into hackneyed script ideas. More decisively, this reflexive beginning serves as spectator address by playing on our interface with the film screen. The frame-within-the-frame position of the monitor and its blue conduction of energy make us mindful of technological mediation. This entrancing blue static—a motif that becomes entangled with supernatural forces and passageways—seems to bear on the assault we do not quite witness. In time, we will discover that this opening insinuates the murder of Teresa Banks (Pamela Gidley)—an uncanny precursor for Laura—at the hands of Laura's father, Leland (Ray Wise), but the feeling, the mood, conveyed by this blue static matters no less.

The ABC series already builds an atmospheric web that entwines the town, the forest, the lumber industry, hydraulic power, the weather, traffic signals, electricity, fire, automobiles, gas stations, a ceiling fan, Indigenous American mythology (invented for the series), and the Black Lodge, an alternate dimension with red-velvet curtains, vertiginous chevron floors, and ghostly figures whose designs on humanity are unclear.[22] *Fire Walk with Me* expands this web in part through relays of blue, the color of flames at peak intensity. The blue TV static resonates with blue vehicles, Teresa Banks's blue eyes, the blue carpet at the FBI's Philadelphia headquarters, and a blue dumpster in the Double R Diner parking lot, where Laura is greeted by envoys from the Black Lodge. The emphatic hum of electricity through utility cables connects many of the film's spaces, with the Fat Trout Trailer Park figuring as a hub of sorts where energy currents crisscross and portals open between worlds. To reassert my notion (sketched in chapter 1) of the endogenous role of style in cinematic atmosphere, *the style of the film is part of this elaborate network of mediation*. Editing transitions, camera movements, and auditory drones are made to feel like conductive operations *within the diegesis*, like fluid waves of atmospheric connectivity relayed from space to space. Tracking shots at the trailer park embody less a point of view, be it authorial or characterological, than a secretive vector of force. When the film dissolves from the park to the flowing of Wind River, we catch the wave as squelchy noise on the soundtrack blends with wind sounds. Michel Chion nicely captures this effect, at once fluid and turbulent, in noting how the film's sonic design "creates a sense of the screen as a fragile membrane with a multitude of currents pressing on it from behind."[23]

Aesthetic discourse tends to define *medium* as "means" of expression, but the term can also be construed as "mediator" and "middle." It refers not just to an object before us but to the mediational process and environment in which we are immersed perceptually.[24] *Fire Walk with Me* affords us the immersive feeling that its spaces are traversed and linked by eerie agential powers. To borrow from Maurice Merleau-Ponty, we feel that "the perceptual 'something' is *always in the middle of something else*, it always forms part of a 'field.'"[25] Any component of the mise-en-scène, any formal gesture on which our attention falls, is implicitly plugged into a complex and indefinitely developing network of mediation, everywhere charged with suspense. What I describe here is not precisely the same thing as traditional plot suspense that turns on a present event anticipating a later, deferred event. In *Fire Walk with Me*, plot-based suspense is eclipsed by atmospheric suspense that is more cosmic in its stress on our slow acclimation to a strangely bifurcated world claimed at all points by insoluble energies of interrelation—energies that ripple outward from Laura Palmer's tragedy to touch on larger historical, ideological, and technological concerns (more on this to come).

This fiery play of mediation is amplified when the film is experienced headphonically. In fact, when we encounter the film that way, we are an "ideal auditor," to use a term Trace Reddell employs in reference to the headphonic spectator of George Lucas's *THX 1138* (1971), who can't evade the science-fictional atmosphere of mind control.[26] With *Fire Walk with Me*, the advantage of experiencing the film with headphones is twofold, in part psychological and in part physical. It reinforces our alignment with Laura's point of view, given that her uncanny and oneiric perceptions more directly lodge themselves "in our head" as well. Consider the nightmarish scene in which BOB's voice speaks to Laura through the atmospheric medium of the ceiling fan in the Palmer household: "I want to taste through your mouth." For the headphonic viewer, the impression of mental and corporeal invasion is even more intense. The sonic waves and vectors of force, instead of affecting our whole bodies by stirring the molecules of air around us in a theater, pipe into the "frame of the skull," as Stevens would put it.[27] Even if the headphonic viewer experiences *Fire Walk with Me* and *The Return* at a typical volume, its murmurs, whooshes, and faint audibility, including room tones and silences, are more prominent—and *closer*. The screen's membrane is more permeable, not because we move *into* a world, but because that world and its "fire" inhabit us.

The Return multiplies yet again the nodes and circuitries of the *Twin Peaks* cosmos, with added locations, characters, conspiratorial liaisons, and otherworldly domains. By turns ominous, funny, solemn, absurd, and contemplative, the series quirkily delays the convergence of its plot lines: the Twin Peaks Sheriff Department's inquiry into new clues regarding the Palmer case; a homicide in Buckhorn, South Dakota; another homicide at a loft in Manhattan where a curious observation room has been installed; an insurance scam in Nevada; and a struggle between different versions of the FBI agent Dale Cooper (all Kyle MacLachlan) that arises when the "bad" one, who has been infested by BOB, refuses an order to go back into the Black Lodge and tries to substitute in his place there yet another Cooper of his creation, insurance agent Dougie Jones. I will soon take up how multilayered suspense accumulates as the series moves toward the pivotal part 8, where the eruption of an atomic bomb accompanies a kind of origin narrative for the *Twin Peaks* universe. But first it must be observed that suspense attends the status of film as medium in this made-for-streaming, shot-on-digital revival.

As Greg Hainge has pointed out in his incisive accounts of Lynch's work, the flickering light and electricity for which the director is known are not just an eccentric authorial signature. The play of luminosity enfolds, implicates, and makes into an "attraction" the film apparatus—the basic elements of cinematic spectacle and "trickery." This reflexive impulse extends to theater curtains and stage acts within the presented world, such as the immortal "no hay banda!" sequence at Club Silencio in *Mulholland Drive* (2001), with its pulsing blue light, smoke, immaterial performers, and "live" sounds that turn out to be a tape recording. Hainge traces this recurring motif to the red draperies of the Black Lodge—"a sign of exhibition" that, like movie theater curtains, "both promises and delays cinematic spectacle." He carefully adds that Lynch's mise-en-scène channels the architectural specificities of old, "pre-multiplex" movie palaces, when the ornately designed lobby, stairways, bathrooms, and exterior were atmospheric supports for the film's attractions.[28]

Part 1 of *The Return*, after the opening titles in which red curtains from the Black Lodge appear (it as if we fall through them into a churning portal), introduces a new site that will later be revealed (across parts 8, 14, and 17) to have overt links to cinema architecture and spectacle. Shown in black-and-white, this space is the home of a tall, elderly man in a tuxedo: a character listed as "???????" (Carel Struycken) in the end credits until part 14, where he names himself "The Fireman." In a lounge that fuses Art Deco, industrial, and science-fictional mise-en-scène, this character instructs Agent Cooper, who is seated nearby, to "listen to the sounds." The man then repeatedly plays a twitchy sound from a gramophone (although this sonic texture doesn't match up with the hiss of a gramophone recording). The man then cryptically says to Cooper, "It is in our house now." He also advises to remember "430" as well as the names "Richard" and "Linda," "two birds with one stone." Addressing the viewer as much as Cooper, the scene primes our aural attention while also alluding to a logic of doubles (Richard and Linda will prove to be multiversal renditions of key characters) and instigating a game of numerical suspense that runs through the series, tempting us with the possible importance of geographical coordinates, motel rooms, phone numbers, addresses, mileage, security codes, dates, and so on.[29] In time, 430 will take on meaning in that the individual numbers in it add up to 7, which resonates with the Lucky 7 Insurance office in Las Vegas, where Dougie Jones is employed. But the sensorial counts in this numbers game, too. The twitch from the gramophone plays seven times, and the tall man's name in the credits comprises seven question marks.[30]

For the headphonic listener who streams the series at home, this early moment of implied spectator address is even more powerful and mysterious. The advice to listen closely relates not just to the noise from the gramophone horn (which, in a surreal twist, resembles an ear canal as the camera tracks toward it)[31] but also to the low drone that imbues the lounge. Layered in with this room tone is an aqueous sound that announces a purple sea outside (to be visually revealed in a later part), an easily lost atmospheric clue that strikes the headphonic listener with greater detail and closeness. The rest of part 1 then sustains suspense by testing our sonic memory and teasing us with noises that slightly recall the gramophone twitch: trees rustling and snapping in the wind, a box cutter opening a shipment of shovels, and the jittering of a computer fingerprint database used by Buckhorn detectives to run a search. The twitch has possible doubles, too, and this game of attention goes beyond the buildup of plot to hint at the importance of sensorial links within and across an interdimensional cosmos.[32]

Moreover, when the tall man states, "It is in our house now," suggesting that the noise he has played has intrusively installed itself, this line takes on added importance for the headphonic encounter. The sound is in our home *and head* now. There is no longer a central speaker behind or underneath the screen to render it sonically emanative, no longer a surround mix (it has been squeezed into two channels),[33] and no longer the spatial separation that most theories of media since Aristotle deem necessary for transmission to happen. Although the characters' gazes still orient us to the gramophone as the source of the noise, the twitch seems to well up from within *our own* bodies: there is a peculiar sense in which the film routes itself through our thoughts and perceptions *from the inside out*, by means of a sonic mediational force for which the screen is a more secondary attachment.

Suspensefully disclosed bit by bit, this space, where The Fireman is joined by a celestial colleague, Señorita Dido (Joy Nash), turns out to be *a film theater*, the design of which conflates computer-generated visuals with architecture reminiscent of movie palaces of the 1920s (fig. 6.1). The actual site used for the auditorium, where The Fireman and Dido interact with lambent images on a screen and perform wonderous rituals to combat sinister forces on Earth, is the Tower Theater in Los Angeles—the same location used for Club Silencio in *Mulholland Drive* (a scene already interwoven with the *Twin Peaks* cosmos through two young women shown in the audience at the club who double not only for *Mulholland Drive*'s two main female characters but also for Laura Palmer and fellow victim Ronette Pulaski). The Tower was downtown LA's first wired-for-sound movie palace, and its French Renaissance interior, modeled on the Paris Opera House, melds cinematic and stage architecture, with a side box on each side of the proscenium.[34] If Lynch's reuse of this space in *The Return* is a citation within his own body of work, and if it pays tribute to the golden age of an exhibition context from which his streaming audience is removed, the place of "film" in this configuration isn't so transparently nostalgic. In the auditorium—which is less a movie theater than an uncanny monitoring station—there are no seats, let alone spectators. There is a spotlight affixed to the back wall, yet no projector beam, despite the flickering nature of the images. The projector is surreally replaced by an overhead contraption of rotating golden pipes and sprockets that look like repurposed components from jazz instruments, clocks, and the gearbox of an engine. The Fireman and Dido somehow pause the image, which a film projection would allow only at the risk of the strip's immolation. Their act of scrutiny is much closer to the actions of a "possessive spectator" in the home-video situation.[35]

The remarkably slow-paced events in this space transform cinema's traditional theatrical apparatus. "Film," as technology, as experience, becomes a matter of suspense as its capabilities flutter between the familiar and the alien, between the anachronistic and the futural. It manifests through intermedial

Figure 6.1 The Fireman and Señorita Dido operate as mystical spectators/creators in their theater in *Twin Peaks: The Return*.

crossings with theater and architecture *as well as through affiliations with electrical devices beyond the auditorium,* from lamps (nodal objects in Lynch's labyrinths that are usually coupled with telephones) to massive, bell-shaped appliances that seem to transfer signals between worlds.[36] At The Fireman's discretion, the windows in the building may serve as screens onto which images from *The Return* that we have already seen resurface. In part 14, after Deputy Andy (Harry Goaz) is transported to the lobby from the forest outside Twin Peaks, The Fireman shows him a murmuring montage of occurrences from

Streaming the Undead Energies of "Film" 197

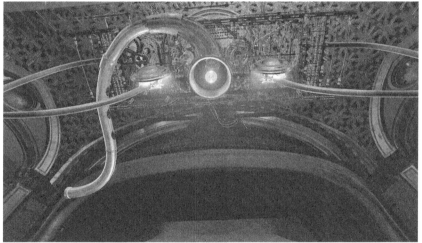

Figure 6.1 (Continued)

earlier parts in the series, including the atomic blast in part 8 and a reminder, for us as much as for Andy, to notice utility cables. This associative montage, which also conjures an event from the future, *streams* on the surface of a circular skylight window above Andy's head through the mechanism of a smoking handheld antenna. This embedded scene of spectatorship is suspenseful in many senses at once. While it tasks us with intuiting relations among disparate clues, it veils in mystery the technical device that powers and displays this stream. Its impact on Andy, our entranced proxy, is unclear at this point,

Figure 6.2 From Andy "streaming" media at The Fireman's lair (*top*) to the Manhattan observation room (*bottom*), enactments of spectatorship abound in *Twin Peaks: The Return*.

though he seems to receive guidance apropos a future crisis. This reflexive scene, in turn, defines as enigmatic our own streaming interface with the small screen (fig. 6.2).

As part of its self-conscious, imaginative, and consistently weird invocations of different media, *The Return* configures "film" as a mobile, *ubiquitous* medium that is neither reducible to celluloid nor confined to a certain architectural arrangement of spectacle and audience adopted from theater.[37] Reflexive inscriptions of media engagement crop up throughout the series, most blatantly in the Manhattan observation room with its glass box that implies a television screen from which spectral bodies may lunge out and attack those who watch.[38] Headphonic spectatorship is reflected in Lynch's reprised performance as FBI chief Gordon Cole, who wears a hearing aid (previously corded, now Bluetooth) that he adjusts with a remote attached to his suit. At some level, his scenes hark back to The Fireman's guidance by reminding us to listen more attentively. And the headphonic viewer who streams *The Return*, when made to alter the taskbar volume as the series fluctuates—sometimes rather joltingly—between extremes of soft and loud, may well find themselves mirroring his prosthetic hypersensitivity. In another parallel with the spectator in headphones, Cole to some extent models for us an intuitive process of detection that is enhanced by his listening device. He is especially tuned into odd stirrings in the atmosphere around spatial thresholds, from his hotel room's doorway to a ramshackle house in Buckhorn, where a whirling and buzzing portal opens in the sky near utility cables yet comically goes unnoticed by all except Cole and the spectator (fig. 6.3).

In *The Return*, the septuagenarian Lynch-as-Cole figure bears certain similarities to Jean-Luc Godard's ludic performances as versions of himself in his late undertakings: though played for laughs on many occasions, these aging directors' onscreen roles embody an alchemical and inquisitive relation to their medium as well as to their imagined viewer.[39] Cole nowhere overtly engages in filmmaker-like activity, but the blinking electronic surveillance equipment with which he is associated strangely stands in for cinematic production gear. *The*

Figure 6.3 Gordon Cole figures as a headphonic listener in *Twin Peaks: The Return*.

Return, moreover, bristles with autoretrospective allusions to Lynch's non–*Twin Peaks* body of work, the key motifs and conundrums of which absorb and reshape the *Twin Peaks* cosmos. Dougie, for instance, appears in shots that directly echo scenes with the timid and awkward protagonist Henry (Jack Nance) in *Eraserhead* (1977), which implies that all the story worlds across Lynch's corpus stand in parallel to one another, not just artistically or thematically but cosmically. To return to Cole's relationship to the ubiquity of "film," electrical sockets, lightning, and the mushroom cloud of a nuclear blast, a large photograph of which adorns the wall behind Cole's bureau desk, are also associated with Lynch's presence in *The Return*. Across *The Return*'s reflexive coalescences of media, "film" is enlaced with gadgetries and powers of transmission that aren't on the surface part of cinematic technology. "Film," including its aesthetic and technical processes, shares an expansive energy grid that is constantly in effect and whose pathways are always ahead of our comprehension. The shifting, multiplying bodies that are routed through this never-quite-mappable circuitry suggest ramifications for the embodied spectator. As we will eventually see, this Lynchian sense of film brings us back around to and asks us to expand our suspense-based conception of the ambiences into which we are drawn.

Transitions, Transductions: *Twin Peaks: The Return*

From my account, *The Return* might seem to be ablaze with overbearing, electrodynamic sensation at every turn, but, on the contrary, the bulk of the series is slow and sparse, its opening and "ending" parts in particular.[40] The widespread, interdimensional energy grid I have noted is *implicitly* operative at all times, yet it moves in and out of our direct perception, surging forth in pyrotechnic bouts and then receding into obscurity, into a metaphysical out of frame that spans, albeit disjunctively, The Fireman's realm and the Black Lodge (where The Arm, a tree-shaped spirit who sparkles with electricity, resides). Transitions from scene to scene sometimes faintly reinstate this energy motif (e.g., the power lines on display in establishing shots for Buckhorn), and abstract cutaways sometimes make this motif conspicuous (e.g., the recurring, spasmodic image of utility wires crackling with electricity at night). Still other transitions and patterns of intercutting involve camera movement, through the air or around physical thresholds, not as a syntactical procedure for maintaining narrative continuity so much as an eerie *inscription and enactment of nonhuman forces* that are astir within the diegesis.[41] At times, these mobile shots—above Ghostwood National Forest or on a vacant road lit by headlights—turn out to be the vantage of a character whose identity is temporarily suppressed, though in other cases the shot is spectral and attributed to no one, less a perspective than an *ingress and tracing of force*. Combined with camera movements, superimpositions occasionally disclose that a scene shares the space–time of another setting. In part 15, a tracking shot that follows "bad" Cooper (a.k.a. Mr. C) as he passes from a secluded 1940s-looking convenience store into a dark maze of corridors is superimposed with another ominous tracking shot through a nocturnal forest as a whooshing wind seems to occupy and mediate both locations. Elsewhere, superimposed images float between oneiric and hallucinatory registers. Comparable to Apichatpong's *Cemetery of Splendor* (2015), this suspenseful stratification of worlds, histories, and subjectivities in *The Return* entails the possibility of dream sharing.[42]

While offering atmospheric clues, Lynch delights in long delays. All the series' games of suspense entail elaborate deferrals as the spectator waits and waits, mostly in vain, for the series to make good on its title's seeming promise to reestablish the *Twin Peaks* we know. When, if ever, will the Agent Cooper we recall from the original ABC show (charismatic man of action and intellect) reemerge from his duplicated, "tulpa" version of himself as the insurance agent Dougie Jones (laconic, childlike, imitative of others, less an agent than a vessel through which outside forces exert themselves)? In addition to delaying the routines of work and middle-class family life and to stalling the momentum of plot, the lags that Dougie unwittingly imposes have the suspenseful effect of miraculous events. Take part 6, where Dougie sits at his kitchen table with case files he has brought home from the agency, an assignment from his boss. Thus far, he has seemed radically unsuited for work of any kind, a reality others have been reluctant to notice in a thread of absurdist comedy. He reaches for a folder labeled "Lucky 7 Insurance," its surface glowing in amber light from a plastic lamp offscreen, the table's centerpiece. When his finger caresses the Lucky 7 insignia, we are transferred, with wind and electrical sputtering, to a traffic light just as it changes from green to yellow to red against a pitch-dark sky.[43] This event of atmospheric enmeshment then cues an intervention: Mike (Al Strobel), a one-armed emissary from the Black Lodge who vies against BOB as well as "bad" Cooper, appears before Dougie by way of a superimposition. Fading into Dougie's living room in front of the *fireplace* (a feature of décor associated with energy, power, mediation), Mike urges, "You have to wake up. Don't die!" He then waves an invisible force into the scene. A whooshing sound morphs into ethereal synth music (Johnny Jewell's "Windswept") as something rather odd and moving happens: Dougie, in a half-conscious trance of intuition, works his way through the case files. His palm-held pencil is guided by shiny digital graphics that materialize, and he scribbles on the documents a series of stairs, ladders, and lines. Later, along with his boss, we will learn these markings are a code that identifies fraud committed by his colleague in cahoots with police detectives—but MacLachlan's nonverbal performance already hints at this finding (fig. 6.4).

Figure 6.4 At Mike's urging from the Black Lodge, Dougie investigates his case files in *Twin Peaks: The Return*.

Beyond its suspense of plot and character, this slow, dilated scene is part of an *energetics* of suspense that here operates in the main through warm color temperatures: yellow, amber, and golden tones vibrantly coordinate the manila file folders, the plastic lamp, Dougie's pencil, the twinkling digital graphics that direct him, the yellow traffic light, and the yellow dinner plates and telephone shown earlier in the scene when Dougie's wife, Janey-E (Naomi Watts), pleads with him to knuckle down for the sake of their family.[44] This chromatic ensemble reverberates beyond the scene by evoking details on display elsewhere in the series, from Dr. Amp's (Russ Tamblyn) motivational, gold-spraypainted shovels ("Shovel your way out of the shit!") to the golden seeds that manufacture tulpas in the Black Lodge and through to the yellow boxing poster behind the desk of Dougie's boss, the former prizefighter Bushnell Mullins (Don Murray), who is paralleled with Agent Cooper's boss, Gordon Cole. Not least, the amber lamp in the middle of Dougie's table, which prominently hugs the edges of the frame throughout the scene, bears the shape of a mushroom, anticipating both the atomic cloud and the screen-filling amber lava into which we are hurled in part 8. The gold pipes in The Fireman's theater and the swirling cosmic dust he secretes from his levitating body in the same part also figure among these color-driven correspondences that reinstate the valence of the New Latin word *electricus*: literally meaning "of amber" in reference to the electrostatic properties of fossilized tree resin.[45] Further, this color-and-energy motif prefigures Agent Cooper's release from Dougie when in part 15 Dougie inquiringly pokes a fork into the kitchen's wall socket.

As with the Kiyoshi Kurosawa films we studied in the preceding chapter, *resonance* of an enveloping, atmospheric kind overtakes meaning. *The Return* acclimates us to webs and powers of interrelation, inscribing at the crux of each shot an increasingly eerie tensile pressure between any inside (be it a physical or mental space) and the gradually multiplying outsides, the reticular elsewheres, that tie in with and potentially shape the inside. Because of repeated colors, textures, sounds, and technical devices, we not only are made attentive to possible threads of intersection that explain the narrative but also pick up on and attempt to track carrier waves of mediational influence. The ambient feel of the film's world is paramount beyond offering us a theme to be interpreted hermeneutically. This ambience streams partially through us, not just in front of us (an effect of immersion all the more heightened when the series is engaged with headphonically). Further like Kurosawa's work, suspense in *The Return* crosses a variety of dramatic moods from wonder and humor to sadness and dread.[46]

Suspense, in this example, is not only about the nextness of narrative action but about the *moreness* of atmosphere—how and why it ongoingly collects and relays energies in the manner that it does. In *The Return*'s images and sounds, there is always a reserve of energetic potential that gestures beyond the delineation of a given place or event. At the Great Northern Hotel in Twin Peaks, a ringing ethereal tone refuses to be located when Ben (Richard Beymer) and his assistant, Beverly (Ashley Judd), search for its source. Initially associated with an amber lamp, Indigenous art, Cooper's returned room key from twenty-five years earlier, *and the very camera movements that underscore these relations*, this aeolian sound, like The Fireman's gramophone twitch, repeats across disparate scenes, assuming new inflections as it points to a larger energy grid and forecasts uncertain futures. This tone will eventually join in the electric stimuli that at last reawaken Cooper in part 16. Energy breeds energy along obscure, transversal pathways that atmospherically signal interrelations.[47]

This is not to argue, however, that this energetics of suspense, so long as we recognize its contours, adds up to a stable system of organization within which clarity replaces confusion. *The Return* baits us into believing, falsely, that if we can just figure out the geometry of connections between worlds, decrypt symbolism, parse a logic of doubles, infer whose dream consciousness certain events are filtered through, and, perhaps, apply information from series coscreenwriter Mark Frost's ancillary novels that supply a "secret history" of Twin Peaks, then we may gain a complete picture of what unfolds.[48] The critic faces a similar temptation to subject the series to an outside explanatory framework—another "narrative" that the audiovisual play of ideas must be made to illustrate with as little friction as possible.[49] In Lynch studies, critics have shrewdly turned to psychoanalysis, phenomenology, affect theory, quantum mechanics, Vedic mysticism (in connection with Lynch's transcendental meditation platform), and many other lenses.[50] But suspense, especially the atmospheric kind, tends to be quashed when the external discourse or approach is leaned on too heavily—when a commentator stages the riddance of uncertainty by handling the film as a text that inevitably translates the concepts of another text to which it is made an accessory. How, then, might a critical response leave intact *The Return*'s energetics of suspense and uphold its atmospheric primacy?

This problem can be negotiated by attending to how *The Return*'s articulation of suspense is *transductive* in its relays of energy. I borrow this term from Gilbert Simondon's philosophy of technology, but I want to show how its meaning is immanent to the atmospheric workings of Lynch's series. The term derives from engineering, where it names the transfer of energy from one form to another, typically as an electrical signal via a transducer.[51] Broadly and inventively deploying the concept across a range of fields from physics, biology, and the social sciences to technics and the arts, Simondon describes transduction as the process through which energetic potential is actualized, moving from phase to phase in a particular domain beset with tensions and disparities. It mobilizes the formation of material beings and objects that are not fixed but vectored into so many further energetic transmutations: any given something is incrementally becoming something else through its emerging and shifting relations to the milieu in which it structurally propagates. Beginning with a basic example, Simondon follows the growth of a crystal from a seed to its physical maturation in contact with the world, each strata laying the structural bases for the next while still carrying and reprocessing the germinal seed. Energy, without discharging all its potentials at once, courses through this operation of "form-taking," as a modulatory force that carries out the fusion of matter and form.[52]

Aside from the felicitous fact that electricity assumes a key place throughout Simondon's examples, this concept of transduction accords with *The Return*'s atmospheric suspense in three crucial respects. First, transduction is tied to what Simondon calls a "metastable" system in the language of thermodynamics: a provisional state of equilibrium that, with a little bit of pressure (exerted either from the inside or from the outside), undergoes new, possibly radical "phase-shifts." In other words, metastability implies and is a catalyst for transductive operations that reopen the system in question onto indefinite paths of becoming.[53] At odds with fixed notions of being and identity, the system is revealed to be "heterogeneous to itself," as Paulo De Assis puts it, not just "capable of" but "necessarily obliged to expand *out of itself*."[54] What makes *The Return* ultimately resistant to the decoding of symbols and to some total mapping of its thematic and topographical parameters is precisely the *metastable* condition of its energetic system of world formation, of being a world in the process of slowly expanding into other worlds, not simply adding realms relative to a fixed, authentic version of itself against which its uncanny reproductions and imposters are measured.

The more *The Return* advances and inflates, the more it becomes eerily and confusingly metamorphic, not quite the continuance of "itself." In parts 17 and 18, after Agent Cooper at last reemerges from Dougie and with the help of Twin Peaks residents at least temporarily defeats his doppelgänger, he moves via transduction between different worlds, what appear to be parallel realities, crossing thresholds marked by fits of electricity that make the image and the bodies it displays quake and fracture (fig. 6.5). We infer *this* Cooper's goal is to track down an alternate version of Laura Palmer—Carrie Page (Sheryl Lee), a diner employee living in Odessa, Texas—and return her to the Palmer household in Twin Peaks, having somehow effaced the horror of Laura's past, including her murder. Yet each transduction leads to radical suspense across the levels of character, world, and temporality. Spaces and identities lose consistency and become "dephased" and diffracted—albeit with eerie degrees of sameness that stem from a continuing yet modulated germ. Cooper is in part himself but also in part "Richard," who, we detect, still harbors residues of the sinister BOB. Diane (Laura Dern), his work partner with whom he was onetime romantically involved—until he, as "Richard," raped her in a motel room—is at once herself and "Linda," the other name The Fireman advised us to remember at the series' outset. Falling in line with this mingling of sameness and difference, Carrie both is and isn't Laura. The Palmers never resided at the household where Cooper/Richard takes Carrie—and yet they did. The atmosphere that conveys these effects of metastability is eerily low key. The whooshing wind and electricity have passed into quiet aural ambiences that set attention on edge, to the point where even the mundane shutting of a car door inflames our

Figure 6.5 Beneath humming electrical towers, Agent Cooper scouts a transductive portal in *Twin Peaks: The Return*.

apprehension. Amid the slowed pacing, words are scarce, and music is almost wholly absent. As we feel *The Return* shift phase, there is no Christopher Nolan–style explanation through dialogue of this world's rules and possibilities in terms of time, space, subjectivity, and perception. With a suddenly bewildered Cooper/Richard's question ("What year is this?") and Carrie/Laura's shriek that becomes absorbed into a black screen, the suspense strands us before a world caught up in an ambiguous series of mutations.

Second, Simondon maintains that the transductions unleashed by a metastable system do not simply construct "links" between already-constituted terms, whose existence and stability are guaranteed by some invariant ontology, or set of principles, that we just take for granted. Rather, transductions create emergent "relations" that *constitute anew the very aspects encompassed by the relations*, returning them to process and making them party to unpredictable phase shifts.[55] *The Return* gives form to this mode of transductivity, using it as a key source of suspense. Each of Cooper's portal crossings destabilizes and reorients the bearings by which we might follow and reason out his crusade relative to where he starts. As I have already begun to explain, it isn't that the *Twin Peaks* cosmos keeps "doubling" itself within a system of parallels and complementary structures that work in terms of originals versus copies or simple variations on a preset pattern. Instead, with each building-out of the world, transductions *change each previously established reference point*, each prior iteration of place and identity, all the way down. Each transductive leap forges new relations that remake origins and futures, a principle of metamorphosis that Lynch started with *Fire Walk with Me*. Scenes from the prequel as well as from the ABC series pilot are sampled (that is, transduced) in *The Return* under the pretext of undoing Laura's past for the better. Our aged, post–Dougie Cooper is spliced into a forest sequence from the evening of young Laura's murder, where he attempts a kind of Orphic rescue, but this temporal loop is ruptured when an eerie sound occasions a phase shift, *a sound we have been trained to recognize*: the gramophone twitch from The Fireman's sitting room. In *The Return*, which lays waste to nostalgia, the act of returning home, to a place that one knows, is an uncanny, not-quite-doable project. Metastability is such that any template of familiarity, any preestablished basis for one's knowledge of self and world, is charged with unsuspected pasts and futures, with vectors of what Alanna Thain calls "anotherness."[56]

There is still a third sense in which Simondon's concept of transduction lends itself to an understanding of atmospheric suspense in *The Return*. He assigns transduction a dual definition by extending it from a process one observes to *the very method by which one accompanies and describes this process*. (The forming of a thought, after all, is a phased process that grows from a germ outward.) As Simondon has it, transduction "is a mental procedure, and even much more than a procedure, it is the mind's way of discovering"—a mode that "consists in *following the being in its genesis*, in accomplishing the genesis of thought at the same time as the genesis of the object is accomplished." By "mental," Simondon doesn't mean the rational activity of a Kantian subject gaining or falling back on existing knowledge. Though transduction does involve problem solving, it differs from both deductive and inductive reasoning. Deduction "go[es] elsewhere to seek a principle to resolve the problem of a domain," trafficking in generalities; induction, even as it immerses itself in specifics of the domain, looks for common features at the expense of singularities that are absolutely elemental but resist being integrated into the terms of logic. By contrast, transduction is less reason based. It names a procedure of "intuition" that descriptively enters into and becomes "contemporary with" the process studied. Rather than falling back onto ontological givens, this more speculative work describes the *ontogenetic* dynamics of being for the purpose not of knowing but of thinking in a manner that is "analogical" to the process at hand.[57] Reflecting on this aspect of transduction in another work, Simondon, in reference to E. T. A. Hoffman's tale "The Mines of Falun," cites a miner who intuitively assumes a "co-natural relation with underground nature." Simondon also finds intuitive couplings—examples of dual transduction—in relational interfaces between humans and a wide array of technical objects, including cinema. For Simondon, writing in the 1950s, even as a film and its audience cannot be simultaneous to each other due to the pastness of the scenes projected, there remains a parallel, albeit nonidentical relationship between "human memory" and the capture/storage capabilities of the photochemical film stock.[58]

This mental part of transduction has resonances with Lynch's own espousal of "intuition" when he discusses his films. By way of intuition, "feeling and thought together" in rhythmic copresence with the onscreen world (a mediated immediacy), we become tuned into the electrical and ontogenetic conditions of Lynchian suspense—though I hesitate to call them "Lynchian" if only because *The Return*'s assumptions of form and lively phase changes are given to feel *self-generated*—that is, powered more by their own embryonic extensions and capricious swerves of atoms than by a creator standing outside the series, notwithstanding Lynch's incredibly robust authorial imprint and diegetic performance as Gordon Cole.[59] Inductive and deductive logics are also necessary—both for us and for the characters—but transduction, insofar as we accede to this mode of discovery, becomes our best compass when those other interpretive protocols fail, when the series' metastability outstrips our capacity to connect dots, when remainders of noise and contradiction keep us from resolving suspense by thinking, for instance, that the series is all just Agent Cooper's guilt-inflected dream—a psychologistic view that *The Return* invites so that this interpretation can be confounded with equal, if not greater, force.[60]

In *The Return*, some characters perform intuition for us and with us to varying degrees of success and spectator surrogacy: each version of Cooper, Dougie included, and especially, in the series' early parts, Deputy Chief Hawk (Michael Horse) in telephonic collaboration with a dying Margaret (Catherine E. Coulson) and her oracular wooden log. Somewhat akin to Laura's role as intercessor in *Fire Walk with Me*, these characters have a hand in guiding us, training us, as their suspenseful situations coincide with ours. But dual transduction runs deeper than this rhetoric of stand-ins. The series' corporeal transductions—its spectacular, identity-diffracting exchanges of bodies through surreal portals between worlds—have a bearing on our spectatorial involvement, speaking as they do to our own relationship to the diegesis as we find ourselves plugged into and implicated by the series' ever-expanding energy grid. This effect is nowhere more salient than in part 8, to which I now turn, while circling back around to the technical and experiential factors of suspense that opened this chapter.

The Tentacles of Ambience: *Twin Peaks: The Return*

A quarter of the way through part 8—following a segment in which "bad" Cooper is shot and left for dead by a gangster associate, only to be resurrected by a swarm of woodsmen whose aura of electrical energy somehow conspires with a subsequent Nine Inch Nails musical performance at the Twin Peaks roadhouse—*The Return* flashes back to an actual event. We are given to witness the Trinity Test, the U.S. Army's initial atmospheric testing of a nuclear device, which, as *The Return*'s documentary-like text onscreen states, took place in White Sands, New Mexico, on July 16, 1945, at 5:29 a.m., Mountain War Time. However, this unanticipated turn to history, though it is signaled with black-and-white cinematography and a time stamp, isn't exactly a flashback. It seems more to coincide with the twenty-first-century present in which the narrative action of *The Return* mostly transpires.

As a countdown ensues (for the launch of this sequence in part 8 as much as for the test detonation), the camera is almost imperceptibly called into motion. The blast then draws this forward movement into the billowing mushroom cloud's peak. What follows—surely the most radical aesthetic experiment to air on Showtime—is the phased dis/continuation of this camera movement through a series of portals: abstract and vorticular forms that make differences of scale as well as divisions of interior and exterior impossible to discern. Mingling arrant digital graphics with evocations of analog film (critics have cited strong resemblances to avant-garde films by Stan Brakhage and Bruce Conner of the 1960s),[61] this "camera movement" is synthetic in that there is no camera present for much of this digitally rendered progression. Accompanied by shrill strings (Krzysztof Penderecki's harrowing *Threnody for the Victims of Hiroshima* [1961]), this phantom ride carries us along a shifting z axis into and through the back of each image. We travel from the cloud to a convenience store of the 1940s with twin gas pumps (a place that, following the explosion, becomes a woodsmen-patrolled gate to the Black Lodge) (fig. 6.6). After a pause, this progression restarts, bursting through the membrane of a fire-produced gold seed and then soaring across the purple sea to The Fireman's fortress. This segment, as many have noted, recalls the immersive stargate sequence in Stanley Kubrick's *2001: A Space Odyssey* (1968). The push through the pitch-dark, rectangular fortress window plays on *2001*'s tracking shot into and through the alien monolith.[62] Yet there is a core difference: in *2001* we have an escort, an astronaut whose point of view mediates our expedition, whereas in *The Return* there is no character, no human perspective, through which our suspense is shared and channeled. The sensory address to the viewer is without a filter, much in the vein of the "cinema of attractions" as famously formulated by Tom Gunning.[63]

When experienced in a theater, this segment of *The Return*, not unlike *2001*'s psychedelic excursion, overwhelms us with aggressive sensations that partake of an aesthetics of the sublime. When watched headphonically and streamed on a more compact screen, however, the experience changes. As the scale of the image reduces and the soundtrack, losing its full-body impact, goes directly into our heads without the medium of air in an acoustic space, we are differently swept up and vehicularized by this phased movement from the blast to The Fireman's lounge. Lynch's intent (much like Kubrick's) is to locate the sensory "power" of the spectacle "on the screen" as much as possible—hence his strict curbing of surround effects in the sonic mix in deference to central loudspeakers

210 Streaming the Undead Energies of "Film"

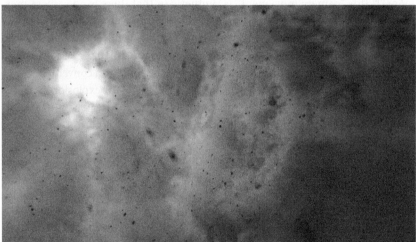

Figure 6.6 In *Twin Peaks: The Return*, a simulated *z*-axis camera movement takes us into an atomic cloud, leading us from station to station until we reach The Fireman's lair.

close to or behind the screen.[64] Such deference is largely tempered for the headphonic listener, who experiences an uncanny spacing that divides the source of the "power" from its visualization. With headphones (technically known as electroacoustic "transducers"), *we* become emanative of this "power," too. As both the partial source of this energy *and* its point of audition, we are sonically haunted from within, our bodies in this way figuring among the portals with uncertain boundaries. Given the scenarios of possession expressed in the series' world, this headphonic situation is not just technical but also

Figure 6.6 (Continued)

aesthetic. And it is the loudness—the intense nearness—of the screechy strings that most viscerally assails us. These sounds and added effects lurk offscreen but, even so, find a frame, a house, between our ears.[65]

Headphonic spectatorship, therefore, differently inflects an experiential question that cuts to the heart of atmospheric suspense in film: What are we, whether in the company of characters or not, presently *in the middle of*, perhaps without knowing it? What powers are we crossed and *middled by*? Atmospheric suspense, beyond its modulations of mood, combines with perceptual suspense to invoke obscure yet diffusely operative energies, forces, agencies, and networks that are never revealed in toto. The z-axis camera movement does reveal a crucial but easy-to-miss fact to us at the end of its voyage in part 8. When The Fireman gazes directly into the camera's eye and acknowledges its arrival at his lair, we begin to understand that the camera's function, all along its route, has been *to capture* the nuclear blast, *trace* its disastrous ripple effects (including the birth of BOB), and then *transport* this evidence to a concerned agent—that is, The Fireman. The synthetic camera, then, *is* a camera after all, an implied recording and courier device *embedded within the film's world*. Dronelike, the camera movement delivers to The Fireman a surveillance report in the form of a signal that is then gradually transduced into the "film" on the screen in his and Señorita Dido's adjacent theater/observation center (a process aided, it seems, by bell-shaped transmitters in each space). As this camera's memory of events has coincided with ours, its flight has made *us* into an unwitting envoy or medium. Perhaps the reconnaissance "film" The Fireman scrutinizes is an extraction of what *we* have perceived and retained along our journey.

Part 8, with its atoms, seeds, and eggs, its rival creations of BOB and Laura, and its childhood scenes from 1956 that cryptically feature Laura's mother in her adolescence, furnishes a history of the *Twin Peaks* cosmos.[66] At the same time, part 8 presents a topological expansion outward from a fiery core (not just a chronological regression within stable coordinates of past, present, and future) that renders all incidents simultaneous as we transductively course through the very molecular stuff out of which the series is composed. With its use of the Manhattan Project and by extension the mid–twentieth century's thermonuclear disasters as the "big bang" from which the series' energy grid is originally derived, part 8 asks the audience to extrapolate points of contact among this traumatic history, *The Return*, and all previous iterations of *Twin Peaks*. In this way, a still more catastrophic underbelly is exposed beneath the conservative middle-class milieu that the ABC television show nearly enshrines with its retro accents and often unchecked nostalgia. *The Return*'s treatment of the bomb, the wellspring of postwar American triumphalism, ties in with a more caustic, multifaceted critique of the American Dream, a shift begun with *Fire Walk with Me*'s slide into horror. Thematically, atmospherically, the bomb lights a spark that takes on more and more layers of social commentary as the concepts of family, home, economic progress and prosperity, patriarchal authority, and so on are revealed to be corrosive shams, false defenses that produce their own violent and devastating threats from within. Through its spreading associations with petroleum (by way of the convenience store and gas station) and a bizarre mutant frog-moth that hatches in the desert (as though it is biologically affected by the radiation), the blast's aftermath raises the specters of resource capitalism and ecological ruin. Related to these thematic concerns is *The Return*'s concerted remapping of the American Dream as a nightmare. If the original series and the prequel had already presented us with dark truths behind the facades of the pristinely rowed neighborhoods with plush lawns in the town of Twin Peaks, *The Return* offers a more well-nigh apocalyptic portrait of American life through the twenty-first-century wasteland of economic collapse, predation, and overextension that is Rancho Rosa Estates, the half-built Las Vegas suburban housing development that shows up intermittently, with a foreclosure sign in front of every other unit. The massive energy grid, as I have called it, thus includes financial and ecological forces that feed into the eerie ambiences in the series. Not all that stirs and textures the atmosphere is otherworldly.[67]

Indeed, in addition to these dimensions of social commentary that are at some level tied to the atomic blast and its widespread ramifications, the fiery, ever-expanding atmospheric and energetic system at play in *The Return* invites us to regard it as *media-technical* and not just as a mystical, thematic armature. Lynch's reflexive treatment of "film" is closely bound up with this media-technical dimension of atmosphere. Questions of mediation and of our interface with the film's world, our dispositive relationship to the screen, remain paramount, not simply as self-conscious themes but also as ambient elements of atmosphere. To fully grasp how the series and its suspense demand to be understood in a media-technical sense that operates on an ambient level, we must carefully delimit three concurrent layers or domains of ambience, enlarging on my earlier definitions of ambience in the book. Let us also take this step with digital streaming specifically in mind.

The first and most prominent layer of ambience is that which imbues the film's world and emanates outward to enwrap the spectator. Sound is vital to this effect, but the feel of ambience is conjured up through multisensory evocations (involving both sonic and visual channels) and through felt tensions between the frame's limited parameters and the sound field's environmental presence. We feel exposed to a mediating force in excess of what is portrayed—a feeling that, in my examples of perceptual and atmospheric suspense, often falls on an affective spectrum from eeriness to dread. We have already seen how this process changes with the use of headphones, but this layer, as discussed in chapter 3, still has a ubiquitous, encircling quality. It makes good on the "spherical" part of atmospheric experience (and complements Lynch's notion of the circle between spectator and film). The second layer—less often recognized—concerns the ambient merger of the aesthetic object with the physical environment in which it is presented. Mikel Dufrenne defines this fusion as the "tentacular nature" by which an artwork "magnetizes" and aesthetically integrates its surroundings in defiance of a rigid frame.[68] Earlier in this book I noted how films such as Antonioni's *The Passenger* (1975), Tsai's *Goodbye, Dragon Inn* (2003), and Apichatpong's *Memoria* (2021), by virtue of their spare ambient styles, uncannily mingle with the space of the film theater and in some cases echo the technical apparatus of projection, claiming it as an integral feature.[69] This "tentacular" layer of ambience becomes much more tenuous and variable under the dispositive conditions of home video and digital streaming as the spectacle's power undergoes what Lynch laments as "extreme putrification," which headphones, however, might counter to some degree.[70] Although the atmospheric (re)turn of film theory has privileged theatrical viewing, it needs to be acknowledged that some films, deliberately or not, cater to this second domain of ambience within the domestic viewing space. One thinks of horror films encountered alone in a house or apartment that begins to murmur more creepily—an effect that may mirror the gothic domestic ambiences of the film's world. J-horror films such as Hideo Nakata's *Ring* (1998) and Kiyoshi Kurosawa's *Pulse* (2001), with their reflexive uses of haunted, contagious, and permeable *small* screens examined by alienated and vulnerable characters, might realize this second layer of ambience more effectively for the viewer who watches in a domestic milieu. Lynch's work—from the unsettling playback of videotapes in *Lost Highway* (1997) to the screens (both televisual and theatrical) nested within screens in *Inland Empire*—likewise charges and "annexes" the domestic viewing space, to use Dufrenne's terminology.[71] One also thinks of Lynch's drawings, lithographs, and paintings in which domestic interiors are electrically abuzz or aflame.[72]

In the dispositive situation of digital streaming in which *The Return* is ensconced, there is a third domain of ambience that, unlike the first two levels, operates chiefly at a remove from our sensory perception, neither readily available to nor correlated with human consciousness. This third layer of ambience ebbs from and eludes phenomenological experience yet still traffics in ubiquity by fueling the work's delivery and encircling us in a networked, albeit hidden fashion. This layer lurks at the technical substrate of what Shane Denson terms "the post-cinematic *dispositif*" in reference to altered and newly emergent interfaces with moving-image media in the wake of digitalization. For Denson, the term *postcinema* doesn't name a technical stage or critical stance situated *after* the demise of a medium presumed to be obsolete. Rather, it orients us to relational factors and possibilities that stem from the *coincidence* of cinema as we know it (that is, as the medium's twentieth-century incarnation remains intact) with its media-technical "envelopment within the larger space of an environment that has been thoroughly transformed by the operation of computational processing." Denson's account of postcinema is in dialogue with a different kind of turn to atmosphere within media studies that film theories of atmosphere have mostly ignored. When Denson, citing the media theorist Mark Hansen, speaks of "atmospheric media," he means not the sensory affordances of a film's world but instead the ubiquitous computing and microtemporal processing networks that now compose the underlying apparatus of the digital moving image—a vast infrastructural environment, the scales and speeds of which are "not cut to human measure."[73] Central to Denson's nuanced claims, however, are the appearance of phenomena during a film's playback that bring forth this computational substrate and "inject" it into the film's surface, making it partially discernable. Certain digital effects (such as artificial lens flares), glitches, and buffering and compression artifacts onscreen serve as sometimes wondrous, sometimes disturbing testaments to ulterior mechanisms that enable the synchronization of our perception with the film's unfolding but that also technically outpace human subjectivity. Such phenomena are the "sensory complements to subperceptual events."[74]

By counting this substrative part of the digital stream as a layer of ambience, I agree with Denson's twofold claim that the technical substrates of media may significantly *bleed into* the formal and aesthetic dimensions of the work, despite film scholars' inclinations to separate the technological apparatus from parameters of form (mise-en-scène, editing, cinematography, and so forth), and that the substrate may exert an influence on the spectator in either conscious or preconscious ways. Indivisible form–substrate relations particular to (if not altogether new with) the digital makeover and repositioning of "film" have been salient features of Lynch's work since his markedly digital *Inland Empire*.[75] What Denson calls the pervasive "digital ether" of today's postcinematic apparatus seems to figure in *The Return* obliquely among the conspiratorial webs and transductions of energy. That is, this media-technical level of ambience figures as another zone of the offscreen, present by dint of its absence and suspensefully involved in corporeal mutations and transferences.[76] Glitchy sonic and visual textures unique to digital media repeatedly punctuate the transit of unstable bodies between different realms, beginning with Cooper's disintegrating exit from The Fireman's lounge early in part 1. In part 8, the sputtering, irregular movements of the woodsmen in and around the convenience store have a glitchy computational feel to them that is allied with the spread of energy from the atomic explosion. Although this effect is by design and therefore not a glitch in the purist technical sense (which would require accident and error),[77] *The Return* more surreptitiously weaves into its scenes little spasms and delays that trouble the distinction between an intended aesthetic device and unwanted hiccups in the streaming signal (indeed, what may initially look to be a stylistic flourish may upon replay turn out to have been an errant digital artifact of compression). The New York observation loft, with its television-like glass box, is an enigmatic space of surveillance where constantly recording digital cameras are hooked up to a tangled mass of exposed cables, sending signals who knows where (we are told merely that the facility is owned by a person of immense wealth) and incorporating this site into ulterior relays of information. The establishing shots of this Manhattan space, from high above the blinking city at night, suggest a circuit board. Reexamined in this light, the synthetic camera's plunge into the atomic cloud in part 8 bears a conceptual, aesthetic, and technical resemblance to the camera movement that tunnels into a wall socket and races along a telephonic fiber-optics channel at the start of Krzysztof Kieslowski's *Three Colors: Red* (1994); or a closer digital-era parallel can be found in the synthetic camera movement that enters a computer screen and follows a cyberattack along the labyrinthine mainframe circuit of a nuclear plant in Hong Kong at the start of Michael Mann's *Blackhat* (2015).[78]

But *The Return*, as part of what I have defined as its medium suspense, here again refuses to firmly anchor "film" in a particular technological era or means of expression, its unmistakably digital patinas of image and sound notwithstanding. Included in the fallout of the atom bomb's detonation in part 8, the partly historical, partly anachronistic, and partly futural play of fire and mediation in which "film" has been embroiled extends to an "old" medium intimately yoked to the aesthetic and technological history of cinema: radio. Following the explosion and a time skip to 1956, a tall, lanky woodsman (played by Abraham Lincoln impersonator Robert Broski) lands from the pitch-black sky in the New Mexico desert and trudges toward a radio station. Along the way, he terrifies a motorist couple as he asks them in a guttural, Freddy Krueger–like growl, "Gotta light?," in reference to his cigarette. A sizzling and flickering aura of electrical power, associated with camera movement and changes of speed, surrounds him.[79] Once inside the station, he kills a receptionist and disc jockey by crushing their skulls in his unnaturally strong hand. Grabbing the microphone and disrupting the broadcast of the Platters' song "My Prayer," he repeats a cryptic mantra over the airwaves that induces sleep in listeners, including young Sarah Palmer (Tikaeni Faircrest), who is now at home, alone in her bedroom, where, after she loses consciousness, the moth-frog shown earlier climbs through a window and into her mouth, a violation synchronized with the woodsman's radio chant: "This is the water, and this is the well. Drink full and descend. The horse is the white of the eyes and dark within" (fig. 6.7).

This horrific and surreal scene—which ends part 8 as the woodsman exits into the night, his departure emphasized by the whinny of an unseen horse—leaves much unexplained. Is this mantra a code awaiting translation into symbolic meaning? Is it perhaps less the content of the words than the chant's somniferous and violent mediational force that most matters here? Why does this woodsman evoke Abraham Lincoln—a suggestion further supported by the heads-up penny that young Sarah Palmer stumbles across minutes earlier? What does this figure and the woodsmen in general, covered as they are in what seems to be soot, tar, and engine oil, have to do with nuclear disaster? Of all people, why are *woodsmen* transient dwellers of the energy grid and servants of evil? What are the implications of the frog-moth's invasion of Sarah, a grotesque happening that prefigures the sexual violence Laura experiences at the hands of BOB in her own bedroom at home?[80]

Figure 6.7 The woodsman delivers his mantra over the airwaves in *Twin Peaks: The Return*.

The suspense of this scene, with its subversive use of the Lincoln figure and the attendant popular myth of an upright "man of the frontier,"[81] provokes us to deduce still further American histories of destruction implied to undergird the universe of *Twin Peaks* and its energy circuit. As other scholars have shown, these histories include land appropriation and genocidal acts against Native American groups in the western United States—communities whose annexed territories and deteriorating health conditions are connected to the New Mexico testing grounds and the radiation released into the atmosphere.[82] The woodsmen in *Twin Peaks*, grimed as they are by the material residues of labor for industries enmeshed in these histories, have been interpreted as avatars of settler violence within Lynch and Frost's implied critique of the American West and its abiding political myths.[83] As for the scene's prefiguration of what later happens to Laura, *The Return* here vaguely implies that her nightmarish situation unfolded behind and was abetted by a narcotizing sense of old-fashioned American values, forged in the aftermath of the bomb: she suffered while a mesmerized and distracted America slept. "You wanna know who killed Laura?" Bobby Briggs (Dana Ashbrook) asks the crowd gathered at Laura's funeral in a soap-operatic scene in season 1. "*You* did! We all did." Given our present concerns, it is no less important to puzzle over the woodsman scene's complex media-technical resonances. After all, the scene offers a dark parable of media transmission and contagion in which film—Lynch's mercurial concept of "film"—is implicated through its relationship to radio.

As described in the screenplay, the woodsman is to speak over the radio "atonal word-like mechanical sounds" in addition to the water-and-well mantra.[84] In the completed work, his speech seems to derive its power not just from the words but from the synthesis of his scratchy voice with the very ground noise of the radio broadcast, the buzz and hiss of which closes out this part of the series as the credits scroll over the sleeping body of Sarah Palmer. Ordinarily in *The Return*, each part concludes with a music performance at the roadhouse, but that routine is cast off as we contemplate the presence and sway of this anempathetic noise, which is made to seem like the ground noise *of the film we are viewing*, as if conditions have quietened enough to let an electrical hiss surface from the medium's substrate. Though aligned with radio, this ending also simulates "a sounding of *film*'s material and technological bases."[85]

The mantra's words do, in fact, signify along these lines. We can conceive of "the water" as the aesthetic work we take in and of "the well" as the technical source and mechanism of its delivery to us. Are *we*, thereby, "the horse" that "drink[s] full and descend[s]" in this immersive transaction? The mantra is too opaque to be reasoned out in its entirety (and I think it would be wrong to assign it a single meaning, like the solution to a riddle), but it matters enormously for our purposes that the water and the well, according to the woodsman, *are elementally the same*. To paraphrase: this is the water, which is also the well. I do not take the two successive deictic expressions of "this" to distinguish different components. At the very least, ambiguities trouble the mantra's delineations. In this reflexive parable of mediation, there is no cleaving of surface from substrate, no clear-cut separation of aesthetic forms from the media-technical apparatuses through which they are channeled. The sonic and visual forms available to our perception retain an elemental affective link to their veiled, substrative means of delivery.

That said, although *The Return* suspensefully gives prominence to mediation as a sensory force and engages us through all three tentacles of ambience, doing so with digital streaming on its mind, it is precisely the series' playful, experimental, and unyielding investment in suspense of an unresolvable kind that deviates from the more technologically deterministic leanings of a postcinema outlook. In spirit, all of Lynch's work—both before and after the arrival of digital media—runs counter to the critical pose of assuming to know exactly what a medium is, what it does, where its energies come from, where its creative and experiential limits fall, how it enters into exchanges with other artistic and technical media, what its histories bode for its current and future configurations, how it affects and involves its spectator, and so forth. *The Return*, through its science-fictional conflations of old and new cinematic forms and environments, enacts on any size or type of screen an "affective suspension of knowledge" regarding the very prospect of a stable medium ontology.[86]

If *The Return* is indeed a film even when we stream its episodes on our computer screen, and if what the series self-consciously presents as "film" encompasses a variety of both real and invented media, then this is because the film medium is taken to be subject to the same strangely metastable conditions that underlie the ontogenetic phase shifts of the *Twin Peaks* cosmos. Not unlike the world of *Twin Peaks* and its characters' identities, our received idea of film is shown to be energetically expanding out of itself into other phases and hybrid incarnations, into newer dimensions of "form-taking" (as Simondon put it) and experience that are at once recognizable and deeply changed. Longing for the immersive darkness and reverberant acoustics of a theater but coping with the less governable streaming situation (which permits the very existence of such a serial "film"), *The Return* extends the purview of "film" in part through surreal remediations of the theatrical experience, from the whirling pipe contraption in The Fireman's auditorium to the "film" scratches and grains in part 8's atomic odyssey. No less often than digital artifacts, such vestiges of film mark transductive passageways, a tendency already found in *Mulholland Drive*'s Club Silencio scene and *Inland Empire*'s portal made of a cigarette burn in silk, a motif inspired by reel-cue dots in a film print that alert the projectionist to a changeover.

A more comprehensive look at medium suspense in *The Return* would need to delve into the changing, increasingly reciprocal aesthetic relationship between film and episodic television in the twenty-first century. *The Return* initially appeared on Showtime in a week-to-week serial format rather than in a single drop of all parts at once. Because binge-watching large swaths of the series wasn't an option until later, its first viewers experienced a suspense of waiting out the weekly intervals between installments, uncertain of which characters and settings would become continuing parts of the series and which would be left behind, consigned to digression and drift. We should not let a cinephilic penchant for film over television divert us from Lynch's reliance on TV genres' serial forms, not just the crime procedural but also the daytime soap opera, with its promise of infinite narrative expansion, which, for Lynch, is a pretext for suspense without end as the slackening of plot allows for (and requires as padding) atmospheric experimentation. Adrian Martin has examined how contemporary cinema and television intriguingly share tactics of delay, expansion, and protraction—through forms for which Martin finds prototypes in post-1945 art cinema.[87] What I have tried to illustrate in this closing chapter is that considerations of atmosphere have no less a critical place in film's confluence with television. Lynch's attempt to relocate the art house on a new frontier of digital streaming is audaciously carried out through an affirmation of the primacy, the sensorial firstness, of atmosphere. *The Return* isn't alone in this sense. Barry Jenkins's Amazon miniseries *The Underground Railroad* (2021), with its slowness and encircling, recurrently gothic sound design used as tools to address the legacy of slavery in the United States, likewise demands a critical vantage that prioritizes atmospheric suspense.[88] It is high time for theories of atmosphere to address the hybridization of film with other media in ways peculiar to the digital era—a broadening of theoretical scope that needs to come to better terms with today's most customary manners of experiencing audiovisual worlds. I have taken steps in this direction by investigating how *The Return*'s atmospheric system lends itself to the *dispositif* of digital streaming and the use of headphones.

The Return further serves as an illuminating example with which to end this book in that its artful orchestration of slow, atmospheric suspense reaches well beyond the clichés that "suspense" has come to be identified with in film culture—clichés I touched on at the very beginning of this study through a reference to Alfred Hitchcock's point that there can be no suspense proper when its stylistic practices become too familiar. Of course, it must be acknowledged that Lynch's approach to generating anxious uncertainty *savors* the generic clichés of suspense, using them as lures that in slow, nonlinear time open onto deeper and more bewildering layers of mystery that cannot be circumscribed by the given precincts of a single genre. The same, in fact, can be said of most of the directors whose films I have keyed on across my chapters—films that maneuver in liminal spaces between art-house and popular idioms, invoking mainstream genre aspects but also setting out to reinvent suspense by other means. As the suspense we have been trained to pigeonhole dissipates, another kind of suspenseful encounter emerges—one with mixed, more delicate affective qualities that fluctuate by degrees between dread and wonder, while running the gamut of a morphology of suspense that goes beyond questions of plot and character identification. As these films restyle suspense, they in turn reconceive the formal and experiential parameters of cinematic slowness, a practice revealed to be much more versatile in its address to and affective involvement of the viewer than polemical arguments either for or against the imposition of slow time have tended to claim. The effects of slowness in art cinema are much too multifarious to be subsumed under a single aesthetic paradigm, and our attention, not to mention our cortisol levels, may oscillate even where boredom and uneventfulness occur.

My goal has also been to demonstrate by example the need to write about suspense from a position internal to its grip, in partial surrender to the experience of bodily felt unknowingness. In much writing about cinema, one discovers an anxiety about suspense itself: suspense must be expeditiously cleared away, overcome, through generic classifications or through the rhetoric of exegesis (the critical counterpart of mainstream filmmaking's premium on dramatic closure). In my arguments, I have found it crucial to let suspense manifest and largely remain *as suspense*, deserving of the name at one or more of its morphological levels. If we have seen erratic progress in the theorization of cinematic suspense, is this because our intellectual customs keep us from valuing the uncertainties of a film that can't be swiftly inducted into scholarly erudition? I have tried to redefine suspense for film studies by writing in solidarity with sonic and visual forms that endeavor to make us into what Jean Louis Schefer once called "custodians of a doubt concerning meaning," a role he ascribes to the immersed cinematic spectator.[89] Throughout this book, I have shadowed, deciphered, and contextualized the films under scrutiny—but I have pursued not meaning so much as atmospheric resonance. An appropriately multitiered account of suspense emerges only when we describe and embrace cinema's evolving powers as an ambient medium.

NOTES

Introduction

1. The clichés of cinematic suspense could be nutshelled by what André Bazin, in his writings on Italian neorealism, disparagingly calls "'doorknob' mise en scène" in reference to melodramatic syntax that reduces an event and its concrete details to an abstract sign. Bazin, *What Is Cinema?*, trans. Timothy Barnard (Montreal: Caboose, 2009), 242. As is well known, Bazin lacked his *Cahiers du Cinéma* disciples' unwavering passion for Hitchcock's body of work. He found Hitchcock's mastery of suspense impressive but unfortunate insofar as it spoils the heightened sensitivity it fosters. Reviewing Hitchcock's *Notorious* (1946), Bazin writes that Hitchcock's style "has extended the limits of the camera's sensitivity, in the sense that we say that a scale is sensitive. Unfortunately, there is something ridiculous about placing the vulgar iron filing of these ready-made psychologists on the scale pan that would register a speck of gold dust." Bazin, *The Cinema of Cruelty: From Buñuel to Hitchcock*, ed. François Truffaut, trans. Sabine d'Estrée (New York: Arcade, 1982), 110. By contrast, the films I discuss in this book make subtler if still virtuosic use of the perceptual sensitivities they display and promote in the spectator. There is a more commensurate use of the ultrasensitive "scale."
2. Pascal Bonitzer traces cinematic suspense further back to before narrative integration. In his view, *The Sprinkler Sprinkled* (Lumiére brothers, 1895) counts as "the first suspense effect": as a gardener waters his plants, a boy enters the frame behind his back and steps on the water hose, stopping the flow and leading the gardener to check the seemingly faulty nozzle; we wait anxiously as the boy removes his foot and the gardener sprinkles himself in the face. Bonitzer intriguingly notes that this abiding tables-are-turned motif—whereby the sprinkler becomes the sprinkled, the hunter becomes the hunted, or the watcher becomes the watched—forms the basis of some of

Hitchcock's more elaborate uses of suspense, as in *Rear Window* (1954). Bonitzer, "Hitchcockian Suspense," trans. Martin Thom, in *Everything You Wanted to Know About Lacan (but Were Afraid to Ask Hitchcock)*, ed. Slavoj Žižek (London: Verso, 2010), 48.

3. François Truffaut, *Hitchcock*, rev. ed., with Helen G. Scott (New York: Simon & Schuster, 1985), 256.
4. As Bonitzer observes, Hitchcockian suspense requires a startling disruption. *The Birds* initially presents an innocent world that presupposes a natural and harmonious order. But it soon shatters this impression of innocence by introducing a "stain," a criminal act or aberrant detail that in turn incites a gaze in which the audience is implicated. Bonitzer, "Hitchcockian Suspense," 20–21. Hitchcock's ambition to conjure suspense out of "nothing" is compromised somewhat by the necessity of a disruptive revelation for which "nothing" is the pretext, hence the dead body in his hypothetical countryside scene.
5. Truffaut, *Hitchcock*, 315.
6. Shigehiko Hasumi, "Adventure: An Essay on Pedro Costa," *Rouge* 10 (2007), http://www.rouge.com.au/10/costa_hasumi.html.
7. Adrian Martin, "There's a Million Stories, and a Million Ways to Get There from Here," *Metro*, no. 142 (2005): 85. The so-called death trilogy that Van Sant directed, including *Gerry* (2002) and *Last Days* (2005), undeniably has a place in accounts of slow-paced suspense, given their lulling, foreboding tones within durationally expanded timescales. See Tiago de Luca, *Realism of the Senses in World Cinema: The Experience of Physical Reality* (London: I. B. Tauris, 2014), 159–231. It isn't just a coincidence that Van Sant dutifully remade *Psycho* (1960) as *Psycho* (1998).
8. Yvette Biró, "The Fullness of Minimalism," *Rouge* 9 (2006), http://www.rouge.com.au/9/minimalism.html; Annette Michelson, "About Snow," *October* 8 (Spring 1979): 118; David Bordwell, *Ozu and the Poetics of Cinema* (London: British Film Institute, 1988), 57–58, 345. Amy Taubin comparably writes that Snow's *Wavelength* (1967) "is like a Hitchcock movie with the narrative pared away so that only the suspense remains." Taubin, "Landscapes with Alienated Figures," *Village Voice*, December 5, 2000.
9. For overviews that cover and add to debates on slow cinema, see Matthew Flanagan, "'Slow Cinema': Temporality and Style in Contemporary Art and Experimental Film," PhD diss., University of Exeter, 2012; Ira Jaffe, *Slow Movies: Countering the Cinema of Action* (London: Wallflower, 2014); Song Hwee Lim, *Tsai Ming-liang and a Cinema of Slowness* (Honolulu: University of Hawai'i Press, 2014); de Luca, *Realism of the Senses in World Cinema*; Tiago de Luca and Nuno Barradas Jorge, introduction to *Slow Cinema*, ed. de Luca and Barradas Jorge (Edinburgh: Edinburgh University Press, 2016), 1–21; Moira Weigel, "Slow Wars: Is This How Cinema Transcends Itself?," *N+1* 25 (2016), https://nplusonemag.com/issue-25/essays/slow-wars/; Katherine Fusco and Nicole Seymour, *Kelly Reichardt* (Urbana: University of Illinois Press, 2017), 51–55; and Emre Çağlayan, *Poetics of Slow Cinema: Nostalgia, Absurdism, Boredom* (Newcastle, U.K.: Palgrave Macmillan, 2018). For a discussion of "over-claiming" on the part of slow cinema's critical champions, see Geoff King, *Positioning Art Cinema: Film and Cultural Value* (London: I. B. Tauris, 2019), 105–39. Karen Beckman (now Redrobe) contributes to this discussion by noting how the polarized distinction between "fast" Hollywood and "slow" international art cinema has fixated primarily on straight male filmmakers and thereby ignored "legacies of feminist, queer, and third cinema engagements with cinematic tempo." Beckman, "The Tortoise, the Hare, and the Constitutive Outsiders: Reframing Fast and Slow Cinemas," *Cinema*

Journal 55, no. 2 (2016): 126–27. Michael Walsh adds to the discussion with *Durational Cinema: A Short History of Long Films* (Cham, Switzerland: Palgrave Macmillan, 2022), where "durational" refers to a history of avant-garde and experimental films that are consanguine with but not categorically identical to slow cinema.
10. For a nuanced defense of "sleepy" spectatorship, see Jean Ma, *At the Edges of Sleep: Moving Images and Somnolent Spectators* (Berkeley: University of California Press, 2022). See also Elena Gorfinkel, "Cinema, the Soporific: Between Exhaustion and Eros," Kracauer Lectures in Film and Media Theory, Goethe University, December 12, 2017, https://www.kracauer-lectures.de/en/winter-2017-2018/elena-gorfinkel/.
11. Adrian Martin, in another rare and insightful act of film criticism, finds suspense in the slow and minimalistic styles of both Tsai Ming-liang and Apichatpong Weerasethakul. Martin, *Mise en Scène and Film Style: From Classical Hollywood to New Media Art* (Basingstoke, U.K.: Palgrave Macmillan, 2014), 98, 199.
12. See Lim, *Tsai Ming-liang and a Cinema of Slowness*. It has become customary to posit slow cinema as a critical and potentially therapeutic response to the circumstances Jonathan Crary identifies under his grim notion of "24/7"—the accelerated imposition of the rhythms of the marketplace and consumption onto every aspect of personal and social being. Crary, *24/7: Late Capitalism and the Ends of Sleep* (London: Verso, 2013).
13. Rosalind Galt and Karl Schoonover, "Introduction: The Impurity of Art Cinema," in *Global Art Cinema: New Theories and Histories*, ed. Galt and Schoonover (New York: Oxford University Press, 2010), 3–27, esp. 6–9.
14. David Andrews, *Theorizing Art Cinemas: Foreign, Cult, Avant-Garde, and Beyond* (Austin: University of Texas Press, 2013); King, *Positioning Art Cinema*.
15. There are good reasons to approach the topic of slow cinema with caution. Tiago de Luca and Nuno Barradas Jorge argue for a selective logic of inclusion that avoids a Eurocentric point of view and refrains from quickly assuming twenty-first-century examples to be the inheritors of earlier European art-cinema styles and traditions. De Luca and Barradas Jorge, introduction to *Slow Cinema*, 9. In the same collection, Lúcia Nagib offers a much-needed corrective to the Eurocentric tendency to regard Gilles Deleuze's notion of the "time-image" as the foundation of an art-cinematic aesthetics of slowness. Nagib, "The Politics of Slowness and the Traps of Modernity," in *Slow Cinema*, ed. de Luca and Barradas Jorge, 25–46. Although these authors rightly challenge the ways in which slow cinema's history tends to be charted, I believe that many of the films in question call for a less protectionist attitude toward slow cinema's roots, legacies, and impure liaisons with popular idioms.
16. For Apichatpong's preparatory notebook reflections, including this mention of *Jaws* (1975), see Apichatpong Weerasethakul, *Memoria* (Berlin: Fireflies, 2021), unpaginated. The pink shirt worn by Tilda Swinton's character even borrows the shade of Richard Dreyfuss's pullover in the *Jaws* scene. While Spielberg's scene furnishes a template of camaraderie and an emphasis on bodily scars from past traumas, Apichatpong makes the corporeal nature of the social bond into a matter of long-drawn-out suspense. See my analysis in chapter 4.
17. There are important precedents for such a critical perspective. In a *Cahiers du Cinéma* roundtable discussion of Alain Resnais's *Muriel, or The Time of Return* (1963) the same year it was released, Claude Ollier reads the art film as a labyrinthine thriller and draws parallels to Hitchcock's *The Birds* (also 1963), arguing that both films court boredom by spacing out their mystery plots with banal situations and characters who lack psychological depth. Also identifying Hitchcockian motifs in Resnais's *Last Year at*

Marienbad (1961), Ollier remarks that this boredom gives way to a "rising anxiety, panic even." Jean-André Fieschi adds to these claims by observing that *Muriel* and *The Birds* incite "a muted sense of terror" that slowly accrues through dull yet dreamlike events. Fieschi also invokes *Vertigo* and maintains that both Hitchcock and Resnais offer "thriller[s] where the enigma is the intention of the film itself and not its resolution." Both delight in an anxious mood that deepens the mystery, keeping it unresolved, and their uses of suspense cooperate with boredom instead of nullifying it. Jean-Louis Comolli, Jean Domarchi, Jean-André Fieschi, Pierre Kast, André Labarthe, Claude Ollier, Jacques Rivette, and François Weyergans, "The Misfortunes of *Muriel*," in *Cahiers du Cinéma, the 1960s: New Wave, New Cinema, Reevaluating Hollywood*, ed. Jim Hillier (Cambridge, MA: Harvard University Press, 1986), 68–81, quotes on 69, 73.

18. One of the definitional problems that surrounds the term *suspense* is whether it denotes a creative practice or a spectatorial state. The answer is that it references both: like *hypnosis*, suspense refers to a technical process *and* the experiential state elicited, encompassing the interface between them when anxious uncertainty is activated. The term describes not just aesthetic operations in the film but also a spectatorial feeling. It is a conceptual couplet.

19. Daniel N. Stern, *The Interpersonal World of the Infant* (London: Carmac, 1998), 73–74, 101–6.

20. Stern, *The Interpersonal World*, 53–61.

21. Alfred Hitchcock, "The Enjoyment of Fear" (1949), in *Hitchcock on Hitchcock: Selected Writings and Interviews*, ed. Sidney Gottlieb (Berkeley: University of California Press, 1997), 120–21. Well before the 1940s, the film industry had given the term *suspense* a particular meaning and sense of dramatic urgency. Some of what Hitchcock said and wrote about suspense had been already outlined in similar terms in the screenwriter-director Denison Clift's published series of lectures, *Dramatic Suspense in the Photoplay* (Los Angeles: Palmer Photoplay, 1920).

22. Hitchcock, "The Enjoyment of Fear," 120–21. See also Truffaut, *Hitchcock*, 73. For a more thorough discussion of Hitchcock's suspense practices as they both conform to and deviate from his public remarks on the subject, see Richard Allen, "Hitchcock and Narrative Suspense: Theory and Practice," in *Camera Obscura, Camera Lucida: Essays in Honor of Annette Michelson*, ed. Richard Allen and Malcolm Turvey (Amsterdam: Amsterdam University Press, 2003), 163–82.

23. David Bordwell, "Murder Culture: Adventures in 1940s Suspense," David Bordwell's Website on Cinema, 2013, http://www.davidbordwell.net/essays/murder.php. See also Bordwell, *Perplexing Plots: Popular Storytelling and the Poetics of Murder* (New York: Columbia University Press, 2023), 157–93. For further historical contextualization of how *suspense* came to be assigned a narrow definition, see Steve Neale, *Genre and Hollywood* (New York: Routledge, 2000), 82–85; and Frank Krutnik, "Theatre of Thrills: The Culture of Suspense," *New Review of Film and Television Studies* 11, no. 1 (2013): 6–33.

24. Bordwell, "Murder Culture."

25. Noël Carroll, "The Paradox of Suspense," in *Suspense: Conceptualizations, Theoretical Analyses, and Empirical Explorations*, ed. Peter Vorderer, Hans J. Wulff, and Mike Friedrichsen (Mahwah, NJ: Lawrence Erlbaum, 1996), 71–92.

26. Julian Hanich, *Cinematic Emotion in Horror Films and Thrillers: The Aesthetic Paradox of Pleasurable Fear* (New York: Routledge, 2010), 205. For another incisive critique of cognitivist descriptions of suspense and their reduction of spectatorship to information processing, see Hauke Lehmann, *Affect Poetics of the New Hollywood:*

Suspense, Paranoia, and Melancholy (Berlin: De Gruyter, 2019), 45–100. For a cognitive analysis that does justice to formal aspects, see Maarten Coëgnarts and Miklós Kiss, "'Look Out Behind You!' Grounding Suspense in the Slasher Film," *New Review of Film and Television Studies* 15, no. 3 (2017): 348–74.

27. Breaking down Hitchcock's methods of suspense into "forms of address" that "determine how we feel by controlling what we know," Susan Smith offers a helpful three-part typology. First, in *vicarious suspense* we grapple with "anxieties and uncertainties" secondhand—"on behalf of a character" who is less privy to story information than we are. We fear *for* a character onscreen who lacks our position of knowledge. (Fear may be dominant, but Smith notes that Hitchcock's suspense entails a fluctuation of emotional tones.) In *shared suspense*, however, we fear *with* characters who know as much or as little as we do, and this enables deeper identification. And, finally, with *direct suspense* we feel suspense in our own right, without any attachment to or identification with a character—that is, without the film folding us into point-of-view structures related to character subjectivity. Smith observes that these forms may compete or combine as the film progresses. Smith, *Hitchcock: Suspense, Humour, and Tone* (London: British Film Institute, 2000), 17–25.

28. Smith, *Hitchcock*, 25. Vittorio Gallese and Michele Guerra make the neuroscientific claim that "the secret magnetism" of cinematic suspense resides not in matters of plot but in low-level motor stimuli delivered by the film's tension-bearing presentation of events. They advance this argument while examining Hitchcock's *Notorious* (1946). Gallese and Guerra, *The Empathic Screen: Cinema and Neuroscience* (New York: Oxford University Press, 2020), 53–83. For a critique of this approach's disinterest in narrative, see Steffen Hven, *Enacting the Worlds of Cinema* (New York: Oxford University Press, 2022), 110–20.

29. There is more to say about this scene's suspenseful and atmospheric use of architecture. Dramatic tension rises the more that our protagonist ascends the windmill's interior. The "escalation" of suspense is made literal by his vertical movement as the cavernous space narrows at the top, leaving him to hang dangerously outside an upper window to avoid being spotted.

30. Alanna Thain, *Bodies in Suspense: Time and Affect in Cinema* (Minneapolis: University of Minnesota Press, 2017), 6–7, 8–49.

31. Thain, *Bodies in Suspense*, 46, 62–70, 118–20. Richard J. Gerrig coined the term *anomalous suspense* in his essay "Suspense in the Absence of Uncertainty," *Journal of Memory and Language* 28 (1989): 633–48. For narrative-centered and psychological treatments of this problem, see Edward Branigan, *Narrative Comprehension and Film* (London: Routledge, 1992), 113; and Carroll, "The Paradox of Suspense."

32. Thain, *Bodies in Suspense*, 62–71, quote on 62, emphasis added to "passage to." As another case in point, take Brian De Palma's *Carlito's Way* (1993), which opens with a depiction of the main character's death by gunshot, revealing the location (a train station) as well as a glimpse of the assailant. Despite having this concrete knowledge of the outcome even during our first viewing, the finale sequence at Grand Central Station, in which Carlito (Al Pacino) flees from mobsters out for revenge, does not fail to deliver an acute suspense that owes mainly to the film's rhythmic orchestration of screen space.

33. Offering a phenomenological discussion of suspense, Julian Hanich explains anomalous or recidivist suspense through his notion of "mimicry," whereby the viewer has "pre-cognitive somatic empathy" with characters onscreen. This situation may arise regardless of the viewer's levels of knowledge vis-à-vis the characters. He also adds

that the viewer may empathize directly with the "body" of the film itself, which is taken as a "subject-object" in its own right. Hanich, *Cinematic Emotion in Horror Films and Thrillers*, 212–13.

34. Robert Sinnerbrink, "*Stimmung*: Exploring the Aesthetics of Mood," *Screen* 53, no. 2 (2012): 148–63; Inga Pollmann, *Cinematic Vitalism: Film Theory and the Question of Life* (Amsterdam: Amsterdam University Press, 2018), 163–205; Hven, *Enacting the Worlds of Cinema*. Hven provides what I take to be the most comprehensive and theoretically rigorous account of cinematic atmosphere that has surfaced. His study was published when my book manuscript was already near completion; otherwise, I would have more extensively cited it. Robert Spadoni, another crucial contributor to this turn, sketches a general overview of new approaches in "What Is Film Atmosphere?," *Quarterly Review of Film and Video* 37, no. 1 (2020): 48–75. In *Atmospheres of Projection: Environmentality in Art and Screen Media* (Chicago: University of Chicago Press, 2022), Giuliana Bruno takes a cross-media approach in considering gallery installations. It is worth bearing in mind that earlier film-theoretical attempts to define film atmosphere, such as Béla Balázs's lyrical and synesthetic accounts in the 1920s, were concerned with the peculiar and unique affordances of a medium whose potentials had yet to be fully discovered, let alone fully understood. Theories of atmosphere spring initially from a kind of exhilarating suspense that surrounded the resources and delights of cinema. Balázs, *Béla Balázs: Early Film Theory*, ed. Erica Carter, trans. Rodney Livingstone (New York: Berghahn, 2010), 22–23.

35. Hven, *Enacting the Worlds of Cinema*, 42–49.

36. Inga Pollmann, "Environmental Aesthetics: Tracing a Latent Image from Early Safari Films to Contemporary Art Cinema," in *Cinema of Exploration: Essays on an Adventurous Film Practice*, ed. James Cahill and Luca Caminati (New York: Routledge, 2021), 107–24; Hven, *Enacting the Worlds of Cinema*, 15–40. For a concept of cinematic atmosphere that is anchored in a politics of race, gender, and transnational affiliation, see Iggy Cortez, "Incestuous Wanderlust: *35 Shots of Rum*'s Atmospheres of Circulation," *Camera Obscura* 37, no. 1 (2022): 61–89.

37. Daniel Yacavone, *Film Worlds: A Philosophical Aesthetics of Cinema* (New York: Columbia University Press, 2015), 190–226. I do not intend to suggest that film atmosphere was altogether off the radar of film scholarship in the years between the end of classical film theory and what I am calling the (re)turn to atmosphere. Touchstones for this debate include Lotte H. Eisner, *The Haunted Screen: Expressionism in the German Cinema and the Influence of Max Reinhardt*, trans. Roger Greaves (London: Thames and Hudson, 1969); Raymond Durgnat, *Films and Feelings* (Cambridge, MA: MIT Press, 1971); and Dudley Andrew, *Mists of Regret: Culture and Sensibility in Classic French Film* (Princeton, NJ: Princeton University Press, 1995).

38. My book was already at press when Steffen Hven and Daniel Yacavone's collected volume *The Oxford Handbook of Moving Image Atmospheres and Felt Environments* (New York: Oxford University Press, forthcoming) was still in development.

39. My concept of negative affects is shaped in part by Sianne Ngai's seminal book *Ugly Feelings* (Cambridge, MA: Harvard University Press, 2005). But her account is ensconced in literary studies and cultural studies without adjusting much for the specificity of film. For instance, when Ngai turns to Alfred Hitchcock's *Vertigo* (1958) as a case study in anxiety, she considers the film only insofar as it can be understood to represent Heidegger's idea of "thrownness" in *Being and Time* (1927), and it is only the anxiety embodied (or, rather, illustrated) by the film's protagonist that interests her reading. Nothing of the aesthetic texture, the multisensory *feel* of the film's world,

Introduction 229

makes its way into her discussion; her chapter on anxiety has little interest in spectatorial anxiety (212–26).
40. Spadoni, "What Is Film Atmosphere?," 48–53, 59, 58. Spadoni's sense of cinematic weather takes cues from Kristi McKim's prescient book *Cinema as Weather: Stylistic Screens and Atmospheric Change* (New York: Routledge, 2013).
41. Spadoni's theory of atmosphere is a work in progress, developed across a series of essays that revolve around horror. See Spadoni, "Horror Film Atmosphere as Antinarrative (and Vice Versa)," in *Merchants of Menace: The Business of Horror Cinema*, ed. Richard Nowell (New York: Bloomsbury, 2014), 109–28; and Spadoni, "Carl Dreyer's Corpse: Horror Film Atmosphere and Narrative," in *A Companion to the Horror Film*, ed. Harry M. Benshoff (Malden, MA: Blackwell, 2014), 151–67.
42. Spadoni, "Horror Film Atmosphere," 110.
43. My thinking about atmosphere is informed by Dylan Trigg, "The Role of Atmosphere in Shared Emotion," *Emotion, Space, and Society* 35 (2020): 1–7, but Trigg doesn't reference cinema in this article. I discuss the emanative qualities of atmosphere in relation to cinematic suspense in my essay "Kubrickian Dread," in *After Kubrick: A Filmmaker's Legacy*, ed. Jeremi Szaniawski (New York: Bloomsbury, 2020), 125–45.
44. Trigg, "The Role of Atmosphere," 3–4.
45. Pertinent here is Francesco Casetti's recent work on the "projection/protection complex" that has been intrinsic to cinema (and to the environment of the movie theater) since at least the 1920s, carrying over to some extent from the earlier Phantasmagoria. The movie theater offers itself as a space of comfortable retreat from threatening realities. At the same time, it provides a mediated encounter wherein "pressures and burdens are only reshaped and relocated." Fears associated with the outside world, then, are not simply escaped but figured on a "loop" by which they enter the spectator's experience in displaced and mediated if still immediate forms. Casetti, *Screening Fears: On Protective Media* (New York: Zone, 2023), esp. 99–106.
46. Trigg, "The Role of Atmosphere," 3–4. Granted, Trigg doesn't mention film in this essay, but his description of atmosphere begs to be applied to the film experience.
47. For a useful overview and critique of literary concepts of tone, see Ngai, *Ugly Feelings*, 38–88.
48. Douglas Pye, *Movies and Tone*, electronic ed. (Warwick, U.K.: *Movie: A Journal of Film Criticism*, 2014), https://warwick.ac.uk/fac/arts/scapvc/film/movie/contents/ebook_moviesandtone.pdf.
49. On this more musical understanding of tone, see Timothy Morton, *Ecology Without Nature: Rethinking Environmental Aesthetics* (Cambridge, MA: Harvard University Press, 2007), 43–45.
50. Pauline Kael, "*McCabe & Mrs. Miller*: Pipe Dream," in *For Keeps: 30 Years at the Movies* (New York: Plume, 1994), 377, emphasis added. Kael's observation here finds a complement in what Barry Jenkins has said about the independent film studio A24: namely, that mood and tone matter more than plot when the studio considers whether to take on a new project: "They don't need to know what it's about. They just need to know how it *feels*." Jenkins, quoted in Zach Baron, "How A24 Is Disrupting Hollywood," *GQ*, May 9, 2017, https://www.gq.com/story/a24-studio-oral-history.
51. Sinnerbrink, "*Stimmung*," 148–56.
52. Spadoni, "What Is Atmosphere?," 50.
53. Cognitive film theorists writing in the 1990s beat phenomenological film theory to the punch in writing extensively about mood, albeit in ways that privileged cognition well above feeling, despite claiming to do the opposite. See Hven's astute critique

of Greg M. Smith's cognitivist "mood-cue" approach, which Hven faults for its atomistic approach to cinematic expression as well as for its failure to factor in embodied perception and environmentality. Hven, *Enacting the Worlds of Cinema*, 50–55.

54. Kiyoshi Kurosawa, *Eiga wa osoroshii* [Film is scary] (Tokyo: Seidosha, 2001).
55. Thomas Elsaesser, "Narrative Cinema and Audience Aesthetics: The *Mise en Scène* of the Spectator" (German orig. 1973), in *The Persistence of Hollywood* (New York: Routledge, 2012), 95–104; Mary Ann Doane, *The Emergence of Cinematic Time: Modernity, Contingency, the Archive* (Cambridge, MA: Harvard University Press, 2002), 13, 160–63, 185; Francesco Casetti, "Why Fears Matter: Cinephobia in Early Film Culture," *Screen* 59, no. 2 (2018): 145–57; Sandy Flitterman, Bill Guynn, Roswitha Mueller, and Jacquelyn Suter, "The Cinematic Apparatus as Social Institution—an Interview with Christian Metz," in *Conversations with Christian Metz: Selected Interviews of Film Theory (1970–1991)*, ed. Warren Buckland and Daniel Fairfax (Amsterdam: Amsterdam University Press, 2017), 185–86.
56. Elsaesser, "Narrative Cinema and Audience Aesthetics," 95–98, 101, 103–4. For strikingly comparable remarks on the inherent anxieties of the theatrical film experience and on the spectator's "expenditure of emotional energy," see John Ellis, *Visible Fictions: Cinema, Television, Video* (New York: Routledge, 1992), 86–88. Ellis directly relates this game with anxiety to narrative suspense (84, 87).
57. Adrian Martin, "A Theory of Agitation, or: Getting Off in the Cinema," *Continuum: Journal of Media & Cultural Studies* 26, no. 4 (August 2012): 519–28. See also Martin, "Slow Burn," *de Film Krant*, March 2011, http://www.filmkrant.nl/world_wide_angle/6524.
58. John David Rhodes, "*L'avventura*," in *Italian Cinema from the Silent Screen to the Digital Image*, ed. Joseph Luzzi (London: Bloomsbury, 2020), 329–34.
59. When faced with "nothing" or extreme rarefaction, the spectator might creatively *supply* a suspense narrative to explain the feeling of anxiety that develops. In an interview concerning his notorious slow film *Twentynine Palms* (2003), Bruno Dumont speaks to this projective capacity: "Today's spectator is so well-versed in film language that all theories about suspense, as argued by Dreyer and Hitchcock, on what makes you scared in cinema, can be ditched. It's the spectator, finally, who's going to construct the menace and the fear. In *Twentynine Palms*, because supposedly nothing is happening, it's impossible, something has to happen. . . . [T]he more elaborate your narrative, the more the spectator shuts up and listens obediently. And if the filmmaker keeps quiet, the spectator will himself project his own assumptions and sentiments onto the screen." Dumont, interviewed in Lizzie Bear, "Bruno Dumont's Lust in the Dust: Talking About *Twentynine Palms*," *IndieWire*, April 9, 2004, https://www.indiewire.com/2004/04/bruno-dumonts-lust-in-the-dust-talking-about-twentynine-palms-79005/. My experience with teaching slow films has affirmed this hypothesis. For example, when I show students Kelly Reichardt's *Old Joy* (2006), it never fails that some of them anticipate a murder at the hot springs to which our two central characters journey, their relationship fraught with subtle tensions that never quite augur such high drama.
60. Sarah Keller, *Anxious Cinephilia: Pleasure and Peril at the Movies* (New York: Columbia University Press, 2020).
61. Of course, there is a much deeper history in which large theatrical screens have been rivaled and displaced by small ones, a history that traces back to the arrival of television.

62. Tiago de Luca, "Slow Time, Visible Cinema: Duration, Experience, and Spectatorship," *Cinema Journal* 56, no. 1 (2016): 23, 28–29, 38.
63. De Luca, "Slow Time, Visible Cinema," 42; Karl Schoonover, "Wastrels of Time: Slow Cinema's Labouring Body, the Political Spectator, and the Queer," in *Slow Cinema*, ed. de Luca and Barradas Jorge, 153–68; Lim, *Tsai Ming-liang and a Cinema of Slowness*, 1–42.
64. For discussions of Barthes's essay that adapt it to the slow-cinema situation and, to my mind, slightly skew its portrait of spectatorship so that it suits an aesthetics and politics of boredom that hinges on inattention to the screen, see de Luca, "Slow Time, Visible Cinema," 27, 40, as well as Karl Schoonover and Rosalind Galt, *Queer Cinema in the World* (Durham, NC: Duke University Press, 2016), 281–86.
65. Philip Watts, *Roland Barthes' Cinema* (New York: Oxford University Press, 2016), 61–76.
66. Roland Barthes, "Leaving the Movie Theater" (French orig. 1975), in *The Rustle of Language*, trans. Richard Howard (Berkeley: University of California Press, 1986), 345–49. For Barthes, one spectatorial body operates according to a "narcissistic" gaze at the screen, while the other more somatically "fetishize[s]" the theater environment.

1. Suspense in Slow Time

1. Martin Rubin, *Thrillers* (Cambridge: Cambridge University Press, 1999), 30–31.
2. François Truffaut, *Hitchcock*, rev. ed., with Helen G. Scott (New York: Simon & Schuster, 1985), 72, emphasis added. Richard Allen disputes Truffaut's point by arguing that the distention of time is not sufficient in and of itself to generate suspense. He cites the Odessa Steps scene in Sergei Eisenstein's *Battleship Potemkin* (1925), which displays temporal distention without being suspenseful at all. Allen, "Hitchcock and Narrative Suspense: Theory and Practice," in *Camera Obscura, Camera Lucida: Essays in Honor of Annette Michelson*, ed. Richard Allen and Malcolm Turvey (Amsterdam: Amsterdam University Press, 2003), 171.
3. Alfred Hitchcock, "Lecture at Columbia University" (1939), in *Hitchcock on Hitchcock: Selected Writings and Interviews*, ed. Sidney Gottlieb (Berkeley: University of California Press, 1997), 272.
4. Julian Hanich, *Cinematic Emotion in Horror Films and Thrillers: The Aesthetic Paradox of Pleasurable Fear* (New York: Routledge, 2010), 161, 206–10.
5. Robert Spadoni, "Carl Dreyer's Corpse: Horror Film Atmosphere and Narrative," in *A Companion to the Horror Film*, ed. Harry M. Benshoff (Malden, MA: Blackwell, 2014), 156–57.
6. Raymond Durgnat, *A Long Hard Look at "Psycho"* (London: British Film Institute, 2002), 169–70, 68, 74.
7. Robert Sinnerbrink, "*Stimmung*: Exploring the Aesthetics of Mood," *Screen* 53, no. 2 (2012): 148–63.
8. Durgnat, *A Long Hard Look at "Psycho,"* 73–74.
9. Noël Carroll, "The Paradox of Suspense," in *Suspense: Conceptualizations, Theoretical Analyses, and Empirical Explorations*, ed. Peter Vorderer, Hans J. Wulff, and Mike Friedrichsen (Mahwah, NJ: Lawrence Erlbaum, 1996), 71–92; Edward Branigan, *Narrative Comprehension and Film* (London: Routledge, 1992), 22–25, 69, 75–76, 81, 113.
10. See David Bordwell, *Poetics of Cinema* (New York: Routledge, 2008), 85–120.

232   1. Suspense in Slow Time

11. Thomas Elsaesser, *The Mind-Game Film: Distributed Agency, Time Travel, and Productive Pathology*, ed. Warren Buckland, Dana Polan, and Seung-hoon Jeong (New York: Routledge, 2021); Alanna Thain, *Bodies in Suspense: Time and Affect in Cinema* (Minneapolis: Minnesota University Press, 2017), 124–25, 156, 257.
12. My sense of character "alignment" is informed by Murray Smith, *Engaging Characters: Fiction, Emotion, and the Cinema* (New York: Oxford University Press, 1995), 142–86.
13. Susan Smith, *Hitchcock: Suspense, Humour, and Tone* (London: British Film Institute, 2000), 17–25. Fear may be dominant, but Smith notes that Hitchcock's suspense entails a fluctuation of emotional tones. She recognizes throughout her book that these different types of suspense flow into one another as the spectator must handle complicated tonal shifts and combinations.
14. Thain, *Bodies in Suspense*, 8–49.
15. Elena Gorfinkel, "Weariness, Waiting: Endurance and Art Cinema's Tired Bodies," *Discourse* 34, nos. 2–3 (Fall 2012): 311–47.
16. Character suspense that follows from obstructed psychological identification can occur even in films that are entirely shorn of popular-genre conventions. Take the opening long take of Nina Menkes's *Queen of Diamonds* (1991), which introduces the protagonist via a close-up on her large, red, lustrous fingernails protruding from under a bedspread, the rest of her body hidden except for her hair and wrist. This slow film offers nothing like conventional suspense as it follows the daily routine of this Las Vegas blackjack dealer, but a less common suspense accretes around her demeanor, stoically resistant to the bland, pseudo-glamorous world in which she works.
17. On the skepticism that the psychiatrist's tidy explanation should arouse, see William Rothman, *Hitchcock: The Murderous Gaze*, 2nd ed. (Albany: State University of New York Press, 2012), 338–47. My sense is that the psychiatrist in *Psycho* (1960) is no more a credible expert than the equally smug ornithologist in *The Birds* (1963).
18. Roland Barthes, *Image—Music—Text*, trans. Stephen Heath (New York: Hill and Wang, 1978), 119. One also thinks of Gwendolyn's line in *The Importance of Being Earnest* (1895): "The suspense is terrible. I hope it will last." Oscar Wilde, *The Importance of Being Ernest*, in *The Importance of Being Ernest and Other Plays*, ed. Peter Raby (Oxford: Oxford University Press, 2008), 304.
19. Robin Wood, *Hitchcock's Films Revisited*, rev. ed. (New York: Columbia University Press, 2002), 152–72.
20. Gilberto Perez shows that Fritz Lang and F. W. Murnau deviated from this implicit guarantee in their uses of cross-cutting to build suspense: Lang in his *Mabuse* films and *Spies* (1928) equates the omniscient view established by this device with villainous control and surveillance, affirming paranoia, while Murnau in *Nosferatu* (1922) uses cross-cutting to drive home the knowledge of imminent death. Perez, *The Material Ghost: Films and Their Medium* (Baltimore, MD: Johns Hopkins University Press, 1998), 131–32. Louis Feuillade's *Les vampires* (1915–1916), I would add, refuses to abide by the moralistic dictates of classical cross-cutting. Joe McElhaney, also discussing Lang's work, in particular *The Thousand Eyes of Dr. Mabuse* (1960), observes how the film purposefully drains cross-cutting of its conventional dramatic and emotional intensity, making the suspense weakly climactic. McElhaney, *The Death of Classical Cinema: Hitchcock, Lang, Minnelli* (Albany: State University of New York Press, 2006), 56. Later films play games with suspenseful cross-cutting that mock its classical functions. Stanley Kubrick's *Dr. Strangelove, or: How I Learned to Stop Worrying and Love the Bomb* (1964) satirically uses the device to make us root for the success of a B-52

mission we know will trigger the Doomsday Machine. Jonathan Demme's *The Silence of the Lambs* (1991) uses cross-cutting to mislead us as to the location of a serial killer relative to an encroaching SWAT team and our protagonist, for the sake of underscoring her situation of danger all the more.
21. With structural suspense, should we make a distinction between how a scholar traces motifs (with an eye toward an argument to be made) and how a less specialized spectator viscerally experiences a film and intuits motifs along the way? Attention to patterns and repetitions, after all, is not inherently colored by suspense. This problem calls for a distinction especially when the scholar's approach doesn't square with the affective contours of a first-time viewing. For instance, when I first saw Carl Th. Dreyer's *Ordet* (1955), I found it suspenseful, but David Bordwell ascribes to the film an "obvious" progression that everywhere stems from narrative causality, an argument I believe he can make only retrospectively, after having seen the film more than once and methodically charted narrational strategies that his book project predisposed him to see. Bordwell, *The Films of Carl-Theodor Dreyer* (Berkeley: University of California Press, 1981), 144–70. This is a tricky matter for anyone examining suspense, but let us not forget that cinematic suspense *grasps us* before we grasp it.
22. Jean-Luc Godard, "The Wrong Man" (originally "Le cinéma et son double," *Cahiers du Cinéma*, June 1957), in *Godard on Godard*, trans. and ed. Tom Milne (New York: Da Capo, 1972), 48–54.
23. Structural suspense can be viewed as an especially anxious version of what Raymond Bellour describes as the "*in vivo* work of active memory" of a viewer who tries to keep pace with a film projected theatrically in the dark while in thrall to its imposed duration, its unstoppable procession of shots that deliver "subtle shocks." Bellour, "The Cinema Spectator: A Special Memory," trans. Adrian Martin, in *Audiences: Defining and Researching Screen Entertainment Reception*, ed. Ian Christie (Amsterdam: Amsterdam University Press, 2012), 211–15.
24. Lesley Stern, *The Scorsese Connection* (London: British Film Institute, 1995), 104–5, 240 n. 76.
25. Cristina Álvarez López and Adrian Martin, "Remarks on the Formation of Abstract Set Theory: *Le cercle rouge*," video essay, *Filmkrant*, March 2018, https://vimeo.com/263221132.
26. Ginette Vincendeau, *Jean-Pierre Melville: "An American in Paris"* (London: British Film Institute, 2003), 186–88, 87.
27. John Carpenter, *The Night He Came Home* (1999), documentary featurette included on the Lionsgate Blu-ray edition of *Halloween* (Carpenter, 1978), 2018. As for the role of suspense in deadpan comedy, the importance of play and the games of attention it entails can be seen in the films of Jacques Tati. For a shrewd account of comic play that could be extended to incorporate apprehension and suspense (though the author does not invoke the term *suspense*, perhaps because of its affiliation with more Hitchcockian styles of film), see Malcolm Turvey, *Play Time: Jacques Tati and Comic Modernism* (New York: Columbia University Press, 2019).
28. Truffaut, *Hitchcock*, 16; Gilles Deleuze, *Cinema 1: The Movement-Image* (French orig. 1983), trans. Hugh Tomlinson and Barbara Habberjam (Minneapolis: University of Minnesota Press, 1986), 201–2.
29. This interpretive protocol by which art-cinematic ambiguity prompts the viewer to refer to a governing authorial presence can be traced to David Bordwell's essay "The Art Cinema as a Mode of Film Practice" (1979), in *The European Cinema Reader*, ed. Catherine Fowler (London: Routledge, 2002).

30. Rothman, *Hitchcock*, 256–347.
31. Countless examples of plot-based suspense require the spectacle of vulnerable characters—a stock convention of allurement and anxiety that goes back to early cinema and *The Perils of Pauline* (1914) and that often sways between sadistic and masochistic viewing positions. But suspenseful films may also pivot on the audience being made to feel vulnerable, as if exposed to an immediate physical threat.
32. Generic suspense comes in other incarnations that I do not have the space to address here. Consider, for instance, the genre-based suspense that crops up whenever a given genre's primary attractive elements are playfully hinted at but suspended—put off so as to make the viewer yearn for them. For instance, it takes what seems like an eternity for Bruce Lee to spring into martial arts action and physical exhibitionism in *The Way of the Dragon* (1972). This teasing delay makes the first fight scene all the more explosive when it erupts. A definition of generic suspense, then, could be enlarged to incorporate the procedures by which a genre film postpones and only gradually makes good on its tacit deliverables. Another variant of generic suspense concerns *the degree to which* a genre film will make good on its promised characteristics. For instance, Philip Brophy describes in his account of body horror a suspense built around the viewer's nervous question: Just "how far is this film going to go" in the way of gruesomely disturbing representation? Brophy, "Horrality—the Textuality of Contemporary Horror Films," in *The Horror Reader*, ed. Ken Gelder (London: Routledge, 2000), 280.
33. Pascal Bonitzer, "Partial Vision: Film and the Labyrinth," trans. Fabrice Ziolkowski, *Wide Angle* 4, no. 4 (1981): 59.
34. Bonitzer, "Partial Vision," 61–63.
35. Stephanie Monohan, "*Skinamarink* Director Kyle Edward Ball on Crafting Homegrown Horror," *Fangoria*, January 10, 2023, https://www.fangoria.com/original/skinamarink-director-kyle-edward-ball-on-crafting-homegrown-horror/.
36. Pascal Bonitzer, "Deframings" (1978), trans. Chris Darke, in *Cahiers du Cinéma*, vol. 4: *1973–1978: History, Ideology, Cultural Struggle*, ed. David Wilson (London: Routledge, 2000), 197–203. Perceptual suspense can be understood as an affectively charged affirmation of the film medium's often suppressed affinities for the blurred, the concealed, the incomplete, and the unclear in the images of the world it presents. Martine Beugnet, introduction to *Indefinite Visions: Cinema and the Attractions of Uncertainty*, ed. Beugnet (Edinburgh: Edinburgh University Press, 2017), 1–8.
37. Pasternak quoted in Robert Bird, *Andrei Rublev* (London: British Film Institute, 2004), 37.
38. Bird, *Andrei Rublev*, 37–38. See also Robert Bird, *Andrei Tarkovsky: Elements of Cinema* (London: Reaktion, 2008), 209–24.
39. Dudley Andrew, *Mists of Regret: Culture and Sensibility in Classic French Film* (Princeton, NJ: Princeton University Press, 1995), 110. My take on *La petite Lise* (1930) is informed by Andrew's analysis, 106–12.
40. Pedro Costa, "A Closed Door That Keeps Us Guessing," transcript of a seminar at Tokyo Film School in 2005, *Rouge* 10 (2007), http://www.rouge.com.au/10/costa_seminar.html.
41. Robert Spadoni, "What Is Film Atmosphere?," *Quarterly Review of Film and Video* 37, no. 1 (2020): 49–53.
42. I borrow the notion of "added value" from Michel Chion, *Audio-Vision: Sound on Screen*, ed. and trans. Claudia Gorbman (New York: Columbia University Press, 1994), 5–12, 20–24.

43. Michael Slowik traces how Hitchcock, across other films prior to *The Birds*, integrates hushed, minimalistic sound into his suspense strategies. Slowik, "'Not for Tourists': Hitchcock's Sparse Sonic Set Pieces," *Hitchcock Annual* 21 (2017): 71–104.
44. Kristen Thompson, "In the Service of Horror—the Lyrical Cinematography of *Picnic at Hanging Rock*," Criterion Channel, n.d., https://www.criterionchannel.com/picnic-at-hanging-rock.
45. Erwin Straus, *The Primary World of Senses: A Vindication of Sensory Experience*, trans. Jacob Needleman (London: Collier Macmillan, 1963), 370–71. For a more recent articulation of the pathic as it bears on philosophical questions of atmosphere, see Tonino Griferro, "Pathicity: Experiencing the World in an Atmospheric Way," *Open Philosophy* 2 (2019): 414–27.
46. My sense of "firstness" is informed by Adrian J. Ivakhiv, *Ecologies of the Moving Image: Cinema, Affect, Nature* (Waterloo, Canada: Wilfrid Laurier University Press, 2013), 52–56, 89, 296, 343. Though atmosphere strikes us first in the film-viewing experience, we are always suspended among catching up with its influence belatedly, tuning into its present modulations, and anticipating its later contours, yet we improve as we go, as the film trains us in the nuances of atmosphere-conscious attention. Instructive here is Daniel Yacavone's account of the *cumulative* and holistic expression of film worlds—how, as immersed viewers, we gradually become acclimated to an atmospheric world sensed *as a whole*. Yacavone, *Film Worlds: A Philosophical Aesthetics of Cinema* (New York: Columbia University Press, 2015), 196–200.
47. Carmen Gray, "High Society: Kleber Mendonça Filho on the Architecture of Loathing," *Sight and Sound*, February 6, 2014, https://www.bfi.org.uk/news-opinion/sight-sound-magazine/interviews/high-society-kleber-mendonca-filho-architecture-loathing.
48. For insightful discussions of the historical, cultural, and geopolitical aspects of *Neighboring Sounds* (2012), see Leslie L. Marsh, "Reordering (Social) Sensibilities: Balancing Realisms in *Neighbouring Sounds*," *Studies in Spanish and Latin American Cinemas* 12, no. 2 (2015): 139–57; and Jack A. Draper III, "'Materialist Horror' and the Portrayal of Middle-Class Fear in Recent Brazilian Film Drama: *Adrift* (2009) and *Neighbouring Sounds* (2012)," *Studies in Spanish and Latin American Cinemas* 13, no. 2 (2016): 119–35.
49. Miguel Penabella has discussed the importance of spectrality in Lav Diaz's slow films as they reckon with Filipino politics and history. Penabella, "Ghostly Temporalities: Spectral Contemplation and Historical Revisionism in Lav Diaz's Slow Films," paper presented at the Society for Cinema and Media Studies Conference, Seattle, March 15, 2019.
50. Bliss Cua Lim, *Translating Time: Cinema, the Fantastic, and Temporal Critique* (Durham, NC: Duke University Press, 2009), 149–89.
51. Some critical defenders of the "slow" style prefer the labels *contemplative* and *durational*. Some object that the term *slow* is disadvantageous because it carries pejorative connotations for many filmgoers. Jonathan Rosenbaum objects that *slow cinema* is "an ahistorical term" ill-suited to historically minded filmmakers such as Kelly Reichardt. Rosenbaum, "Crossing Kelly Reichardt's Wilderness," Jonathan Rosenbaum (website), December 2022, https://jonathanrosenbaum.net/2022/12/crossing-kelly-reichardts-wilderness/. I would counter that *slow*, when used responsibly, allows us to address the *experiential tensions* a spectator feels when confronted by a film whose pacing, rhythm, and economy of narrative disclosure depart in drastic ways from the speeds and intensities by which contemporaneous popular cinema (and even some examples

of art cinema) progress. Asbjørn Grønstad has been careful to note that perceptions of slowness evolve over time and may come into play retrospectively when, say, today's spectators watch films produced during an earlier era. Grønstad, *Screening the Unwatchable: Spaces of Negation in Post-millennial Art Cinema* (Basingstoke, U.K.: Palgrave Macmillan, 2012), 67. It should also be observed that what registers as "slow" may differ widely across cultures.

52. For a concise survey of the critical reception of slow cinema and its controversies, see Erika Balsom, *Ten Skies* (Victoria, Australia: Fireflies, 2021), 67–75. A constant reference in these debates about slowness is David Bordwell's articulation of a polar-opposite aesthetic tendency in mainstream films in "Intensified Continuity: Visual Style in Contemporary American Film," *Film Quarterly* 55, no. 3 (2002): 16–28.

53. For nuanced handlings of the functions of slow cinema, see Song Hwee Lim, *Tsai Ming-liang and a Cinema of Slowness* (Honolulu: University of Hawai'i Press, 2014); Moira Weigel, "Slow Wars: Is This How Cinema Transcends Itself?," *N+1* 25 (2016), https://nplusonemag.com/issue-25/essays/slow-wars/; and Katherine Fusco and Nicole Seymour, *Kelly Reichardt* (Urbana: University of Illinois Press, 2017), 51–55. For a larger rundown of critical debates surrounding this kind of filmmaking, see note 9 in the introduction.

54. On contemporary art cinema's use of negative affects, particularly as they intertwine banality, boredom, duration, and extreme violence in slow films such as Bruno Dumont's *Twentynine Palms* (2003), see Grønstad, *Screening the Unwatchable*; and Allison Taylor, *Troubled Everyday: The Aesthetics of Violence and the Everyday in European Art Cinema* (Edinburgh: Edinburgh University Press, 2017).

55. Tarkovsky quoted in Bird, *Andrei Tarkovsky*, 197. In numerous interviews and some of her writings, Chantal Akerman theorizes a durationally inflected cinematic image that begins to oscillate between concrete and abstract dimensions in the spectator's consciousness. See Akerman's televisual self-portrait *Chantal Akerman par Chantal Akerman* (1996) as well as the interview of her included on the Criterion Collection's Blu-ray edition of *Jeanne Dielman 23 quai du Commerce, 1080 Bruxelles* (1975), 2017.

56. Nöel Burch, *Theory of Film Practice*, trans. Helen R. Lane (Princeton, NJ: Princeton University Press, 1981), 25.

57. David Bordwell, "Murder Culture: Adventures in 1940s Suspense," David Bordwell's Website on Cinema, 2013, http://www.davidbordwell.net/essays/murder.php.

58. Christophe Wall-Romana, *Jean Epstein: Corporeal Cinema and Film Philosophy* (Manchester, U.K.: Manchester University Press, 2016), 54.

59. Wall-Romana, *Jean Epstein*, 55.

60. Wall-Romana, *Jean Epstein*, 199. Also relevant here is Nico Baumbach's claim that Hitchcock's suspense merely seems to privilege the economical functioning of cause-and-effect narrative, while in fact "suspending suspense": "Hitchcock's genius might be seen to lie not in narrative economy, as is often believed, but rather in his use of repetition and stoppage to neutralize the cause and effect of narrative logic and render it, like the law in Kafka, as 'in force without significance.' He is the master of suspending suspense." This argument suggests there is a closer affinity between Hitchcock's practice and Jean Epstein's concept of "suspension" than is usually noted. Baumbach, *Cinema/Politics/Philosophy* (New York: Columbia University Press, 2018), 159.

61. *Oxford English Dictionary*, s.v. "suspension (n.)," December 2023, https://doi.org/10.1093/OED/5526042745.

62. Durgnat, *A Long Hard Look at "Psycho,"* 169–70. Let us not exclude Douglas Gordon's *24 Hour Psycho* (Tramway Art Centre in Glasgow, Scotland, and Kunst-Werke Institute for Contemporary Art in Berlin, 1993), a video installation that many scholars writing about aesthetic slowness have enthusiastically considered. The piece removes all sound from Hitchcock's film, projects the images in their original sequence on a screen viewable on either side, and expands the running time to the length of entire day. Events no longer flow but incrementally lurch forward at a rate of around two frames per second. As Lutz Koepnick writes, this deceleration converts the whole of *Psycho* into one long take insofar as the cuts become less frequent and harder to remember. Lutz Koepnick, *The Long Take: Art Cinema and the Wonderous* (Minneapolis: University of Minnesota Press, 2017), 48–52. See also Koepnick, *On Slowness: Toward an Aesthetic of the Contemporary* (New York: Columbia University Press, 2014), 256–61. Gordon indeed does away with Hitchcock's original rhythm and renders the narrative less climactic, yet the resulting experiment in suspension *bears forth suspense of another kind*. There emerges a more contemplative, less tightly controlling version of what Hitchcock liked to call "pure cinema," where the images alone, free of dialogue, articulate events and wield an absorbing power. For a distillation of Hitchcockian pure cinema, see Bruce Isaacs, *The Art of Pure Cinema: Hitchcock and His Imitators* (New York: Oxford University Press, 2020), 15–40.
63. Vivian Sobchack, *Carnal Thoughts: Embodiment and Moving Image Culture* (Berkeley: University of California Press, 2004), 102–3.
64. Robert Bird, "The Suspended Aesthetic: Slavoj Žižek on Eastern European Film," *Studies in East European Thought* 56 (2004): 370, 379–80, 377–78.
65. Adrian Martin, *Mysteries of Cinema: Reflections on Film Theory, History, and Culture 1982–2016* (Amsterdam: Amsterdam University Press, 2019), 173–75.
66. Martin, *Mysteries of Cinema*, 176, 188–91.
67. Perez, *The Material Ghost*, 368. The key term here for Perez is *withholding*. Paul Schrader comparably offers in his survey of contemporary slow cinema—a new addition to his book on transcendental style—a list of devices that "withhold" and thus create "dissonance," but he refrains from invoking "suspense," which in his taxonomy includes only traditional narrative suspense—that is, something to be stanchioned off from the "introspective" and boredom-inducing practice of slow cinema. Schrader, *Transcendental Style in Film: Ozu, Bresson, Dreyer* (1972), with a new introduction (Berkeley: University of California Press, 2018), 11–21. I use the term *withholding* in reference to suspenseful operations, but when it comes to the kind of radical suspense Antonioni's art cinema enacts and provokes, is it indeed correct to say the film withholds? Something "withheld" is implied to be something known. Doesn't the term risk assuming masterly knowledge on the part of the film and its authorial-rhetorical discourse? Aren't some examples of suspense in art cinema, including Antonioni's, more to do with *relinquishing* the epistemological pretense of mastery and its promise to end uncertainty?
68. Pascal Bonitzer, "The Disappearance (on Antonioni)," trans. Chris Beyer, Gavriel Moses, and Seymour Chatman, in *L'avventura: Michelangelo Antonioni, Director*, ed. Seymour Chatman and Guido Fink (New Brunswick, NJ: Rutgers University Press, 1989), 215–18; Umberto Eco, *The Open Work*, trans. Anna Cancogni (Cambridge, MA: Harvard University Press, 1989), 115–18. See also Peter Wuss, "Narrative Tension in Antonioni," in *Suspense*, ed. Vorderer, Wulff, and Friedrichsen, 51–70.
69. Perez, *The Material Ghost*, 369–70.

238   1. Suspense in Slow Time

70. Michelangelo Antonioni, *The Architecture of Vision: Writings and Interviews on Cinema*, ed. Carlo di Carlo and Giorgio Tinazzi, U.S. ed., ed. Marga Cottino-Jones (New York: Marsilio, 1996), 346.
71. This suspenseful conflict between character and the actor's persona can also be found in Viggo Mortensen's role in Alonso's slow film *Jauja* (2014), which I examine in chapter 3.
72. Chion, *Audio-Vision*, 9.
73. Emre Çağlayan, *Poetics of Slow Cinema: Nostalgia, Absurdism, Boredom* (Newcastle, U.K.: Palgrave Macmillan, 2018), 203, 208–12.
74. Çağlayan reports that Ceylan's film takes inspiration from Chekhov's work and intersperses quotations from a number of his short stories. Çağlayan, *Poetics of Slow Cinema*, 207. The reasons behind the doctor's decision to falsify the autopsy report can be inferred by the attentive viewer.
75. There is more to say here than I have space to explore regarding how slow, atmospheric suspense and suspension enact uncommonly graded, morphing transitions between what we think of as "still" and what we think of as "moving." A starting point for this discussion would be Jordan Schonig's account of "durational metamorphoses" in slow cinema. See Schonig, *The Shape of Motion: Cinema and the Aesthetics of Movement* (New York: Oxford University Press, 2022), 74–98.
76. Grønstad, *Screening the Unwatchable*, 57–83; Linda Williams, "Film Bodies: Gender, Genre, and Excess," *Film Quarterly* 44, no. 4 (1991): 2–13.
77. Taylor, *Troubled Everyday*, 61–77. Critiquing received conceptions of everydayness in film—namely, the positions advanced by Paul Schrader and Andrew Kleven—Taylor makes a persuasive case that the line that separates the dramatic from the undramatic can be so thin as to be nearly impossible to determine (39–43). She cites Robert Bresson's *L'argent* (1983) and Michael Haneke's *The Seventh Continent* (1989) to shore up her claim.
78. The phrase "rhetoric of boredom" is from Grønstad, *Screening the Unwatchable*, 58.
79. Saige Walton, "Cruising the Unknown: Film as Rhythm and Embodied Apprehension in *L'iconnu du lac / Stranger by the Lake*," *New Review of Film and Television Studies* 16, no. 3 (2018): 239–46, 246–53.
80. Spadoni, "What Is Film Atmosphere?," 60, emphasis added.
81. Hanich, *Cinematic Emotion in Horror Films and Thrillers*, 180–82; see also 104, 119, 155, 173, 193–94, 210, 217.
82. Davina Quinlivan, *The Place of Breath in Cinema* (Edinburgh: Edinburgh University Press, 2012), 1–40.

2. Minimal Thrills

1. Martin Rubin, *Thrillers* (Cambridge: Cambridge University Press, 1999), 5–8.
2. Reichardt quoted in Katherine Fusco and Nicole Seymour, *Kelly Reichardt* (Urbana: University of Illinois Press, 2017), 115.
3. Rubin, *Thrillers*, 30–31. Here Rubin enlarges on terminology used by Lars Ole Sauerberg.
4. Bresson's disclaimer at the outset of *Pickpocket* (1959) has also led commentators to rule out suspense as an aesthetic concern. Onscreen text, in concert with elegant baroque music by Jean-Baptiste Lully, proclaims: "The style of this film is not that of a thriller [*policier*]. The filmmaker strives to express, with images and sounds, the

nightmare of a young man whose weaknesses lead him to commit acts of theft for which nothing destined him. However, this adventure, and the strange path it takes, bring together two souls who may otherwise never have met." We should grasp Bresson's French term *policier* in its local context. Not quite a catch-all for thrillers of any stripe, it encompasses police procedurals, tales of crime and detection, as well as gangster films. For Bresson, it references the lurid and moody crime films that cropped up in high numbers in France after World War II—films that staged a transatlantic dialogue with American film noir. In distinguishing *Pickpocket* from the "style" of the *policier*, Bresson's statement doesn't proscribe suspense. It tells his late 1950s audience not to expect yet another film depicting violent crimes and the Paris underworld in the more melodramatic fashion of this postwar cycle that had already become overly familiar.

5. Susan Sontag, "Spiritual Style in the Films of Robert Bresson" (1964), in *Against Interpretation and Other Essays* (New York: Picador, 1966), 183, 180.
6. Paul Schrader, *Transcendental Style in Film: Ozu, Bresson, Dreyer* (1972), with a new introduction (Berkeley: University of California Press, 2018), 196; Brian Price, "The End of Transcendence, the Mourning of Crime: Bresson's Hands," *Studies in French Cinema* 2, no. 3 (2002): 131.
7. "Should we talk of suspense?," Eric Rohmer asks. "No, not if what we mean by that word is a clever arrangement of good or bad omens. Yes, if it is true that nothing can distract us from the one thought: escape." Rohmer, "Le miracle des objets," *Cahiers du Cinéma*, no. 65 (December 1956): 43, my translation. François Truffaut locates suspense in *A Man Escaped*'s (1956) command of our attention through a nontraditional orchestration of time: "The suspense . . . is created naturally, not by stretching out the passage of time, but by letting it evaporate." For Truffaut, suspense develops not because time is elasticized in the manner of Hitchcock but because scenes in seeming real time "evaporate" before we can fully apprehend them. But in the aggregate, he explains, these fleeting scenes lend the impression that we share a cell with Fontaine for two months instead of ninety minutes. Truffaut, "*Un condamné à mort s'est échappé*" (1956), trans. Leonard Mayhew, in *Robert Bresson*, ed. James Quandt (Toronto: Toronto International Film Festival Group, 1998), 586.

   For more recent commentary on suspense in *A Man Escaped*, see Mirella Jona Affron, "Bresson and Pascal: Rhetorical Affinities," in *Robert Bresson*, ed. Quandt, 169–70; Jonathan Rosenbaum, "The Last Filmmaker: A Local, Interim Report," in *Bresson*, ed. Quandt, 20; Adrian Martin, "*A Man Escaped*," Film Critic: Adrian Martin (website), April 2003, https://www.adrianmartinfilmcritic.com/reviews/m/man_escaped.html; Tony Pipolo, *Robert Bresson: A Passion for Film* (New York: Oxford University Press, 2010), 117–18; Gwendolyn Audrey Foster, "*A Man Escaped*," *Senses of Cinema* 62 (March 2012), https://www.sensesofcinema.com/2012/cteq/a-man-escaped/; and Darragh O'Donoghue, "*A Man Escaped*," *Cineaste* 38, no. 4 (Fall 2013): 60.
8. To his commentators who too quickly imposed intellectual frameworks onto his films, Bresson had this to say: "I have much more confidence in the real public, the one that feels, than in the small-minded audience that seeks to exercise its intelligence before feeling." Bresson, "To Get to the Mystery" (1960), in *Bresson on Bresson: Interviews 1943–1983*, ed. Mylène Bresson, trans. Ana Moschovakis (New York: New York Review of Books, 2016), 75.
9. Robert Bresson, *Notes on the Cinematograph* (French orig. 1975), trans. Jonathan Griffin (1977; reprint, New York: New York Review of Books, 2016), 28, 5, 37, 56, 59 ("One does not create by adding but by taking away. . . . Empty the pond to get the fish"), 62, 86.

10. Robert Bresson, "To Create Life Without Copying It" (1966), in *Bresson on Bresson*, 162.
11. I determined the average shot length of *A Man Escaped* using the calculation tool available at Yuri Tsivian's website Cinemetrics, http://www.cinemetrics.lv/.
12. Michel Chion, *Film: A Sound Art*, trans. Claudia Gorbman (New York: Columbia University Press, 2009), 256.
13. Inevitability can *increase* suspense regardless of our knowledge levels. Even when we watch, say, *Carrie* (Brian De Palma, 1976) for the first time, we know—even if we haven't read the Stephen King novel or seen the posters and trailers—that the bucket of blood *will fall* during the crowning of the prom queen, but the unbearably slow, atmospheric protraction of the interval of waiting activates suspense all the same.
14. Germane to the point I am chasing here is André Bazin's contemporaneous review of Henri Clouzot's *The Wages of Fear* (1953), where he argues that the film's finely milled attention to process upstages "dramatic complications in the plot." Suspense works as "an epic of imminence" that nonetheless delays plot through an excruciating, incrementalist emphasis on detail. Bazin, "*Le salaire de la peur*: A Masterly Work by Henri Clouzot" (1953), in Bazin, *French Cinema from the Liberation to the New Wave, 1945–1958*, ed. and trans. Bert Cardullo (New Orleans: University of New Orleans Press, 2012), 175–76.
15. P. Adams Sitney, "The Rhetoric of Robert Bresson: From *Journal d'un curé de campagne* to *Une femme douce*," in *Robert Bresson*, rev. ed., ed. James Quandt (Toronto: Toronto International Film Festival Group, 2011), 129, emphasis added.
16. Gregory Flaxman, "Film Philosophy and Fideism: Bresson and the Fifties," manuscript in progress, chap. 2. Flaxman develops the concept of "zerocularity" through an engagement with the narratological theory of François Jost and specifically in relation to Bresson's films *Diary of a Country Priest* (1951), *A Man Escaped*, and *Pickpocket*.
17. Flaxman, "Film Philosophy and Fideism," chap. 2.
18. Flaxman, "Film Philosophy and Fideism," chap. 2.
19. Salomé Aguilera Skvirsky, *The Process Genre: Cinema and the Aesthetic of Labor* (Durham, NC: Duke University Press, 2020), 1–49, 101–2, 104–14.
20. Chion, *Film*, 389.
21. Colin McArthur, "Mise en Scène Degree Zero: Jean-Pierre Melville's *Le Samouraï*," in *French Film: Texts and Contexts*, 2nd ed., ed. Susan Hayward and Ginette Vincendeau (New York: Routledge, 2000), 191–93, 198.
22. McArthur, "Mise en Scène Degree Zero," 191, 198.
23. Sitney, "The Rhetoric of Robert Bresson," 119.
24. A larger Bressonian school of suspense falls beyond this chapter's scope, although spiritual elements don't necessarily find expression across its examples. Among its practitioners are Michael Haneke, Christian Petzold, Angela Schanelec, Valeska Grisebach, Céline Sciamma, Olivier Assayas, Ognjen Glavonić, and Andreas Fontana of the remarkable yet underseen *Azor* (2021). Directors I address in later chapters—namely Lisandro Alonso, Pedro Costa, and, to a lesser extent, Kiyoshi Kurosawa—also newly devise techniques of Bressonian suspense.
25. For accounts that regard such delays in editing continuity as hallmarks of slow cinema, see Matthew Flanagan, "Towards an Aesthetic of Slow in Contemporary Cinema," *16:9*, November 2008, http://www.16-9.dk/2008-11/side11_inenglish.htm; and Paul Schrader, "Rethinking Transcendental Style," introduction to *Transcendental Style in Film*, 12. The critic, novelist, and poet Gilbert Adair once noted that delays

involving doors in the films of Jean-Marie Straub and Danièle Huillet constituted a "contemplative" variety of screen "suspense": the trace of an action completed and vanished is no less suspenseful than a door about to open in "a horror movie." Adair, "Amerikana: *Class Relations*," *Sight and Sound* 54, no. 2 (1985): 144. On the importance of repetition in minimalism, see Yvett Biró, *Turbulence and Flow in Film: The Rhythmic Design*, trans. Paul Salamon (Bloomington: Indiana University Press, 2008), 129–50.
26. Nöel Burch, *Theory of Film Practice*, trans. Helen R. Lane (Princeton, NJ: Princeton University Press, 1981), 17.
27. Chion, *Film*, 253–54.
28. Here I borrow Tonino Griffero's concept of the quasi-thingness of atmospheric expression, a quality of space not attaining to the ontology of an object yet all the more powerful and positive *because of* its evanescence. Griffero, *Atmospheres: Aesthetics of Emotional Spaces*, trans. Sarah De Sanctis (Burlington, VT: Ashgate, 2010), 108–12. Griffero's take on this concept comes from the neophenomenology of the philosopher Hermann Schmitz.
29. Bresson, "To Get to the Mystery," 75.
30. Rubin, *Thrillers*, 30–31; Steve Neale, *Genre and Hollywood* (New York: Routledge, 2000), 84–85.
31. Nicole Brenez, "Chantal Akerman: The Pajama Interview," *Lola* 2 (June 2012), http://www.lolajournal.com/2/pajama.html. See also the director's self-portrait made for television, *Chantal Akerman par Chantal Akerman* (1996).
32. Akerman, in Brenez, "Chantal Akerman."
33. Akerman, in Brenez, "Chantal Akerman."
34. Akerman's filmography technically includes two versions of *La chambre*. In addition to the version of 1972, the version I reference is the one included in late 2023 on the Criterion Channel, the streaming service of the Criterion Collection.
35. Miriam Rosen, "In Her Own Time: Miriam Rosen in Conversation with Chantal Akerman," *Artforum* 42, no. 8 (April 2004): 122. See also Akerman's televisual self-portrait *Chantal Akerman par Chantal Akerman* and the interview of Akerman included on the Criterion Collection's Blu-ray edition of *Jeanne Dielman 23 quai du Commerce, 1080 Bruxelles* (1975), 2017.
36. Manny Farber, "*Wavelength, Standard Time*, , and *One Second in Montreal*," *Artforum* 8, no. 5 (January 1970): 81. For Farber, these extremely subtle elements of form ascend to the role of "new actors," supplanting human actors. See also Manny Farber and Patricia Patterson, "Kitchen Without Kitsch" (1976), in *Farber on Film: The Complete Film Writings of Manny Farber*, ed. Robert Polito (New York: Library of America, 2009), 762–69. Here Farber and Patterson examine *Jean Dielman* in relation to a wide range of minimalist film and art-world practices, including the work of Bresson, Yasujirō Ozu, Michael Snow, and Andy Warhol.
37. Ivone Margulies, *Nothing Happens: Chantal Akerman's Hyperrealist Everyday* (Durham, NC: Duke University Press, 1996), 56–60. Margulies, although handling Akerman's affinities with Jean-Luc Godard, Carl Th. Dreyer, and Andy Warhol, aligns Akerman with Bresson in terms of a closely shared minimalist, antinaturalist, antipsychological, and antididactic "aesthetics of homogeneity," whereby the forms and corporeal figures do not refer beyond themselves for the sake of Brechtian quotation but rather remain locked within metonymic patterns that evoke the mechanical, automatic properties of the film medium. Margulies also crucially identifies another influence on Akerman's ostensibly Bressonian practice: the *nouveau roman*, in

242   2. Minimal Thrills

particular the prose of Alain Robbe-Grillet and its focus on quotidian physical details (69–72).
38. Margulies, *Nothing Happens*, 64.
39. Margulies, *Nothing Happens*, 23.
40. Chantal Akerman, "Chantal Akerman on *Jeanne Dielman*" (2009), featurette included on the Criterion Collection's Blu-ray edition of *Jeanne Dielman* (1975), 2017.
41. Mary Ann Doane, "Woman's Stake: Filming the Female Body," *October* 17 (Summer 1981): 35, emphasis added.
42. Margulies, *Nothing Happens*, 80.
43. Margulies, *Nothing Happens*, 79, emphasis added.
44. Margulies, *Nothing Happens*, 23–24, 65–66, 75.
45. Marion Schmid, *Chantal Akerman* (Manchester, U.K.: Manchester University Press, 2019), 153, 154. This statement plays down the fact that Akermanian suspense exists in its own right without Hitchcockian elements having to be in the equation.
46. For a survey of the genre that informs my arguments, see Linda Ruth Williams, *The Erotic Thriller in Contemporary Cinema* (Bloomington: Indiana University Press, 2005).
47. *La captive* (2000) incorporates and recontextualizes the clichés of erotic thrillers. The shot of a nude woman bathing behind fogged glass or fabric is everywhere in the genre, especially in its installments in the 1980s and 1990s.
48. James Naremore, "Spies and Lovers: *North by Northwest*," in *An Invention Without a Future: Essays on Cinema* (Berkeley: University of California Press, 2014), 170.
49. See, for example, Colleen Glenn, "Complicating the Theory of the Male Gaze: Hitchcock's Leading Men," *New Review of Film and Television* 15, no. 4 (2017): 496–510. *La captive* anticipates this rethinking of the male gaze in that Simon, no less than Ariane, is the "captive" named in the film's title, done in, rather than empowered, by the workings of the gaze and his compulsion to control.
50. Akerman excitedly makes this comparison to *Eyes Wide Shut* (1999) in an interview by Dominique Païni, included as a special feature on the Image Entertainment DVD edition of *La captive* (2000), 2004.
51. Cristina Álvarez López and Adrian Martin, "Each in a Place Apart: *La captive* (Chantal Akerman, 2000)," *Multimedia Lectures on Film*, episode 2, October 22, 2021, https://vimeo.com/ondemand/multimedialectures2. Lancelin's cinematographic flair for low-key suspense in slow cinema is also on display in Manoel de Oliveira's *The Strange Case of Angelica* (2010).
52. Álvarez López and Martin, "Each in a Place Apart." This part of the lecture is voiced specifically by Álvarez López.
53. Richard Dyer, "Making Sense of Noise and Silence in *La captive*," in *The Oxford Handbook of Cinematic Listening*, ed. Carlo Cenciarelli (New York: Oxford University Press, 2021), 241–51. See also Bérénice Reynaud, "Alluring Absence: *La captive*," *Senses of Cinema* 31 (April 2004), https://www.sensesofcinema.com/2004/cteq/la_captive/.
54. Akerman, interview by Païni, special feature on the Image Entertainment DVD edition of *La captive*. On the significance of sleep in the film, see Emma Wilson, "Unknown Deaths in *La captive*," in *Chantal Akerman: Afterlives*, ed. Marion Schmid and Emma Wilson (Cambridge: Legenda, 2019), 92–95. For another crucial discussion of the motif of sleep in the film, see Christine Smallwood, *La captive* (Victoria, Australia: Fireflies, 2024), which appeared after my book was already at press.
55. Indeed, Akerman's engagement with Hitchcock's oeuvre and its gender dynamics goes beyond *Vertigo* (1958). The car scene late in *La captive* when Simon, after insisting they

2. Minimal Thrills   243

end their relationship, drives Ariane to her aunt's countryside home, along the way still quizzing and lecturing her, vividly recalls the extended car scene in Hitchcock's *Marnie* (1964) when Mark (Sean Connery) reveals to "Marnie" (Tippi Hedren) that he has hunted and captured her and plans to keep her under his "care." The vehicle in both films figures as a prison for the female passenger, as does Hitchcock's and Akerman's similar uses of a frontal two-shot through the windshield.

56. Álvarez López and Martin, "Each in a Place Apart." For Martin's invaluable discussion of cinematic *dispositifs*, which informs my perspective here, see Adrian Martin, *Mise en Scène and Film Style: From Classical Hollywood to New Media Art* (Basingstoke, U.K.: Palgrave MacMillan, 2014), 178–204.
57. Brenez, "Chantal Akerman."
58. See Kate Rennebohm, "Approaching the Other as Other: A Study of the Ethical Nature of Chantal Akerman's Films," MA thesis, Concordia University, 2011, 112–30. On Akerman's Levinas-influenced conception of the image, see Kate Rennebohm, "'A Pedagogy of the Image': Chantal Akerman's Ethics Across Film and Art," *Moving Image Review & Art Journal* 8, nos. 1–2 (2019): 41–53.
59. Narrative suspense still claims this ending. Martine Beugnet intriguingly argues that the shape of *La captive*'s trajectory is keyed to Ariane's liberatory "becoming mermaid" as she merges with the sea and thus eludes Simon for good. Beugnet, *Cinema and Sensation: French Film and the Art of Transgression* (Cambridge: Cambridge University Press, 2013), 132–37. This reading is as compelling and plausible as any, but the tone of the scene feels much bleaker to me.
60. Akerman's suspenseful practice makes good on Hugo Münsterberg's early theory of cinematic attention: "A faint light to which we turn our attention does not become the strong light of an incandescent lamp. No, it remains the faint, just perceptible streak of lightness, but it has grown more impressive, more distinct, more clear in its details, more vivid. It has taken a stronger hold of us." Münsterberg, *The Photoplay: A Psychological Study* (New York: Appleton, 1916), 84.
61. Akerman quoted in Adam Roberts, "'Like a Musical Piece': Akerman and Musicality," in *Chantal Akerman*, ed. Schmid and Wilson, 138 n. 11.
62. Kelly Reichardt, "Kelly Reichardt's Top 10," Criterion Collection, May 9, 2020, https://www.criterion.com/current/top-10-lists/370-kelly-reichardt-s-top-10.
63. James Ponsoldt, "Lost in America: Kelly Reichardt's *Meek's Cutoff*," *Filmmaker Magazine*, November 23, 2011, https://filmmakermagazine.com/35034-lost-in-america-kelly-reichardts-meeks-cutoff/; Vadim Rizov, "'Why Don't We All Go Blow Stuff Up?' Kelly Reichardt on *Night Moves*," *Filmmaker Magazine*, May 30, 2014, https://filmmakermagazine.com/86114-why-dont-we-all-go-blow-stuff-up-kelly-reichardt-on-night-moves/; Kelly Reichardt, "Kelly Reichardt Q&A—*Night Moves*," Film Society Lincoln Center, July 31, 2014, https://www.youtube.com/watch?v=18zzyN9FRew.
64. Fusco and Seymour, *Kelly Reichardt*; Elena Gorfinkel, "Exhausted Drift: Austerity, Dispossession, and the Politics of Slow in Kelly Reichardt's *Meek's Cutoff*," in *Slow Cinema*, ed. Tiago de Luca and Nuno Barrados Jorge (Edinburgh: Edinburgh University Press, 2015), 123–36.
65. In 2020, Reichardt curated a film series for the Brooklyn Academy of Music around the release of her film *First Cow* (2019). The series comprised films that informed her approach to *First Cow*, a revisionist Western, and included Melville's heist film *Le cercle rouge* (1970).
66. Fusco and Seymour, *Kelly Reichardt*, 2.
67. Fusco and Seymour, *Kelly Reichardt*, 2.

68. Adrian J. Ivakhiv, *Ecologies of the Moving Image: Cinema, Affect, Nature* (Waterloo, Canada: Wilfrid Laurier University Press, 2013), 341–45.
69. Ivakhiv, *Ecologies of the Moving Image*, 52–56, 89, 296, 343.
70. Reichardt in Zachary Wigon, "Interview: Kelly Reichardt on the Nuance of *Night Moves*," *Tribeca News*, May 29, 2014, https://tribecafilm.com/news/interview-kelly-reichardt-night-moves.
71. Ivakhiv, *Ecologies of the Moving Image*, 62–63, 254.
72. Fusco and Seymour, *Kelly Reichardt*, 26.
73. On the matter of the perceptibility of the "slow violence of environmental degradation," see Fusco and Seymour, *Kelly Reichardt*, 74–75.
74. Graig Uhlin, "Feeling Depleted: Ecocinema and the Atmospherics of Affect," in *Affective Ecocriticism: Emotion, Embodiment, Environment*, ed. Kyle Bladlow and Jennifer Ladino (Lincoln: University of Nebraska Press, 2018), 283–87.
75. Amy Dawes, "The Journey Is the Destination," *DGA Quarterly*, Fall–Winter 2016–2017, https://www.dga.org/Craft/DGAQ/All-Articles/1701-Winter-2017/Independent-Voice-Kelly-Reichardt.aspx.
76. On the film's unnerving soundscape as it renegotiates its thrillerness, see E. Dawn Hall's rich discussion of *Night Moves* (2014) in *ReFocus: The Films of Kelly Reichardt* (Edinburgh: Edinburgh University Press, 2018), 114–19.
77. Fusco and Seymour, *Kelly Reichardt*, 73–74. Offering a different take on the film's treatment of negative affects, Matthew Holtmeier examines how it explores a type of paranoia for which no real material basis and no linear chain of events emerge. Holtmeier, "Communicating Cascadia: Reichardt's Three Ecologies as Bioregional Medium," *Screen* 58, no. 4 (Winter 2017): 495–96.
78. Sianne Ngai, *Ugly Feelings* (Cambridge, MA: Harvard University Press, 2005), 299, 19–20.
79. Thomas Elsaesser, *The Mind-Game Film: Distributed Agency, Time Travel, and Productive Pathology*, ed. Warren Buckland, Dana Polan, and Seung-hoon Jeong (New York: Routledge, 2021), 50.
80. Cynthia Freeland, "Horror and Art-Dread," in *The Horror Film*, ed. Stephen Prince (New Brunswick, NJ: Rutgers University Press, 2004), 189–205, esp. 191–92. I return to this concept in greater detail in my discussion of Kiyoshi Kurosawa's work in chapter 5.
81. No doubt Reichardt's environmental soundscape is informed by Todd Haynes's *Safe* (1995), a film she teaches in her sound-design course at Bard College. Haynes is an executive producer for *Night Moves* and several other Reichardt-directed projects.
82. What I discuss in this chapter as a thrilling minimalism could be further essayed in conversation with Andrew Klevan's book *Disclosure of the Everyday: Undramatic Achievement in Narrative Film* (Wiltshire, U.K.: Flicks, 2000), in particular his conceptions of repetition and "invigorating the commonplace" (40–41), although Klevan puts suspense on the chopping block where I would consider structural suspense to be in effect. To my mind, one of the most supreme examples of the invigoration of the quotidian occurs in Abbas Kiarostami's *Close-Up* (1990) when the reporter kicks an aerosol can in the street, an object to which we have been acoustically sensitized minutes earlier, albeit at the threshold of attention. See Gilberto Perez, *The Material Ghost: Films and Their Medium* (Baltimore, MD: Johns Hopkins University Press, 1998), 263–64.
83. See Aaron Smuts, "The Desire-Frustration Theory of Suspense," *Journal of Aesthetics and Art Criticism* 66, no. 3 (2008): 281–90.

84. On suspense as an idiom that forces viewers to reckon with their multilayered lack of control, see Hauke Lehmann, "Suspense in the Cinema: Knowledge and Time," in *The Fascination with Unknown Time*, ed. Sibylle Baumbach, Lena Henningsen, and Klaus Oschema (Cham, Switzerland: Palgrave Macmillan, 2017), 251–71.

3. The Ambient Landscape

1. See Catherine Fowler, "Obscurity and Stillness: Potentiality in the Moving Image," *Art Journal* 72, no. 1 (2013): 64–79; Fowler, "Slow Looking: Confronting Moving Images with Georges Didi-Huberman," in *Indefinite Visions: Cinema and the Attractions of Uncertainty*, ed. Martine Beugnet (Edinburgh: Edinburgh University Press, 2017), 241–54.
2. Scott MacDonald, "Surveying James Benning," in *James Benning's Environments: Politics, Ecology, Duration*, ed. Nikolaj Lübecker and Daniele Rugo (Edinburgh: Edinburgh University Press, 2018), 28.
3. Courtney Duckworth, "Got Milk," *Artforum*, March 5, 2020, https://www.artforum.com/film/courtney-duckworth-on-kelly-reichardt-s-first-cow-2019-82356.
4. Martin Lefebvre, "Between Setting and Landscape in Cinema," in *Landscape and Film*, ed. Martin Lefebvre (New York: Routledge, 2006), 28–29, 30, 38–44. For Lefebvre's more recent discussion of *Gerry* (2002), see Lefebvre, "On Landscape in Narrative Cinema," *Canadian Journal of Film Studies* 20, no. 1 (Spring 2011): 65–66.
5. Christophe Wall-Romana, *Jean Epstein: Corporeal Cinema and Film Philosophy* (Manchester, U.K.: Manchester University Press, 2013), 54–55; Robert Spadoni, "Horror Film Atmosphere as Anti-narrative (and Vice Versa)," in *Merchants of Menace: The Business of Horror Cinema*, ed. Richard Nowell (London: Bloomsbury, 2014), 109–28.
6. Jean-Paul Thibaud, "A Brief Archaeology of the Notion of Ambience," *Unlikely* 6 (2020), https://unlikely.net.au/issue-06/notion-of-ambiance. In philosophical accounts, the terms *ambience* and *atmosphere* are sometimes taken to be interchangeable and sometimes not, and the variances may depend on differences in language. The German thinker Gernot Böhme predominantly uses *atmosphere* (*Atmosphäre*) but invokes *ambience* (*Ambiente*) to emphasize that in discussing atmosphere we are talking not just about space but also about qualitative *presences*. Böhme, "Atmosphere as an Aesthetic Concept," in *The Aesthetics of Atmospheres*, ed. Jean-Paul Thibaud (New York: Routledge, 2017), 25–26.
7. Paul Roquet, *Ambient Media: Japanese Atmospheres of Self* (Minneapolis: University of Minnesota Press, 2016), 3–5, 18. Where Roquet casts "ambient" as a vector of "subjectivation," my account argues otherwise. Slow atmospheric suspense, in our three case studies in this chapter, partakes of a bewildering process of *de*subjectivation.
8. Leo Spitzer, "*Milieu* and *Ambiance*: An Essay in Historical Semantics," *Philosophy and Phenomenology* 3, no. 1 (September 1942): 2, 13 n. 3, 9–10, 4 (emphasis added), 34–35, 41.
9. Antonio Somaini, "Walter Benjamin's Media Theory: The *Medium* and the *Apparat*," *Grey Room* 62 (Winter 2016): 8. In this essay, Somaini also makes the key point about early German-language film theorists such as Béla Balázs never using the word *Medium* in reference to "the film medium" so much as to define the "medium of perception" (27). See also Somaini, "The Atmospheric Screen: Turner, Hazlitt, Ruskin," in *Screen Genealogies: From Optical Device to Environmental Medium*, ed. Craig

246   3. The Ambient Landscape

Buckley, Rüdiger Campe, and Francesco Casetti (Amsterdam: Amsterdam University Press, 2019), 159–86, esp. 167–68, where Somaini traces the conception of *media diaphana* back to Aristotle's *De anima* (c. 350 BCE).
10. See my discussion of Kiyoshi Kurosawa's work in chapter 5 for a lightly gothic example of this imbrication of elemental media involving cinema.
11. Giuliana Bruno, *Atmospheres of Projection: Environmentality in Art and Screen Media* (Chicago: University of Chicago Press, 2022), 22–27.
12. James J. Gibson, *The Ecological Approach to Visual Perception* (1986; reprint, New York: Psychology Press, 2015), 41, 44–46, 58. Gibson prioritizes vision in this study, but his concept of ambience also includes listening to sonic vibrations in the surrounding air (13).
13. Gibson, *The Ecological Approach to Visual Perception*, 255–89.
14. For an instructive overview, both historical and theoretical, of the sonic aspects of atmosphere and the transition "from a vococentric to a noise-centric" sound experience in contemporary cinema, see Steffen Hven, *Enacting the Worlds of Cinema* (New York: Oxford University Press, 2022), 121–43, 133.
15. On Remington's evocations of carnage, see Maurizia Natali, "The Course of the Empire: Sublime Landscapes in the American Cinema," in *Landscape and Film*, ed. Lefebvre, 103.
16. Adrian Martin observes how *Jauja* (2015), as a transition from Alonso's earlier films, "enters into an extremely rich, flowing, unforced dialogue with certain key forms and traditions in cinema history." Martin, "Jauja," *Sight & Sound*, May 2015, 66. Martin mentions Pier Paolo Pasolini's *Oedipus Rex* (1967), Valeria Sarmiento's *Our Marriage* (1984), David Lynch's *Inland Empire* (2006), Apichatpong Weerasethakul's work, and Miguel Gomes's *Tabu* (2012) as films that compare to *Jauja*.

Alonso lists Herzog's *Aguirre, the Wrath of God* (1972) and Andrei Tarkovsky's *Stalker* (1979) among his ten favorite films submitted to *Sight & Sound* in 2012, https://www2.bfi.org.uk/films-tv-people/sightandsoundpoll2012/voter/1035. Alonso also includes on the list canonical slow films such as Tsai Ming-liang's *The River* (1997) and Carlos Reygadas's *Silent Light* (2007). It is clear that Alonso self-consciously approaches slow cinema as a field of artistic experimentation within an international community of kindred artists.
17. See, for example, Jenny Barrett, "(Not) John Wayne and (Not) the US-American West," in *Transnationalism and Imperialism: Endurance of the Global Western Film*, ed. Hervé Mayer and David Roche (Bloomington: Indiana University Press, 2022), 214–29.
18. Timothy Morton, *Ecology Without Nature: Rethinking Environmental Aesthetics* (Cambridge, MA: Harvard University Press, 2007), 41–43. For Morton, "the Aeolian provokes anxiety, because built into it is a hesitation between an *obscure* source and *no* source at all" (43). Furthermore, "a disembodied Aeolian sound emanates 'from the background' but appears 'in the foreground.' With Aeolian events, we have a paradoxical situation in which background and foreground have collapsed in one sense, but persist in another sense. . . . The Aeolian attempts to undo the difference between a perceptual event upon which we can focus, and one that appears to surround us and which cannot be directly brought 'in front of' the sense organs without losing its environing properties" (47).
19. The suspenseful effects of ambient sound that I examine in this chapter and throughout this book more generally attest to what Danijela Kulezic-Wilson has called the "musicalization" of sound design—practices that are more aesthetic than strictly representational as they render hazy the perceptible differences among score, effects,

and noise. See Kulezic-Wilson, *Sound Design Is the New Score: Theory, Aesthetics, and Erotics of the Integrated Soundtrack* (New York: Oxford University Press, 2020). Of particular relevance to my study is Kulezic-Wilson's discussion of "sensuous" aesthetic design and experience in slow-cinematic experiments by Gus Van Sant (99–105), Béla Tarr (105–10), and Hou Hsiao-hsien (117–23).
20. Raymond Durgnat, *A Long Hard Look at "Psycho"* (London: British Film Institute, 2002), 169.
21. Nicolas Rapold, "Interview: Lisandro Alonso," *Film Comment*, March 25, 2015, https://www.filmcomment.com/blog/interview-lisandro-alonso-jauja/.
22. John Belton speaks to the "anxiety" that attends the 4:3 frame given its palpable restrictedness as a field of action flanked by absences, whereas the widescreen format slows and suppresses the viewer's awareness of the frame's limitations. Belton, *Widescreen Cinema* (Cambridge, MA: Harvard University Press, 1992), 196–97.
23. Chelsea Birks, "Objectivity, Speculative Realism, and the Cinematic Apparatus," *Cinema Journal* 57, no. 4 (Summer 2018): 23.
24. Gilles Deleuze, *Cinema 1: The Movement-Image* (French orig. 1983), trans. Hugh Tomlinson and Barbara Habberjam (Minneapolis: University of Minnesota Press, 1986), 17.
25. André Breton, "Manifesto of Surrealism" (French orig. 1924), in *Manifestoes of Surrealism*, trans. Richard Seaver and Helen R. Lane (Ann Arbor: University of Michigan Press, 1972), 16.
26. Also relevant to *Jauja* and its surrealism is Buñuel's devilish, self-critical dissection of the colonial gaze in his pseudo-travelogue essay film *Land Without Bread* (1933).
27. Luis Buñuel, "Notes on the Making of *Un chien andalou*," trans. Grace L. McCann Morley (trans. orig. pub. 1947), in *Art in Cinema: Documents Toward a History of the Film Society*, ed. Scott MacDonald (Philadelphia: Temple University Press, 2006), 102. Buñuel goes even further to claim that the images in *Un chien andalou* (1929) "are as mysterious and inexplicable to the two collaborators [Buñuel and Dalí] as to the spectator" (102). This admonition to be wary of symbolic interpretation usefully applies to much of cinematic surrealism. Not unlike David Lynch and Apichatpong Weerasethakul, the Alonso of *Jauja* is a custodian of the insoluble who regards the film medium as a site for experimentation beyond the director's knowledge, too. As he states in an interview, "The film breaks itself a little bit and starts to have distortions in time, space, and reality. I'm not sure what it is, but I don't really want to know. Not yet." Rapold, "Interview: Lisandro Alonso."
28. Adam Lowenstein, *Dreaming of Cinema: Spectatorship, Surrealism, and the Age of Digital Media* (New York: Columbia University Press, 2015), 181–82. See also Jacques Brunius, "Crossing the Bridge," and Ado Kyrou, "The Fantastic—the Marvelous," in *The Shadow and Its Shadow: Surrealist Writings on the Cinema*, 3rd ed., ed. and trans. Paul Hammond (San Francisco: City Lights, 2000), 99–102, 158–60.
29. Brunius, "Crossing the Bridge," 101–2. This piece is taken from Brunius's book *En marge du cinéma français* (Paris: Arcanes, 1954).
30. Kyrou, "The Fantastic—the Marvelous," 158–60. This chapter is excerpted from Kyrou's book *Le surréalisme au cinéma* (Paris: Éditions le Terrain Vague, 1963).
31. One could find countless other examples of such atmospheric "bridge crossing" in surrealist cinema in what Adrian Martin has called its "eternal" phase—that is, its global continuation well beyond its French interwar heyday. See Martin, "The Artificial Night: Surrealism and Cinema," in *Surrealism: Revolution by Night* (Canberra: National Gallery of Australia, 1993), 190–95.

The not exactly adversarial relationship between neorealism and surrealism warrants further attention in the context of slow-cinematic suspense than I can offer here. An important text in this regard is Luis Buñuel's essay "The Cinema, Instrument of Poetry" (1958), which Buñuel wrote following the success of his film *Los olvidados* (1950). He takes Italian neorealism to task for excluding "mystery and the fantastic" but also praises the scenarist and theorist Cesare Zavattini for "raising the anodyne act to the level of a dramatic category." Buñuel points to the celebrated sequence in *Umberto D.* (1952), scripted by Zavattini and directed by Vittorio de Sica, in which the pregnant maid awakes in the middle of the night and performs a series of wordless gestures in the kitchen—a scene that many discussions of slow, contemplative cinema have cited as a key prototypical sequence. "Despite the triviality of these situations," writes Buñuel, "the action is followed with interest and even with *suspense*." Buñuel, "The Cinema, Instrument of Poetry" (1958), in *The Shadow and Its Shadow*, ed. and trans. Hammond, 115, emphasis added.

32. The role of suspense within surrealist cinema more generally calls out for further discussion. Across several examples, much of the suspense unfolds as a balancing act between registers of expression in tension with one another. Of use here is the concept of "aesthetic suspense" that V. F. Perkins develops in his little-discussed analysis of Nicholas Ray's Western melodrama *Johnny Guitar* (1954). Perkins uses the phrase *aesthetic suspense* in reference to the viewer's supple appreciation for stylistic feats that teeter on the cusp of absurdity. Perkins, "*Johnny Guitar*," in *The Movie Book of the Western*, ed. Ian Cameron and Douglas Pye (London: Studio Vista, 1996), 221–28. "Aesthetic suspense," then, refers not simply to the aesthetic impact of suspense but instead to a more specialized critical and spectatorial consciousness of the risky aesthetic strategy of the film as it develops, leaving us to wonder where it is headed and whether the patterned arc of development will find an elegant and resonant way to complete itself despite the air of ridiculousness (this is close in spirit to what I theorize as "structural suspense" in my suspense morphology). Alex Clayton writes in his helpful expansion on Perkins's concept, "Aesthetic suspense results from the perception that we are only a whisker away from risibility." Turning to Gus Van Sant's *Elephant* (2003), Clayton finds that aesthetic suspense stems from how the slow film tensely "walks the line between aestheticism and naturalism, mystification and cliché, subjective alignment and autonomy of viewpoint." Clayton, "V. F. Perkins: Aesthetic Suspense," in *Thinking in the Dark: Cinema, Theory, Practice*, ed. Murray Pomerance and R. Barton Palmer (New Brunswick, NJ: Rutgers University Press, 2016), 214. Aesthetic suspense of this sort builds up around *Jauja*'s eleventh-hour surrealism and applies to what I have termed, drawing on Jacques Brunius, "crossing the bridge."

33. André Bazin, *What Is Cinema?*, trans. Timothy Barnard (Montreal: Caboose, 2009), 241.

34. On Martel's stylistic relationship to slow cinema and its sensorial dimensions, see Deborah Martin, *The Cinema of Lucrecia Martel* (Manchester, U.K.: Manchester University Press, 2016), 7–8, 43, 127.

35. In an interview, Lucrecia Martel connects this theme of waiting (*esperar* in Spanish, which means both "to wait" and "to hope") to Catholicism, which promises eventual reward for the suffering body. But Martel stresses that in making *Zama* (2017) she stripped away nearly all signs of Catholicism to the point of historical inaccuracy in order to remove hope as a possibility in the film's affective texture. Gerd Gemünden

and Silvia Spitta, "'I Was Never Afraid': An Interview with Lucrecia Martel," *Film Quarterly* 71, no. 4 (2018): 37.
36. Steven Connor, "Sounding Out Film," in *The Oxford Handbook of New Audiovisual Aesthetics*, ed. John Richardson, Claudia Gorbman, and Carol Vernallis (New York: Oxford University Press, 2013), 116 (emphasis added), 113, 109–10. The capacity of the spectator's body for acoustic absorption (both direct and reverberant sound) isn't just theoretical but a property of physics. The size of the crowd will affect the sound field's levels as the film is shown: the greater the number of absorptive bodies, the louder the volume will need to be set. See "Sound Level," in *The Art of Film Projection: A Beginner's Guide*, ed. Paolo Cherchi Usai, Spencer Christiano, Catherine A. Surowiec, and Timothy J. Wagner (Rochester, NY: George Eastman Museum, 2019), 227.
37. The sound design of *Zama* refuses to be dictated by the image in part through sonic devices of panning (the apparent source of a noise moves position from one stereo channel to another) and raising the volume for thematic and affective emphasis rather than in terms of sound perspective (i.e., the closeness of a sound source relative to the camera).
38. The atmospheric import of insects across my three case studies in this chapter calls for further consideration. In *Jauja*, a shot of Dinesen distortedly reflected in a murky puddle buzzing with flies serves as a crucial image of his dissipating identity and harks back to the fly visible on Ingeborg's dress in the film's otherwise pristine opening shot. In *Zama*, gossip surrounding the spider-wasp lends a feeling of dread, as does the tremolo of insect and frog noises that comes to replace the Shepard tone. Further, Zama's quarters at the outpost are, in bleakly comic fashion, being eaten away by termites in a superior display of colonization. *Under the Skin* (2013), for its part, affiliates ants and flies with the alien protagonist and her/its perceptual system. These insectile motifs give each film a surrealist tinge, the history of which can be traced to the nominal start of surrealist cinema with Luis Buñuel and Salvador Dalí's *Un chien andalou*, with its famous use of ants and a death's-head moth.
39. Martel in Paul Dallas, "The Politics of Waiting: Lucrecia Martel on *Zama*," *Filmmaker*, March 8, 2018, https://filmmakermagazine.com/104946-the-politics-of-waiting/.
40. Michel Chion, *Audio-Vision: Sound on Screen*, ed. and trans. Claudia Gorbman (New York: Columbia University Press, 1994), 20.
41. Ambient sonic ubiquity has commonalities with the acousmatic voice (a voice whose source is suppressed) described by Michel Chion, which often implies the powers of omnipresence and omniscience. Chion, *Audio-Vision*, 130. For a thorough discussion of ubiquitous sound not only in cinema but in real-world environments, see "Ubiquity," in *Sonic Experience: A Guide to Everyday Sounds*, ed. Jean-François Augoyard and Henry Torque, trans. Andra McCartney and David Paquette (Montreal: McGill-Queen's University Press, 2005), 130–44.
42. Martel in José Teodoro, "Interview: Lucrecia Martel," September 26, 2017, https://www.filmcomment.com/blog/interview-lucrecia-martel/.
43. Adrian J. Ivakhiv, *Ecologies of the Moving Image: Cinema, Affect, Nature* (Waterloo, Canada: Wilfrid Laurier University Press, 2013), 161. See also Gerd Gemünden, *Lucrecia Martel* (Urbana: University of Illinois Press, 2019), 124–28.
44. In this respect, *Zama* bears similarities to the treatment of colonial history in Miguel Gomes's *Tabu* (2012), which was shot by the same cinematographer, Rui Poças, and which likewise has salient gaps in its fabric. See Lucia Nagib, *Realist Cinema as World*

250   3. The Ambient Landscape

Cinema: Non-cinema, Intermedial Passages, Total Cinema (Amsterdam: Amsterdam University Press, 2020), 107–26.

45. Jean-Pierre Oudart, "Cinema and Suture" (French orig. 1969), trans. Kari Hanet and Henry Seggerman, in *Cahiers du Cinéma*, vol. 3: *1969–1972: The Politics of Representation*, ed. Nick Browne (London: Routledge, 1990), 45–57.
46. Trace Reddell, *The Sound of Things to Come: An Audible History of the Science Fiction Film* (Minneapolis: University of Minnesota Press, 2018), 91–190.
47. Given *Under the Skin*'s explorations of gender and sexuality, the alien may nevertheless serve as a powerful locus of identification. Take Ara Osterweil's response: "I have never before so identified with a female protagonist in a feature film. Watching Scarlett Johansson's character gaze with impunity at the men she pursues, I remember what it feels like to experience the world through a lens of uninhibited sexual desire. This resonance astonishes me. Through her, I recall the pleasure of imagining random strangers, however oddly comported, as lovers. Whereas her alien mission gives her license to act upon this taboo impulse, watching her, I feel suddenly and terribly constrained by my various pledges to refuse the world's seductive energy. I may be of this Earth, but I too am curious about the shape of strangers' bodies under their clothes, and wonder how a random passerby might react to a thinly veiled solicitation. How might a calculated intervention transform an anonymous encounter into an intimate ritual? Only by witnessing someone becoming human for the very first time do I realize how many aspects of 'being human' I have relinquished. Must one be an alien to behave as she does? Is there any space on this Earth in which one can freely explore taboo sexual desire without incurring censure or violence?" Osterweil, "*Under the Skin*: The Perils of Becoming Female," *Film Quarterly* 67, no. 4 (Summer 2014): 47. Accounts of the film differ as to whether the alien bears a name. The script identifies her as "Laura," but the character is never referenced by name in the finished film, a choice that needs to be honored critically.
48. Brian Eno, liner notes for *Ambient 1: Music for Airports* (Polydor Records, 1978). Eno recounts a story of listening to harp music on a gramophone through defective speakers while he was recovering from a serious accident (he had been run over by a taxi), which blended with the sounds of rain through the window as well as with his vague, trauma- and painkiller-induced wooziness. See John T. Lysaker, *Brian Eno's Ambient 1: Music for Airports* (New York: Oxford University Press, 2019), 81–83.
49. David Toop, "How Much World Do You Want? Ambient Listening and Its Questions," in *Music Beyond Airports: Appraising Ambient Music*, ed. Monty Adkins and Simon Cummings (Huddersfield, U.K.: University of Huddersfield Press, 2019), 2.
50. Michel Chion, *Kubrick's Cinema Odyssey*, trans. Claudia Gorbman (London: British Film Institute, 2001), 77–81.
51. Jonathan Glazer, "Director's Statement," in Walter Campbell and Glazer, *Under the Skin*, screenplay, Filmnation Entertainment, n.d., https://static1.squarespace.com/static /5d78f7aafa2a676e1fcddfe9/t/5e87096b6d595f7cba98a926/1585908079163/Under+the +Skin.Fierce.pdf.
52. Jean Louis Schefer, *The Ordinary Man of Cinema* (French orig. 1980), trans. Max Cavitch, Paul Grant, and Noura Wedell (South Pasadena, CA: Semiotext(e), 2016), 104, translation modified, emphasis added.
53. For a more detailed analysis of Glazer's borrowings from Kubrick in *Under the Skin*, see Rick Warner, "Kubrickian Dread: Echoes of *2001: A Space Odyssey* and *The Shining* in Works by Jonathan Glazer, Paul Thomas Anderson, and David Lynch," in *After*

Kubrick: A Filmmaker's Legacy, ed. Jeremi Szaniawski (London: Bloomsbury, 2020), 125–45.
54. Annette Michelson, "Bodies in Space: Film as 'Carnal Knowledge,'" *Artforum* 7, no. 6 (February 1969): 54–63.
55. On "foreground music" in the context of Kubrick's *The Shining* (1980), see K. J. Donnelly, *The Spectre of Sound: Music in Film and Television* (London: British Film Institute, 2005), 36–54.
56. Osterweil, "Under the Skin," 47.
57. Chion, *Kubrick's Cinema Odyssey*, 99.
58. On the "vehicularization" of the spectator, see Gregory Flaxman, "Once More, with Feeling: Cinema and Cinesthesia," *SubStance* 45, no. 3 (2016): 181–86.
59. Elena Gorfinkel, "Sex, Sensation, and Nonhuman Interiority in *Under the Skin*," *Jump Cut* 57 (Fall 2016), https://www.ejumpcut.org/archive/jc57.2016/-GorfinkelSkin/index.html.
60. The "beehive" description comes from Mica Levi in Larry Fitzmaurice, "Jonathan Glazer and Mica Levi," *Pitchfork*, March 31, 2014, https://pitchfork.com/features/interview/9366-under-the-skins-jonathan-glazer-and-mica-levi.
61. See Karla Oeler, *A Grammar of Murder: Violent Scenes and Film Form* (Chicago: University of Chicago Press, 2009).
62. An indirect link emerges between the murder of the alien and the murder of Marion in *Psycho* (1960). It occurs intertextually through Kubrick's reworking of the earlier film's famous shower scene. In *The Shining* (1980), when Jack Torrance visits room 237 and finds a ghostly nude woman in the bathtub, who soon transforms into a putrefied living corpse of an elderly woman, Kubrick stages a volte-face of Hitchcock's shower scene by having the nude woman approach and assail the man. Kubrick's bathroom scene is understatedly referenced by the murder of the alien in *Under the Skin*. When the camera wraps around the woodsman's stunned gaze to show the alien's back-turned figure, her/its posterior wound exactly duplicates that of the old woman Jack Torrance sees in the mirror. Glazer in this way reenacts the foiling of male fantasy in *The Shining* but recasts the "monstrous" woman as a victim in a human world of entrenched violence: the focus falls not on a scary zombie but on a defenseless Other in retreat.
63. Gorfinkel, "Sex, Sensation, and Nonhuman Interiority."
64. Michel Faber, *Under the Skin* (San Diego: Harcourt, 2000), 310–11. I quote the passage from the novel at greater length here than Gorfinkel does in "Sex, Sensation, and Nonhuman Interiority."
65. In *Under the Skin*, the earlier scenes that directly follow the prologue already summon the "beyond the infinite" journey of Kubrick's *2001* (1968). The Scottish Highlands countryside in effect stands in for the strange, electronically filtered landscapes over which Bowman glides when he passes through the stargate. Indeed, that sequence bears on Glazer's imagery when we cut to a frontal close-up of the speeding motorcyclist, whose glossy black helmet rhymes with the eyeball constructed at the beginning of the film and reflects colored streaks of light from passing vehicles. The scene is thus rendered abstract and made to resemble an interstellar flight.
66. Immanuel Kant, *Observations on the Feeling of the Beautiful and Sublime* (German orig. 1764), trans. Paul Guyer, in *Observations on the Feeling of the Beautiful and Sublime and Other Writings*, ed. Patrick Frierson and Paul Guyer (Cambridge: Cambridge University Press, 2011), 65–204; and Kant, *Critique of the Power of Judgment* (German

252   3. The Ambient Landscape

orig. 1790), trans. Paul Guyer and Eric Matthews (Cambridge: Cambridge University Press, 2000), 128–59.
67. Jennifer Wild, "Distance Is [Im]material: Epstein Versus Etna," in *Jean Epstein: Critical Essays and New Translations*, ed. Sarah Keller and Jason N. Paul (Amsterdam: Amsterdam University Press, 2012), 115–42.
68. For an edifying reconsideration of *photogénie*, see Sarah Keller, "Gambling on *Photogénie*: Epstein Now," *Photogénie*, October 25, 2012, https://photogenie.be/gambling-on-photogenie-epstein-now/.
69. For an example of Glazer's investment in *photogénie*, look no further than his television commercial for the Nike Air Jordan XII sneaker for the Wieden+Kennedy advertising agency in 1996.
70. Glazer in Danny Leigh, "*Under the Skin*: Why Did This Chilling Masterpiece Take a Decade?," *The Guardian*, March 6, 2014, emphasis added, https://www.theguardian.com/film/2014/mar/06/under-the-skin-director-jonathan-glazer-scarlett-johansson.
71. In discussing computerized point-of-view interfaces in narrative cinema as "technological patina[s]," Alexander R. Galloway explains how this device, as used in science-fiction films such as *The Terminator* (1984) and *RoboCop* (1987), "acts as a buffer to mediate the shock of the subjective shot" belonging to a nonhuman character yet also produces an effect of alienation in the viewer. Galloway, "Origins of the First-Person Shooter," in *Gaming: Essays on Algorithmic Culture* (Minneapolis: University of Minnesota Press, 2006), 53–56. *Under the Skin* now and then enters an abstract register of image and sound that suggests alien subjectivity, but for most of its duration the film functions as a minimalist—and far more radically suspenseful—variation on this point-of-view device. Instead of using an overlay that denotes "alien vision and subjectivity," Glazer's film *more furtively and vaguely* enlists its optical, graphic, and sonic techniques as mediations that place us in the clutches of an alien perceptual apparatus. Galloway refers in passing to the inscription of HAL's point of view in *2001*, noting that wide-angle lenses with pronounced distortion serve as another example of technological patina to express a "digital" nonhuman viewpoint ("Origins of the First-Person Shooter," 54). I would add here that because wide-angle lenses, unlike computerized overlays, are optical devices already associated with analog cinema, there is a closer affinity between HAL's artificial perception and the operations of the traditional film medium.
72. *2001* implicates cinema as an alien intelligence in part through conflating the black alien monolith with the film's own black screens. In *Under the Skin*, Glazer craftily reenacts Kubrick's famous tracking shot into and through the monolith by having the camera follow the alien as she lures victims into and through the blackened, rectangular doorway to her ramshackle house.
73. Murray Pomerance, *Uncanny Cinema: Agonies of the Viewing Experience* (London: Bloomsbury, 2022), 87.
74. The quoted phrase comes from Robert Spadoni, "What Is Film Atmosphere?," *Quarterly Review of Film and Video* 37, no. 2 (2020): 60.
75. My understanding of these films' sonic destabilization of subjectivity, be it that of a character or that of the spectator, is informed by Jean-Luc Nancy, *Listening*, trans. Charlotte Mandell (New York: Fordham University Press, 2007).
76. Hermann Schmitz, *New Phenomenology: A Brief Introduction*, trans. Rudolf Owen Müllen (Milan, Italy: Mimesis International, 2019), 89–94.
77. Michelson, "Bodies in Space."

4. Ailing Bodies on the Threshold of Action

1. Benedict Morrison, *Complicating Articulation in Art Cinema* (Oxford: Oxford University Press, 2021), 10–14, 13–20. In art cinema's scholarly reception since David Bordwell's influential approach, the director, understood as a guiding narrational presence, is also posited as an explanatory agent in the face of ambiguity and formal eccentricity. Bordwell, "The Art Cinema as a Mode of Film Practice" (1979), in *The European Cinema Reader*, ed. Catherine Fowler (London: Routledge, 2002). I don't object to factoring in the inscribed presence of the filmmaker, but one must be careful not to disband purposefully unresolved suspense in the process.
2. My call for a more suspense-friendly conception of character is informed by Adrian Martin's reflections on this problem in relation to Terrence Malick's films. "One of the worst habits of film commentary amounts to an ultra-conventional congealing of all the different levels that create a cinematic character into a single, coherent, univocal, common-sense 'personhood'—with every imaginable metamorphosis of that character, every structuring contribution made by the multi-levels of cinematic artifice, and every 'spacing' or complication in relation made possible by the actor's performance, thinned out into a banal, psychologistic humanism." Martin, "Approaching *The New World*," in *The Cinema of Terrence Malick*, 2nd ed., ed. Hannah Patterson (London: Wallflower, 2007), 213.
3. Elena Gorfinkel, "Weariness, Waiting: Endurance and Art Cinema's Tired Bodies," *Discourse* 34, nos. 2–3 (Fall 2012): 311–47; Ira Jaffe, *Slow Movies: Countering the Cinema of Action* (London: Wallflower, 2014), 15–44, 87–108.
4. The postures and states of being enacted by the figures in Andy Warhol's films also warrant mention here as a genealogical reference for slow cinema. Gorfinkel, "Weariness, Waiting," 311, 339.
5. Let me add that these three films are not designed as diagnostic representations of known illnesses or disabilities. Two of the actors in question (Ventura and Jenjira Pongpas Widner) manifest ailments that they have in real life, whereas one actor (Tilda Swinton) doesn't (she embodies a syndrome that the director, Apichatpong, had while making *Memoria* [2021]). But in all three cases, suspense and supernatural possibilities render the undiagnosed ailments obscure.
6. Gilles Deleuze, *Cinema 2: The Time-Image* (French orig. 1985), trans. Hugh Tomlinson and Robert Galeta (Minneapolis: University of Minnesota Press, 1989), 20.
7. For Pascal Bonitzer, "this should be formulated as a law or as an axiom: any suspense implies a labyrinth. Inversely, the labyrinth from the point of view of narrative implies necessarily an enigma or suspense." Bonitzer, "Partial Vision: Film and the Labyrinth," trans. Fabrice Ziolkowski, *Wide Angle* 4, no. 4 (1981): 59.
8. On Pedro Costa's collaborative process with nonprofessional actors, see Nuno Barradas Jorge, *ReFocus: The Films of Pedro Costa: Producing and Consuming Contemporary Art Cinema* (Edinburgh: Edinburgh University Press, 2020), 128–32.
9. All three case studies presented in this chapter undertake projects in line with what Marcia Landy calls "counter-history" in *Cinema and Counter-History* (Bloomington: Indiana University Press, 2015).
10. In interviews regarding *Horse Money* (2014) and its sequel, *Vitalina Varela* (2019), Costa has stressed that his small productions are in step with the slow tempos and contingencies of delay that define his participants' lives—illnesses, the time it takes to walk long distances and use public transportation, and so on. Costa describes this

unhurried pace as being *"with* time, on the side of time," as opposed to the hasty work routines of the film industry. See "Pedro's Rules," Locarno Film Festival, August 15, 2019, https://www.youtube.com/watch?v=yHGD47_sIeQ. The shantytown Fontaínhas, it should be noted, no longer exists. Its replica appears in *Horse Money*, rebuilt from memory. For a detailed account of the Fontaínhas community and Costa's involvement with its members, see Michael Gaurneri, "Pedro Costa: Documentary, Realism, and Life on the Margins," interview, *BOMB Magazine*, July 16, 2015, https://bombmagazine.org/articles/pedro-costa/.

11. The extent to which Géricault's depictions of Africans depart from and critique the status quo racist views of his era is open to debate. Albert Alhadeff argues that the painter's drawings of Black subjects show an ambivalence—now stereotypical, now challenging of contemporaneous practices. Géricault's portraiture, like the example in *Horse Money*, removes persons of color from the exoticizing scenes found in the work of Delacroix, Girodet, and Gros and portrays the subject in contemporary western European attire, attempting "a more direct and empathetic mode" as the model appears in a quotidian pose. Furthermore, Géricault uniquely portrays Blackness through "layers of classicism" thought to be the "exclusive province" of white hegemony. See Albert Alhadeff, *Théodore Géricault, Painting Black Bodies: Confrontations and Contradictions* (New York: Routledge, 2020), 6–7. Jacques Rancière astutely considers how Costa imports genres of painting into the Fontaínhas community without aestheticizing poverty in an exploitative sense. See Rancière, "Pedro Costa's Politics," in *The Intervals of Cinema*, trans. John Howe (London: Verso, 2014), 127–42.

12. On the concept of "shared anthropology," see Paul Henley, *The Adventure of the Real: Jean Rouch and the Craft of Ethnographic Cinema* (Chicago: University of Chicago Press, 2010), 310–37.

13. Jacques Rancière, "The Ghost Road," *Sight and Sound* (October 2015): 50–51.

14. Gorfinkel, "Weariness, Waiting," 318–23, 311–13, 316–17. Gorfinkel's essay focuses mainly on marginalized female characters in these slow art films, but her concept of "endurance" lends itself to other situations of dispossession where race, sexuality, and class are the most pronounced concerns.

15. Gorfinkel, "Weariness, Waiting," 318.

16. My conception of *Horse Money*'s nocturnal style is informed by María DeGuzmán, *Buenas Noches, American Culture: Latina/o Aesthetics of Night* (Bloomington: Indiana University Press, 2012), 1–16.

17. Édouard Glissant, *Poetics of Relation*, trans. Betsy Wing (Ann Arbor: University of Michigan Press, 1997), 189–94.

18. Robert Bresson, *Notes on the Cinematograph* (French orig. 1975), trans. Jonathan Griffin (1977; reprint, New York: New York Review of Books, 2016), 64, 58, capitalization in the original.

19. A term more common to art-critical studies of painting, *tenebrism* is sometimes conflated with *chiaroscuro*. Both terms refer to dramatic contrasts of light and dark, but in the case of tenebrist paintings, such as those by Caravaggio and Georges de la Tour, a more extreme intensity of occlusive darkness is involved.

20. Pedro Costa, "Pedro Costa Interview," *The Seventh Art*, September 6, 2016, https://www.youtube.com/watch?v=C1kCwAOoUqk&t=3035s.

21. Pedro Costa, "Pedro Costa on Finding the Shadows of Humanity," Film at Lincoln Center, February 28, 2020, https://www.youtube.com/watch?v=FoKRCUzz2eA&t=8s.

22. Pedro Costa, "A Closed Door That Leaves Us Guessing," trans. Downing Roberts, *Rouge* 10 (2007), http://www.rouge.com.au/10/costa_seminar.html.

23. Béla Balázs, *Béla Balázs: Early Film Theory*, ed. Erica Carter, trans. Rodney Livingstone (New York: Berghahn, 2010), 102–4. For Balázs, "microphysiognomy" refers to little tics and spasms in the face of an actor that are caught by the camera—physical indications of internal thoughts and feelings.
24. Minimalistic styles do not, as a rule, efface atmospheric qualities of the performer. Bresson aspired for his "models" to become "phosphorescent" despite the reduction of affect well below popular cinema's standards. He referred to this process as a chemical reaction dependent on temporal accumulation and the interplay of figure and form: "Your images will release their phosphorous only in aggregating. (An actor [as opposed to a model] wants to be phosphorescent right away)." Bresson, *Notes on the Cinematograph*, 56.
25. Rancière, "Pedro Costa's Politics," 136–42, quotes on 140.
26. Here again, Glissant's evolving concept of *opacité* pertains to the aesthetic and political dimensions of suspense in *Horse Money*—opacity as a socially shared poetic practice that undermines Western epistemologies and their imposed insistence upon transparency and universality. Glissant, *Poetics of Relation*, 191.
27. James Quandt, "Exquisite Corpus: An Interview with Apichatpong Weerasethakul," in *Apichatpong Weerasethakul*, ed. Quandt (Vienna: SYNEMA, 2009), 130.
28. Adrian Martin, *Mise en Scène and Film Style: From Classical Hollywood to New Media Art* (London: Palgrave, 2014), 199.
29. As Apichatpong's published sketches and notebooks make clear, he avidly reads scientific journals, mining them for studies of sleep, perception, disease, brain activity, and ecological concepts that he converts into motifs for his films and gallery installations. See Apichatpong Weerasethakul, *Memoria* (Berlin: Fireflies, 2021).
30. See "Apichatpong Weerasethakul," List of Favorite Films, *LaCinetek*, La Cinémathèque des Réalisateurs, n.d., https://www.lacinetek.com/fr/la-liste-de/apichatpong-weerasethakul.
31. Jean Ma, *At the Edges of Sleep: Moving Images and Somnolent Spectators* (Berkeley: University of California Press, 2022), 82–93.
32. This encounter calls back to the climax of Apichatpong's film *Tropical Malady* (2004), where two men in front of flags that represent the Thai nation lick each other's hands.
33. The therapeutic interactions in *Cemetery of Splendor* (2015) are eroticized (and made partly comical) in several other ways I have not mentioned. Jen says that a medicinal cream she uses, just prior to the extended oneiric "threesome" with Itt and Keng, smells of semen and causes her breasts to "perk up." In an earlier scene, Keng and Jen notice and laugh at Itt's erection during his sleep, with Keng going as far as to flip it like a springboard. In multiple scenes, including the conclusion of the climax, the neon-light tubes are, through Apichatpong's framing, situated in direct alignment with the midsections of the sleeping soldiers, a motif subtle enough that it is likely to go unnoticed.
34. The goddesses' shrine is geographically associated with the lake, suggesting that the water turbines and the gigantic amoeba are connected to a spiritual force at work in the atmosphere.
35. Lesley Stern, "Ghosting: The Performance and Migration of Cinematic Gesture, Focusing on Hou Hsiao-hsien's *Good Men, Good Women*," in *Migrations of Gesture*, ed. Carry Noland and Sally Ann Ness (Minneapolis: University of Minnesota Press, 2008), 185–215, esp. 192.
36. Lutz Koepnick, *The Long Take: Art Cinema and the Wonderous* (Minneapolis: University of Minnesota Press, 2017), 1–32.

256   4. Ailing Bodies on the Threshold of Action

37. Karl Schoonover and Rosalind Galt, *Queer Cinema in the World* (Durham, NC: Duke University Press, 2016), 281–84.
38. *Oxford English Dictionary*, s.v. "suspension (n.)," December 2023, https://doi.org/10.1093/OED/5526042745.
39. Filmed in and around Bogotá, *Memoria* stands as Apichatpong's first feature film made outside of Thailand. Starring Tilda Swinton, *Memoria* also marks a transition from Apichatpong's use of mostly nonprofessional actors to the use of a professional actor, although Swinton has stated that her approach was to follow suit with Pongpas Widner's role as a self-effacing receiver of sensations in Apichatpong's films. "Apichatpong Weerasethakul and Tilda Swinton on *Memoria*," *Film Comment Podcast*, December 9, 2021, https://www.filmcomment.com/blog/the-film-comment-podcast-apichatpong-weerasethakul-tilda-swinton-on-memoria-interview/. In the same discussion, Swinton states that when she and Apichatpong began to imagine what the film might become, they were interested primarily in what she calls "an atmosphere of lostness" or "suspension" more than in plot. See also the interview of Swinton included in Apichatpong, *Memoria*, the published collection of his preparatory notes and sketches, unpaginated.
40. Swinton describes Jessica as less a "character" than a puzzling "predicament." "Apichatpong Weerasethakul and Tilda Swinton on *Memoria*," *Film at Lincoln Center Podcast*, October 2021, https://soundcloud.com/filmlinc.
41. As has been widely reported, Apichatpong was suffering from "exploding head syndrome" while planning and making *Memoria*. In his words, "It feels like someone snapping a rubber band inside your skull. Your skull seems to be made of metal. The immense noise reverberates around the brain, but instead of waking you up fully, it puts you in a semi-conscious state, listening, anticipating. . . . Soon I familiarized myself with its rhythm. I was able to initiate the 'bang' and tune it into different tones, as if I were a conductor or an animal trainer. This sonic companion dutifully emerged at sunrise and prompted me to listen to the sound of the city." Apichatpong, *Memoria*, unpaginated.
42. Apichatpong's reference to Tourneur's *I Walked with a Zombie* (1943), also a key source for Costa, which he remade as *Casa de lava* (1994), informs the opening mise-en-scène of *Memoria*—the densely patterned shadows, the faintly billowing fabrics. A more local reference for the film's suspenseful visual design is the work of the Colombian artist Ever Astudillo, in particular the motif of a dark, silhouetted figure blocking the camera's point of view.
43. "Apichatpong Weerasethakul," List of Favorite Films.
44. Michel Chion, *Audio-Vision: Sound on Screen*, ed. and trans. Claudia Gorbman (New York: Columbia University Press, 1994), 29–33, citing Schaeffer.
45. Apichatpong's work in general tends to atmospherically stress the somatic, tactile qualities of sound in relation to memory. For a shrewd analysis of this practice that could be extended to *Memoria*, see Philippa Lovatt, "'Every Drop of My Blood Sings Our Song. There, Can You Hear It?': Haptic Sound and Embodied Memory in the Films of Apichatpong Weerasethakul," *New Soundtrack* 3, no. 1 (2013): 61–79.
46. *Oxford English Dictionary*, s.v. "contemplation (n.)," July 2023, https://doi.org/10.1093/OED/1943320353.
47. Mikel Dufrenne, *The Phenomenology of Aesthetic Experience*, trans. Edward S. Casey (Evanston, IL: Northwestern University Press, 1973), 57–58.
48. Walter Benjamin, "The Work of Art in the Age of Its Technological Reproducibility: Second Version" (German orig. 1936), in *Selected Essays*, vol. 3: *1935–1938*, ed. Howard

Eiland and Michael W. Jennings, trans. Edmund Jephcott, Howard Eiland, and others (Cambridge, MA: Belknap Press of Harvard University Press, 2002), 108, 118–20, 132 n. 33. As Miriam Bratu Hansen has clarified, Benjamin's use of the term *distraction* likely refers less to a transhistorical condition of cinema than to "a type of cinema experience still patterned on the variety format" of early film presentation—"that is, the programming of shorter films (interspersed with or framed live performances) on the principle of maximum stylistic or thematic diversity." Hansen, *Cinema and Experience: Siegfried Kracauer, Walter Benjamin, and Theodor W. Adorno* (Berkeley: University of California Press, 2012), 86.

49. Koepnick, *The Long Take*, 19–21.
50. Raymond Bellour, "The Pensive Spectator," trans. Lynne Kirby, *Wide Angle* 9, no. 1 (1987): 6–10; Koepnick, *The Long Take*, 21–28.
51. Benjamin, "The Work of Art in the Age of Its Technological Reproducibility," 120.
52. Gilles Deleuze, *Difference and Repetition* (French orig. 1968), trans. Paul Patton (New York: Columbia University Press, 1994), 71–79.
53. James Williams, *Gilles Deleuze's Philosophy of Time: A Critical Introduction and Guide* (Edinburgh: Edinburgh University Press, 2011), 38–39.
54. Williams, *Gilles Deleuze's Philosophy of Time*, 73–74.
55. Deleuze, *Difference and Repetition*, 77, 74 (emphasis added), 76 (emphasis added), 71. As Deleuze phrases it earlier in his book, "Every organism, in its receptive and perceptual elements, but also in its viscera, is a sum of contractions, of retentions and expectations. At the level of this primary vital sensibility, the lived present constitutes a past and a future in time" (73).
56. Gilles Deleuze and Félix Guattari, *What Is Philosophy?* (French orig. 1991), trans. Hugh Tomlinson and Graham Burchell (New York: Columbia University Press, 1994), 211–12, 169.
57. "Apichatpong Weerasethakul and Tilda Swinton on *Memoria*," *Film Comment Podcast*; "Apichatpong Weerasethakul and Tilda Swinton on *Memoria*," *Film at Lincoln Center Podcast*.
58. Apichatpong, it seems, will always find a way to work "monsters" and paranormal events into his films, from the "monstrous" amoeba and dinosaurs in *Cemetery of Splendor* to this strangely organic yet technological spacecraft. The use of computer-generated imagery in this manner is not without precedent in slow art cinema. One thinks of the unexpected alien spacecraft launch in Jia Zhang-ke's *Still Life* (2006). The Chinese director, Jia, served as a producer for *Memoria*.
59. James Wham, "Sounds of History," *Sidecar* (blog for *New Left Review*), January 18, 2022, https://newleftreview.org/sidecar/posts/sounds-of-history.
60. In *Cemetery of Splendor*, Apichatpong's indirect social commentary is a way of sidestepping the Thai government's strict censorship laws, against which he previously had run afoul. Suspense of an atmospheric nature may serve a political purpose when direct critique isn't an option.
61. For an account that embraces Apichatpong's nontraditional, "para-ethnographic" work and its suspensions of explanatory and contextual protocols, see Isaac Marrero-Guillamón, "The Politics and Aesthetics of Non-representation: Re-imagining Ethnographic Cinema with Apichatpong Weerasethakul," *Antípoda* 33 (2018): 13–32.
62. Swinton quoted in Apichatpong, *Memoria*, unpaginated.
63. See Apichatpong's comments on his preference for film over digital in "Seeing the World Through Film and 'Memoria,'" *Filmmaker Stories* (Kodak Motion Picture blog), July 15, 2021, https://www.kodak.com/en/motion/blog-post/memoria.

258   4. Ailing Bodies on the Threshold of Action

64. NEON, tweet, Twitter, October 5, 2021, https://twitter.com/neonrated/status/144542 5759107969024?lang=en.
65. Tiago de Luca, "Slow Time, Visible Cinema: Duration, Experience, and Spectatorship," *Cinema Journal* 56, no. 1 (Fall 2016): 23–42; Schoonover and Galt, *Queer Cinema in the World*, 276–77. While fascinating and to some degree consonant with my own experience of viewing certain slow films, such arguments could benefit from factoring in the more nuanced appraisal of collective viewing in Julian Hanich, *The Audience Effect: On the Collective Cinema Experience* (Edinburgh: Edinburgh University Press, 2018).
66. Dufrenne, *The Phenomenology of Aesthetic Experience*, 151–54. It may seem contradictory to bring Dufrenne's phenomenological approach into a discussion in which Deleuze, a staunch opponent of phenomenology, has played a crucial role. However, Deleuze mentions Dufrenne in a favorable light in the first of his cinema books, where he calls for a promising comparison between Charles S. Peirce's concept of "Firstness" and Dufrenne's "material or affective *A-priori.*" Gilles Deleuze, *Cinema 1: The Movement-Image* (French orig. 1983), trans. Hugh Tomlinson and Barbara Jabberjam (Minneapolis: University of Minnesota Press, 1986), 231 n. 16.

5. Gothic Uncertainty, Bordering on Horror

1. "Zombie-like" from Jean Ma, *Melancholy Drift: Marking Time in Chinese Cinema* (Hong Kong: Hong Kong University Press, 2010), 99, 117. For an argument that extensively relates *Goodbye, Dragon Inn* (2003) to horror and the "zombie" figure, see G. Andrew Stuckey, *Metacinema in Contemporary Chinese Film* (Hong Kong: Hong Kong University Press, 2022), 38–60.
2. Ma, *Melancholy Drift*, 103. *Goodbye, Dragon Inn*'s reflexive connections between ghostliness and the obsolescence of photochemical film are surveyed in Nick Pinkerton, *Goodbye, Dragon Inn* (Victoria, Australia: Fireflies, 2021). For a theoretically rigorous dive into this subject, see Elizabeth Wijaya, "Screening Today: The Visible and Invisible Worlds of Tsai Ming-liang's *Goodbye, Dragon Inn*," *Discourse* 43, no. 1 (Winter 2021): 65–97. See also Nicholas de Villiers, *Cruisy, Sleepy, Melancholy: Sexual Disorientation in the Films of Tsai Ming-liang* (Minneapolis: University of Minnesota Press, 2022), 35–52.
3. For the two most compelling and nuanced arguments for interpreting slow, durational art cinema as a realist mode, see Lúcia Nagib, *World Cinema and the Ethics of Realism* (London: Continuum, 2011); and Tiago de Luca, *Realism of the Senses in World Cinema: The Experience of Physical Reality* (London: I. B. Tauris, 2014).
4. In *El Sur* (1983), a poster for *La sombra de una duda* (Hitchcock's *Shadow of a Doubt*, 1943) can be seen outside the movie theater to which the young girl protagonist follows her mysterious father. Hardly a minor reference, the poster compels the camera to push in and hold on it at length before the scene shifts. Confirming the intertextual link between these gothic-inflected coming-of-age dramas, *El Sur* later stages a conversation scene between daughter and father at a hotel café while sounds from a wedding reception in a neighboring banquet room filter in from out of frame. This scene, in which the "couple" finally has a frank conversation, alludes to the symbolic "marriage" and "divorce" scenes between Uncle Charlie (Joseph Cotten) and his niece Charlie (Teresa Wright) in *Shadow of a Doubt* that occur at the Till-Two Bar.

5. Jerrold E. Hogle, "The Gothic–Theory Conversation: An Introduction," in *The Gothic and Theory: An Edinburgh Companion*, ed. Hogle and Robert Miles (Edinburgh: Edinburgh University Press, 2019), 1–30.
6. Stacey Abbott and Simon Brown, "Gothic and Silent Cinema," in *The Cambridge History of the Gothic*, vol. 3: *Gothic in the Twentieth and Twenty-First Centuries*, ed. Catherine Spooner and Dale Townshend (Cambridge: Cambridge University Press, 2021), 22–42. See also Elizabeth Bronfen, "The Gothic at the Heart of Film and Film Theory," in *The Gothic and Theory*, ed. Hogle and Miles, 165–81. Bronfen goes as far as to suggest that films invoke the gothic in order to theorize the basic conditions and possibilities of the film medium.
7. Robert Spadoni's consideration of the atmospheric uncanniness of early horror films, such as Todd Browning's *Dracula* (1931), that resulted from the technological transition to sound is of relevance to my perhaps seemingly strained connection between classical horror films and contemporary slow art-house films. Spadoni, *Uncanny Bodies: The Coming of Sound Film and the Origins of the Horror Genre* (Berkeley: University of California Press, 2007), 61–92.
8. Because Rivers sustains a mood of slow, tense eeriness in the first half of the montage, there are several omitted jump scares, as will be apparent to viewers familiar with the original films. For instance, near the eleven-minute mark, while sampling a scene from *Halloween* (Carpenter, 1978), Rivers cuts away just before the moment in which Michael Myers in the original film attacks an unsuspecting victim from the backseat of a car. In Rivers's re-edit, the assault is voided out.
9. Rivers quoted in Francesa Steele, "What Is Driving the Rise in Extreme Cinema?," *The Spectator*, March 2, 2020, emphasis added, https://www.spectator.co.uk/article/what-is-driving-the-rise-in-extreme-cinema.
10. "Slow," for Davis, is more than a metrical trait limited to long takes and a presumed animus toward the mainstream. It comprises reductions and hiatuses in narrative delivery as well as a dampening of traditional affective intensities. Slowness isn't necessarily a matter of shot length, and it doesn't exclude "the gradual winching of tension and suspense." His examples encompass exploitation horror in which lethargic, ambiguity-laden durations reflect a lack of financial resources (e.g., Greydon Clark's *Without Warning* [1980] and Thom Eberhardt's *Night of the Comet* [1984]); films that exist between "art-house" and "popular" labels and defy provincial taste distinctions (e.g., Georges Franju's *Eyes Without a Face* [1960], Roman Polanski's *Repulsion* [1965], Paul Morrissey's *Flesh for Frankenstein* [1973], and Michael Almereyda's *Nadja* [1995]); and more recent entries in the independent sector (e.g., Ti West's *The House of the Devil* [2009] and Ana Lily Amirpour's *A Girl Walks Home Alone at Night* [2014]). All these works belong to a "historical pedigree" of films "whose narratives drag, in which 'not much happens'; in which tension is dissipated or attenuated rather than tightly wound and clinically deployed; films where anticipated genre pay-offs are not delivered, or are notably stripped back." Glyn Davis, "The Speed of the VCR: Ti West's Slow Horror," *Screen* 59, no. 1 (Spring 2018): 41–42, 45–46, 48–58. Davis opens the door to ways of rethinking slowness in the context of horror and horror-adjacent films. Plenty of other candidates come to mind. Given the loose art-house ambit of my study, one thinks of Jim Jarmusch's vampire romance *Only Lovers Left Alive* (2013) and Lucile Hadzihalilovic's maritime experiment in body horror *Evolution* (2015). If select passages from films may count as slow horror, then what about the eerily protracted downtime in Werner Herzog's *Nosferatu the Vampyre* (1979)? So-called elevated horror of the twenty-first century, such as Ari Aster's *Midsommar* (2019) and Robert

260 5. Gothic Uncertainty, Bordering on Horror

Eggers's *The Lighthouse* (2019), have a place in this opened-out terrain of slowness, as does Oz Perkins's less hubristic *The Blackcoat's Daughter* (2015). One also thinks of erotic-horror exploitation films such as Jean Rollin's *The Iron Rose* (1973) as well as of experimental documentaries, beyond Rivers's work, that integrate horror atmospherics, such as Mauro Herce's *Dead Slow Ahead* (2015). For a more expansive study of the shifting forms, affects, and matters of taste that define contemporary art-house horror cinema, see David Church, *Post-horror: Art, Genre, and Cultural Elevation* (Edinburgh: Edinburgh University Press, 2021), esp. 27–67.

11. Bordwell doesn't invoke slow cinema in discussing Kiyoshi Kurosawa's work, but he associates the director's art-house films with long-take shooting styles and minimalist poetics. David Bordwell, *Figures Traced in Light* (Berkeley: University of California Press, 2005), 292; Bordwell, "The Other Kurosawa: *Shokuzai*," *Observations on Film Art: Kristin Thompson and David Bordwell* (blog), July 21, 2013, http://www.davidbordwell.net/blog/2013/07/21/the-other-kurosawa-shokuzai/.

12. Chika Kinoshita, "The Mummy Complex: Kurosawa Kiyoshi's *Loft* and J-horror," in *Horror to the Extreme: Changing Boundaries in Asian Cinema*, ed. Jinhee Choi and Mitsuyo Wada-Marciano (Hong Kong: Hong Kong University Press, 2009), 118–19.

13. Let me remind the reader that what I consider "generic suspense" is not to be confused with suspense reduced to a neat genre category. In generic suspense, one or more genre possibilities hang in the balance, but the film doesn't commit firmly to any one of them.

14. Kiyoshi Kurosawa, in "The Making of *Before We Vanish*," special feature included on the Arrow Video Blu-ray edition of *Before We Vanish* (2017), 2019.

15. In an especially eerie scene in the slow, nightmarish *Carnival of Souls* (1962), the protagonist, a woman who may or may not have survived an automobile accident at the start of the film goes to a bus station in an attempt to leave town but is disregarded by the attendant, as though she isn't there. *Barren Illusion* (1999) reworks this scene when one of its disaffected youths goes to the airport and is ignored, the suggestion being that there is no escape from Japan despite the epidemic.

16. Aaron Gerow, "The Empty Return: Circularity and Repetition in Recent Japanese Horror Films," *Minikomi* 64 (2002): 24.

17. Aaron Gerow, "Kiyoshi Kurosawa," in *Directory of World Cinema: Japan 2*, ed. John Berra (London: Intellect, 2012), 46.

18. For an indispensable discussion of the *kaiki* film, see Michael Crandol, *Ghost in the Well: The Hidden History of Horror Films in Japan* (London: Bloomsbury, 2021), 19–62.

19. Charles Shirō Inouye, "Japanese Gothic," in *A New Companion to the Gothic*, ed. David Punter (Malden, MA: Blackwell, 2012), 442–53. Shirō Inouye explains the belatedness of the transliterated word *goshikku* (gothic) by suggesting that "the Japanese world" was already so thoroughly gothic that it had no need for the term (443–44).

20. Kurosawa quoted and translated in Crandol, *Ghost in the Well*, 39.

21. Kiyoshi Kurosawa, *Mon effroyable histoire du cinéma* [My horrifying history of cinema], interviews by Makoto Shinozaki, trans. Mayumi Matsuo and David Matarasso (Pertuis, France: Rouge Profond, 2008), 11–68. Given its transnational expanse, the Japanese *kaiki* category bears strong resemblance to the French *fantastique*.

22. The influence of older *kaiki* films (including international, not just Japanese, examples) on J-horror calls for further discussion. Disputing the idea that J-horror is specifically Japanese, Hiroshi Takahashi states that he and Kiyoshi Kurosawa were most heavily inspired by Robert Wise's British gothic horror film *The Haunting* (1963), which

was adapted from Shirley Jackson's novel *The Haunting of Hill House* (1959). Takahashi, interview by Chika Kinoshita, J-Horror and the Archiving of Global Horror Studies, July 26, 2001, virtual conference hosted by the University of Pittsburgh, Global Horror Studies Research and Archival Network.
23. Gerow, "Kiyoshi Kurosawa," 46. In a key observation on the same page, Gerow writes: "At the end of some Kurosawa films we are often left confused, unsure if *Loft* (*Rofuto*, 2005) or *Retribution* (*Sakebi*, 2006) should be considered as horror films or comedies. The absurdity of such films has confused plenty of viewers . . . but beyond reflecting Kurosawa's long-time admiration for Godard, it underlines the fact that our uncertainty over the very status of his films is part of what haunts us."
24. Kiyoshi Kurosawa's debt to the genre of the Western is an overlooked dimension of his filmmaking. He has long named Sam Peckinpah's *The Ballad of Cable Hogue* (1970) as a major source of inspiration—a surprising choice that provokes awkward silence in critics interviewing him, who expect a more horror-based answer. The duster that the detective wears in *Charisma* (1999), coupled with the plot of an outsider who wanders into a local dispute, evokes Clint Eastwood's Westerns (those in which he stars and/or directs), albeit semiparodically. The garnet color of the duster as well as the tone and luminosity of the landscape cinematography recall Eastwood's ghostly *Pale Rider* (1985), one of Kurosawa's favorite films. See "Kiyoshi Kurosawa," List of Favorite Films, *LaCinetek*, La Cinémathèque des Réalisateurs, n.d., https://www.lacinetek.com/fr/la-liste-de/kiyoshi-kurosawa. Kurosawa's preference for dark lighting schemes arguably takes cues from Bruce Surtees's cinematographic collaborations with Eastwood.
25. Tim Palmer, among other critics, attributes a stark ecocritical platform to *Charisma*. He contends that whereas Japanese films of the postwar era delight in a "classical garden aesthetic" with pristine images of natural beauty, *Charisma* contributes to a fin de siècle streak of "environmental pessimism" in Japanese films that emphasize ecological devastation, "with little or no human agency capable of intervening." Palmer, "The Rules of the World: Japanese Ecocinema and Kiyoshi Kurosawa," in *Framing the World: Explorations in Ecocriticism and Film*, ed. Paula Willoquet-Maricondi (Charlottesville: University of Virginia Press, 2010), 209–24.
26. As David Toop has illustrated, accounts of the uncanny, including Freud's, tend to omit sound despite its supremely uncanny and haunting aspects. Toop, *Sinister Resonance: The Mediumship of the Listener* (London: Continuum, 2010), 125–78.
27. See Murray Pomerance, *Uncanny Cinema: Agonies of the Viewing Experience* (London: Bloomsbury, 2022). Pomerance's account of uncanniness is a key intervention precisely because it defines cinema and our encounter with it as uncanny in myriad ways beyond the overly familiar gothic examples. One could perhaps take issue with the fact that Freud's famous essay isn't dealt with in Pomerance's book, but I would counter that Pomerance gifts film studies with a much-needed description of the uncanny that is not anchored in a framework of psychoanalysis.
28. On Dreyer, see Abbott and Brown, "Gothic and Silent Cinema."
29. Sigmund Freud, *The Uncanny* (German orig. 1919), trans. David McClintock (London: Penguin, 2003), 123–25.
30. Dylan Trigg, "The Uncanny," in *The Routledge Handbook of Phenomenology of Emotion*, ed. Thomas Szanto and Hilge Landweer (New York: Routledge, 2020), 556.
31. Stanley Kubrick in Vincente Molina Foix, "An Interview with Stanley Kubrick" (1980), in *The Stanley Kubrick Archives*, ed. Alison Castle (Cologne, Germany: Taschen, 2016), 678.

32. Mark Fisher, *The Weird and the Eerie* (London: Repeater, 2016), 9–10 (emphasis added), 8.
33. Fisher, *The Weird and the Eerie*, 61, 8, 15, 61–62 (emphasis added on "suspense"), 110–21 (on *Stalker* [1979]).
34. Cynthia Freeland, "Horror and Art-Dread," in *The Horror Film*, ed. Stephen Prince (New Brunswick, NJ: Rutgers University Press, 2004), 189, 191–93.
35. Freeland, "Horror and Art-Dread," 191, 193–97, 202.
36. Fisher, *The Weird and the Eerie*, 13.
37. Pascal Bonitzer, "Deframings" (French orig. 1978), trans. Chris Darke, in *Cahiers du Cinéma*, vol. 4: *1973–1978: History, Ideology, Cultural Struggle*, ed. David Wilson (London: Routledge, 2000), 198–201. Adrian Martin instructively observes that deframing, as Bonitzer is well aware, "is constantly co-opted, used by the classical system of representing and narrating." One should be careful, warns Martin, not to "confuse genuine deframing with mere obliquity" that "sucks us in, like a whirlpool, to the screen center." Martin, "Frame," in *Global Cinema Networks*, ed. Elena Gorfinkel and Tami Williams (New Brunswick, NJ: Rutgers University Press, 2018), 48. As Martin notes, countless thrillers resort to pseudo-deframings without destabilizing screen space. Kiyoshi Kurosawa's place in this discussion is especially complex because his compositions oscillate between radical deframings and more ornamental or symbolic types of scenic obfuscation that can be found in gothic melodramas, horror, and film noir.
38. Kurosawa on *The Innocents* (Jack Clayton, 1961), which he paired with his film *Séance* (2000) in a retrospective of his work that he curated for the Entrevues Belfort Film Festival in 2014: "I see *The Innocents* as the first film that managed to make visible a blurry, uncertain existence—to make that somehow real. It's the first film that shows ghosts as being *present*, existing truly, irrefutably." In Diane Arnaud and Lili Hinstin, "Entrevues Belfort 2014—a Certain Genre: Double Feature Kiyoshi Kurosawa," interview of Kiyoshi Kurosawa, trans. Eléonore Mahmoudian, October 9, 2014, https://www.festival-entrevues.com/sites/default/files/images/archives/interview_kurosawa_hd.pdf.
39. Keiko McDonald, "Noh Into Film: Kurosawa's *Throne of Blood*," *Journal of Film and Video* 39, no. 1 (Winter 1987): 36–41.
40. If Yabuike is lucky to be alive after having eaten the mushrooms poisoned by Charisma, this can be understood as a riff on the genre cliché of the detective's affinity with the serial killer. Yabuike's tolerance for Charisma's hypnotic poisoning is not unlike how the detective in *Cure* (1997) seems to have a tolerance for the hypnotic possession exerted by the villain and seems to have become a dispenser of hypnotic influence by the film's end.
41. Aaron Gerow, "Kurosawa Kiyoshi, Dis/continuity, and the Ghostly Ethics of Meaning and Auteurship," in *The Global Auteur: The Politics of Authorship in 21st Century Cinema*, ed. Seung-hoon Jeong and Jeremi Szaniawski (New York: Bloomsbury, 2016), 346–51.
42. As part of *Charisma*'s games of absence and presence, some of the offscreen sonic noises are belatedly associated with diegetic sources: airplanes overhead, satellites that emit a zapping sound. But even this "de-acousmaticization" process, as Michel Chion would call it, refuses to confirm itself in the film. Chion, *Audio-Vision: Sound on Screen*, ed. and trans. Claudia Gorbman (New York: Columbia University Press, 1994), 72, 86, 130–31. For an invaluable discussion of ambient sound in Kurosawa's horror films, see Steven T. Brown, *Japanese Horror and the Transnational Cinema of Sensations* (Basingstoke, U.K.: Palgrave Macmillan, 2018), 27–84.

43. Gerow, "Kurosawa Kiyoshi, Dis/continuity, and the Ghostly Ethics of Meaning and Auteurship," 350.
44. To the accompaniment of a droll, exuberant score that seems out of place, *Charisma* at times veers into absurd comedy, including farcical action with guns and a samurai sword, filmed from a great distance. I return to the matter of absurdity at the end of this chapter.
45. *Oxford English Dictionary*, s.v. "charisma (n.)," July 2023, https://doi.org/10.1093/OED/8504496144.
46. See, for example, Kurosawa's comments in Paul Matthews, "Kiyoshi Kurosawa," *Reverse Shot*, October 20, 2005, http://reverseshot.org/interviews/entry/1503/kiyoshi-kurosawa.
47. Kurosawa admiringly discusses the finale to Carpenter's *Escape from L.A.* in *Mon effroyable histoire du cinéma*, 84.
48. Bonitzer, "Deframings," 200.
49. Crandol, *Ghost in the Well*, 58–59; Kurosawa, *Mon effroyable histoire du cinéma*, 43.
50. Mayumi Matsuo and David Matarasso, translators' introduction to Kurosawa, *Mon effroyable histoire du cinéma*, 9, my translation to English.
51. Matsuo and Matarasso, translators' introduction to Kurosawa, *Mon effroyable histoire du cinéma*, 9, my translation to English.
52. At this reflexive level, Kurosawa's concept of cinema as a "machine of fate" could be further elaborated in terms of suspense and dread. Take Nicolas Roeg's *Don't Look Now* (1973), where John Baxter's (Donald Sutherland) fate is manifestly known by the mind of the film long before he confronts his death in Venice. Ambiguously entangled with his clairvoyant perception, the whole film is a fatal mechanism that pushes him toward this outcome, as if already knowing that he will ignore all the stark warning signs offered along the way.
53. Kurosawa, *Mon effroyable histoire du cinéma*, 43–49.
54. "Broken Circuits: A New Interview with Director Kiyoshi Kurosawa," special feature included on Arrow Video's Blu-ray special edition of *Pulse* (2001), 2017.
55. "Broken Circuits." See also Kurosawa, *Mon effroyable histoire du cinéma*, 16–20.
56. Katarzyna Ancuta, "Asian Gothic," in *A New Companion to the Gothic*, ed. Punter, 430.
57. Kurosawa quoted in Alec Morgan, "Visible Silence: Kiyoshi Kurosawa's Cinematic Representation of Contemporary Japanese Characters," *Film International* 16, no. 3 (2018): 87.
58. Kiyoshi Kurosawa, "Director's Statement," included in booklet for the Eureka! Masters of Cinema Blu-ray edition of *Journey to the Shore* (2015), 2016.
59. Jean-Luc Godard's influence on Kurosawa warrants a more thorough consideration than it has received so far. Kurosawa has listed Godard's films *One Plus One* (a.k.a. *Sympathy for the Devil*, 1968), *Detective* (1984), *Notre musique* (2006), and *Goodbye to Language* (2014) among his favorite films. Kurosawa's penchant for reflexivity with respect to media technologies and matters of genre is markedly Godardian. See "Kiyoshi Kurosawa," List of Favorite Films. *Goodbye to Language* appears in Kurosawa's list of best films of the 2010s submitted to *Cahiers du Cinéma*.
60. Eyal Peretz, *The Off-screen: An Investigation of the Cinematic Frame* (Stanford, CA: Stanford University Press, 2017), 81.
61. For a detailed overview of the Kyoto School and this concept, elaborated in dialogue with (and partially against) Western philosophies of being, see Bret W. Davis, "The Kyoto School," in *The Stanford Encyclopedia of Philosophy* (Stanford, CA: Stanford

University Press, Summer 2019), https://plato.stanford.edu/archives/sum2019/entries/kyoto-school.
62. Pascal Bonitzer, "Off-screen Space" (French orig. 1972), trans. Lindley Hanlon, in *Cahiers du Cinéma*, vol. 3: *1969–1972: The Politics of Representation*, ed. Nick Browne (London: Routledge, 1990), 293.
63. Raymond Bellour, *Le corps du cinéma: Hypnoses, émotions, animalités* (Paris: P.O.L., 2009), 23–123.
64. Bellour quoted in Hillary Radner and Alistair Fox, *Raymond Bellour: Cinema and the Moving Image* (Edinburgh: Edinburgh University Press, 2018), 158.
65. Given the importance of spectatorial states on the fringes of sleep in discourse on slow cinema, Bellour's distinction of the hypnotic experience from sleep proper has a bearing on this scholarly debate: "More generally, at the level of a comparative phenomenology of the two experiences"—that is, hypnosis and the film experience—"I was greatly inspired by an American study that was noteworthy and very innovative in its time, 'The Process of Hypnotism and the Nature of the Hypnotic State.' Its two authors, Lawrence Kubie and Sydney Margolin, maintain that it is necessary to distinguish two phases in the hypnotic process, the process of induction that leads the subject toward sleep as a result of a generalized regression, and the hypnotic state proper, in which, contrary to what happens during the first phase, a manifest relation is established between the subject and his or her hypnotist, and with the external world—as if, once asleep, the subject regains a full capacity for coherency. The situation with cinema thus seemed, to me, like a permanent superimposition of these two states, since the spectator is always led by the marriage of the film and the *dispositif* toward a state that is close to sleep, *while being kept awake by the film itself,* which has *intercepted the sleep.*" Bellour quoted in Radner and Fox, *Raymond Bellour*, 156–57, emphasis added. Granted, Bellour appears to have in mind popular cinema in this formulation, not extreme versions of slow cinema.
66. *Creepy*'s (2016) constellation of hypnosis and financial precarity deserves a fuller analysis than I can venture here. Nishino, we learn, preys on overextended households, turning family members against each other. His hypnotically enabled foreclosure-and-disappearance operation—which involves a hidden gothic warehouse-like space in his home and the shrink-wrapping of dead bodies—is a kind of industrial enterprise. In much of Kiyoshi Kurosawa's work, capitalism is among the tentacular forces and circuitries that bear on the lives of characters. Consider the important scene in *Bright Future* (2002) when the protagonist learns from a television report that the venomous red jellyfish has mutated and multiplied and that scores of jellyfish are swimming throughout Tokyo's canal system (another atmospheric circuit) and lethally stinging humans. Just before this report, the program airs a segment about the ongoing economic downturn and politicians unable to stem its tide. Economic forces in Kurosawa's films are not just structures we are given to think about but eerie environmental pressures we feel. For Fisher, capital is an eerie force par excellence: "conjured out of nothing, capital nevertheless exerts more influence than any allegedly substantial entity." Fisher, *The Weird and the Eerie*, 11.
67. The eerie way in which Kurosawa's mobile "camera"—always a ghostly thing, present in absentia—seems both inside and outside the world of the film at once resonates with Daniel Morgan's account of the games that camera movements play. See Morgan, *The Lure of the Image: Epistemic Fantasies of the Moving Camera* (Berkeley: University of California Press, 2021), 57–87.

68. On the middle-class home in Kurosawa's work, see Kinoshita, "The Mummy Complex," 107, 117–20.
69. These subtle, almost disguised hints of horror to come are a low-key version of the intrusive "stain" in Hitchcockian suspense, as Pascal Bonitzer defines it. For Bonitzer, Hitchcock films initially establish a "humdrum" atmosphere of normality, only to disturb it with a small, anomalous detail or graphic form that undercuts this false feeling of comfort and stability. Bonitzer, "Hitchcockian Suspense," trans. Martin Thom, in *Everything You Always Wanted to Know About Lacan but Were Afraid to Ask Hitchcock*, ed. Slavoj Žižek (London: Verso, 2010), 20–21.
70. Considering how central curtains are to Kurosawa's atmospheric style, he has a gothic place in what Joe McElhaney terms "the cinema of fabric," which concerns not only mise-en-scène but also the film medium more generally. McElhaney, *Luchino Visconti and the Fabric of Cinema* (Detroit: Wayne State University Press, 2001), 1–16.
71. The gently seductive, tranquil use of natural light and foliage testifies to the creative input of Akiko Ashizawa, the director of photography. Her contribution to *Creepy* and other Kurosawa films adds a lyrical feel to the cinematography that is pointedly absent in Kurosawa's work before her addition to his usual production team with *Loft* in 2005.
72. Kurosawa's staging techniques could be further studied through recourse to Adrian Martin's Alain Bergala–inspired consideration of spatial "intervals" between bodies onscreen, a parameter of style Martin relates to his conception of *dispositifs*. Martin, *Mise en Scène and Film Style: From Classical Hollywood to New Media Art* (Basingstoke, U.K.: Palgrave Macmillan, 2014), 59–67, 207–15.
73. This motif, insofar as it works as spectator address, is compounded by Kurosawa's recurrent use of shadowy, more or less entranced extras who haunt the backgrounds and borders of offices, libraries, waiting rooms, and other institutional spaces in *Creepy* and *Pulse*. The extras signify a fundamental ghostliness at the heart of humanity. My thanks to Joe McElhaney for pointing out this staging device to me.
74. If eeriness and dread traffic in obscure ambiences, this encounter with Nishino might seem to terminate those affective modes by instituting a terror of directness, or what Julian Hanich has called "direct horror." Hanich, *Cinematic Emotion in Horror Films and Thrillers: The Aesthetic Paradox of Pleasurable Fear* (New York: Routledge, 2010), 81–103. However, Nishino, in our example, is a mere shadow figure, the mechanism of his hypnotic control still undisclosed. If a heightening of fear occurs here for the viewer, it does so against the backdrop of enduring eerie qualities that never wholly subside.
75. A no less pertinent comparison can be drawn here to the nocturnal tunnel effect by which the foreground of the screen world and our viewing space in the theater are made to correspond. Think of Jacques Tourneur's films. Paul Willemen, citing examples in *I Walked with a Zombie* (1943), *The Leopard Man* (1943), and *Night of the Demon* (1957), observes how Tourneur's mise-en-scène "consists of the insertion of a shadow barrier between the space of the viewer and that of the diegesis, as if the real interval between the audience and the screen were insufficient, or perhaps not sufficiently visible and had to be re-presented in the form of a barrier." Willemen argues that such patches of darkness redouble the physical boundary and inscribe a threatening "lack" within the image. Willemen, "Notes Towards the Constructions of Readings of Tourneur," in *Jacques Tourneur*, ed. Claire Johnston and Paul Willemen (Edinburgh: Edinburgh Film Festival, 1975), 23–24. By contrast, I see in both Tourneur's and Kurosawa's films the atmospheric and rhetorical negotiation of a porous boundary.

76. Noël Burch outlines six dimensions of offscreen space: the four that surround the sides of the frame (left, right, top, bottom), a fifth that lies "behind the camera," and a sixth "behind the set," referring to implied spaces of action in back of profilmic objects. Burch, *Theory of Film Practice*, trans. Helen R. Lane (Princeton, NJ: Princeton University Press, 1981), 17. Kurosawa's uncanny address to and inclusion of the spectator vis-à-vis the world of the film calls for a refinement of Burch's "behind the camera" dimension, for the experiential space the viewer occupies is not behind the camera per se. The addition of sound to our experience of the out of frame on *this side of the screen* only complicates matters. I return to this problem in chapter 6.
77. As Gilberto Perez explains, there is a notable difference between a fair number of "Brechtian" film theories and Brecht's attitude toward questions of emotion, immersion, alienation, activity, and passivity. Brecht's sense of reflexivity is not a total disruption of our emotional investment in dramatic narrative so much as a modulation within interplays of immersion and estrangement, the former being vital to the latter. Perez, *The Material Ghost: Films and Their Medium* (Baltimore, MD: Johns Hopkins University Press, 1998), 291.
78. Jonathan Crary, *Suspensions of Perception: Attention, Spectacle, and Modern Culture* (Cambridge, MA: MIT Press, 2001), 70, 64–72.
79. Trigg, "The Uncanny," 558–61.
80. Dylan Trigg, *The Memory of Place: A Phenomenology of the Uncanny* (Athens: Ohio University Press, 2012), 324–25, 164–66.
81. Jean Louis Schefer, *The Ordinary Man of Cinema* (French orig. 1980), trans. Max Cavitch, Paul Grant, and Noura Wedell (South Pasadena, CA: Semiotext(e), 2016), 10–11, 101, 111.
82. Gilles Deleuze invokes Blanchot's concept of the Outside when discussing aesthetic and philosophical transformations of the out of frame in post-1945 modern cinema. Deleuze, *Cinema 2: The Time-Image* (French orig. 1985), trans. Hugh Tomlinson and Robert Galeta (Minneapolis: University of Minnesota Press, 1989), 180–81, 311 n. 37. Schefer's account of the medium and spectatorship in *The Ordinary Man of Cinema* indispensably informs Deleuze's notion of the "spiritual automaton," which Deleuze delineates in part in reference to hypnosis. Deleuze's curious Scheferian sense of the film awakening an alien entity or an "unknown body" located "in the back of our heads"—a "mechanical man without birth who brings the world into suspense" while "dispossessed of his own thought ... through the intermediary of hypnosis" (263)—resonates, in more than just a superficial sense, with Kiyoshi Kurosawa's one-behind-the-other blocking patterns that evoke hypnotic possession.
83. Shigehiko Hasumi is also one of the most astute champions of Kurosawa's work. See Hasumi, "*Bright Future*," trans. Linda Hoaglund, *Film Comment* 39, no. 2 (2003): 18.
84. Ryan Cook, "An Impaired Eye: Hasumi Shigehiko on Cinema and Stupidity," *Review of Japanese Culture and Society* 22 (December 2010): 130.
85. Cook, "An Impaired Eye," 130–33.
86. Cook, "An Impaired Eye," 132–36.
87. Hasumi quoted in Cook, "An Impaired Eye," 137.
88. Bonitzer, "Deframings," 200 (emphasis added), 201. Bonitzer derives his sense of deframing more generally from "the unmastered space of modern art ... replete with lacunae" (198).

6. Streaming the Undead Energies of "Film"

1. Neta Alexander argues that "speed watching" is a practiced skill that requires extraordinary focus and results in a possibly deeper state of immersion than theatrical viewing. She makes this claim while acknowledging that the digital spectator's option to raise the playback speed is anathema to many filmmakers. Alexander, "Speed Watching, Efficiency, and the New Temporalities of Digital Spectatorship," in *Compact Cinematics: The Moving Image in the Age of Bit-Sized Media*, ed. Pepita Hesselberth and Maria Poulaki (New York: Bloomsbury, 2017), 103–12. How might speed watching change our experience of suspense? For Alexander, whether the speed-watcher misses something is a question of plot, the uptake of narrative action and dialogue (104–9). But in almost any film there is more to catch than narrative information. Speed watching may give us the illusion of missing nothing when we in fact miss affective nuances and intensities that depend on a film's preset rhythms, from comic timing to the emotional contours of melodrama and horror. In a different article, though it doesn't focus on suspense, Alexander makes important inroads into understanding anxieties peculiar to the streaming experience. See Alexander, "Rage Against the Machine: Buffering, Noise, and Perceptual Anxiety in the Age of Connected Viewing," *Cinema Journal* 56, no. 2 (2017): 1–24.
2. Caetlin Benson-Allott, *Killer Tapes and Shattered Screens: Video Spectatorship from VHS to File Sharing* (Berkeley: University of California Press, 2013); Glen Creeber, *Small Screen Aesthetics: From TV to the Internet* (Basingstoke, U.K.: Palgrave Macmillan, 2013); John Ellis, *Visible Fictions: Cinema, Television, Video* (New York: Routledge, 1992); and John Ellis, *Seeing Things: Television in the Age of Uncertainty* (London: I. B. Tauris, 2000). For other texts relevant to this history of shifting and converging *dispositifs*, see Timothy Corrigan, *A Cinema Without Walls: Movies and Culture After Vietnam* (New Brunswick, NJ: Rutgers University Press, 1991); Barbara Klinger, *Beyond the Multiplex: Cinema, New Technologies, and the Home* (Berkeley: University of California Press, 2006); and Laura Mulvey, *Death 24x a Second: Stillness and the Moving Image* (London: Reaktion, 2006).
3. Creeber focuses on *Twin Peaks* in its ABC incarnation in 1990–1991 as an example of hybridity between film and television, while also noting, in a passage relevant to suspense, that the show's infinite and unresolvable mysteries invited the viewer to rewatch recorded episodes and repeatedly study key scenes, using the VCR as an investigative instrument. Creeber, *Small Screen Aesthetics*, 93. On cinematic "gaze" versus televisual "glance" aesthetics, see Ellis, *Visible Fictions*, 24–25, 47–50, 128–29, 137. See also Ellis, *Seeing Things*, 100–101. For an overview and analysis of how *Twin Peaks*, from its initial incarnation to *Twin Peaks: The Return* (2017), plays with and defies the formulas of dramatic television, see Martha P. Nochimson, *Television Rewired: The Rise of the Auteur Series* (Austin: University of Texas Press, 2019), 31–61, 237–68.
4. Julian Hanich, "An Invention with a Future: Collective Viewing, Joint Deep Attention, and the Ongoing Value of the Cinema," in *The Oxford Handbook of Film Theory*, ed. Kyle Stevens (New York: Oxford University Press, 2022), 591.
5. Hanich, "An Invention with a Future," 591–92.
6. I am referring specifically to the initial distribution pattern set by NEON in the United States. *Memoria* (2021) has been available for purchase on Blu-ray in other regions.

7. According to David Lynch and members of the production crew, *Twin Peaks: The Return* was approached as one long "feature film" rather than as a series having the structural and technical specificities of serial television (camera setup, narrative shape within each episode, etc.). Peter Deming, the cinematographer, reports that the eight-month shoot worked from a 550-page script by Lynch and co-creator Mark Frost that was not broken into separate episodes. This "film" was shot digitally using the ARRI Amira camera system at 3.2K resolution and in postproduction upped to 4K to comply with Showtime's requirement as well as the effects team's requirements. Deming also reports that Lynch considered shooting the whole series on iPhones. "Peter Deming—Cinematographer," *Team Deakins Podcast*, April 2021, https://teamdeakins.libsyn.com/peter-deming-cinematographer.
8. Given my emphasis on dispositive consciousness, it could be argued that the internet culture of memes, fan and journalistic reviews, and discussion sites forms an integral part of the streaming experience. See, for example, Brigid Cherry, "'The Owls Are Not What They Meme': Making Sense of *Twin Peaks* with Internet Memes," in *Critical Essays on* Twin Peaks: The Return, ed. Antonio Sanna (Cham, Switzerland: Palgrave Macmillan, 2019), 69–84. A simple internet search will lead to various, remarkably detailed fan writings and videos attempting to explain, as if once and for all, the series' hidden meanings.
9. David Lynch, *Catching the Big Fish: Meditation, Consciousness, and Creativity* (New York: Jeremy P. Tarcher/Penguin, 2007), 17.
10. David Lynch, interview included in "Stories," special feature of the Rhino Special Edition DVD of *Inland Empire* (2006), 2007.
11. David Lynch, "Consciousness, Creativity, and the Brain," public appearance, Emerson College School of Arts, Boston, October 1, 2005.
12. Lynch, "Consciousness, Creativity, and the Brain." See also Lynch, *Catching the Big Fish*, 21–22.
13. Dean Hurley, interview by Jon Dieringer and John Klacsmann, *Screen Slate Podcast*, April 20, 2022, https://www.screenslate.com/articles/episode-6-dean-hurley.
14. Lynch in Noel de Souza, "David Lynch: 'Silence Is so Powerful and It's Missing in the World,'" interview, *Open Magazine*, June 28, 2017, https://openthemagazine.com/columns/hollywood-reporter/david-lynch-silence-is-so-powerful-and-its-missing-in-the-world/.
15. Kyle Stevens, "Headphones, Cinematic Listening, and the Frame of the Skull," in *The Oxford Handbook of Film Theory*, ed. Stevens, 339, 345–46.
16. It is not my intention here to delve into the specifics of different kinds of headphones (ear buds versus circumaural headphones, and so on). To avoid needless complications tangential to my argument, let us assume a spectator whose use of headphones allows the soundtrack of the film to play with high quality and to dominate auditory perception.
17. On Lynch's preoccupation with electricity, as "explained" in his own words, see David Lynch, *Lynch on Lynch*, interviewed by Chris Rodley, ed. Chris Rodley, rev. ed. (London: Faber and Faber, 2005), 72–73.
18. Saige Walton, "The Electricity of Blue Roses: Shorting the Senses and Sensing Film Mood in *Twin Peaks: Fire Walk with Me*," in *From Sensation to Synaesthesia in Film and New Media*, ed. Rossella Cantanese, Francesca Scotto Lavina, and Valentina Valente (Newcastle upon Tyne, U.K.: Cambridge Scholars, 2019), 151–66.
19. In criticism and fan discussions, it has become customary to refer to this character as "BOB" in all caps, an acronym that evokes "Beware of Bob" and accords with

Laura's diary. I will follow suit in calling this character "BOB," but the end credits of *Fire Walk with Me* (1992) list him as "Bob," as do the credits for both the ABC show and *Twin Peaks: The Return*. More pivotal than the issue of capitalization is the name's palindromic aspect as it relates to language games and mirror motifs associated with the Black Lodge. The degree to which BOB controls Leland Palmer's actions becomes more uncomfortably ambiguous in *Fire Walk with Me*, where the family patriarch seems closer to Jack Torrance of *The Shining* (Stanley Kubrick, 1980) or to the equally deranged and malevolent Ed Avery (James Mason) in *Bigger Than Life* (Nicholas Ray, 1956).

20. *Fire Walk with Me* tends to be described as a plunge into Laura's point of view, something that the original TV series, which begins with her already murdered, denies. But the prequel, to my mind, still partakes largely of the type of character suspense that *obstructs* our access to a screen figure's psychological interiority. Despite our closeness to her point of view, Laura remains in large measure unknowable beneath the clichéd identities that others project onto her. She remains defined by her elusiveness. Indeed, the film is about her escaping, albeit through death or a kind of death and transfiguration, abuse at the hands of Leland and BOB, the latter of whom feeds on what denizens of the Black Lodge call "garmonbozia," or the pain and sorrow of humanity. Laura's elusiveness also wards off the spectator who—desiring what character-driven narrative usually offers—seeks a gratifying experience of psychological identification. Such a spectator, it must be said, feasts on "garmonbozia," too.

21. Directors hired for *Twin Peaks* episodes in 1990–1991 couldn't introduce blue mise-en-scène unless Lynch approved. Brad Dukes, *Reflections: An Oral History of Twin Peaks* (Nashville, TN: Short/Tall Press, 2014), 280. Blue delineates zones of liminality between different worlds in *Twin Peaks*, much as it does in *Mulholland Drive* (2001).

22. For an astute audiovisual essay and accompanying text that explores the relays of electrical energy across the original series, *Fire Walk with Me*, and *Twin Peaks: The Missing Pieces* (2014), see Cristina Álvarez López and Adrian Martin, "Short-Circuit: A 'Twin Peaks' System," *MUBI Notebook*, May 12, 2015, https://mubi.com/notebook/posts/short-circuit-a-twin-peaks-system.

23. Michel Chion, *David Lynch*, trans. Robert Julian, 2nd ed. (London: British Film Institute, 2006), 142.

24. See Antonio Somaini, "Walter Benjamin's Media Theory: The *Medium* and the *Apparat*," *Grey Room* 62 (Winter 2016): 6–41.

25. Maurice Merleau-Ponty, *The Phenomenology of Perception* (French orig. 1945), trans. Colin Smith (New York: Routledge University Press, 2002), 4.

26. Trace Reddell, *The Sound of Things to Come: An Audible History of the Science Fiction Film* (Minneapolis: University of Minnesota Press, 2018), 293. Reddell's claim for the headphonic "ideal auditor" is also predicated on the viewer's alignment with *THX 1138*'s (1971) protagonist, a control-center employee who wears headphones for his surveillance work.

27. Stevens, "Headphones," passim.

28. Greg Hainge, "Red Velvet: David Lynch's Cinemat(ograph)ic Ontology," in *David Lynch in Theory*, ed. François-Xavier Glezon (Prague: Litteraria Pragensia, 2010), 33–35. See also Richard Martin, *The Architecture of David Lynch* (London: Bloomsbury, 2014), 59–61.

29. In part, Lynch's game of numbers here nods to the suspense-laden fascination with numbers, coordinates, and identities in Hitchcock's espionage thriller *North by*

Northwest (1959), a film whose famous scenes are directly channeled in *The Return* more than once.

30. For a reading of the gramophone motif in Lynch's work as it evolves from *Eraserhead*(1977) on, see Holly Rogers, "The Audiovisual Eerie: Transmediating Thresholds in the Work of David Lynch," in *Transmedia Directors: Artistry, Industry, and New Audiovisual Aesthetics*, ed. Carol Vernallis, Holly Rogers, and Lisa Perrott (London: Bloomsbury, 2019), 18–27.

31. The forward-pushing camera that crosses a threshold and passes between dimensions is, of course, one of the primal expressive gestures in Lynch's style. The viewer conversant with his work can't help but think of the camera movement into the severed ear discovered in a field in *Blue Velvet* (1984). This gesture, eerier and more ambiguously cosmic in *Eraserhead*, always performs a kind of double movement whereby we move into the onscreen world *while it moves into us*. The spectator's body is thus implied to be a threshold, too, which the headphonic listener experiences in an especially acute way.

32. This sound-oriented game of structural, perceptual, and atmospheric suspense is borne along by what Danijela Kulezic-Wilson calls a fully integrated, "musicalized" sound design, wherein subtleties of noise, score, and effects blend together rhythmically. For Kulezic-Wilson, who invokes *Twin Peaks: The Return* as part of this increasingly widespread principle of design in contemporary film and television, such musicalization of sound was greatly assisted by the arrival of digital audio workstations in the 1990s but can be traced back to Lynch's acoustic experiments with Alan Splet on the production of *Eraserhead*. Kulezic-Wilson, *Sound Design Is the New Score: Theory, Aesthetics, and Erotics of the Integrated Soundtrack* (New York: Oxford University Press, 2020), 1–26. Lynch's key collaborators in crafting the digitally "musicalized" sound design of *Twin Peaks: The Return* were Dean Hurley and Ron Eng.

33. Some types of headphones are manufactured to provide a "surround sound" experience, either through multiple speakers emitting sound at different angles from each earcup or through the use of algorithms that, so it is claimed, offer a virtual surround experience. Neither of these options, however, manages to cancel out the slightly awkward separation of sound between the screen and the ear canal or to re-create the particular ambient feel of proper surround sound and the much wider tonal range that larger loudspeakers provide.

34. Martin, *The Architecture of David Lynch*, 59.

35. On the "possessive spectator," see Mulvey, *Death 24x a Second*, 161–80.

36. In *Mulholland Drive*, for example, a conspiratorial network, with designs on the casting of a particular lead actress in a Hollywood production, is expressed through a series of spaces relayed by telephone calls, the phone subtended visually by a lamp in each location. The combination of lamps, phones, and ashtrays on nightstands or side tables often serves as a still-life that has a nodal position within an elaborate circuitry.

37. Lynch's work has understandably served as a lightning rod in recent debates about intermedial relationships. See Anne Jerslev, *David Lynch: Blurred Boundaries* (Cham, Switzerland: Palgrave Macmillan, 2021). My conception of "medium suspense" means to underscore the fundamentally enigmatic, anxious, surreal, and wondrous ways in which "film" figures vis-à-vis its complex entwinements with other media. My thinking is shaped by what Jihoon Kim theorizes as the "nesting" of media within media, a condition that aesthetically involves a negotiation between medium specificity and media hybridity rather than simply the supplantation of the former by the latter. See

Kim, *Between Film, Video, and the Digital: Hybrid Moving Images in the Post-media Age* (New York: Bloomsbury, 2016), 8–9, 25–28.

38. *The Return* borrows this idea in part from Francis Bacon (1909–1992) paintings. Although the glass box evokes a television monitor, it seems to have been inspired by the floating transparent boxes that enclose figures in grotesque states of dissolution and anguish in Bacon's "Screaming Popes" series of oil paintings. *Seated Figure* (1961) and similarly styled renderings of boxed figures in domestic interiors that are distantly called to mind by the Red Room of the Black Lodge are also key references here. Lynch's debt to Bacon's work has been widely acknowledged. In part 1 of *The Return*, when the figure abstractly emerges from the glass box, the box's dimensions are flush with our screen, which suggests the figure breaches the boundary between spectator and spectacle.

39. See Jonathan Foltz, "David Lynch's Late Style," *Los Angeles Review of Books*, November 12, 2017, https://lareviewofbooks.org/article/david-lynchs-late-style/. The comparison to Godard in this late-period sense is my own.

40. Dean Hurley, sound mixer and supervising sound editor for *The Return*, remarks that Lynch, upon rewatching the finale of season 2 of the ABC series, complained that there was "way too much music in it" and not enough silence. Lynch's more minimalistic approach to sound in *The Return* indeed marks a dramatic shift away from the sound design of the original TV series. "Night Electricity Theme with Dean Hurley," *The ION Pod*, September 2021, https://podtail.com/en/podcast/the-ion-pod/ep-38-night-electricity-theme-with-dean-hurley-unl/.

41. Within his conception of film atmosphere, Steffen Hven considers how camera movement (a key example comes from Mikhail Kalatozov's *The Cranes Are Flying* [1957]) doesn't stand outside the diegetic world but instead "enacts" a "dynamic change of viewpoint" as a "quality of sensation" that shapes (and, in effect, *is*) "the diegesis anew." What the camera embodies in the scene Hven analyzes is not the subjectivist substitute of a perceptual gaze for character or audience but a nonanthropomorphic perspective. Hven, *Enacting the Worlds of Cinema* (New York: Oxford University Press, 2022), 118–19. Lynch's camera movements in *The Return*, in particular those that patrol thresholds between realms, often play on ambiguities between human and nonhuman perspectives and agencies. *Camera*, I must say, is a misleading term insofar as we don't see a physical camera so much as we experience an articulation of force, as if riding an invisible energy current. Here again, we encounter an operation of style that assumes an endogenous atmospheric role within the film's world.

42. In part 14 of *The Return*, Gordon Cole recounts a dream he had in which the Italian actress Monica Bellucci tells him at a Paris café: "We are like the dreamer who dreams and then lives inside the dream. But who is the dreamer?" This line reworks a passage from the Upanishads: "We are like the spider. / We weave our life and then move along in it. / We are like the dreamer who dreams and then lives in the dream. / This is true of the entire universe." Quoted in Lynch, *Catching the Big Fish*, 139. In *The Return*, Bellucci's added question to this Vedic passage raises the possibility of dream sharing that happens unawares.

43. An operative concept here is "intersection." This traffic light, which harks back to an eerily inserted sound-image that recurs periodically in the original TV series, is not just an abstract, free-floating shot, as it is sometimes described. Rather, it specifically marks the intersection of Highway 21 and Sparkwood Road in the town of Twin Peaks, the fateful intersection where Laura Palmer was last seen by James Hurley (James

Marshall) as she ran into the woods on the night of her murder, a specific location that *The Return* revisits in surreal, metamorphic ways.

44. Inspired by the colors of a traffic light (and thus the idea of intersection), this scene's yellow/red/green color logic, which extends to Janey-E's cardigan and Dougie's green jacket, returns in part 16 when Dougie, now reconstituted as Agent Cooper, awakens at the hospital. Sonny Jim (Pierce Gagnon), their son, wears a yellow sweatshirt; Janey-E has a red purse and red, yellow, and green in her sweater, not to mention blond hair and red lipstick.

45. *Oxford English Dictionary*, s.v. "electric (adj. & n.)," December 2023, https://doi.org/10.1093/OED/1136251700.

46. As an example of tragic pathos associated with this electricity motif in *The Return*, consider the scene, also in part 6 (and somehow on the same grid as Dougie's discovery of the insurance scam), where a young boy playing a game with his mother is struck and killed by a maniacal gangster henchman who runs a stop sign. A spark from the boy's dying body drifts toward power lines and dissipates in the air, connecting this disaster to the electrical circuitry of the series and its interdimensional cosmos. This scene culminates a thread of motifs initiated, albeit obliquely, by Dougie's miraculous work on his case files. The event also happens at the same intersection where in *Fire Walk with Me* Laura is accosted by Mike, the one-armed man, who screams a warning at her, almost unintelligibly, while revving his engine.

47. On this score, Brian Massumi's process-based philosophical account of atmosphere informs my thinking of *The Return*'s atmospherics: "There is always activity, energising more activity—action upon action.... The word 'transduction' would be better than transmission, because the self-completion of a pulse of experience is the springboard for a next that will differ from it." Massumi, "Dim, Massive, and Important: Atmosphere in Process," in *Music as Atmosphere: Collective Feelings and Affective Sounds*, ed. Friedlind Riedel and Juha Torvinen (London: Routledge, 2020), 292. Massumi's reference to the concept of "transduction" is a nod in the direction of the philosopher Gilbert Simondon, to whom I soon turn in this chapter.

48. Mark Frost, *The Secret History of Twin Peaks* (New York: Flatiron, 2016); Frost, *Twin Peaks: The Final Dossier* (New York: Flatiron, 2017).

49. Hainge observes that scholars writing about Lynch's practice go to extreme lengths to convert its nonsignificatory noise into meaning that corresponds to the terms and principles imposed by an outside discursive system or "narrative." Resistant to this narrativization of noise and spectacle is what Hainge describes as Lynch's "cinema of attractions" in reference to Tom Gunning's famous elaboration of this concept of early cinema's forms of address. Hainge, "Red Velvet," 25–27. See also Greg Hainge, *Noise Matters: Towards an Ontology of Noise* (London: Bloomsbury, 2013), 177–208. For what it is worth, Lynch, when speaking to the matter of interpretation, states: "You don't need anything outside of the work." Lynch, *Catching the Big Fish*, 19.

50. For a reading of Lynch's work in relation to quantum physics, see Martha P. Nochimson, *David Lynch Swerves: Uncertainty from* Lost Highway *to* Inland Empire (Austin: University of Texas Press, 2013).

51. To be more precise, Jean-Hugues Barthélémy traces Simondon's use of the term *transduction* back in part to the writings of the Swiss developmental psychologist Jean Piaget, where it refers to a mental operation by which the child makes sense of the world. Transduction differs, however, from both induction and deduction—a distinction Simondon also takes on board. Barthélémy, "Glossary: Fifty Key Terms in the Work of Gilbert Simondon," trans. Arne De Boever, in *Gilbert Simondon: Being and*

Technology, ed. Arne De Boever, Alex Murray, Jon Roffe, and Ashley Woodward (Edinburgh: Edinburgh University Press, 2011), 230.
52. Gilbert Simondon, *Individuation in Light of Notions of Form and Information* (French orig. 1964/1989), trans. Taylor Adkins (Minneapolis: University of Minnesota Press, 2020), 1–17.
53. Simondon, *Individuation*, 5–16, 65–82.
54. Paulo De Assis, "Gilbert Simondon's 'Transduction' as Radical Immanence in Performance," *Performance Philosophy* 3, no. 3 (2017): 705.
55. "Relation," writes Simondon, "is a modality of being; it is simultaneous with respect to the terms whose existence it guarantees. A relation must be grasped as a relation in being, a relation of being, a manner of being, and not a simple rapport between two terms that could be adequately known via concepts because they would have an effectively prior, separate existence." Simondon, *Individuation*, 12.
56. Alanna Thain, *Bodies in Suspense: Time and Affect in Cinema* (Minneapolis: University of Minnesota Press, 2017), esp. 119–76.
57. Simondon, *Individuation*, 14–16.
58. Gilbert Simondon, *On the Mode of Existence of Technical Objects* (French orig. 1958), trans. Cecile Malaspina and John Rogove (Minneapolis: Univocal, 2017), 129, 135–38.
59. Jean-Hugues Barthélémy notes that *transductive operations*, as Simondon uses the term, may involve "*auto*-complexifiction." Barthélémy, "Glossary," 230, emphasis added. It is tempting to adapt this notion to Lynch's autoreferential tendencies and self-inscriptive performance across the different iterations of *Twin Peaks*.
60. Those who characterize Lynch's late works as "puzzle films" tend to want to work out all the snags and noisy remainders. When discussing his film *Lost Highway* (1997) and the difficulties it poses to an audience, Lynch remarks that "the clues are all there for a correct interpretation" but also that "a few things" are "a hair off." Lynch, *Lynch on Lynch*, 227. This "hair-off-ness," which no doubt applies also to *The Return* and its split identities, time loops, and parallel worlds, needs to be kept intact in critical discussions of Lynch-directed work. This hair-off-ness is essential to the suspenseful "world-feeling," as Daniel Yacavone would put it, of Lynch's films. Yacavone, *Film Worlds: A Philosophical Aesthetics of Cinema* (New York: Columbia University Press, 2015), 190–226, especially 220–21, where Yacavone invokes the singular qualities of Lynch's film worlds.
61. See, for example, Donato Totaro, "*Twin Peaks: The Return*, Part 8: The Western, Science-Fiction, and the BIG BOmB," *Offscreen* 21, nos. 11–12 (December 2017), https://offscreen.com/view/twin-peaks-the-return-part-8-the-western-science-fiction-and-big-bomb; and Nick Pinkerton, "*Twin Peaks: The Return*, or What Isn't Cinema? (Part One)," *Reverse Shot*, January 29, 2018, http://reverseshot.org/features/2417/twin_peaks_one.
62. The underexplored affinities between Lynch and Kubrick warrant more extensive attention than I can offer here. For an essay that begins to mine this connection, see Rick Warner, "Kubrickian Dread: Echoes of *2001: A Space Odyssey* and *The Shining* in Works by Jonathan Glazer, Paul Thomas Anderson, and David Lynch," in *After Kubrick: A Filmmaker's Legacy*, ed. Jeremi Szaniawski (New York: Bloomsbury, 2020), 125–45.
63. Tom Gunning, "The Cinema of Attraction[s]: Early Film, Its Spectator, and the Avant-Garde," in *The Cinema of Attractions Reloaded*, ed. Wanda Strauven (Amsterdam: Amsterdam University Press, 2006), 381–88. For the relevance of this argument to Lynch's work, see Hainge, "Red Velvet," 26–27, 33–34.

64. Dean Hurley, sound mixer and supervising sound editor for *The Return*, telephone interview by the author, September 23, 2022. Indeed, the sound mix of *The Return* is almost closer to mono than to stereo in its avoidance of the kind of surround effects we found in Martel's *Zama* (2017) in chapter 3. For the headphonic listener, though the full-bodied reverberance is lost, less is lost in terms of audio directionality.

65. Stevens, "Headphones."

66. Where the young Sarah Palmer (née Novack) in part 8 is concerned, Mark Frost's novels, which disclose this girl's identity, are necessary intertexts. Nothing internal to part 8 confirms her identity, leaving this connection in suspense. Frost, *Twin Peaks: The Final Dossier*, 133–36.

67. Kate Rennebohm points to *The Return*'s registrations of the opioid epidemic through "a parade of women in various degrees of deterioration." Rennebohm, "A Little Night Music: *Twin Peaks: The Return*, Part Eight," *Cinema Scope* 72 (2017): 61. I would add that our being made to feel atmospherically caught up in the various mediational currents of *The Return* is at least in part *implicatory* on ethical grounds. The suggestion is that horrible things happen *on our watch* when we are in thrall to the ideology of the American Dream—things including Laura's abuse, rape, and murder.

68. Mikel Dufrenne, *The Phenomenology of Aesthetic Experience*, trans. Edward S. Casey (Evanston, IL: Northwestern University Press, 1973), 152–54.

69. Lynch's earlier projects merit reference in this respect. *Eraserhead*, which sometimes appears in overviews of slow cinema, features abstract mechanical whirs that resonate not only with industrial mise-en-scène but with the hum of the projector, the system noise of the film apparatus. Writing of *Lost Highway*'s sonic ambience, Philip Brophy remarks that it "lugubriously bleeds into the air-conditioned atmosphere of the cinema itself." Brophy, *100 Modern Soundtracks* (London: British Film Institute, 2004), 156.

70. Lynch, interview included in "Stories," special feature.

71. Dufrenne, *The Phenomenology of Aesthetic Experience*, 152–53, 179–80.

72. See Jean-Charles Vergne, Pierre Zaoui, and Mathieu Potte-Bonneville, *David Lynch: Man Waking from Dream* (Clermont-Ferrand, France: FRAC Auvergne, 2012); David Lynch, *David Lynch: Someone Is in My House*, ed. Stijn Huijts (Munich: Prestel, 2021). As has been carefully documented by fans in social media, many of *The Return*'s images are adapted from earlier drawings and paintings by Lynch. For example, The Fireman's levitation scene in part 8 is inspired by such drawings as the chalk-on-paper *Floating Figure* (1985). The digital-effects house BUF worked directly from Lynch's charcoal drawings. See "Twin Peaks #3—BUF Making of," https://vimeo.com/251488637.

73. Shane Denson, *Discorrelated Images* (Durham, NC: Duke University Press, 2022), 1–17, 41–43, 2, 3, 37–39.

74. Denson, *Discorrelated Images*, 3–4.

75. In my view, Denson's discussion of "discorrelation"—that is, the severing of images and their substrative speeds and structures from human consciousness and subjectivity—could be more carefully historicized. His account opens with a description of a camera movement in the TV show *Lost* (2004–2010) that diverges from the human point of view it initially seems to embody. Denson, *Discorrelated Images*, 4–8. Such stylistic gestures of discorrelation, of course, abound in the various European and East Asian modern cinemas that sprouted after 1945, well before the technical advent of digital media and its computational infrastructures in relation to cinema, and they can also be found even in mainstream Hollywood cinema of the classical

era. Indeed, Anthony Mann's Western *The Man from Laramie* (1955) features such a camera movement, even more disorienting than the one in *Lost*, in its opening minutes (my thanks to Gregg Flaxman for calling this example to my attention). What is more, indivisible form–substrate relations are arguably just as salient under the traditional cinematic *dispositif*, where the technical apparatus may assert itself in such a way as to become part and parcel of the projected film's atmospherics. I concur that the nature of the relationship between form and substrate changed radically with the digital, but the disruptive and aesthetic intrusions of the traditional substrate call for a more thorough acknowledgment in this debate.

76. For "digital ether," see Denson, *Discorrelated Images*, 38.
77. See Nathan Allen Jones, *Glitch Poetics* (London: Open Humanities Press, 2022). On Lynch's aesthetic and conceptual use of technological malfunctions, see Thain, *Bodies in Suspense*, 148.
78. For a striking example of a film that *atmospherically* interrelates its forms with its media-technical substrate, take Lana and Lilly Wachowski's *The Matrix* (1999) and the implicit affective relationship between its greenish neo-noir atmosphere, the green liquidlike computational coding generated by the AI entity known as the Matrix within the diegesis (an entity also responsible for the greenish neo-noir synthetic world in the first place), and the "digital ether" (as Denson might put it) or computational matrix toward which the film gestures. When the ambient digital ether materializes before Neo (Keanu Reeves) at the film's end, it is green, too. This inclusion of the media-technical substrate is, granted, more allegorical than literal, but it attests to the multifaceted role of atmosphere in this aesthetic and technological context.
79. The mobile frame and the film's editing style in this scene are vaguely correlated with the woodsman's point of view. But notice how when the woodsman approaches the motorist couple, what initially seems to be a point-of-view shot brings his figure into the frame, thus detaching, or discorrelating, the camera from his point of view. As Greg Hainge has noted, the difference in speeds is important here, too, in that the woodsman moves and speaks to a speed that is incommensurable with yet combined in one space with the temporal frame inhabited by the motorists. Hainge, "When Is a Door Not a Door? Transmedia to the Nth Degree in David Lynch's Multiverse," in *Transmedia Directors*, ed. Vernallis, Rogers, and Perrott, 279–80.
80. On the relationship of the film's atmospherics to gender violence and the screams and gasps of women, see Monique Rooney, "Air-Object: On Air Media and David Lynch's 'Gotta Light?' (*Twin Peaks: The Return*, 2017)," *New Review of Film and Television Studies* 16, no. 2 (2018): 123–43.
81. Robert Gordon Joseph, "Lincoln the Woodsman: Native Americans and Obscene Patriarchs in Frost and Lynch's *Twin Peaks*," *Quarterly Review of Film and Video*, published online September 25, 2022, 16, https://doi.org/10.1080/10509208.2022.2124096.
82. Joseph, "Lincoln the Woodsman," 21–23.
83. The woodsmen are slightly less one-dimensional in their alignment with colonial-settler and patriarchal violence than Joseph's argument indicates. Moreover, although Joseph is quick to credit Frost as the primary if not sole author of this line of social and historical commentary, the woodsmen initially surface in the film *Fire Walk with Me*, which Lynch coscripted with Robert Engels, without Frost's involvement. Joseph writes that the woodsmen are "unambiguously White" ("Lincoln the Woodsman," 14), but in *Fire Walk with Me* one of them, a character credited as "The Electrician," is Black (and played by the Bahamian American stage and film actor Calvin Lockhart). The woodsmen in *The Return* seem to be an amalgam of the traits Joseph

emphasizes and their former iteration in *Fire Walk with Me*, which also includes a grime-covered, seemingly unhoused person, a woman who mysteriously stalks the Fat Trout Trailer Park when FBI agents are there to investigate. The woodsmen thus bear some connection to destitution and precarity, not unlike the grime-covered figure lurking behind the dumpster in *Mulholland Drive*.

84. Pages of the screenplay can be glimpsed in Boiler Room's interview with Dean Hurley, "He Heard a Wind: Behind the Sound Design in *Twin Peaks*," May 9, 2018, https://www.youtube.com/watch?v=CPeiUFybVUs.
85. Andy Birtwistle, *Cinesonica: Sounding Film and Video* (Manchester, U.K.: Manchester University Press, 2010), 86, emphasis added.
86. Regarding the "affective suspension of knowledge" through cinema, see Thain, *Bodies in Suspense*, 123.
87. Adrian Martin, "The Challenge of Narrative: Storytelling Mutations Between Television and Cinema," *Cineaste* 44, no. 3 (Summer 2019): 22–27.
88. Onnalee Blank, supervising sound editor and re-recording mixer for *The Underground Railroad*, affirms that the series sound design has a "*Twin Peaks* vibe." "*The Underground Railroad*'s Joi McMillon, Onnalee Blank Featured," *The Hollywood Reporter Behind the Screen* (podcast), May 28, 2021, https://www.hollywoodreporter.com/tv/tv-features/underground-railroad-joi-mcmillon-onnalee-blank-thr-behind-the-screen-1234960497/.
89. Jean Louis Schefer, *The Ordinary Man of Cinema* (French orig. 1980), trans. Max Cavitch, Paul Grant, and Noura Wedell (South Pasadena, CA: Semiotext(e), 2016), 117.

INDEX

absence–presence interaction, 137, 157, 162, 164, 171, 174, 262n42; cinema as gothic medium and, 156
action thrillers, 52, 55–56
aesthetics of night, 127, 129, 132
affect theory, 11, 20, 204
Affron, Mirella Jona, 54
After Hours (Scorsese, 1985), 28
Agee, James, 127
agency, political, 80, 126, 131
Agger, Vililbjørk Malling, 91
Aguirre, the Wrath of God (1972), 91, 246n16
Akbari, Mania, 109
Akerman, Chantal, 3, 18, 31, 34, 76, 77, 88; on *dispositif* in *La captive*, 72; gothic notes in films of, 155; instinctive kinship with Bresson's approach, 65; on metamorphic capabilities of long take, 40; minimalistic thriller of, 53; on structural films of Snow, 64; on suspense and nervous expectation, 66; theory of durational image in spectator's consciousness, 65, 236n55
Á la recherche du temps perdu [*In Search of Lost Time*] (Proust), 67, 68
Alexander, Neta, 267n1
Alhadeff, Albert, 254n11

Allen, Richard, 231n2
Almayer's Folly (Akerman, 2011), 92
Almereyda, Michael, 259n10
Alonso, Lisandro, 3, 18, 90, 92, 238n71, 240n24
Alphaville (Godard, 1965), 109
alterity, 74, 104–5, 112, 132, 162
Altman, Robert, 14
Álvarez López, Cristina, 28, 70, 72
ambience, 12, 13, 85, 86, 115, 245n6; ambient music genre, 90; atmospheric perception and, 90; definition of, 106; ecological use of, 49; etymology of, 89; headphonic sound and, 19, 203; relation to atmosphere, 88–89, 245n6; "sensory point of view" and, 18, 88; suspenseful functions of landscape and, 88. *See also* atmosphere
Ambient Media (Roquet), 88–89
Amenábar, Alejandro, 31, 163
Amirpour, Ana Lily, 32, 259n10
Ancuta, Katarzyna, 171–72
Andersson, Roy, 29
Andrei Rublev (Tarkovsky, 1966), 32
Andrew, Dudley, 34
Andrews, David, 5
anempathetic effect, 45, 73, 84

Angelopoulos, Theo, 157
Annihilation (Garland, 2018), 169
"anotherness," 11, 25, 207
Antonioni, Michelangelo, 5, 16, 22, 88, 109; deframing and, 164; fog in films of, 112; media diaphana and, 90; suspension used by, 42–45
anxiety, 28, 84, 120, 220, 228–29n39; "anxious cinephilia," 17; from concealment and protraction, 64; dispositive, 16; dread compared with, 163; excessive "nothing" and, 15–20; 4:3 Academy ratio and, 247n22; suspension and, 46
Apichatpong, Weerasethakul, 3, 6, 19, 182, 225n11, 225n16, 246n16; Buddhist outlook of, 135; doubling used by, 29, 97; "exploding head syndrome" of, 256n41; interest in science and science fiction, 135, 255n29; media diaphana and, 90; sound in relation to memory in work of, 256n45; surrealism and, 97; switch to use of professional actors, 256n39
architecture, 13, 32, 37, 67
Argento, Dario, 36
Aristotle, 89, 195
Army of Shadows (Melville, 1969), 28–29
art cinema, 5–6, 16, 146, 219, 237n67; denial of identification in, 25; Eurocentrism and, 225n15; everydayness in, 49; plot ambiguities in, 24
art-house films, 2, 3, 12, 19, 88, 120
Asano, Tadanobu, 172
Ashbrook, Dana, 217
Ashizawa, Akiko, 265n71
Assassin, The (Hou, 2015), 4, 86, 93
Assayas, Olivier, 240n24
Aster, Ari, 259n10
Astudillo, Ever, 256n42
Atlantics (Diop, 2019), 30, *31*
atmosphere, 2, 11, 19, 32, 46; aesthetic and ecological senses of, 76; atmospheric turn of film theory, 11–15, 89; character and, 122, 133, 148; discreet uses of, 35; ecological senses of, 20, 76; endogenous role of film style within, 35, 112, 192, 271n41; etymology of, 14; in *The Fall of the House of Usher*, 35; in *Foreign Correspondent*, 10; gothic mode and, 155; in *Jauja*, 92; media hybridity and, 220; narrative and, 13, 40, 42, 78; in *Neighboring Sounds*, 37, 38; plot and, 32; relation to ambience, 88–89, 245n6; sensorial "firstness" of, 36, 78, 80, 175, 219, 235n46; sensory details and, 40; in *The Spirit of the Beehive*, 42; styled, 34; "surfaceless space" as core feature of, 118; in *Twin Peaks: The Return*, 203, 205, 213. *See also* ambience
Atmosphères (Ligeti), 10
atmospheric suspense, 11, 32–38, 86, 136, 153, 238n75; headphonic spectatorship and, 211–12; in *Jeanne Dielman*, 34; in *Memoria*, 142, 150; in *The Passenger*, 44; source of dread and, 183; in *Stranger by the Lake*, 50; in *Twin Peaks: The Return*, 190; temporality in, 36–38; in *Zama*, 100, 101
aura, 12
avant-garde cinema, 5, 41, 209, 225n9; Akerman and, 67; structural films of Snow as, 64–65
Azor (2021), 240n24

Back and Forth (<--->, Snow, 1969), 64
Bacon, Francis, 169, 271n38
Bacurau (Mendonça Filho and Dornelles, 2019), 30
Badalamenti, Angelo, 191
Balázs, Béla, 12, 129, 228n34, 245n9, 255n23
Ball, Kyle Edward, 31
Ballad of Cable Hogue, The (Peckinpah, 1970), 261n24
Barradas, Nuno, 225n15
Barren Illusion (Kurosawa, 1999), 157, 158, 260n15
Barthélémy, Jean-Hugues, 272n51
Barthes, Roland, 18, 27, 146, 231n66
Basic Instinct (Verhoeven, 1992), 69
Battleship Potemkin (Eisenstein, 1925), 231n2
Baumbach, Nico, 236n60
Bava, Mario, 159
Bazin, André, 98, 223n1, 240n14
Becker, Jacques, 61
Beckman, Karen, 224n9
Before We Vanish (Kurosawa, 2017), 158, 179, 182, 260n14
Being and Time (Heidegger), 228n39

Bellour, Raymond, 28, 146, 175–76, 264n65
Bellucci, Monica, 271n42
Belton, John, 247n22
Benedetto, Antonio di, 100
Benjamin, Walter, 12, 89, 146, 257n48
Benning, James, 87, 88
Benson-Allott, Caetlin, 187
Bergala, Alain, 265n72
Beugnet, Martine, 243n59
Beymer, Richard, 203
biomorphic dimension, 78, 79
Bird, Robert, 32, 42
Birds, The (Hitchcock, 1963), 2, 43, 225–26n17, 232n17; atmospheric suspense in, 35; fourth wall revoked in, 29–30; "horror of not knowing" in, 27; startling disruption in, 224n4
Birks, Chelsea, 93
Biró, Yvette, 4
Birsel, Taner, 47
Blackcoat's Daughter, The (Perkins, 2015), 260n10
Blackhat (Mann, 2015), 216
Blade Runner (Scott, 1982), 110
Blanchot, Maurice, 183, 266n82
Blissfully Yours (Apichatpong, 2002), 133, 134
blockbusters, hyperspectacular, 118
Blow-Up (Antonioni, 1966), 43, 88
Blue Velvet (Lynch, 1984), 270n31
Blu-ray, 188, 233n27, 236n55, 241n35, 260n14, 267n6
Bodies in Suspense: Time and Affect in Cinema (Thain), 10–11, 24–25, 207, 275n77
Böhme, Gernot, 12, 245n6
Bong Joon-ho, 30
Bonitzer, Pascal, 30, 31, 169, 223n2, 224n4, 253n7; on deframing, 164, 184, 262n37, 266n88; on "double register of lack," 174; on Hitchcockian suspense, 265n69
Bordwell, David, 4, 9, 157, 233n21, 253n1, 260n11
boredom, 4, 12, 40, 47, 220, 225–26n17; "communal viewing" and, 140; rhetoric of, 49, 238n78; slow cinema as sphere of, 18, 237n67; "slow seeing" and, 49; suspension and, 42, 46, 48
Borges, José Tavares (alias Ventura), 122

Brakhage, Stan, 209
Branigan, Edward, 23
breath/breathing, suspense and, 49–50, *50*, 110
Brecht, Bertolt, 54, 266n77
Brenez, Nicole, 64, 74
Bresson, Robert, 18, 76, 84, 85, 88, 238n77; antinaturalism and, 65; on art and suggestion, 54; on audiences, 239n8; Bressonian close-up, 57, 91; deframing and, 164, 169; doctrine of film actor as "model," 57, 255n24; on "margin of indefiniteness," 127; modernist art cinema of, 123; relation to suspense, 53–54; stylistic austerity of, 53; transcendental style of, 54
Bressonian lineage of suspense, 25, 62, 122; Akerman and, 64, 65, 68; *Jauja* and, 91; Reichardt and, 79
Breton, André, 95, 98
Bright Future (Kurosawa, 2002), 160, 163, 264n65
Brophy, Philip, 234n32, 274n69
Broski, Robert, 216
Brown, Irma, 37
Browning, Todd, 156
Brunius, Jacques, 98, 247n29
Bruno, Giuliana, 12, 90, 228n34
Buñuel, Luis, 97–98, 102, 247n26, 248n31
Burch, Noël, 40, 62, 266n76
Burchfield, Charles E., 82
Burnett, Charles, 25
Burning (Lee, 2018), 35
Burr, Raymond, 29
Bust of a Black Man (Géricault painting), 125

cable networks, 187
Caché (Haneke, 2005), 38
Çağlayan, Emre, 47, 238n74
Cahiers du Cinéma (journal), 188, 223n1, 225n17, 263n59
Cameron, James, 117
Campion, Jane, 69, 188
capitalism, 76, 126, 140, 264n65
Carlito's Way (De Palma, 1993), 227n32
Carnival of Souls (Harvey, 1962), 158, 260n15
Carpenter, John, 29, 37, 142, 169
Carrie (De Palma, 1976), 240n13

Carroll, Noël, 9, 23
Casa de lava (Costa, 1994), 256n42
Casas, Fabián, 92
Casetti, Francesco, 15, 229n45
Cassavetes, John, 8
Cat People (Tourneur, 1942), 163
Cemetery of Splendor (Apichatpong, 2015), 19, 122, 132–40, 141, 144, 148, 150; coexistence of ordinary and supernatural in, 255n32; digital format of, 151; eroticized therapeutic dream-sharing motif, 136–37, *138*, 143, 255n33; indirect social commentary in, 257n60; interplays of figure and environment in, 134, *135*; "monsters" in, 257n58; *Twin Peaks: The Return* compared with, 201
center–periphery relation, 14
Certain Women (Reichardt, 2016), 76
Ceylan, Nuri Bilge, 5, 23, 46, 47
Cézanne, Paul, 148
Chabrol, Claude, 69
Chaplin, Charlie, 23
character alignment, 24, 232n12
character-based suspense, 19, 24–27, 121, 151, 153; in *La captive*, 73–74; "focalizing" in response to ambiguity, 121–22, 253n1; in *Memoria*, 142; in *The Passenger*, 44; psychological identification and, 25, 232n16; in *Stranger by the Lake*, 50; suspension of, 41; in *Twin Peaks: The Return*, 202
Charisma (Kurosawa, 1999), 19, 157, 160–69, 182, 184, 262n40; absence and presence in, 262n42; comic aspect of, 168, 263n44; deframing and dis/continuity in, 167–68, 177; forested "hotel" in, 165–66, *166*; gothic spaces in, *165*, 167; *Stalker* references in, 162, 166; Western genre and, 261n24
Chekov, Anton, 48, 238n74
chiaroscuro lighting, 45, 58, 254n19
Chion, Michel, 45, 55, 58, 108, 249n41, 262n42; on *2001: A Space Odyssey*, 110; on *A Man Escaped*, 62–63; on *Twin Peaks: Fire Walk with Me*, 192
Christie, Agatha, 9
Cicero, 89
"Cinema, The: Instrument of Poetry" (Buñuel), 248n31

"cinema of process," 60, 61
cinematography/cinematographers, 31, 92, 215, 249n44, 265n71
Clainche, Charles le, 62
Clark, Greydon, 259n10
Clayton, Alex, 248n32
Clayton, Jack, 13, 159, 164
Clift, Denison, 226n21
climate catastrophe, 168
"Closed Door That Leaves Us Guessing, A" (Costa), 128
Close-Up (Kiarostami, 1990), 244n82
Clouzot, Henri, 79, 240n14
cognitivism, 9
Coincoin and the Extra-humans (Dumont, 2018), 188
Colombia, civil war in, 149
colonialism, 90, 104, 106, 107, 129, 155, 249n44; colonial gaze, 91, 247n26; colonial-settler violence, 275n83; Indigenous peoples subjugated by, 148; logics of, 92, 93; modern economic oppression and, 38; Portuguese, 125; postcolonial cinema, 30, 38; racial exoticization and, 129; surrealist critique of, 97, 99
color, 26, 66, 139, 202–203, 272n44
Colossal Youth (Costa, 2006), 132
comedy and humor, 27, 30, 72, 154, 201, 203, 233n27; absurdist, 158, 201, 263n44; dark humor, 25, 29; deadpan, 233n27; narrative suspension and, 47; structural suspense and, 29; surrealist humor, 97
computer-generated imagery, 149, 195, 257n58
Conner, Bruce, 209
Connor, Steven, 101
contemplation, 19, 48, 100, 116, 151; ambient music and, 107; cinematic, 141, 145–46; dead time and, 88; definitions of, 145; slow cinema and, 140, 146; suspense as "ecstasy of contemplation," 41, 140–41, 144
Conversation, The (Coppola, 1974), 82, 83, 142
Coppola, Francis Ford, 82, 142
Corman, Roger, 169, 170
Costa, Pedro, 3, 19, 93, 122, 153, 240n24, 256n42; "closed door" metaphor of

suspense, 34; on ethics of suspense, 128; influences on, 123–24; pictorial tenebrism of, 127, 129, 254n19; on slow tempos and delays, 253–54n10; stylistic hybridity of, 124
Cotten, Joseph, 258n4
Cranes Are Flying, The (Kalatozov, 1957), 271n41
Coulson, Catherine E., 208
Creeber, Glen, 187, 267n3
Creepy (Kurosawa, 2016), 19, 157, 175–82, 265n71; doubling in, 178–79; hypnotic forces in, 175–76, 177, *178*, 182, 264n65; one-behind-the-other staging motif, 179, *180*, 265n73
Cremonini, Leonardo, 169
crime thrillers, 52, 239n4
cross-cutting, 27, 30, 232n20
"crossing the bridge" metaphor in surrealism, 98, 247n31
Cruise, Tom, 27
cult cinema, 30
Cure (Kurosawa, 1997), 157, 160, 163, 175, 176, 182, 262n40

Daguerrotype (Kurosawa, 2016), 171
Dalí, Salvador, 97
Dark Waters (Haynes, 2019), 36
Dassin, Jules, 58
Davies, Terence, 121
Davis, Glyn, 157, 259n10
Day Night Day Night (Loktev, 2006), 5, 52
Day of the Jackal, The (Zinnemann, 1973), 56
Days (Tsai, 2020), 4–5, 6
Dead Slow Ahead (Herce, 2015), 260n10
De Assis, Paulo, 205
Death in the Land of Encantos (Diaz, 2007), 155
Debucourt, Jean, 35
deframing, 164, 167, 169, 184, 262n37, 266n88
Dekalog, The (Kieslowski, 1988), 42
Deladonchamps, Pierre, 49
Deleuze, Gilles, 11, 19, 29, 57, 258n66; on "actor-mediums," 122; "any-space-whatever" concept, 70; on offscreen as "radical Elsewhere" beyond homogenous space-time, 94; Schefer's concept of Outside and, 183, 266n82; on time and contemplation, 147–48, 257n55
Delon, Alain, 25, 60
de Luca, Tiago, 17, 224n7, 225n15
Deming, Peter, 268n7
Demme, Jonathan, 11, 233n20
Denis, Claire, 48
Denson, Shane, 214–15, 274n75, 275n78
De Palma, Brian, 227n32, 240n13.
Deren, Maya, 24, 41
Dern, Laura, 205
Descartes, René, 89
De Sica, Vittorio, 248n31
Detective (Godard, 1984), 263n59
Devigny, André, 55
Devil, Probably, The (Bresson, 1977), *77*, 79, 84
Diary of a Country Priest (Bresson, 1951), 64, 240n16
Diaz, Lav, 39, 55, 90, 155
diegesis, 32, 35, 83, 97, 265n75, 271n41, 275n78; ambient sound and, 84; in *Cemetery of Splendor*, 135, 142; contemplation within, 146; in *Creepy*, 176, 181; as environment, 12; Shepard tones in *Zama*, 104, 106; in *Twin Peaks*, 192, 200, 208
Difference and Repetition (Deleuze, 1968), 147, 257n55
digital media, 19, 154, 190, 215, 218, 274n75. *See also* streaming, digital
Diop, Alice, 150
Diop, Mati, 30
"direct suspense," 10, 227n27
Disclosures of the Everyday: Undramatic Achievement in Narrative Film (Klevan, 2000), 244n82
dispositif, 17, 72, 118, 151, 187, 275n75; defined, 15; of digital streaming, 19, 188, 214, 220; hypnosis and, 175–76; postcinematic, 214; spatial intervals and, 265n72; theatrical, 17, 118, 189
Doane, Mary Ann, 15, 66
Dr. Mabuse the Gambler (Lang, 1922), 176
Dr. Strangelove, or: How I Learned to Stop Worrying and Love the Bomb (Kubrick, 1964), 232–33n20
Dōguchi, Yoriko, 167
Don't Look Now (Roeg, 1973), 28, 263n52

Dornelles, Juliano, 30
Dostoevsky, Fyodor, 100
doubling and doppelgängers, 28, 29, 97, 160, 178, 205, 206
Dracula (Browning, 1931), 156, 259n7
Dragon Inn (King Hu, 1967), 154
Dramatic Suspense in the Photoplay (Clift, 1920), 226n21
dread, 19, 22, 37, 83–84, 107, 168, 182; ambient sound and, 142; anxiety deepened into, 15; environmental dread, 84, 157, 163; gothic horror and, 163; as negative feeling, 12
Dreyer, Carl Theodor, 161, 230n59, 233n21, 241n37
Dreyfuss, Richard, 225n16
Dufrenne, Mikel, 145, 151, 213, 214, 258n66
Dullea, Keir, 109
Dumont, Bruno, 5, 41, 48, 52, 188, 230n59
Dunkirk (Nolan, 2017), 102
Durgnat, Raymond, 22, 23, 42, 51, 93
DVDs, 187, 188
Dyer, Richard, 70

Eastwood, Clint, 261n24
Eberhardt, Thom, 259n10
ecological crises, 78, 79, 80, 83, 84, 212
ecothrillers, 79
eeriness, 161–62, 168, 170
Eggers, Robert, 32, 259–60n10
Egoyan, Atom, 8
Eisenberg, Jesse, 77
Eisenstein, Sergei, 231n2
Elephant (Van Sant, 2004), 4, 248n32
El Eternauta (serial comic), 106
Ellis, John, 187
Elsaesser, Thomas, 15, 16, 24, 83
El silenciero (Benedetto, 1964), 100
El sur (Erice, 1983), 155, 258n4
Emerald (Apichatpong, 2007), 133
"endurance," 126, 130, 254n14
Eng, Ron, 270n32
Engels, Robert, 275n83
En marge du cinéma français (Brunius, 1954), 247n29
Eno, Brian, 107, 250n48
Epstein, Jean, 12, 32, 35, 40, 88, 126, 236n60
Eraserhead (Lynch, 1977), 200, 270nn31–32, 274n69

Erice, Victor, 42, 155
erotic thrillers, 52, 53, 69, 242n47
Escape from Alcatraz (Siegel, 1979), 63
Escape from L.A. (Carpenter, 1996), 169, 263n47
espionage thrillers, 52
Evans, Walker, 127
Evolution (Hadzihalilovic, 2015), 259n10
existentialism, 60
Exotica (Egoyan, 1994), 8
expressionism, German, 13
exterior–interior distinction (mental and/or spatial), 14, 35, 45, 144, 164–165
Eyes Wide Shut (Kubrick, 1999), 70, 242n50
Eyes Without a Face (Franju, 1960), 159, 171, 259n10

Faber, Michel, 107
Faircrest, Tikaeni, 216
Fall of the House of Usher, The (Epstein, 1928), 32, 35
Fanning, Dakota, 76
Fantômas (Feuillade, 1913), 2
Farber, Manny, 65, 241n36
Fassbinder, R. W., 8, 161
Fehér, György, 34
feminism, 66, 69, 224n9
Ferroni, Giorgio, 159, 169
Feuillade, Louis, 2, 232n20
Fieschi, Jean-André, 226n17
Fight for the Watering Hole (Remington painting), 91
"film" (beyond or in absence of celluloid) 19, 188, 195, 212, 268n7; atmosphere and, 213; digital makeover of, 215; as environment, 151; gadgetries and energy grid of, 200; headphonic viewer/listener and, 90, 189; home-viewing technologies and, 186, 198; radio linked to, 216; variety of media encompassed by, 219, 270n37. *See also* medium suspense; streaming, digital; *Twin Peaks: The Return*
Film Is Scary (Kurosawa), 15
film noir, 13
film theory: atmospheric turn of, 11–15, 228n37; classical, 20, 228n37; phenomenological, 229n53
First Cow (Reichardt, 2019), 76, 87, 243n65
First Reformed (Schrader, 2017), 62, 93

Fisher, Mark, 107, 161–62, 163, 183
Fisher, Terence, 159, 169
Five Dedicated to Ozu (Kiarostami, 2003), 87
Flaherty, Robert, 58
Flaxman, Gregory, 57, 240n16, 251n58, 275n75
Flesh for Frankenstein (Morrissey, 1973), 259n10
Fly, The (Neumann, 1958), 171
focus pulls, 28, 35, 116
Fog, The (Carpenter, 1980), 142
Fonda, Henry, 132
Fontaínhas shantytown (Lisbon), 124, 126, 132, 254n10
Fontana, Andreas, 240n24
Ford, John, 91, 123, 132
foreground–background relation, 14
Foreign Correspondent (Hitchcock, 1940), 9–10, 227n29
Foster, Gwendolyn Audrey, 54
Foster, Jodie, 11
fourth wall, 29
4:3 Academy ratio, 91, 93, 247n22
framing: in *Foreign Correspondent*, 10; in *The Headless Woman*, 32; in *A Man Escaped*, 57; in *The Passenger*, 45; in *Stranger by the Lake*, 49
Franju, Georges, 159, 259n10
Frankenstein (Whale, 1932), 155
Freeland, Cynthia, 83, 163
Freud, Sigmund, 160, 161, 182, 261nn26–27
Friedrich, Caspar David, 114
Frost, Mark, 204, 268n7, 274n66, 275n83
Fukatsu, Eri, 172
Funhouse, The (Hooper, 1981), 170
Furtado, Tito, 125
Fusco, Katherine, 76, 82

Gagnon, Pierce, 272n44
Gallese, Vittorio, 227n28
Galloway, Alexander R., 252n71
Galt, Rosalind, 5
García Morales, Adelaida, 155
Garland, Alex, 169
generic suspense, 30, 158, 172, 234n32, 260n13
genre fusion, 30
geomorphic dimension, 78
Géricault, Théodore, 125, 254n11
Gerow, Aaron, 158, 159, 168, 261n23

Gerry (Van Sant, 2002), 88, 224n7
Ghost Story of Yotsuya, The (Nakagawa, 1959), 159, 171
Gibson, James J., 90, 246n12
Gidley, Pamela, 191
Gilroy, Tony, 41
Giménez Cacho, Daniel, 99
Girl Walks Home Alone at Night, A (Amirpour, 2014), 32, 259n10
Glavonić, Ognjen, 240n24
Glazer, Jonathan, 3, 18, 34, 90, 121, 251n62; nostalgia for *photogénie*, 116–17, 252n69; the uncanny and, 161
Glissant, Édouard, 127, 255n26
global art cinema, 5
Glover, Danny, 25
Goaz, Harry, 196
Godard, Jean-Luc, 24, 109, 173, 199, 241n37
Gomes, Miguel, 92, 246n16
Goodbye, Dragon Inn (Tsai, 2003), 17, 122, 154–55, 156, 213
Goodbye to Language (Godard, 2014), 263n59
Gordon, Christine, 141
Gordon, Douglas, 257n62
Gorfinkel, Elena, 25, 76, 112, 114–15, 126, 254n14
Gorgon, The (Fisher, 1964), 159, 169
gothic, the, 155, 157, 167, 259n6; *goshikku* (Japanese transliteration), 159, 260n19; gothic horror films, 13, 25, 109, 163; Japanese *kaiki* films, 158–59, 168, 169, 260nn21–22; Kiyoshi Kurosawa and, 158–59; reflexivity and, 156; as spatial-temporal regime of mood, 159; Western literary associations of, 155, 159
Grace, Jeff, 79
Grandrieux, Philippe, 41, 70
Grant, Cary, 2, 72
Grapes of Wrath, The (Ford, 1940), 132
Grémillon, Jean, 33
Griffero, Tonino, 241n28
Griffith, D. W., 2, 27
Grisebach, Valeska, 240n24
Grønstad, Asbjørn, 48–49, 236n51
Guattari, Félix, 147, 148
Guerra, Michele, 227n28
Guiraudie, Alain, 5, 23, 49
Gunning, Tom, 209, 272n49

Hadzihalilovic, Lucile, 259n10
Hainge, Greg, 193, 272n49
Halloween (Carpenter, 1978), 37, 233n27
Hammer films, 159, 169
Hammershoi, Vilhelm, 45
Hammid, Alexander, 24
Haneke, Michael, 38, 238n77, 240n24
Hanich, Julian, 9, 227–28n33, 265n74; on breathing and "somatic empathy," 49; on "challenging films" and theatrical spectatorship, 187; on suspense and speed, 22
Hansen, Mark, 214
Hansen, Miriam Bratu, 257n48
Harvey, Herk, 158
Hasumi, Shigehiko, 3, 4, 5, 158, 183–84
Haunting, The (Wise, 1963), 260–61n22
Haunting of Hill House, The (Jackson), 261n22
Haynes, Todd, 36, 244n81
Headless Woman, The (Martel, 2008), 5, 25, 32, *33*, 40
headphonic viewer/listener, 19, 190, 194, 199, *199*, 210–11; "intracranial aesthetics" and, 189; mediation and, 192–93; "surround sound" simulation, 270n32
Heidegger, Martin, 228n39
Hellman, Monte, 5
Herce, Mauro, 260n10
Herzog, Werner, 91, 106, 246n16, 259n10
Hitchcock, Alfred, 2, 2–3, 44, 220, 223n1, 225n17, 230n59; avoidance of clichés, 1, 8; doubled components used by, 28; fantasies of control over spectators, 21; genre fusion and, 30; influence on later filmmakers, 2; minimalist approach to suspense, 1, 2; on "pure cinema," 257n62; refusal of closure and, 27; on suspense versus surprise, 8–9; suspension of suspense and, 236n60
Hitchcockian suspense, 3, 7, 40, 45, 121, 133, 265n69; aesthetic experience and, 9–10; Akerman and, 69, 70, 73; audience vulnerability and, 38; Bressonian approach as alternative to, 63; camera gestures, 177; fourth wall revoked in, 29; minimalism as challenge to, 4; spectators' apprehensive attention and, 28; spectators situated ahead of characters in, 79, 85; *Stranger by the Lake* as queer version of, 49
Hoffmann, E. T. A., 207
Hogg, Joanna, 39
Hollywood cinema, 2, 23, 60, 123, 274–75n75; global dominance of, 92; regulation of anxiety and, 16
Holtmeier, Matthew, 244n77
Hong Sang-soo, 29
Hooper, Tobe, 169, 170
Hopper, Edward, 45
horror genre, 30, 37, 155; "American canon" of, 172; atmosphere and, 12; as corporealized spectacle, 49; films bordering on, 157, 181; Japanese (J-horror), 156, 157, 158, 171, 214; science fiction hybrid with, 90, 107, 115; "slow horror," 157, 158. *See also* gothic, the
Horse, Michael, 208
Horse Money (Costa, 2014), 19, 93, 122, 123–32, *124*, *130*; *Cemetery of Splendor* compared with, 133, 139; Géricault painting of Black man in, 125, 254n12; Glissant's *opacité* and, 255n26; gothic accents in, 155; indefinite elements in, 127–28; *Memoria* compared with, 141; monologues in, 150; time of waiting in, 126
Hotel Monterey (Akerman, 1972), 65
Hou Hsiao-hsien, 4, 86, 93; as long-take specialist, 157; media diaphana and, 90
House (Rivers, 2005–2007), 156
House of the Devil, The (West, 2009), 259n10
Hoyt, Harry O., 135
Hu, King, 154
Huillet, Danièle, 123, 241n25
Humanité (Dumont, 1999), 5, 52, 62, 122
Hurley, Dean, 189, 270n32, 271n40, 274n64
Hutton, Peter, 87, 88
Hven, Steffen, 12, 228n34, 271n41
hybrid categories, 52, 90
hypnosis, 175–76, 177, 181–82, 264n65

Ida (Pawlikowski, 2013), 93
Identification of a Woman (Antonioni, 1982), 43, 109, 112
identity, 112, 160; change or switch of, 44, *46*; genre identity, 30; multiplied and

disfigured by suspense, 11; plot-based suspense and, 24; suppression of character identity, 25
I Don't Want to Sleep Alone (Tsai, 2006), 126
Ikeuchi, Hiroyuki, *165*
imperial-spectacular gaze structure, 106
Importance of Being Earnest, The (Wilde), 232n18
Inception (Nolan, 2010), 136
Indigenous peoples: in *Jauja*, 91, 92, 94, 100; in *Memoria*, 148, 149; in *Zama*, 104, 105–6
information, withholding of, 43, 237n67
Inland Empire (Lynch, 2006), 24, 31, 189, 214, 215, 219, 246n16
Innocents, The (Clayton, 1961), 13, 159, 164–65, 179, *180*, 262n38
In the Cut (Campion, 2003), 69
In Vanda's Room (Costa, 2000), 126
Iron Rose, The (Rollin, 1973), 260n10
Ivakhiv, Adrian J., 78, 79
I Walked with a Zombie (Tourneur, 1943), 141–42, 163, 256n42, 265n75

Jackson, Shirley, 261n22
Jahn, Gustavo, 37
James, Henry, 13, 164
Jarmusch, Jim, 259n10
Jauja (Alonso, 2015), 18, 90, 91–99, 112, 238n71, 246n16; boundless perceptual space in, 118; figure disappearing into landscape horizon, 93, *94*; 4:3 Academy ratio in, 91, 93; gothic accents in, 155; *Stalker* references in, 95, 96, 97, 106; surrealism and, 95, 96, 97–99, 122, 247nn26–27, 248n32; *Zama* compared with, 99, 100, 105, 249n38
Jaws (Spielberg, 1975), 6, 7, 88, 93, 168, 225n16
Jeanne Dielman, 23 quai du Commerce, 1080 Bruxelles (Akerman, 1975), 65–67, *68*, 76, 109, 123, 241n36; atmospheric suspense in, 34; "endurance" in, 126; *A Man Escaped* compared with, 66
Jenkins, Barry, 219, 229n50
Jia Zhangke, 5, 39, 257n58
Johansson, Scarlett, 107, 108, 110, 250n47
Johnny Guitar (Ray, 1954), 248n32

Journey to the Shore (Kurosawa, 2015), 19, 157, 169–74, *170*, *173*, *174*, 182
Judd, Ashley, 203

Kael, Pauline, 14–15, 229n50
Kafka, Franz, 100
Kagawa, Teruyuki, 176
kaiki films, 158–59, 168, 260nn21–22; *mitoru* concept and, 172–73; temporal blurring in, 171; *unmei no kikai* ("machine of fate"), 169, 171, 263n52
Kalatozov, Mikhail, 271n41
Kaurismäki, Aki, 92
Kawaguchi, Haruna, 178
Keller, Sarah, 17
Kiarostami, Abbas, 41, 48, 87, 109, 244n82
Kieslowski, Krzysztof, 42, 43, 216
Killing of a Chinese Bookie, The (Cassavetes, 1976), 8
Kim, Jihoon, 270n37
King, Geoff, 5
King, Stephen, 240n13
Kinoshita, Chika, 157
Kinski, Klaus, 91
Klevan, Andrew, 238n77, 244n82
Klute (Pakula, 1971), 31
knowledge of outcome, suspense and, 11, 227nn31–32. *See also* spectatorship and spectators' experience
Koepnick, Lutz, 146, 257n62
Kon, Satoshi, 136
Kore-eda, Hirokazu, 157
Kracauer, Siegfried, 12
Kubie, Lawrence, 264n65
Kubrick, Stanley, 31, 50, 70, 108, 109, 232n20; affinities with David Lynch, 209, 273n62; *Blade Runner* as tribute to, 110; on the uncanny, 161
Kulezic-Wilson, Danijela, 246–47n19
Kurosawa, Kiyoshi, 14, 15, 19, 29, 203, 214, 240n24; atmospheric style of, 177, 181, 265n70; deframing technique and, 164, 262n37; "fatal mechanisms" and, 169–71, 181; Godard's influence on, 173, 263n59; horror genre and, 156–57; *kaiki* genre and, 158–59; media diaphana and, 90
Kyoto School philosophy, 174
Kyrou, Ado, 98

La captive (Akerman, 2000), 18, 64, 67–75, 72, 74, 85, 243n59; erotic thriller genre and, 69, 242n47; male gaze in, 69, 69, 242n49; *Marnie* compared with, 242–43n55; *Notorious* compared with, 72, 73; as structuralist experimental film, 75; *Vertigo* compared with, 53, 68–69, 70, 71, 74

Lancelin, Sabine, 70, 242n51

La chambre (Akerman, 1972), 64–65, 241n34

landscape, 13, 32, 79–80, 87, 149; exoticism and, 92; figure disappearing into, 93, 94, 112, 113, 114–15, 115; Patagonian desert, 91, 94, 96, 97

Land Without Bread (Buñuel, 1933), 247n26

Landy, Marcia, 124

Lang, Fritz, 2, 176, 184, 232n20

La petite Lise (Grémillon, 1930), 33–34

La région centrale (Snow, 1971), 64

L'argent (Bresson, 1983), 238n77

LaserDiscs, 187

Last Days (Van Sant, 2005), 224n7

last-minute rescue sequence, 27

Last Wave, The (Weir, 1977), 98, 106

Last Year at Marienbad (Resnais, 1961), 24, 225–26n17

L'avventura (Antonioni, 1960), 16, 22, 43

"Leaving the Movie Theater" (Barthes, 1975), 18

Le cercle rouge (Melville, 1970), 28, 243n65

Lee, Bruce, 234n32

Lee, Sheryl, 190, 205

Lee Chang-dong, 35

Lefebvre, Martin, 88

Leopard Man, The (Tourneur, 1943), 265n75

Le samouraï (Melville, 1967), 25, 26, 60

Les vampires (Feuillade, 1915–1916), 2, 232n20

Le tempestaire [The storm tamer] (Epstein, 1947), 41–42

Leterrier, François, 55

Le trou [The hole] (Becker, 1960), 61, 63

Let Us Now Praise Famous Men (Agee), 127

Levi, Mica ("Micachu"), 107, 108

Levinas, Emmanuel, 74

Ligeti, György, 108

Lighthouse, The (Eggers, 2019), 32, 260n10

Li'l Quinquin (Dumont, 2014), 188

Lim, Bliss Cua, 38

Lloyd, Danny, 37

Lockhart, Calvin, 275n83

Loden, Barbara, 76, 126

Loft (Kurosawa, 2005), 261n23

Loktev, Julia, 5, 52

Lomnoi, Banlop, 136

Long Day Closes, The (Davies, 1992), 121

long take, 5, 7, 257n62, 260n11; in *Charisma*, 164, 168; "contemplative viewing" and, 146; in East Asian films, 157; in *Jeanne Dielman*, 66; metamorphic capabilities of, 40; mobile, 4

Lontano (Ligeti), 108

Los olividados (Buñuel, 1950), 98, 248n31

Los suicidas (Benedetto novel), 100

Lost Highway (Lynch, 1997), 25, 30, 214, 273n60, 274n69

Lost World, The (Hoyt, 1925), 135

Lovecraft, H. P., 161, 162

Lowenstein, Adam, 98

Lucas, George, 193

Lynch, David, 11, 19, 24, 25, 31, 185; on auditory "power" of his films, 188–89; on circle of spectator and film, 213; clichés of suspense and, 220; as diegetic actor in *Twin Peaks: The Return*, 190, 199, 199, 208; tendency of critics to explain his work through "narratives" drawn from elsewhere, 204, 272n49; forward-pushing camera style, 194, 270n31; on intuition, 208; labyrinths of, 190, 196; surrealism and, 97; the uncanny and, 161

MacDonald, Scott, 87

MacLachlan, Kyle, 193

male gaze, 69, 242n49

Malick, Terrence, 253n2

Man Escaped, A (Bresson, 1956), 18, 53–63, 59, 60; average shot length in, 55, 240n11; *Jeanne Dielman* compared with, 66; minimalist style of suspense in, 56; offscreen sound in, 58, 63; orchestration

of time in, 239n7; uncertainty repressed in, 55, 58
Man from Laramie, The (Mann, 1955), 275n75
Man from London, The (Tarr, 2007), 5
Mangolte, Babette, 64, 65
Mann, Anthony, 275n75
Mann, Michael, 8, 216
Mapuche people, in Argentina, 91, 94–95
Marathon Man (Schlesinger, 1976), 82
Margolin, Sydney, 264n65
Margulies, Ivone, 65, 66–67, 241n37
Marnie (Hitchcock, 1964), 2, 41, 243n55
Marshall, James, 271–72n41
Martel, Lucrecia, 3, 5, 18, 25, 90; on theme of waiting in *Zama*, 248n35
Martin, Adrian, 4, 16, 28, 43, 54, 225n11; on Apichatpong's films, 133; on deframing, 262n37; on focalizing tendency of criticism, 253n2; on *Jauja*, 246n16; on *La captive*, 70, 72; on shared tactics of cinema and television, 219; on surrealist cinema, 247n31; on suspension, 42
Massumi, Brian, 11, 272n47
mastery, pretense of, 20, 184, 237n67
Matarasso, David, 170
Matrix, The (Wachowski and Wachowski, 1999), 275n78
Matsuo, Mayumi, 170
McArthur, Colin, 60–61
McCabe & Mrs. Miller (Altman, 1971), 14
McCrae, Joel, 9
McElhaney, Joe, 232n20, 265n70
McQuarrie, Christopher, 27
media diaphana, 89–90, 115
mediation, 14, 20, 89, 139, 192; aesthetic, 32; ambience and, 90, 117; in atmospheric suspense, 19, 36, 116, 150, 190; hypnotic, 177; Kurosawa and, 19; sonic, 195; technological, 150, 191; in *Twin Peaks: The Return*, 19, 192, 213, 218
medium suspense, 19, 150, 190–200, 270n37. *See also* "film"; headphonic viewer/listener
Meek's Cutoff (Reichardt, 2010), 76, 93
Melancholia (Diaz, 2008), 155
melodrama, 2, 13, 25, 49
Melville, Jean-Pierre, 25, 28, 60, 243n65

Memento (Nolan, 2000), 24
Memoria (Apichatpong, 2021), 19, 122, 140–53, *152*, 253n5; Apichatpong's syndrome during making of, 256n41; contemplation in, 144–48; "detective film" premise of, 141; enigmatic ambient sound in, 142–43, *143*; home-viewing technologies and, 187, 267n6; *Jaws* scene evoked in, 6, *7*, 144, *145*, 225n16; spare ambient style of, 213; Swinton as professional actor in, 256n39
Mendonça Filho, Kleber, 5, 30, 37, 155
Menkes, Nina, 232n16
Merhar, Stanislas, 67
Merleau-Ponty, Maurice, 192
Meshes of the Afternoon (Deren and Hammid, 1943), 24
Metz, Christian, 15
Miami Vice (Mann, 2006), 8
Michael Clayton (Gilroy, 2007), 41
Michelson, Annette, 4, 110
Midsommar (Aster, 2019), 259n10
milieu, 12, 89, 105; in *La captive*, 67; character as atmosphere and, 122; in *Creepy*, 177; in *Goodbye, Dragon Inn*, 154; in *Night Moves*, 82; in *La petite Lise*, 34; plot-based suspense and, 23; transduction and, 204; in *Twin Peaks: The Return*, 212
"Milieu and Ambiance" (Spitzer, 1942), 89
Mill of the Stone Women (Ferroni, 1960), 159, 169, 171
Mimicry (motor, neurological), 227n33
"mind-game film," 24
"Mines of Falun, The" (Hoffmann), 207
mise-en-scène, 3, 13, 17, 28, 31, 156, 274n69; of *Barren Illusion*, 158; of *La captive*, 72; of *Cemetery of Splendor*, 139; of *Charisma*, 166; of *The Fall of the House of Usher*, 35; of *Memoria*, 256n42; of *Night Moves*, 80, 82; suspension and, 42; technological apparatus and, 215; of *Twin Peaks: The Return*, 192, 194; of *Zama*, 100
Mission, The (To, 1999), 56
Mission: Impossible—Rogue Nation (McQuarrie, 2015), 27

mood, 35, 80, 226n17, 229n53, 259n8; agency and, 89; atmosphere and, 13, 15, 32; atmospheric suspense and, 211; in *Charisma*, 168; cognitive film theory and, 229n53; elevated above narrative, 33, 157; "enduration" and, 126; the gothic and, 156, 163; in *Horse Money*, 130; in *Hotel Monterey*, 65; in *Jauja*, 95; in *Journey to the Shore*, 172; in *A Man Escaped*, 55; in *Once Upon a Time in Anatolia*, 47; of paranoia, 67, 83; perceptual regime of, 159; reflective, 44; in *Under the Skin*, 114; slowness as modifier of, 7; in *Stranger by the Lake*, 50; suspension and, 41; of tension, 62; tone and, 14, 229n50; in *Twin Peaks: The Return*, 191. See also *Stimmung*

Morgan, Daniel, 264n67

Morrison, Benedict, 121

Morrissey, Paul, 259n10

Mortensen, Viggo, 91, 92, 238n71

Morton, Timothy, 92, 246n18

Mouchette (Bresson, 1967), 64

movie theater, 17, 129, 151, 213–14, 229n45; boredom of slow cinema and, 18; darkness of, 110, 152, *181*; *dispositif* and, 15; immersive experience of, 118–19; Lynch's tribute to golden age of, 195, *196–97*; sound of projectors, 45; space of encounter in, 118

Mulholland Drive (Lynch, 2001), 193, 195, 219, 269n21, 270n36, 276n83

Mummy, The (Fisher, 1959), 169

Münsterberg, Hugo, 243n60

Muriel, or The Time of Return (Resnais, 1963), 225–26n17, 226n17

Murnau, F. W., 98, 156

Murray, Don, 203

music, 13, 26, 92; ambient, 90, 107; in *La captive*, 72; nondiegetic, 35, 61, 63; Shepard tones in film musical scores, 102; in *Twin Peaks: The Return*, 201, 208, 209

Music for Airports (Eno album), 107, 250n48

Muybridge, Eadweard, 112

My Horrifying History of Cinema (Kurosawa), 159, 169

Nadja (Almereyda, 1995), 259n10

Nagib, Lúcia, 225n15, 249n44, 258n3

Nakagawa, Nobuo, 159, 171

Nakata, Hideo, 156, 171, 214

Nance, Jack, 200

Nanook of the North (Flaherty, 1922), 58, 76

narrative, 36, 224n8; atmosphere and, 13, 40, 42, 78; gendered codification of suspense and, 66; halting of narrative continuity, 65; "landscape gaze" against, 88; momentum of, 2; suspension of, 41, 42; teleological drive of, 40, 64; time and energy management in, 16

"Narrative Cinema and Audience Aesthetics" (Elsaesser, 1973), 16

Nash, Joy, 195

negative affects/feelings, 12, 19, 40, 76, 80, 84, 163, 228n39

Neighboring Sounds (Mendonça Filho, 2012), 5, 37–38, *39*, 40, 51, 155

neorealism, 25, 98, 122, 223n1, 248n31

Neumann, Kurt, 171

neuroscience, 227n28

New Hollywood, 82

Newton, Isaac, 89

Ngai, Sianne, 83, 228n39, 229n47, 244n78

Nicholson, Jack, 25, 44

Night Moves (Penn, 1975), 82

Night Moves (Reichardt, 2014), 18, 53, 75–84, 85; deforested landscape in, 76, 80, *81*, 87; processual mode of attention in, 78; stationary long take in, 77–78, *77*

Night of the Comet (Eberhardt, 1984), 259n10

Night of the Demon (Tourneur, 1957), 265n75

nihilism, 174

Nishijima, Hidetoshi, 176

Noh theater, 166

Nolan, Christopher, 24, 102, 136, 206

Nørby, Ghita, 95

North by Northwest (Hitchcock, 1959), 2, 31, 40, 269–70n29

Nosferatu (Murnau, 1922), 98, 156, 232n20

Nosferatu the Vampyre (Herzog, 1979), 259n10

nostalgia, 83, 116–17, 154, 195, 207, 212

Notes on the Cinematograph (Bresson, 1975), 54, 127

Nothing Happens: Chantal Akerman's Hyperrealist Everyday (Margulies, 1996), 65

Notorious (Hitchcock, 1946), 72, 73, 223n1, 227n28

Notre musique (Godard, 2004), 173, 263n59
nouveau roman (new novel), 60, 241–42n37
Nouvelle vague (Godard, 1990), 24

objective-subjective distinction, 13, 45
O'Donoghue, Darragh, 54
Old Dark House (Rivers, 2003), 156
Old Dark House, The (Whale, 1932), 32
Old Joy (Reichardt, 2006), 79–80, 84, 230n59
Oliveira, Manoel de, 242n51
Ollier, Claude, 225–26n17
Once Upon a Time in Anatolia (Ceylan, 2011), 5, 23, 46–48, *47*, 51, 238n74; steppe landscape in, 87; thriller genre and, 52
One Plus One, a.k.a. *Sympathy for the Devil* (Godard, 1968), 263n59
Onetto, María, 25
On Land (Eno album), 107
Only Lovers Left Alive (Jarmusch, 2013), 259n10
On Top of the Whale (Ruiz, 1982), 97
Ordet (Dreyer, 1955), 233n21
Ordinary Man of Cinema, The (Schefer), 183, 266n82
Ossos (Costa, 1997), 3, 16
Osterweil, Ara, 250n47
otherness, 70, 105, 112, 169, 183. See also "anotherness"
Others, The (Amenábar, 2001), 31, 163
Our Marriage (Sarmiento, 1984), 246n16
Oxford Handbook of Moving Image Atmospheres and Felt Environments, The (Hven and Yacavone, eds.), 12
Ozon, François, 69
Ozu, Yasujirō, 4, 40, 128, 157, 184, 241n36

Pabst, G. W., 2
Pacifiction (Serra, 2022), 5, 7–8
Pacino, Al, 227n32
Païni, Dominique, 72, 242n50
Painlevé, Jean, 97
Pakula, Alan J., 8, 31
Pale Rider (Eastwood, 1985), 261n24
Palmer, Tim, 261n25
Paou, Christophe, 49
Paprika (Kon, 2006), 136
Parallax View, The (Pakula, 1974), 8
parallel editing, 56

paranoia, 31, 38, 72, 81; film apparatus and, 15, 18; as negative feeling, 12; Ngai's definition of, 83; thriller genre and, 53
Parasite (Bong, 2019), 30
Pasolini, Pier Paolo, 246n16
Passenger, The (Antonioni, 1975), 5, 25, 43, 46, 51; reduction of suspense in, 44–45; spare ambient style of, 213; thriller genre and, 52
Pasternak, Boris, 32
Patterson, Patricia, 241n36
Pawlikowski, Pawel, 93
Peckinpah, Sam, 261n24
Penderecki, Krzysztof, 209
Penn, Arthur, 82
perceptual ecology, 78
perceptual suspense, 19, 30–32, 136, 153, 234n36; in *Charisma*, 169; in *Cemetery of Splendor*, 133; in *Horse Money*, 132; in *Journey to the Shore*, 174; in *Memoria*, 142; in *The Passenger*, 44; in *Stranger by the Lake*, 50; in *Zama*, 100, 101
Perez, Gilberto, 42–43, 232n20, 237n67, 266n77
Perils of Pauline, The (Gasnier and MacKenzie, 1914), 234n31
Perkins, Anthony, 26
Perkins, Oz, 260n10
Perkins, V. F., 248n32
Petzold, Christian, 69, 240n24
phenomenology, 12, 32, 42, 74, 137, 182, 187, 204, 214
Phoenix (Petzold, 2014), 69
photogénie, 12, 117, 252n69
photography, 146
Piaget, Jean, 272n51
Pickpocket (Bresson, 1959), 62, 64, 238–39n4
Picnic at Hanging Rock (Weir, 1975), 35–36
Pipolo, Tony, 54
Pit and the Pendulum, The (Corman, 1961), 170
Plato, 89
plot-based suspense, 23–24, 27, 28, 51; in *A Man Escaped*, 56; in *The Passenger*, 44; spectacle of vulnerable characters in, 234n31; in *Stranger by the Lake*, 50; suspension of, 41; in *Twin Peaks: The Return*, 192, 202; in *Zama*, 100
Poças, Rui, 249n44

point of view, 24, 26, 48, 58, 256n42; ambience and, 18, 88, 90; in *La captive*, 70, 75; in *Cemetery of Splendor*, 139; confounded by deframing, 164, 184; direct suspense and, 227n27; discorrelation and, 274n75; in *Foreign Correspondent*, 10; in *Jauja*, 94; labyrinth and, 253n7; in *A Man Escaped*, 57; in *Night Moves*, 77; in *Once Upon a Time in Anatolia*, 48; in *Under the Skin*, 110, 114, 252n71; in *Stranger by the Lake*, 50; in *The Terminator*, 117; in *Twin Peaks*, 192, 193, 269n20, 275n79; in *2001: A Space Odyssey*, 209, 252n71; wide-angle lenses and, 252n71; in *The Wrong Man*, 58; in *Zama*, 103, 104, 106
Polanski, Roman, 259n10
policier thrillers, 238–39n4
Polley, Sarah, 150
Pollmann, Inga, 12
Pomerance, Murray, 117, 261n27
Pongpas Widner, Jenjira, 122, 133, 134, 253n5, 256n39
popular cinema, 6, 25, 41, 75, 140, 235n51; action in, 122; narrative suspense as instrument of time management, 16; processual cinema and, 61; shopworn vocabulary of suspense in, 2
pornography, 49
Portugal, Carnation Revolution in (1974), 124, 125, 131
postcinema, 214, 215
poststructuralism, 183
Potter, Sally, 66
Price, Brian, 54, 58
Primary World of Senses, The (Straus), 36
process genre, 58, 76
"projection/protection complex" (Casetti), 229n45
protagonist characters, identification with, 9, 25, 40, 132, 184, 227n27
Proust, Marcel, 67, 68
Psycho (Hitchcock, 1960), 2, 30, 45, 93, 114, 186, 224n7, 251n62; Apichatpong's work and, 133; *Creepy* compared with, 179, 181; Gordon video installation *24 Hour Psycho*, 237n62; psychiatrist's report in, 26, 232n17; *Under the Skin* compared with, 114, 251n62; *Stimmung* in, 22–23

Psycho (Van Sant, 1998), 224n7
psychoanalysis, 204, 261n27
Pulse (Kurosawa, 2001), 157, 159, 160, 163, 171, 265n73; atmospheric suspense in, 175; *Barren Illusion* as companion to, 158; reflexive use of small screen in, 214
Pye, Douglas, 14

Quandt, James, 133
"quasi-thing," 63, 241n28
Queen of Diamonds (Menkes, 1991), 232n16
Querelle (Fassbinder, 1982), 8
Quinlivan, Davina, 50–51

radio, 144, 149, 150; as "old" medium linked to cinema, 216; radio plays (1940s), 9; woodsman's incantation on radio in *Twin Peaks: The Return*, 216–18, 217
Ramsay, Lynne, 25
Rancière, Jacques, 125, 132, 254n12
Ray, Nicholas, 248n32, 269n19
Rear Window (Hitchcock, 1954), 2, 29–30, 224n2
Reddell, Trace, 192, 269n26
Red Desert (Antonioni, 1964), 112
Reeves, Keanu, 275n78
reflected-light motif, 5, 6
reflexivity, 109, 156, 170, 182, 214; Brechtian, 181, 266n77; in *Jauja*, 91; and Kiyoshi Kurosawa's "machine of fate" concept, 170–71; of *Under the Skin*, 110, 115; in *Twin Peaks: The Return*, 190
Refn, Nicolas Winding, 188
Reichardt, Kelly, 3, 18, 88, 120, 126, 230n59; durational aesthetics and, 75; genre play and, 76; importance of landscape to, 87–88; on minimalistic thriller, 53
Reis, António, 123
Remington, Frederic, 91
Rennebohm, Kate, 243n58, 274n67
repetition, 8, 29, 236n60, 244n82; contemplation and, 147, 148; cyclical, 62; sonic, 142; "strange magnetism" of, 28; traumatic, 177. *See also* structural suspense.
Repulsion (Polanski, 1963), 259n10
Resnais, Alain, 24, 225–26n17
Retribution (Kurosawa, 2006), 157, 159, 261n23

Return of W. De Rijk, The (Soderbergh, 2015), 110
Reygadas, Carlos, 122, 246n16
Rhodes, John David, 16
Rififi (Dassin, 1955), 58, 76
Right Now, Wrong Then (Hong, 2015), 29
Riis, Jacob, 125
Rilla, Wolf, 36
Ring (Nakata, 1998), 156, 171, 175, 214
River, The (Tsai, 1997), 246n16
Rivers, Ben, 156, 259n8, 260n10
Road to Nowhere (Hellman, 2010), 5
Robbe-Grillet, Alain, 242n37
RoboCop (Verhoeven, 1987), 252n71
Roeg, Nicolas, 28, 97, 263n52
Rohmer, Eric, 54, 239n7
Rollin, Jean, 260n10
Roquet, Paul, 88–89
Rosenbaum, Jonathan, 54, 235n51
Rossellini, Roberto, 123
Rothman, William, 30
Rouch, Jean, 123–24, 125
Rubin, Martin, 21, 22, 52, 53
Ruiz, Raúl, 97
Russell, Kurt, 169

Safe (Haynes, 1995), 244n81
Saint Omer (Diop, 2022), 150
Salminen, Timo, 92
Sarmiento, Valeria, 246n16
Sarsgaard, Peter, 76
satellite dishes, 187
Schaeffer, Pierre, 142
Schanelec, Angela, 240n24
Schefer, Jean-Louis, 109, 183, 221
Schlesinger, John, 82
Schmid, Marion, 68–69
Schmitz, Hermann, 12, 118
Schonig, Jordan, 238n75
Schoonover, Karl, 5, 17, 231n64
Schrader, Paul, 54, 62, 93, 237n67, 238n77, 240n25
Sciamma, Céline, 240n24
science fiction, 90, 106, 107, 109, 115; Apichatpong's work and, 135, 136, 143; *Twin Peaks: The Return* and, 218
Scorsese, Martin, 28
Scott, Ridley, 110
Séance (Kurosawa, 2000), 157, 159

Searchers, The (Ford, 1956), 91
Serra, Albert, 5, 7, 39
Seventh Continent, The (Haneke, 1989), 238n77
sexuality, 48, 49, 101, 254n14
Seymour, Nicole, 76, 82
Seyrig, Delphine, 65, 66
Shadow of a Doubt (Hitchcock, 1943), 28, 155, 258n4
"shared suspense," 10, 227n27
Shaw, Robert, 6, *7*
Shepard, Robert, 102
Shepard tones, 101–5, *103*, 106
Shimizu, Koichi, 134
Shining, The (Kubrick, 1980), 31, 37, 38, 108, 251n62
Shinozaki, Makato, 159
Shirō Inouye, Charles, 159, 260n19
shot/countershot editing, 95
Shout, The (Skolimowski, 1978), 35, 36
Shyamalan, M. Night, 24, 163
Silence of the Lambs, The (Demme, 1991), 11, 50, 233n20
Silent Light (Reygadas, 2007), 122, 246n16
Silva, Henry, 191
Simondon, Gilbert, 204–5, 206, 207, 219, 272n51, 273n55
Sinnerbrink, Robert, 12, 22
Sitney, P. Adams, 56
Sixth Sense, The (Shyamalan, 1999), 163
Skinamarink (Ball, 2022), 31–32
Skolimowski, Jerzy, 35
Skvirsky, Salomé Aguilera, 58, 60, 76
slow cinema, 3, 4, 11, 225n9; alternate names for, 235n51; boredom induced by, 18, 237n67; capitalism and, 17; colonial logic undermined by, 91–92; as contemplative cinema, 140, 146; as critical response to consumption rhythms, 225n12; durational metamorphoses in, 238n75; epistemological slowness, 7; Eurocentrism and, 225n15; global art cinema and, 5; humor in, 29; hybridity of, 75; immersive experience of movie theater and, 118–19; as landscape art for meditation, 86; "nothing" in plot action, 17; suspension in, 38–45; thriller genre and, 43
Slowik, Michael, 235n43

small roads (Benning, 2011), 87
smartphones, 186
Smith, Susan, 10, 24, 227n27, 232n13
Snow, Michael, 4, 31, 64, 224n8, 241n36
Sobchack, Vivian, 42
Soderbergh, Steven, 110
Sokurov, Alexander, 90
Solha, W. J., 37
Somaini, Antonio, 89–90, 245n9
Sombre (Grandrieux, 1998), 70
Song Hwee Lim, 17
Sontag, Susan, 54
sound, 13, 19, 26; atmospheric suspense and, 34; gothic sensibility and, 164; memory and, 144, 256n45; Shepard tones, 101–3; sources of, 92; spectator's body and, 101
sound, ambient, 31, 49, 246n19; acousmatic voice and, 249n41; Aeolian, 92–93, 246n18; ambient music, 107–9; in *La captive*, 70; in *Charisma*, 167; in *Jauja*, 92–93, 94; in *A Man Escaped*, 63; in *Memoria*, 142, 149; in *Neighboring Sounds*, 37; in *Night Moves*, 84; sonic repetition, 142; in *Stranger by the Lake*, 50; in *Zama*, 103
Spadoni, Robert, 12–13, 22, 228n34; atmosphere distinguished from scenery, 88; on early horror films' atmospheres, 259n7; on film audiences and breathing, 49; on stylization of film atmosphere, 34–35
spaghetti Westerns, 30
spectatorship and spectators' experience, 4, 17, 48, 115, 127, 186; anomalous (recidivist) suspense and, 11; cinematic gesture and, 140; contemplation and, 146; double-bodied viewer, 18; durational lures and, 110; enacted in *Twin Peaks: The Return*, 197–98, *198*; experiential tension in slow cinema, 235n51; home-viewing technologies and, 195; identification of viewer and protagonist, 90; Kantian subject and, 145; outward emanation of film atmosphere and, 14; sadomasochistic enjoyment, 53, 234n31; sound and spectator's body, 101, 249n36; suffering of audience, 21; time duration, 3. *See also* headphonic viewer/listener

Spielberg, Steven, 6, 225n16
Spies (Lang, 1928), 232n20
Spirit of the Beehive, The (Erice, 1973), 42, 155
Spitzer, Leo, 89, 90
Sprinkler Sprinkled, The (Lumière brothers, 1895), 223n2
Stalker (Tarkovsky, 1979), 47, 97, 162, 166, 246n16
Standard Time (Snow, 1967), 64
Stern, Daniel N., 8
Stern, Lesley, 28, 140
Stevens, Kyle, 189
Stewart, James, 69
Still Life (Jia, 2006), 257n58
Stimmung, 12, 13, 14–15, 22
Story of a Love Affair (Antonioni, 1950), 43
Strange Case of Angelica, The (Oliveira, 2010), 242n51
Stranger by the Lake (Guiraudie, 2013), 5, 23, 49–51, *50*, 52
Straub, Jean-Marie, 123, 241n25
Straus, Erwin, 36
streaming, digital, 17, 187, 198, 268n8; ambience and, 213, 215, 218; *dispositif* of, 19, 188, 214, 220; as culturally dominant form of movie watching, 186
Strobel, Al, 201
structural suspense, 27–30, 49, 87, 153, 233n21, 233n23, 244n82, 248n32; Akerman and, 67; in *Creepy*, 178; in *A Man Escaped*, 61–62; in *Memoria*, 142; as play, 29; in *Stranger by the Lake*, 50
Struycken, Carel, 194
subjectivity, 10, 27, 77, 116, 174; absence of character subjectivity, 110; camera movement and, 44; destabilization of, 118, 252n75; digital media culture and, 215; hypnosis and, 182; imperial-spectacular gaze structure and, 106; limits of, 175; listening experience and, 189; oneiric, 69; perceptual suspense and, 139; time of waiting and, 100; "zerocularity" and, 57
sublime, Kantian formulation of, 116
surrealism, 19, 25, 38, 60, 90, 91, 95, 97, 102, 104, 106, 122, 123, 131, 134, 135, 139, 194–195, 208, 216, 247n26, 248n32, 249n38; "crossing the bridge" metaphor

Index   293

and, 98–99, 247n31; horror genre and, 159; neorealism and, 98, 248n31
suspense: anomalous (recidivist), 11, 227n31, 227n33; assurances in, 26–27; clichés of, 1, 35, 220; as creative practice and spectatorial state, 226n18; as deprivation, 34, 58, 79; Durgnat's suspense gradient, 42, 51; ecstatic contemplation and, 19, 41, 88, 140–41, 144; emotional manipulation and, 3; etymology of, 21; expanded morphology of, 23–38; as "game with structure," 27; gendered codifications of, 66; generic suspense, 30, 142, 158, 172, 234n32, 260n13; "gnostic" and "pathic" elements of, 36; identity and, 11; labyrinth and, 30–31, 85, 253n7; minimalist, 76, 84, 120; multiple types of, 22; phasing of, 63–64; pseudo-suspense, 44; redefined, 3, 8–11, 18, 221; without rescue, 27. *See also* atmospheric suspense; character-based suspense; generic suspense; medium suspense; perceptual suspense; structural suspense
Suspense (Weber, 1913), 2, 27
suspension, 23, 38–45, 88, 236n60; contemplation and, 146; as "ecstasy of contemplation," 41; transition from "still" to "moving" and, 238n75
Sutherland, Donald, 263n52
Swinton, Tilda, 6, 122, 141, 225n16, 253n5; on "Jessica" character in *Memoria*, 149, 150–51, 256n40; working relationship with Apichatpong, 256n39
Syndromes and a Century (Apichatpong, 2006), 29, 133–34
Syntax (cinematic), 57, 66, 69, 139, 223n1

Tabu (Gomes, 2012), 92, 246n16, 249n44
Takeuchi, Yūko, 176
Tamblyn, Russ, 203
Tarkovsky, Andrei, 32, 40, 42, 43, 157, 161, 246n16
Tarr, Béla, 5, 34, 55
Tati, Jacques, 233n27
Taubin, Amy, 224n8
Taylor, Allison, 49, 238n77
Tehuelche people, in Argentina, 91
television, 187, 188, 191, 219, 230n61

Ten (Kiarostami and Akbari, 2002), 109
tenebrism, 127, 129, 254n19
Ten Skies (Benning, 2004), 87
Terminator, The (Cameron, 1984), 117, 252n71
Terror! (Rivers, 2007), 156
Testud, Sylvie, 67
texture, 13, 26, 35, 41, 65, 70, 116, 203, 215
Thailand: censorship laws in, 257n60; political and economic despotism in, 136, 140
Thain, Alanna, 10, 11, 24, 25, 207
That Night's Wife (Ozu, 1930), 4
therapy motif, 19, 123, 129–30, 136–37, 141, 143, 182
Thesis (Amenábar, 1996), 31
13 Lakes (Benning, 2004), 87
Thompson, Kristen, 36
Thousand Eyes of Dr. Mabuse, The (Lang, 1960), 232n20
Three Colors: Red (Kieslowski, 1994), 216
Three Monkeys (Ceylan, 2008), 47
Threnody for the Victims of Hiroshima (Penderecki, 1961), 209
Thriller (Potter, 1979), 66
thriller genre, 30, 46, 52–53, 120, 239n4; detective film, 141; excess as distinguishing feature of, 52
THX 1138 (Lucas, 1971), 193, 269n26
time/temporality, 123, 140, 149, 205; acceleration of, 22; atmospheric suspense and, 36–37, 235n46; boredom and, 4, 225n17; contemplation and, 147; cycling of, 77; dilation of, 65; distention of, 2, 4, 21; layering of, 38; linear, rational space-time, 95; narrative and time management, 16; offscreen "Elsewhere" beyond homogenous space-time, 94; temporal suspensions, 66; *temps morts* (dead time), 22, 88
To, Johnnie, 56
tone, 14
Too Old to Die Young (Refn, 2019), 188
Toop, David, 261n26
Top of the Lake (Campion, 2013), 188
To Sleep with Anger (Burnett, 1990), 25
Touch of Sin, A (Jia Zhangke, 2013), 5
Tourneur, Jacques, 31, 123, 141, 163, 256n42, 265n75

transduction, 204–8, 215, 272n47, 272n51
traumatic history, 19, 25, 38, 65, 150; in *Charisma*, 161; in *Twin Peaks: The Return*, 212
Trigg, Dylan, 182–83, 229n43
Tropical Malady (Apichatpong, 2004), 255n32
Trouble Every Day (Denis, 2001), 48
Truffaut, François, 2, 54, 231n2; on Hitchcock's style, 21; on *A Man Escaped*, 239n7; on suspense as game, 29
Tsai Ming-liang, 4, 17, 55, 126, 225n11, 246n16
Turn of the Screw, The (James novella, 1898), 13, 164
24 Frames (Kiarostami, 2017), 87
24 Hour Psycho (Gordon, 1993), 237n62
Twentynine Palms (Dumont, 2003), 48, 49, 230n59
Twilight (Fehér, 1990), 34
Twin Peaks [TV series] (Lynch et al., 1990–1991), 187, 267n3, 269n21
Twin Peaks: Fire Walk with Me (Lynch, 1992), 188, 190–93, 207, 208, 269nn19–20, 272n46; slide into more aggressive horror, 212; woodsmen characters, 275–76n83
Twin Peaks: The Missing Pieces (Lynch, 2014), 188
Twin Peaks: The Return (Lynch, 2017), 19, 267n3; ambience in, 208–21; American Dream as nightmare in, 212–13, 274n67; "BOB" character, 191, 193, 212, 268–69n19; camera movements in, 201, 203, *210–11*, 212, 215–16, 271n41; color motifs in, 203, 272n44; dream sharing in, 201, 204, 271n42; energetics of suspense in, 202–204; embedded spectatorship in, 197–98, *198*; as feature film, 188, 268n7; images adapted from Lynch's artwork, 214, 274n72; medium suspense in, 190–200, 271n38; metamorphosis in, 205, 206–7, 272n43; sound design of, 194, 270n32, 271n40; soundtrack, 189; transition and transduction in, 200–208, *202*, *206*, 272n47; woodsmen characters, 216, *217*, 218, 275–76n83

See also "film"; headphonic viewer/listener; streaming, digital
2 or 3 Things I Know About Her (Godard, 1967), 109
2001: A Space Odyssey (Kubrick, 1968), 50; *Under the Skin* allusions to, 108, 109–10, 115, 251n65, 252nn71–72; *Twin Peaks: The Return* compared with, 209

Ugly Feelings (Ngai, 2005), 83, 228n39
Uhlin, Graig, 80
Umberto D. (De Sica, 1952), 248n31
Umwelt, 12
uncanny, the, 155, 160, 261nn26–27; affective modes related to, 161–62; "phenomenological uncanny," 182–83
Uncanny Cinema (Pomerance, 2022), 117, 261n27
uncertainty, 10, 55, 63, 97, 226n18, 237n67, 261n23; ambient music and, 107; clichés of suspense and, 220; contemplative style and, 43; dread and, 156; offscreen elements and, 93; refusal of closure and, 27; riddance of, 121, 204, 237n67; spectators' experience and, 183; supension and, 100; suspense as game of, 8
Un chien andalou (Buñuel and Dalí, 1929), 97–98, 247n27
Uncle Boonmee Who Can Recall His Past Lives (Apichatpong, 2010), 134
Underground Railroad, The (Amazon miniseries, 2021), 219–20, 276n88
Under the Skin (Faber novel), 107, 114–15, 117, 251n64
Under the Skin (Glazer, 2013), 18, 90, 106–18, *108*, 156; alien perceptual apparatus in/of, 110; allusions to other films, 109, 115, 251n65, 252nn71–72; audience lured into rupture from human perception, 110, *111*, 112, 252n71; figure disappearing into landscape, 112, *113*, 114–15, *115*; gender and sexuality in, 250n47; gothic notes in, 155, 161; Levi's ambient musical score, 107–9, 110, 112, *113*; *photogénie* evoked in, 117
Undine (Petzold, 2020), 69
Urrego, Juan Pablo, 142
Uzuner, Muhammet, 47

Vampyr (Dreyer, 1932), 161
Van Sant, Gus, 4, 88, 224n7, 248n32
Varela, Vitalina, 127, 129, *130*
VCR (video cassette recorder), 187
Ventura (José Tavares Borges), 123, 124–25, *124*, 128, 131–32, *131*, 155, 253n5; as "actor-medium," 22; as atmospheric screen entity, 129, *130*; as author of *Horse Money*, 124; "enduration" and, 126, 127, 130; hand spasms of, 130–31
Ventura, Lino, 28
Verhoeven, Paul, 69
Vertigo (Hitchcock, 1958), 2, 11, 53, 225–26n17; as case study in anxiety, 228n39; evoked in *La captive*, 68–69, 70–71, 74, 242n55; *Under the Skin* compared with, 109
Village of the Damned (Rilla, 1960), 36
Vincendeau, Ginette, 28, 29
Vitalina Varela (Costa, 2019), 253n10
vitality affects, 8
voice-over, 24, 55, 56, 58

Wachowski, Lana and Lilly, 275n78
Wages of Fear, The (Clouzot, 1953), 79, 240n14
Wakasugi, Katsuko, 171
Wall-Romana, Christophe, 40–41, 42, 43
Walton, Saige, 49
Wanda (Loden, 1970), 76, 126
Warhol, Andy, 241nn36–37, 253n4
Watts, Naomi, 202
Wavelength (Snow, 1967), 4, 31, 67, 224n8
Way of the Dragon, The (Lee, 1972), 234n32
"weather system," film atmosphere as, 12–13
Weber, Lois, 2, 27
Weimar cinema, 2
Weir, Peter, 35, 98, 106
Weird and the Eerie, The (Fisher, 2016), 161
weirdness, 161–62
Wendy and Lucy (Reichardt, 2008), 126
We Need to Talk About Kevin (Ramsay, 2011), 25–26
West, Ti, 259n10

Western genre, 76, 90, 91, 243n65; Kiyoshi Kurosawa and, 261n24; widescreen, 93
Whale, James, 32, 155
What Is Philosophy? (Deleuze and Guattari, 1991), 147
Whip and the Body, The (Bava, 1963), 159
Whitehead, Alfred North, 148
Willemen, Paul, 265n75
Williams, Linda, 49
Wise, Ray, 191
Wise, Robert, 260n22
Without Warning (Clark, 1980), 259n10
Woman in the Silver Plate, The (also known as *Daguerrotype*, Kurosawa, 2016), 171
women-directed films, 66
Women Talking (Polley, 2022), 150
Wood, Robin, 27, 43
"Work of Art in the Age of Its Technological Reproducibility, The" (Benjamin, 1936), 146
Wright, Teresa, 258n4
Wrong Man, The (Hitchcock, 1956), 28, 58

Yacavone, Daniel, 12, 235n46, 273n60
Yakusho, Kōji, 160, 175
Yang, Edward, 157
You, the Living (Andersson, 2007), 29
Young, Vernon, 43
You Were Never Really Here (Ramsay, 2017), 25–26

Zaillian, Steven, 79
Zama (Benedetto novel, 1956), 100
Zama (Martel, 2017), 18, 90, 99–106, *102*, *105*, 112; boundless perceptual space in, 118; Shepard tones in, 102–5, *103*, 106; sound design of, 101, 249n37, 274n64; theme of endless waiting in, 248n35
Zavattini, Cesare, 248n31
"zerocularity" (Flaxman), 57, 61, 240n16
Zimmer, Hans, 102
Zinnemann, Fred, 56
Zone of Interest, The (Glazer, 2023), 34

Printed and bound by CPI Group (UK) Ltd, Croydon, CR0 4YY
02/12/2024
14603652-0002